Night Comes to the Cumberlands

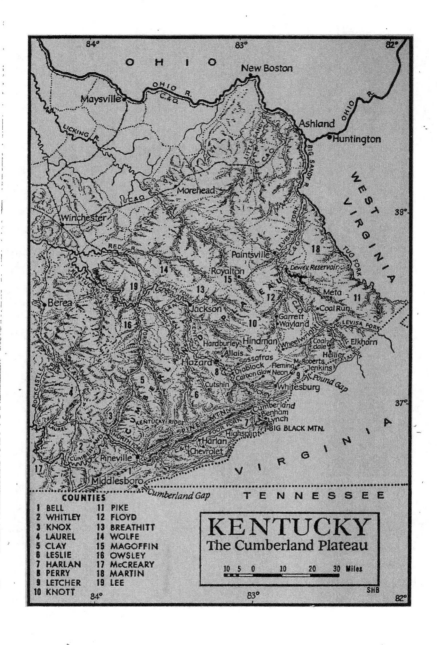

KENTUCKY
The Cumberland Plateau

COUNTIES

1	BELL	11	PIKE
2	WHITLEY	12	FLOYD
3	KNOX	13	BREATHITT
4	LAUREL	14	WOLFE
5	CLAY	15	MAGOFFIN
6	LESLIE	16	OWSLEY
7	HARLAN	17	McCREARY
8	PERRY	18	MARTIN
9	LETCHER	19	LEE
10	KNOTT		

10 5 0   10   20   30 Miles

SHB

Night Comes to the Cumberlands

A Biography of a Depressed Area

by HARRY M. CAUDILL

with a foreword by

STEWART L. UDALL

An Atlantic Monthly Press Book

LITTLE, BROWN AND COMPANY · BOSTON · TORONTO

This book is dedicated with affection and respect to my wife, Anne, without whose assistance and insistence it would never have been written, and to the Kentucky coal miners whose trials and tragedies are its central theme.

Foreword

THREE HUNDRED MILES west of the national capital lies the Cumberland Plateau of the Appalachians, a mountainous region of flat-topped ridges and steep-walled valleys, richly endowed by nature with dense forests, winding rivers, abundant game, loamy soils, and thick veins of coal.

This is Daniel Boone country, where Indians and then fiercely independent frontiersmen found in these isolated valleys the elements that sustained a vigorous life. Yet it is one of the ironies of our history that many of their descendants live there today in bleak and demoralizing poverty almost without parallel on this continent.

Harry Caudill, a young Kentucky ex-legislator with roots generations deep in the Cumberland coves, tells here the pathetic and disturbing story of these forgotten backcountry people — a tragic tale of the abuse and mismanagement of a resource heritage, and the human erosion that is always the concomitant of shortsighted exploitation.

Caudill's book is a story of land failure and the failure of men. It is reminiscent of such earlier works as Sinclair's *The Jungle*, Steinbeck's *The Grapes of Wrath*, and Agee's *Let Us Now Praise Famous Men*. Although one may differ with details of interpretation, in probing dark areas of American life such books as these and *Night Comes to the Cumberlands* speak eloquently to the American conscience.

Life on the Cumberland Plateau today is an anachronism, a remnant of an ugly chapter of our history. In the nineteenth century we recklessly plundered our continent, raiding it for beaver, for buffalo, for timber, for gold, for grass, laying waste to forests and hillsides and river valleys, without regard for the needs of future generations. A national movement of protest finally slowed the pace of exploitation, and Gifford Pinchot and Theodore Roosevelt led the American people onto the uphill road of conservation. Today we are all conservationists — or, in our pride, so we would have it seem. Yet Harry Caudill's book tells us that in some parts of the United States the raider spirit of the last century is still abroad, wasting irreplaceable resources and demeaning human lives.

Although Caudill has called his book "A Biography of a Depressed Area," it is also the story of what other parts of America might have been, if we had not developed a land ethic and formulated a systematic conservation program. Ironically, not far away from the dark and bloody ground of the Cumberland Plateau is the Tennessee Valley Authority, the nation's highest benchmark in land use and regional planning of resources. But a few years ago the Congress drew a wall around TVA, and its proximity only serves now to dramatize the contrast between the social health and well-being that accompany wise development of resources, and the poverty of land and spirit that can occur in absence of such planning.

Mr. Caudill has constructive proposals for the rehabilitation of his homeland — but it will take deep concern by people in Washington and Frankfort to bring them to fruition.

This book is the story of what happens when men betray their responsibilities as land stewards. The price we pay for wanton spoliation is sure and certain. In the highest sense, conservation of the land is the conservation of human life. The two have always been, and will always be, inseparable.

— STEWART L. UDALL

Introduction

THE CUMBERLAND PLATEAU region of Kentucky is a serrated upland in the eastern and southeastern part of the state. Its jagged hills and narrow winding valleys cover some ten thousand square miles. It embraces nineteen counties and portions of a dozen others. These units of government were created by the caprice of governors and legislators and, with one exception, were named for the state's heroes of statecraft and battlefield: Bell, Breathitt, Clay, Floyd, Harlan, Knott, Knox, Laurel, Lee, Leslie, Letcher, McCreary, Magoffin, Martin, Owsley, Perry, Pike, Whitley and Wolfe. Few of the heroes deserved so high an honor and few of the counties were worthy of creation. Only Pike County has proved to be sufficiently large and wealthy to discharge even fairly well the responsibilities inherent in local government.

The plateau's half million inhabitants are among the earth's most interesting folk. Their European ancestry and American adventures constitute a remarkable page in the history of mankind. The American public is prone to think of them as quaint hillbillies, a concept sociologists have neglected to explain or explore. In truth, the Kentucky mountaineer is drawn from some of the oldest white stock to be found north of Florida. His forebears had dwelt in or on the edge of the Southern Appalachians for generations before the Declaration of Independence was penned. In their long residence on this continent they left behind a unique, checkered and violent history. Their past created the modern mountaineers and the communities in which they live, and resulted in a land of economic, social and political blight without parallel in the nation. The purpose of this work is to trace the social, economic and political forces which produced the vast "depressed area" of eastern Kentucky. .

Much of the region's story is the story of coal. Geologists tell us that two hundred million years ago it was a plain that had risen from the floor of a long-dry inland sea. Then the tortured crust of the earth cracked and "faulted," rearing the Pine Mountain. This long, steep, ragged ridge now stretches from the Breaks of the Big Sandy River on the Virginia line some hundred and thirty miles south-westerly into northern Tennessee. It parallels the Cumberland (or Big Black) Mountain, the southern boundary of the plateau. Water flowing away from its base over a great fan-shaped territory carved the channels of three of the state's major streams and chiseled thousands of narrow valleys — the creeks and hollows of today.

After the shallow sea receded it left a vast bog where vegetation flourished, died, piled up in deep beds, turned to peat and finally, aeons later, to coal. When the streams carved out the mountains and ridges of today they sliced through magnificent seams of coal, a mineral the steel age would esteem more highly than rubies.

Coal has always cursed the land in which it lies. When men begin to wrest it from the earth it leaves a legacy of foul streams, hideous slag heaps and polluted air. It peoples this transformed land with blind and crippled men and with widows and orphans. It is an extractive industry which takes all away and restores nothing. It mars but never beautifies. It corrupts but never purifies.

But the tragedy of the Kentucky mountains transcends the tragedy of coal. It is compounded of Indian wars, civil war and intestine feuds, of layered hatreds and of violent death. To its sad blend, history has added the curse of coal as a crown of sorrow.

What I have written is drawn from experience — from seeing, hearing and working with mountaineers. In a land with few books and pens many tales are transmitted from father and mother to son and daughter. Such tales and legends breathe out a rich past to anyone patient enough to hear them. From my grandmothers and scores of other ancient storytellers were acquired many of the incidents and impressions I have related. After all, people of my blood and name have lived in the plateau from the beginning. My grandfather's grandfather, James Caudill, was the first white man to call what is now Letcher County his home. He built his cabin in 1792. Another of my forebears was scalped by an Indian raiding party when he was two years old. The redskins killed his parents, brothers and sisters and left him for dead in the corner of a rail fence a few yards from their burned cabin. A hunter found him, nursed him back to health, reared him with his own children and gave him his name. My grandfather, Henry Caudill, served four years as a lieutenant in the Confederate Army, was wounded and totally pauperized in the process. My mother's grandfather fought on the other side, a fact which caused me to be indoctrinated from both directions. In more recent times, my father lost an arm in a mining accident. Still later my only brother was seriously disabled in a similar mishap. Since 1948 I have practiced law in mountain courthouses. Three times I have been elected to represent my county in the Kentucky Legislature. This personal background is mentioned, pardonably I hope, as evidence that my narrative is not founded on hasty first impressions.

In the 1960 preferential primary, Senator — now President — John F. Kennedy campaigned across West Virginia and saw at first hand the conditions existing in the coalfields of that state. The spectacle of mass misery and of mass surrender to it appears to have deeply impressed him, because in the general election campaign he repeatedly referred to the hunger and depression he had seen there. West Virginia is not far from the great population centers of the eastern seaboard where Mr. Kennedy grew up, and it may be cause for wonder that this inquisitive and well-educated young man could have been unaware of the deplorable situation in which the West Virginia highlander finds himself in the seventh decade of the twentieth century. However, the fact is that a million Americans in the Southern Appalachians live today in conditions of squalor, ignorance and ill health which could scarcely be equaled in Europe or Japan or, perhaps, in parts of mainland Asia. For example, the 1960 census disclosed that 19 per cent of the adult population of the Southern mountain region can neither read nor write. Bell County, Kentucky, with a total population of 35,336, was found to contain 17,213 citizens twenty-five years of age or older. Of these adults 1018 had never attended school at all. In addition, 3884 had attended school four years or less. Thus, 4902 persons — substantially more than 25 per cent — were classified, for all practical purposes, as functional illiterates.

A plethora of articles and feature stories have been written in national magazines and metropolitan newspapers about this paradox of medieval stagnation in the midst of twentieth-century prosperity and progress, but none of them has traced the long road over which the Southern mountaineer has traveled to the helplessness and hopelessness which so frequently marks him today.

The people of the Southern mountains share a similar history and background and, with local variations, they have journeyed together into the tragedy which now enfolds them. The same geologic processes which culminated in the Kentucky coal seams produced similar deposits in a small corner of Maryland, and in Virginia, West Virginia, Alabama and Tennessee. The mining industry developed in each of these states along the same general lines though during somewhat different periods of time. Few of the deep social and economic forces which afflict a people stop at lines drawn on political maps, and the pressures which have undermined the character and independence of the Kentucky coalfield mountaineer have been at work with similar results in other states. What I shall say about the Kentucky coal miner applies, with local modifications, to the entire coal-producing area of the Southern highlands.

The mountaineer can present no enigma to a world which is interested enough to look with sympathy into the forces which have made him. And look we must, because with his fruitful wife and brood of untamed children he presents a problem to the nation which is many-faceted and which will deepen in complexity during the ensuing decades. As the nation moves toward the challenges of a new century and a world ringing with change, it cannot afford to leave huge islands of its own population behind, stranded and ignored. Idleness and waste are antipathetic to progress and growth, and, unless the Cumberland Plateau is to remain an anchor

dragging behind the rest of America, it — and the rest of the Southern Appalachians — must be rescued while there is yet time.

In the spring of 1960 I was invited to serve as commencement
speaker at an eighth-grade graduation in a coal camp school. The
seven graduates received their diplomas in the dilapidated two-room
building which had sheltered two generations of their forebears. A
shower sent a little torrent of water through the ancient roof onto
one of the scarred desks. The worn windows rattled in their frames
and the paper decorations which had been prepared by the seventh-
graders fluttered in drafts admitted by the long-unpainted walls. Outside, the grassless playground lay in the shadow of an immense slate
dump and was fringed by a cluster of ramshackle houses. One of the
graduates had been orphaned by a mining accident, and the father of
another wheezed and gasped with silicosis. The fathers of three
others were jobless.

The little ceremony was opened with the singing of "America the
Beautiful," our most stirring patriotic hymn. The irony of the words,
sung so lustily in such a setting, inspired the writing of this book. Perhaps it may help a little to bring the sad reality and the splendid
dream a little closer together, for my friends, my kinsmen, my fellow mountaineers.

Contents

PART I

The Wilderness Seed

CHAPTER ONE

———•———

Our Disinherited Forebears

SYSTEMATIC and orderly migration onto the shores of North America began, as every schoolboy knows, in the early 1600s and persisted thereafter at an ever-rising tempo for more than three hundred years. Europeans came to the New World for many reasons and under a great diversity of circumstances. In New England whole families came from England and settled small but entire villages. A shipload of settlers was likely to contain representatives from a dozen crafts. Thus a community life sprang up which was patterned closely after the social order from which the people had migrated. Some of the settlers came to avoid religious inhibitions, some were adventurers in quest of fame, and others were seeking political freedom and economic opportunity not to be found in Europe. But, for whatever reasons, they came freely and willingly. These essential premises are evidenced by the fact that, within thirty years after the first settlements, a considerable number of chartered towns had sprung up over a wide area in New England. More often than not the newcomer to these Northern shores brought his wife and a steadily augmenting number of children. Most of the settlers were from the middle class, and not a few were landed gentry, perhaps in most instances sons whose inheritance was insufficient to maintain them in the Island Kingdom. Even the similarity of climate contributed to perpetuation of a minuscule England along these rockbound coasts. Thus it turned out that the foundations were laid for a cohesive, well organized and disciplined society. This society, as it grew and strengthened, was able to clear the forests, sow the fields, build the towns and then the cities which were to become the powerhouses of American industry and civilization.

Essentially, this is the schoolboy conception of the origins of America, and when applied to New England it is doubtless true as a generalization.

New England was settled by farmers and villagers, but the climate and soil of the Southland did not entice such settlers. The economic value of the Southern region was discovered by planters, and there a plantation society was established and nurtured. As Europeans became habituated to nicotine, the demand for tobacco expanded at an astronomical rate. Tobacco was a cash crop and producers sought to manufacture it from the soil in the most efficient and least expensive way. Thus there grew up along the tobacco coasts a spangle of plantations, the majority originally quite small, embracing at most a few thousand acres. Slaves were imported from Africa to work the land, and then more slaves and still more. But so rapidly did the demand for the product grow that not even by the mightiest exertions could the slave traders keep up with the demand for black field hands. As the plantation economy strengthened and as the cotton plant appeared in the same regions, the labor shortage became acute and the planters turned to the teeming cities of England.

The cities and greater towns of Britain were not places of beauty or comfort for anyone in the seventeenth and eighteenth centuries — not even for the most favored classes. And for many — indeed, for most — they were nauseous hell holes of crime and venality. The streets were unlighted by night and swarmed with footpads, pickpockets, thieves, robbers and prostitutes at all hours. Hideous open sewers contaminated air and water and helped to make life both unpleasant and short. Constables were able to maintain only a semblance of order in such a setting, even though, with the help of the assize judges, gibbets and scaffolds were seldom bare of their grisly fruit. It was an age in which a child of seven could be hanged for stealing a loaf of bread; an age in which the father of a large brood of children could be locked in a cell for life if he was so unfortunate as to incur debts which he could not pay. It was also an age in which many men were slain in perilous occupations, and in which many others went to the scaffold or died in military service or of recurring plagues. It was an age in which countless mothers died of "childbed fever" and other complications arising from pregnancy. These and many other factors resulted in great hordes of orphans, who roamed the streets of towns and cities and the countryside itself, and whose care and protection the Crown was wholly unprepared to assume.

It was to these orphans and to the debtors' prisons which the labor-hungry planters of the Southern coasts turned. Parliament wanted to get rid of these social outcasts, who so proliferated and burdened the respectable classes of England, and the agents of the plantation owners were able to paint glowing pictures of the wonderful new world waiting beyond the Atlantic, where the weather was sunny and where men might perform honest labor under wholesome conditions. The inevitable result was a series of Parliamentary acts making it possible to transport street orphans, debtors and criminals to the New World, their transportation costs to be paid by the planters. Of course, these wretched outcasts were obliged by law to repay the generous planter with the sole commodity they could produce — their labor. The period of indentureship was usually seven years, though sometimes it was much longer.

And so for many decades there flowed from Merry England to the piney coasts of Georgia, Virginia and the Carolinas a raggle-taggle of humanity — penniless workmen fleeing from the ever-present threat of military conscription; honest men who could not pay their debts, pickpockets and thieves who were worth more to the Crown on a New World plantation than dangling from a rope, and children of all ages and both sexes, whose only offense was that they were orphans and without guardians capable of their care.

Not all persons who came to the New World under such circumstances were brought legally, even by the loose standards prevailing at the time. Not all children who found themselves in a ship's hold outward bound for Charleston were orphans. Gangs of thieves prospered in the sordid business of stealing or "nabbing" children for the plantations. In the parlance of their day they were called "kidnabbers," a term later converted by Cockney English to "kidnapers."

But the peril of kidnaping was not restricted to hapless boys and girls. Judging from an ancient song, adults, too, were shanghaied, and sometimes under truly agonizing circumstances:

> The night I was a-married,
>   And on my marriage bed,
> There come a fierce sea captain
>   And stood by my bed stead.
>
> His men, they bound me tightly
>   With a rope so cruel and strong,
> And carried me over the waters
>   To labor for seven years long.

It is apparent that such human refuse, dumped on a strange shore in the keeping of a few hundred merciless planters, was incapable of developing the kind of stable society under construction in the Puritan North. Instead of the hymn-singing pilgrim to whom idleness was the badge of shame, we must start with the cynical, the penniless, the resentful and the angry. Many of them died on the plantations under the whips of taskmasters. Some ran away and became pirates whose Jolly Rogers terrorized the oceans. A few, perhaps, rose over the heads and shoulders of their suffering fellows to become planters themselves. Others — and it is these with whom we are concerned — ran away to the interior, to the rolling Piedmont, and thence to the dark foothills on the fringes of the Blue Ridge. These latter were joined by more who came when their bonds had expired. And here we have the people — few in number, but steadily gaining recruits, living under cliffs or in rude cabins — who were the first to earn for themselves the title of "Southern mountaineers."

Slowly, in the last quarter of the seventeenth century and throughout the eighteenth, these backwoodsmen increased in number. Steadily, newcomers pushed in from the coastal regions and the birth rate must have been, as it still is, prodigious. Thus by 1750 or 1775 there was thoroughly established in the fringes of the Southern Appalachian chain the seed stock of the "generations" * whose descendants have since spread throughout the entire mountain range, along every winding creek bed and up every hidden valley. The family names found in eastern Kentucky today are heard over the entire region of the Southern mountains. They bespeak a peasant and yeoman ancestry who, for the most part, came from England itself and from Scot-

* In the colloquial parlance of the Highlands, this term is used to denote a blood line bearing the same surname.

land and Ireland: Adams, Allen, Anderson, Baker, Begley, Boatwright, Brown, Burke, Cable, Callihan, Campbell, Caudill*, Collier, Collins, Combs, Cook, Cooper, Cornett, Day, Fee, Fletcher, Frazier, Freeman, Gilley, Gilliam, Hale, Hall, Hampton, Hensley, Holbrook, Halcomb, Huff, Ison, Knuckles, Langley, Lewis, Little, Long, Martin, Mason, May, Morgan, McIntosh, Miller, Moore, Noble, Nolan, Perkins, Pigman, Potter, Reynolds, Rose, Scott, Sexton, Shell, Shepherd, Sizemore, Smith, Spencer, Spicer, Stamper, Sturgill, Sumpter, Taulbee, Thomas, True, Turner, Ward, Watts, Webb, Wells, White, Williams, Workman, Wright.

The Antebellum South was filled with romantic legends in which handsome young men left baronial halls and came to the New World to establish spacious manor houses of their own and to preserve the chivalry and gallantry of Sir Walter Scott's fantastic novels. Coats of arms were duly supplied to bolster these outlandish claims, and they hang today on thousands of walls, attesting to the hereditary splendor of imaginary ancestors. But, alas, in contrast the Southern mountaineer is by his very name fenced off from such pretensions, for his cognomen has come down with him from his first outcast ancestors on these shores and marks him indelibly as the son of a penniless laborer whose forebears, in turn, had been, more often than not, simply serfs.

It is conventional history that after Dr. Thomas Walker and a number of other explorers had entered the Kentucky country, Daniel Boone and James Harrod led the first crop of permanent settlers to found a fortress village called Harrodstown. But a realistic appraisal of the character of the men and women then gathering in the valleys of the Blue Ridge make it most likely that at least a scattering of

* A tradition gives to this surname an interesting and unusual history. Apparently Spanish, it is unusual in a land of Scotch-Irish-English extraction. The story is told that when the Spanish Armada passed the coasts of Northern Scotland some of the unfortunate galleons were wrecked on off-shore rocks. The sailors and soldiers straggled ashore and a few, at least, were permitted to survive by the fierce Scots. When the Scots attempted to talk to them, the Spaniards pointed out an officer as their spokesman, and referred to him as "El Caudillo." In time the Scots came to apply this term derisively to all the castaways, in much the same spirit of jest in which we are likely to refer to all Indians as Chiefs. The name stuck, and eventually through intermarriage there grew up a strain of "black Scotch" — people with swarthy complexions, heavy black beards and coal-black eyes, who contrast sharply with the brown hair and eyes and ruddy skin of the Scots generally.

backwoodsmen had preceded them into the region. By the time of
the Harrodstown (now Harrodsburg) settlement, much of the pioneer society in this mountainous region had resided in the wilderness for three or four generations. They had already become thoroughly adapted to their environment. They had acquired much of
the stoicism of the Indians and inurement to primitive outdoor living had made them almost as wild as the red man and physically
nearly as tough. The white backwoodsman had learned, perhaps
from the Cherokees, how to build cabins,* and had improved the
structure by the addition of a crude chimney. His "old woman"
could endure hardships and privation as well as the Indian squaw,
and was far more fruitful. Having never been exposed to the delights
of civilization, she was willing to follow her husband wherever
wanderlust and a passion for untrammeled freedom might take him.
And the mountaineer needed few implements and skills to live by
kingly standards (to him) anywhere in the Appalachians, or in the
rolling meadowlands beyond. He had learned to clear the narrow
bottoms for the cultivation of Indian corn, squash, potatoes, beans
and tobacco, and from the sale of skins and other forest products he
had acquired an ax and the Pennsylvania "Dutch" rifle and lead and
powder. Salt could be obtained at natural licks, and all other things
essential to his well-being could be acquired in the forest.

Recently discovered archives from the files of the Royal Government of Virginia disclose that more than a generation before
Walker's expedition an exploring party sent out by the governor
stumbled upon a family living near the present town of Pound, Virginia, on the edge of the Cumberland Plateau — some two hundred
miles in advance of the westernmost forts. The family had survived,
on friendly terms with occasional bands of prowling Indians, and it
is hardly likely that this wild frontiersman and his wife and children
were the only ones to penetrate so far into the vast wilderness.

Be that as it may, the Piedmonters and Blue Ridge mountaineers
had attained considerable numbers by the onset of the Revolutionary War, and, inspired by a folk memory of ancient wrongs endured
at the hands of British Royal authority, they threw themselves into
the war against the Crown. At the Battle of Kings Mountain their
sharpshooters decimated the royalists and their strutting officers,

* A skill the Indian had probably acquired from French trappers.

and won for themselves the gratitude of the Continental Congress. When the war ended, the new nation was unable to pay its heroes the wages they had earned, so, when the disorders of the Confederation were past, Congress promptly provided for the allotment of "western lands" to the unpaid veterans.

The lure of free land was certainly a powerful magnet which attracted many mountaineers deeper into the hinterland of the range, and a few of them farther westward into the "open country." But it must not be supposed that the enticement of land ownership was the most important cause of the new westward migration. While the population was sparse, indeed, by modern standards, these wild woodsmen had begun to yearn for escape from a land so crowded that neighbors could be found within a few miles of the cabin door. They had "gone wild" in the still solitudes of their forests, and they hungered for new expanses of virgin wilderness where their lives might be unrestricted by even the frail inhibitions imposed by the meager society that had coalesced around them. It was largely for this reason that, in the years after the close of the Revolution, the mountaineers began to move westward in ever-increasing numbers.

Much of the western migration within the mountains was determined quite by accident. The few existing trails had been worn by wild animals and the occasional bands of wild men who hunted them. "Long hunters" had prowled through much of the western Appalachians before the general westward migration began. Nevertheless, it was essentially unexplored country, and the usual newcomer simply strapped his few possessions onto the back of a mule or horse and, with wife and children plodding behind, crossed the hills, creeks and valleys until he found an area which suited his fancy.

A number of factors may have influenced a newcomer's decision to stop, but it is almost certain that the most important consideration was the availability of game and of soil that could be easily cleared for a corn patch. I remember talking to an aged mountaineer who explained how his ancestors had chanced to settle near the mouth of Turkey Creek in Letcher County. His grandfather as an old man had recounted the tale to him. After passing through the dense forests for many days, they came to a place "whar they had been a big forest fire. Hit had burnt down all the big timber trees. Hit was in the early spring of the year, and young cane sprouts was a-growin' up everywhar wild amongst the stumps and dead trees. And Pap said, 'We'll stop here and dig up the cane and plant corn.' And so that's how we happened to be here instead of sommers else and our folks have ben here ever since. Besides, they was a-plenty of game, and while us young'uns and the women put in the corn, Pap was able to hunt and kill a-plenty of fresh meat."

This venerable mountaineer also explained one of the cogent reasons why his ancestors had moved into this new region two or three hundred miles from their starting place. His grandfather had told him "game was skase in North Kerliner, and so we just follered the game track into Kentucky."

So it is clear that the people who settled the Kentucky mountains were not inspired Europeans determined to cross the dangerous oceans and found a citadel of religious and economic freedom in the New World. They were native North Americans with deeply engrained mores, habits and social outlook. The Kentucky mountaineer, as a type, was already thoroughly established. He had simply moved over a few hundred miles to find unplowed creek bottoms, a more plentiful supply of game, and to get away from his neighbors.

The migration into the virgin Kentucky mountain wilderness continued at a steady pace for about twenty-five years after 1787. Steadily, the fresh valleys filled with people until about 1812, when the flow of newcomers began to decline. At that time the country was by no means filled with people, in any modern sense of the word; but over most of the region the backwoodsman could find neighbors within five or ten miles of his cabin. Though the influx from the east diminished, it did not cease, but continued sporadically until about 1830. By that year all the parent stock of the basic population had arrived, and few settlers came into the region after that date.

CHAPTER TWO

———•———

A Harsh New Land Becomes
Home Sweet Home

WITHIN the span of years mentioned in the last chapter, the Blue
Ridge mountaineer had become a farmer, dependent upon crops
and herded livestock rather than the forests for his livelihood, and
willing, in some measure at least, to break with the old, unstable
frontier tradition of hunting and Indian-style agriculture. Society in
the Blue Ridge had undergone softening refinements, and there
were few large tracts of new land to be found in the western mountains. So the long trickle of immigrants dried up, and the scattered
inhabitants of the Cumberlands were left alone.

The trek from the Blue Ridge to the Cumberland Plateau was
not an easy one, even for the rugged borderers. The escarpments of
Pine and Black Mountains, straight as walls and almost as steep,
were baffling barriers. Many passed through Cumberland Gap. Some
came by way of less famous passes — the Scuttle Hole, the Doubles,
or Pound Gap. Some of their troubles were embalmed in songs which
a wrinkled fiddler will still occasionally saw out:

> In Cumberland Gap it got so cold
> I couldn't keep from freezin' to death to save my soul.

> Cumberland Gap is a dry old place,
> Ye can't find water there to wash ye' face.

> In the Cumberland Gap the cattle all died,
> The men all swore and the women all cried.

The fierce Choctaws from Tennessee and the hunted, wandering Shawnees from their villages in Ohio still prowled the plateau and southwestern Virginia, especially in Indian Summer, that hazy, still season just after the earliest frost. Then the young braves set out to find scalps to boast of during the long months of winter. For protection against these "red devils" the borderer fetched not only his rifle but a huge military-type musket or a long-barreled "polk-stalk" shotgun. (These were stuffed with rifle balls or hard creek stones, and could work fearful execution from a cabin window or porthole.) And the borderer and his family brought fierce allies to warn them of any impending assault — a pack of a dozen or more evil-natured, vicious feist and mongrel dogs. Fed on raw flesh and taught a savage hatred of Indians from puppyhood, they constituted a snarling, implacable outguard against roaming war parties. And sad, indeed, was the case of the unfortunate warrior who found himself wounded and helpless beneath their fangs.

It is unlikely that history will ever again record the appearance of a man who, as a type, will possess the hardihood, the sturdy self-reliance and the fierce independence of the American frontiersman in the forty years preceding the turn of the ninteenth century, and in the next decade or two thereafter. He was an uncouth brawler, wholly undisciplined and untamed, and it was practically impossible to direct or control his energies in any sustained undertaking, but when objectives were within his grasp and were approved by him, the frontiersman multiplied by any considerable number constituted a well-nigh irresistible force on the North American continent.

This fact was best demonstrated in the incredible Battle of Kings Mountain in 1780. Major Patrick Ferguson, the British commander, referred to the frontier militiamen as "barbarians," but in the battle that followed, the outnumbered borderers killed or captured all the 1104 officers and men who wore the King's Coat — including the unfortunate Ferguson. Twenty-eight of the "barbarians" perished in the brief engagement.

In most American frontier areas the pioneer sought to create the comforts and safety of a stable society for himself and his neighbors. To him, the frontier was simply a passing phase which must precede the establishment of civilization with its opportunity to enjoy security and to amass wealth. However, in the middle South, specifically in the Blue Ridge, the frontiersman, rooted in the background which we have already noted, did not regard the frontier era as a passing phase through which he must journey to a better time. To the contrary, he cherished the freedom and the savage harshness of his primitive existence. A passionate lover of a freedom that was licentious, he was resolved to avoid even the mildest limitations on his liberty required by any kind of organized society. Any manifestation of government was abhorrent to his lawless soul. Far from seeing the frontier as a galling time of hardship and privation, he viewed it as a golden age which he lusted to retain. Instead of moving westward to find new lands in which to build snug farms and bustling towns, he sought to remain on the frontier in order to keep away from the advancing influences and restrictions of civilization. This essential difference in fundamental psychology, projected through a half-dozen intervening generations, accounts in part, at least, for the singular "apartness" of the Southern highlander from the rest of the nation to this day. Thus the frontier of the middle and upper South became the spawning ground of such heroic American scouts as Daniel Boone, Simon Kenton, John Colter, Kit Carson, Jim Bridger, and scores and hundreds of others who, in buckskin jacket and leggings, with butcher knife, tomahawk and rifle, marked the trails for a century of westward migration.

It was here on the frontier of the middle and upper South that the Indian wars rose to their fiercest and cruelest pitch. Here the savage was taught his lessons in perfidy by masters of the trade. Here the childish, superstitious red man was brought abruptly cheek to jowl with a population born of embittered rejects and outcasts from the shores of Europe — as cynical, hardened and bitter a lot as can be imagined outside prison walls. They were free hands with fists, knife and rifle, illiterate, uncouth and hard-drinking. And to them the Indian was no more than another animal to be hunted in the same spirit and relish with which the bear was tracked down and slain — for the fierce pleasure of the sport. The Indian, simple savage that he was, quickly reacted to the frontiersman's harsh treatment, and in backwoods vernacular, "the fur flew." In the long border wars that followed the Indian inevitably lost, because he fought an opponent who had adopted the red man's skills and tactics and used them with greater tenacity and persistence. The white man became, almost, a pale-faced Indian. He ate the Indian's corn and "jerked" meat. He wore the Indian's deerskin clothes. He even adopted his tomahawk, and here only, on the rampaging frontier, the white border man collected scalps with all the zest of the Choctaw brave.

Sometimes the pale-faced borderer actually chose Indian society in preference to his own and joined a tribe as an adopted member. The most infamous of these renegades was Simon Girty, who took a Shawnee wife and was perhaps the cruelest raider ever to harry the frontier. He is known to have participated in diabolical torture of white captives and was present at the prolonged siege of Boonesborough in 1778. Chief Benge, the "Shawnee Devil" who between 1777 and 1794 raided and plundered in southwestern Virginia and along the Big Sandy and the upper reaches of the Kentucky River in the Cumberland Plateau, was a half-breed. His confidant and loyal supporter was a murderous white man named Hargis. Simon Kenton, the magnificent Virginian whose prowess as a woodsman was unsurpassed, first heard tales about "Kaintuckee" from George Yeager, an Indian-reared white man.

In the autumn of 1960 I persuaded a ninety-two-year-old resident of Leslie County to take down his battered fiddle and play some ancient dance tunes for tape recording. When the tapes were finished we fell into a discussion of his ancestry. The dark pigmentation of his eye sockets, his high cheekbones and hooked nose, betrayed at least one Indian forebear not too many generations removed. His explanation of how his Shawnee blood was acquired tells a deeper story — of a people's character in those long-ago years when George Washington was President of an infant nation.

My grandmammy was half Indian and half white and she told me how it come to be, just as her mammy told her. Ye see, when our folks had fust come here from North Kerliner they wuz a-livin' on Rockhouse Creek under a big cliff they had sort of fronted up with poles and mud daubin'. Well, the men was buildin' a log house and one of the girls went out into the woods to gether a basket of chestnuts. She was about fourteen years old and while she was out there by herself she was grabbed by two Indians and kerried off to the Ohio country. Indians liked young-'uns, but fer some reason Indian wimmen didn't have many babies. So one of the Indian men fell in love with her and decided to keep her fer his wife. She seed she never could get back to her people unless she used her head so she played up to him and made him think she loved him. They spent the winter in a Indian town and the next spring she begged him to let her go home. She promised to stay with him always and to love him and have children fer him if he would just let her see her pap and mammy one more time. So he believed her and trusted in her and brought her back here to this country. Well, sir, when they got here on this creek he killed a wild turkey and cooked it and they eat it. Afterwards he laid down on a mossy place and went to sleep and she slipped off and run away. She knowed she was close to home and shore enough, in a little while she seed the house. She run up to hit and her daddy wasn't at home but her mammy and brother was. She told them what happened and her brother axed her to pint out the way she had come after she left the Indian. Then he took a gun and went out and hid in a little ivy thicket and waited real still. In a few minutes here come the Indian, slippin' along trackin' the girl. Her brother shot him and killed him afore he knowed what was a-happenin'.

In about three months the girl had a baby by that Indian. Hit was a girl and growed up to be my grandmammy, and that's how come I am part Indian.

In woodcraft the white men were little less skillful than the red. In other respects, however, they were sharply dissimilar. The Indian was grave and calm and loved ceremony and ritual. He was deeply religious and was respectful of many time-sanctioned customs and taboos. The white man, however, was, more often than not, loud-mouthed, profane, vulgar and short-tempered. He honored few memories and generally disdained religion short of the deathbed. In some important respects he was less civilized than his red foe.

I have heard highland fiddlers and banjo-"pickers" play and sing a hoary ballad which they called "Grand-Pap's Trip to New Orleens." A good many Kentuckians made the long trip to Louisiana with Andy "By-God" Jackson, and their sharpshooting helped to shatter the ordered ranks of valiant English infantry. If the balladeer did not exaggerate unduly — and I doubt that he did — John Bull's soldiers were vanquished by an enemy who combined the most savage traits of both races.

We made a bank just nipple high
  Behind which we was layin',
And when the Redcoats come in sight
  We started out a-slayin'.

We fed them lead fer breakfast,
  And we fed them lead fer dinner,
And the ones that didn't say their prayers
  Went straight to hell a sinner.

We shot them in their big round eyes,
  We shot their chins and noses,
We shot all the buttons off
  Their coats as red as roses.

When we first went to New Orleens
  They said, 'John Bull's a-comin',
When we'd been there a mighty short time
  They said, 'John Bull's a-runnin'.'

When we got through a-shootin' them
  Ye should of heerd 'em cryin',
Cause we went out and got their hair
  And set their skelps to dryin'.

And, while he fought the Indian as a beast, the frontiersman unhesitatingly mated with the red man's squaws. White women and
girls were frequently in short supply and great demand, and the frontier standards of beauty could not be high. By capture and by woo-
ing, great numbers of dusky aborigine women found their way into the
pole cabins of the borderers — to bear broods of unruly half-breed
children. Most of them were Cherokees or Choctaws, and as the migration westward proceeded into Kentucky, the acquisition of Indian
blood continued unabated. To this day countless mountaineeers display the high cheekbones and coppery skin of Indian forebears, and
one hears repeated over and over from old men and women, "My
grandmother told me that her mother was a full-blooded Cherokee
Indian," or, "My daddy always said his grandmother was a Choctaw
squaw." The deed books of Eastern Kentucky counties abound with
such names as Golden Hawk Hall, Mingo Halcomb, Black Fish

Thomas and Choctaw Ingram — cognomens almost certainly bestowed by proud squaws on the sons of their white husbands.

The folk who settled the Kentucky mountains were part and parcel of this stock, and shared fully its psychology and point of view. In short, they were by inclination permanent frontiersmen. They were exasperating "trash" to the Ohio- and Illinois-bound farmer — settlers whose wagon trains passed their cabins along the Wilderness Road through Cumberland Gap and on the banks of the Ohio in northern Kentucky.

A European, Karl Anton Postl, writing under the pseudonym of Charles Sealsfield, traveled extensively through the American West in 1823 and 1824. He was a sort of nineteenth-century John Gunther, and his travel book (*The Americans as They are: Described in a Tour Through the Valley of the Mississippi*) undertook to give the low-down on the states through which he passed. His praise of the industrious Ohio farmers was lavish but his opinion of most Kentuckians was low indeed. Though by that time the frontier had advanced far beyond Kentucky, the tenacious frontier mentality of the Piedmont and Blue Ridge was still little diluted. The widely traveled author, who had already written *Austria As It Is*, declared about Kentucky:

The productions of this beautiful country might, if properly cultivated, become inexhaustible sources of wealth and prosperity to its inhabitants; tobacco is a staple article, excelling in quality even that of Virginia, if properly managed: cotton thrives well in the southern parts of the state. Corn yields from forty to ninety bushels; wheat from thirty to sixty; melons, sweet potatoes, peaches, apples, plums, &c, attain a superior degree of perfection. One of the principal articles of trade is hemp, the culture of which has been brought to a high state of improvement; it constitutes one of the chief articles of export to New Orleans. Kentucky has not such extensive plains as Ohio, but is equally fertile, and less exposed to bilious and ague fevers. The stratum, which is generally limestone, is a sure sign of inexhaustible fertility. Hills alternating with valleys form landscapes, which though consisting of native forests, are in the highest degree picturesque. There are parts about Lexington and its environs, which nothing can exceed in beauty of scenery. Even Louisville, with its three islands, the majestic Ohio, and the surrounding little towns, possesses charms seldom rivaled in any country. Kentucky is, without the least exaggeration, one of the finest districts on the face of the earth. The climate is equal to that of the south of France; fruits of every kind arrive at the highest perfection; and it would be difficult to quit this country, did not the character of the inhabitants lessen one's regret at leaving it. But notwithstanding these natural advantages, the population has not increased either in wealth or numbers, in proportion to the more recent state of Ohio. The inhabitants consist chiefly of emigrants from Virginia, and North and South Carolina, and of descendants from backwood settlers — a proud, fierce, and overbearing set of people. They established themselves under a state of continual warfare with the Indians, who took their revenge by communicating to their vanquishers their cruel and implacable spirit. This, indeed, is their principal feature. A Kentuckian will wait three or four weeks in the woods, for the moment of satiating his revenge; and he seldom or never forgives. The men are of an athletic form, and there may be found amongst them many models of truly masculine beauty. The number of inhabitants is now 57,000, including 15,000 slaves. Planters are among the most respectable class, and form the mass of the population. Lawyers are next, or equal to them in rank, no less than the merchants and manufacturers. Physicians and ministers are a degree lower; and last of all, are those mechanics and farmers not possessed of slaves. These are not treated better than the slaves themselves. The constitution inclines towards federalism, landed property being required to qualify a man for a public station. Ministers, of whatever form of worship, are wholly excluded from public offices. Kentucky is not a country that could be recommended to new settlers; slavery; insecure titles to land; the division of the courts of justice into two parts, furiously opposed to each other; an executive, whose present chief is a disgrace to his station, and whose son would be hung in chains, had he been in Great Britain; the worst paper-currency, &c., are serious warnings to every lover of peace and tranquility. We abstain from farther particulars, as our purpose is to give a characteristic description of the Union, which would assuredly not gain by a faithful representation of the state of things in this country, during the last ten years. The Desha family, the emetic scene, the proceedings of the legislature, and of the courts of justice, Sharp's death, &c., are facts which belong rather to the history of the tomahawk savages, than to that of a civilised state. Passions must work with double power and effect, where wealth, and arbitrary sway over a herd of slaves, and a warfare of thirty years with savages, have sown the seeds of the most lawless arrogance, and an untameable spirit of revenge.

The literary institutions, the Transylvania University of Lexington, and the college of Bairdstown, have hitherto exercised very little influence over these fierce people. But a still worse feature observable in them, is an utter disregard of religious principles. Ohio has its sects, thereby evincing an interest in the performance of the highest of human duties. The Kentuckian rails at these, and at every form of worship; certainly a trait doubly afflicting and deplorable in a rising state.

It must be kept in mind that our reporter had confined his journeys to the better and most progressive portions of the state. He saw a relatively open country whose people were engaged in commerce and plantation agriculture of a sort. Imagine if you can the consternation he would have felt if he had ridden a mule into the untamed jungle of the plateau.

In the wrinkled landscape of the Kentucky mountains these folk found a splendid frontier environment. It offered rich lands, ample for their limited agricultural needs, and it swarmed with myriads of wild beasts, birds and fish. Its vast size, intricately compartmented by its numberless valleys, afforded isolation for decades, and the illusion of isolation for more than a century. It remained an island of frontier life and circumstances far behind the real frontier and time forgot and ignored it for a hundred years. Here the Blue Ridgers were well content to remain.

But society does not remain wholly static even in the most primitive and isolated environment. Changes came, though sometimes by stages so slow as to be almost imperceptible.

The settler in the hollows of the Cumberland Plateau wore deerskin shirts, breeches and moccasins, topped with a coonskin cap, and his woman and children were dressed in similar rough attire. Such materials were abundantly available in the forests around them. Skins of beasts could be manufactured into raiment far more easily than could fibers of cotton or linen. His first dwelling was usually a cliff or "rockhouse," faced up in front with a row of leaning poles. Within a year or so, this gave way to a pole cabin which his father had taught him to make after the Cherokee fashion. This shelter was low, usually with walls no more than six feet high. Its walls were built of round poles notched in the corners to fit together as tightly as possible, and with the remaining cracks chinked with mud. The roof consisted of rude boards rived out by hand. This cabin possessed no floor except the dirt on which it stood, and its chimney was built of mud-coated sticks laid up in the same fashion as the log walls.

In the half-century that followed, this structure underwent important aesthetic and practical refinements. A puncheon or split-log floor replaced the packed earth. The walls grew higher and each log was hewed into a six-inch-thick plank. The structure acquired a second floor, or loft, in which the children slept on corn-shuck beds. The dangerously inflammable wooden chimney gave way to one of stone, which drew a much better draft. And, as the larger game grew less abundant, leather garments were supplanted by cotton and linsey-woolsey — home grown, home carded and home made. The later immigrants from the older settlements brought bundles of seed, and small crops of cotton and flax began to bloom in the fertile creek bottoms. To this day, numerous localities bear such names as Flax Branch and the Cotton Patch. The spinning wheel, the card, and the loom came to occupy a prominent corner in each of these improved cabins.

Changes came also in the field of diet. Whereas in the early years venison and squirrel, fish and corn bread occupied the table, now pork held first place. To the active, far-ranging borderer, fat, greasy pork had long been the foremost delicacy; he had eaten deer and other "varmints" only because they were plentifully available and their hunting offered a challenge. But when a real repast was desired fried "hog meat" took precedence over all else. The first settlers brought no domestic animals other than the pack of savage dogs and a few pack horses or mules. But in later years herds of sheep and hogs were driven in front of the family caravan. The latter were turned loose to feed on mast of acorn, chestnut and beech, and soon vast herds of wild swine proliferated on the timbered hillsides. The sheep, too, multiplied and were protected because of their wool, which could be made into warm and serviceable cloth.

In this half-century there grew up farther west, in the Bluegrass, the first of the distilleries which were eventually to make the word "Kentucky" synonymous with bourbon whiskey. Scotsmen had brought to the Blue Ridge the science of distilling firewater from rye and barley, and in their new environment they quickly learned to substitute Indian corn for these Old World grains. Alcohol could break the tedium of a harsh and dangerous life and the mountaineer was prompt to establish a primitive "still" capable of turning out ample whiskey for his household. Money was almost nonexistent, and to get some cash the mountaineer soon learned to manufacture a few barrels of the colorless and raw corn whiskey to be floated downstream on a raft for sale to the distilleries at Louisville or Frankfort. This source brought him practically his only money income for a period of more than fifty years, and ingrained in him a habit so deeply tenacious that generations of revenue officers have been unable to root it out.

If order of even the most rudimentary sort is to be maintained over a region, its sections must be distinguished by place names. The mountaineer, living almost unto himself and supremely self-sufficient, never got around to bestowing names, as such, on his valleys or mountains. Names of places as they are known today simply grew out of generations of use by reference. For example, if on a certain stream there was a large overhanging cliff in which the mountaineer and his family had found shelter, he was likely to call it "the rockhouse creek." In time this would be shortened and formalized to "Rockhouse Creek." Not until surveyors for railroads and coal companies arrived and insisted on a single name for a single place did such appellations crystallize with any certainty. In the picturesque names which these people offhandedly applied to their beautiful streams and valleys one may read much of their history and their harsh and bitter experiences in the loneliness of a grim new frontier: Greasy, Stinking, Little Bullskin, Beefhide, Hell for Certain, Thousand Sticks, Kingdom Come, Little Betty Troublesome, Cutshin, Dead Injun, Devil's Jump, Frozen, Frying Pan, War Branch, and Hell Mountain.

The first immigrants had been frontiersmen pure and simple, but toward the end of the period of settlement relatively solid farmers began to appear. These latter had accumulated some little wealth and brought wagonloads of farm implements, spinning wheels, looms, candle molds, household utensils, and sometimes a few slaves to help clear the forests. The utility and value of the Negro was speedily recognized, and the established settlers began to convey some of their land to the newcomers in return for slaves. A deed recorded in the 1830s, for example, recited that two thousand acres of land were conveyed "in consideration of a buck Negro 30 years of age named Tom, and his wife Julie."

And what of this new land itself — this mother earth which has nurtured some of mankind's most clannish and enigmatic folk? It is a baffling profusion of hills and mountains with ridges and spurs running off them at close intervals. Between these great and small mountains lie narrow valleys, some no more than a dozen yards across and, even at the widest, seldom more than a few hundred yards. Untold generations of fallen forest giants had enriched the land with their decay, and moldering black humus carpeted the floor of the forests from the banks of the creeks almost to the tops of the spurs. Occasionally, an intruder encountered small natural clearings caused by fire, but these were rare and far between. The entire region was matted with an immense primeval forest, so dank and so dense as to amount almost to a jungle. Huge tulip poplars rose straight as arrows and centuries old. Beech, oak, walnut, chestnut, and scores of other species grew in the wildest profusion on hillside, cove and valley floor. Immense tangles of wild grapevine clung to the tops of these forest patriarchs and the combined foliage of tree and vine was so dense as to almost exclude the light from the ground beneath, casting in the hollows and valleys a deep perpetual gloom. In the branches of these great trees, thriving on the mast, were swarms and myriads of squirrels, the foremost delicacy known to the frontier palate. On the ground lurked the bear and the mountain lion — the dread "painter," whose wailing cry so chilled the occupants of lonely cabins that the folk memory of it has assumed supernatural overtones. The streams, especially the longer rivers and creeks, were deep and crystal-clear and teemed with fish and frogs.

Wherever the pioneer could manage to get down a few trees and burn them, the soil produced a profusion of corn, squash, beans, onions, potatoes, and tobacco, almost without labor after it was planted, for this was a land yet without weeds. In the autumn the backwoodsman's wife dried beans, still in their hulls, against winter need. Strings of beans, rings of dried pumpkin and strips of meat hung drying in the smoke of every chimney. These crude delicacies were so succulent that, even in this age of supermarkets and deep-frozen foods, hundreds of mountain women diligently hang up strings of "shucky beans" and "pokes" of dried apples for frontier-style banquets at Thanksgiving and Christmas.

When the migration to the Southern coasts began, agriculture had already achieved the status of a fine art in some parts of Europe. In Holland, Denmark and Scandinavia, and in portions of Germany, France and England, the science of soil conservation and replenishment was fully established and far advanced and even then a field was able to produce food and fiber generation upon generation. Wasteful agricultural methods were resorted to in New England and much of the land was speedily worn out, but this resulted in great measure from the abundance of land rather than from the lack of essential knowledge. After all, such conservative farming techniques were intensive in nature, requiring close care and persistent effort, a system not feasible with much land and little labor. Doubtless many of the emigrants into New England were excellent farmers, long used to the soil and able to bring many tested and proven techniques to the New World. Soon Old World crops were growing side by side with the maize and squash of the Algonquins. Here, for instance, wheat remained the staff of life. The homely corn cake of the Indians was resorted to only when wheat was in short supply.

But the people who came to the Blue Ridge were, for the most part, from the teeming and iniquitous cities of England, with a rich dash of Scotch and Irishmen. These city dwellers, by and large, knew little or nothing about the agricultural way of life. Many of them had spent most of their lives on the cobblestones. Even our Scotch and Irish, while sprung from heath and moor, came certainly from areas on the fringe of European science and learning — areas by no means renowned for successful and remunerative agriculture. Nor were the years spent by many of them on the plantations of any instruction to them, because there the soil was literally mined for the cash crops that could be wrung from it. Finding themselves upon the frontier, they were compelled to resort to the soil, and to the stream and forest, for their sustenance. Having no better teachers to learn from, they perforce learned from the Indians. Since the Indians kept no livestock except the dog, they needed no cribs or barns. Their meat came from the wilderness. They wandered from place to place and seldom planted the same field twice. Usually the squaws planted clearings which had resulted from forest fires, or, finding none, created them by setting fire to the woods. They had no knowledge of soil conservation and the white newcomers who learned from them could contribute none.

So the white man who moved into the rich forests of the Cumberland Plateau brought with him a form of Stone Age agriculture which, with the natural game, was able to provide him with all his essential needs. Corn and meat were the staples — and the two were certainly of equal rank. With scalding water and a little salt his wife could take the pounded corn and bake a tough but nutritious bread. The grains were parched or made into hominy. Few other vegetables or grains found their way into his diet, but in the spring his wife picked "sallets" of crowsfoot, shawnee, poke and countless other wild greens. The frontiersman and his wife had acquired a passionate addiction to tobacco, or as they sometimes called it, "the Indian weed." The women smoked it in clay and corncob pipes and the men both chewed and smoked. A not uncommon practice was to pack one's jaw with a heavy "chew" of the leaf before tamping and lighting one's pipe. The nicotine habit was passed on to children at an early age, and the frontier was fairly splotched with ambeer and wreathed in gray tobacco smoke. The tobacco patch was planted close to the cabin and was tended with even greater care than was devoted to the foodstuffs.

As the wild game declined the mountaineer turned to milk cows, hogs and sheep, and chickens began to roost in the trees about his cabins. The corn patches grew larger but the essential methods and attitudes remained. His agricultural techniques remained rooted deeply in the rudimentary Stone Age concepts, and with the same unfailing results. Tract by tract he was able to cut down the great forests, sometimes burning the trees for their value as fertilizer. He possessed neither the knowledge nor the inclination to prevent any of his land from becoming exhausted or to renew the fertility of any that had already worn out.

The transocean movement did not begin in earnest until the Church of England was already firmly established and its anti-papacy propaganda had found a deep root in the popular mind. If our shanghaied seamen, our street orphans and our insolvent debtors held anything in common besides their misery and resentment, it was likely to be a firm conviction that if heaven were to be acquired it must be reached by a road which avoided Rome. But the Church of

England, as formal and as haughty as the Roman Church, ministered principally to the landed and the wealthy. Its spiritual blessings, such as they were, reached the lower classes largely by a process of downward osmosis. In Scotland the Calvinist Church, while rejecting much of the formality and dogma of Anglican and Roman orders, was nevertheless aloof from a great part of the proletariat.

The point is that the Church — Calvinist, Anglican or radical sect — was wholly unprepared to follow the emigrant and his sons westward with the disorderly and rampaging frontier. The vicars, the parsons, the priests and the preachers would have recoiled from frontier conditions as fire withdraws from water, and the frontier was a hundred years old before any serious effort was made to give spiritual instruction to its sons and daughters. This attempt was first made in the trans-Appalachian country by Methodists and other reform groups after the turn of the nineteenth century. Consequently the frontiersman, in the Blue Ridge and in his wanderings across the intervening mountains to the Cumberland Plateau, had passed from five to ten decades out of contact with the Christian Church in any organized form. The King James Bible was relatively new when his fathers reached the New World, and the borderer retained a fierce respect for it as the Word of God. But many cabins were without a copy, and few of the inhabitants could read it, so that its contents more often than not came down to the frontiersman in garbled snatches from the preceding generation. There was no religious discipline, and the isolation of the frontiersman made it practically impossible for any semblance of religious instruction to be transmitted. Even when a wandering preacher found occasion to pass a night in a cabin, he was likely to find his opinions resented and rejected because the frontiersman believed that one man knew as much about the road to paradise as another. The tradition of the oral transmission of biblical lore is still encountered in the highlands, where one may hear an assertion that such-and-such a statement is "somewhere between the covers of the Bible" — frequently a statement which not even the most diligent Biblical research can verify. While the Good Book occupied an honored place in many frontier households, in a society which was almost wholly illiterate it was seldom read.

Thus the frontiersman was cast adrift in a wilderness with a garble of Christian tradition and half-remembered beliefs. Unable to find fulfillment for inevitable spiritual needs at the altar, and without priest, parson or preacher to console him, he turned in many instances to his old enemy and teacher — the red man.

The frontiersman had brought with him to the New World innumerable Old World superstitions, and these were augmented by additions from Africa acquired from Negro slaves on the plantations. To this mixture was added a formidable assortment of Stone Age superstitions acquired from squaw mothers and wives. In the loneliness and amid the brooding silences of the great forest, this hodgepodge of superstition was called upon to give the explanations of the mysteries and the consolations for the miseries for which mankind has, in all ages, turned to his priests.

Much of life on the frontier had superstitious overtones, and countless commonplace occurrences were carefully studied for meaning or portent. Witchcraft enjoyed widespread credence and misfortune was likely to be attributed to a spell. This in turn called for much conjecture on the question of the witch's identity.

A staple of furniture was the four-legged, straight-backed, cane-bottomed chair. This sturdy hickory implement was believed to have a singular role in the witch's nefarious activities. She had but to seize it by one of the upright posts, tilt it slightly forward and turn it round and round with only one leg touching the floor to cause the devil "to come a-runnin' " — and any child who absentmindedly indulged in this thoughtless gesture was likely to be sternly rebuked.

The mirror, too, had great potency, and seven years of bad luck were visited upon anyone so unwise or clumsy as to break one. Mirrors in the bedroom were so arranged that a person in the bed could not see his reflection. It was well known that to see oneself in a "looking-glass" before arising was to risk incurring the harshest kind of ill luck until the next snowfall.

The black cat was, of course, an evil symbol, but his repute was only a little blacker than that of the owl. This feathered wanderer of the night was believed to be in the service of the devil, and his approach was viewed with dismay. Some thought he was a spy for the Evil One and he was not infrequently greeted with a charge of shot. Generally, though, it was thought best not to offend him. His conduct near a habitation was carefully remarked. If he flew off to the left of the cabin door, bad luck was in store. Perhaps the cabin would burn, or the crops would blight, or the livestock sicken and die. If the owl flew directly over the house, death was coming soon to one of its occupants. But if the bird flapped his great wings and flew off to the right, the household was spared and a run of good luck was sure to ensue.

Spider webs, on the other hand, were spun by creatures friendly to the righteous, and if a man rose in the dawn and found the filmy net stretched across his door, it was a warning that he must not cross the threshold until after sunrise.

In what was, perhaps, a curious blending of the superstitions of the white man with those of the aborigine, it was believed that a child born on certain days — Old Christmas (January 6th) or his father's birthday — was endowed with the power to understand the conversation of wild beasts.

In addition to the invisible bonds of superstitious ritual and observances within which he dwelt, the frontiersman felt the influence of innumerable occult personalities and presences. His European forebears had believed in the existence of ghosts and banshees, and his associations with the Indians strengthened his own opinion that the "spirits" of the dead lived on to torment the living. These ghostly presences frequented the forest trails and hovered near the fords of streams. Sometimes their unearthly cries could be heard at night from some windswept crag. Such mysterious manifestations, or the fear that they might be encountered, could give wings to the feet of a stalwart who, under other circumstances, and armed only with an ax or a butcher knife, would unflinchingly give battle to an enraged bear. Many a frontiersman or his wife had encountered such "spirits," and countless "hainted" places may still be pointed to by their descendants.

The devil, too, was a very real personage, capable of assuming tangible form. This evil one wandered the valleys and hills, his malevolent eyes, red as coals and large as saucers. At lonely bends in a trail he would sometimes spring onto the rump of an agitated horse and accompany the unwilling rider for a mile or so — holding his victim fast all the while in his great black arms. At other times he could be heard late at night passing the door of a lonely cabin, accompanied by the bloodcurdling clank of the chains which he carried for his victim.

Dreams were regarded with awe, and their fulfillment in actual experience was confidently expected. They were believed to be "warnings" of things to come, imparted in some vague way by the spirits of the departed. To dream of muddy water was an omen of impending death. When encountered in dreams, a distinct significance was attached to fire, blood, birds and countless other things. And "to dream of things out of season" would bring "bad luck out of reason."

The moon, too, was thought to exert strong supernatural influences on the lives of men. The phases of the moon were carefully noted and, to a considerable degree, life was regulated by its growth and decline. Some crops could be planted only when the moon was new, while others must be withheld from the soil until an old moon arrived. Meat would spoil even in the coldest weather if the animal was slain when the moon was new. If boards for a cabin roof were rived "when the moon is wrong," they would curl and split. The moon was even believed to influence the birth of children, and the frontier wife was likely to hope that her child would be born when the moon was a tiny crescent. Such good timing was thought to insure strength and a good mind in the baby.

Lacking medicines and physicians, the frontiersman was compelled to rely upon a combination of superstitions and Indian remedies for treatment of illnesses. Wild herbs, barks and roots were hunted and boiled as remedies for practically every ailment. But these "teas" and "poultices" were inadequate, and more potent supernatural medicines were frequently relied on. "Madstones" were carefully preserved and transmitted through the generations. One of these curious formations, sometimes found in the stomach of a sheep or deer, if rubbed on the wound resulting from the bite of a dog was believed to ward off rabies. Incantations were carefully remembered, and Huckleberry Finn with his dead cat in the graveyard was resorting to a remedy firmly believed in by thousands of highlanders before and since Huck's time.

A cult grew up about persons gifted with unusual powers. A seventh son sometimes had the power to cure the sick or injured by laying his hands on them. A woman who had borne seven children in seven years had the power to cure "thrash" — an inflammation of the mouth and throat — by simply blowing into the victim's mouth.

Disease was sometimes banished by exiling the evil into some plant or seed. A person afflicted with rheumatism carried a buckeye or two about his person. In a little while the "trouble" would enter the buckeye and the aching joints would become well. If a person suffered from a painful sore which refused to heal, he could cure it by squeezing a drop of blood from the ulcer onto a bean. The bean was buried in the earth and by the time it sprouted the sore would heal. It was believed steel was abhorrent to pain, and when a woman entered the pangs of childbirth her husband was likely to place an ax under her bed "to cut the pain." And birthmarks — those banes to womanly beauty — could be caused to disappear by simply rubbing them with the cold dead hands of a corpse.

These and countless other folk remedies and superstitions provided the only safeguards against ill health for at least one hundred and fifty years.

It is unlikely that any sizable portion of the original immigrants into the Blue Ridge were artisans or possessed of significant mechanical skills. Smiths, masons, wood carvers, weavers and the like commanded decent wages in the Old World, but relatively few such mechanics were required on the plantations where raw labor was at a premium, and those artisans who came were prone to remain in the prospering ports of entry. These skilled workmen were undei little temptation — in the language of an aphorism still current in the mountains — to "take off for the tall timber," and to lose themselves in the vast beckoning hinterland.

So it came to pass that the influx to the Blue Ridge was composed almost entirely of the unskilled or the little-skilled. They were men and women who, with rare exception, had known little or no experience with artfully wrought things of beauty. They had not owned or lounged upon skillfully carved chairs or beds and, as a generality, they were not people who had ever been called upon to maintain or create graceful or attractive things. They had lived in Europe in crowded, ill-lighted and rudely furnished hovels and tenements, and in the wilderness they found their red-skinned mentors dwelling in crude pole cabins little worse if at all. The Indian sat on the ground and slept wrapped in a blanket on his earthen floor. The white newcomer added a stool and later a roughly carved, straight-backed chair with a seat of woven cane strips or hickory withes. He contrived a simple bedstead laced with sinew ropes on which he laid a bed of corn shucks or feathers. He and his wife learned how to weave the red man's baskets in which to store shelled corn and chestnuts, but they never equaled the skill of the squaws in this respect. His every effort at manufacture was crude in the extreme, and his descendants through the intervening generations have been unable to add either design or skill to his meager handicrafts.

The women brought with them a knowledge of weaving, and they tended to repeat endlessly the same patterns remembered from the Old World. Little of real beauty was added by them. And while in later generations they acquired the habit of patchwork quilting, their patterns most frequently were garish and overlarge. Their needlework was never fine or intricate.

The white man, however, enjoyed one skill which the aborigine wholly lacked, and that was the ability to do primitive blacksmithing. With charcoal made from the hardwood trees, and low-grade iron ore found here and there in the mountains, he could fashion hoes, knives, plows, nails and eventually even a facsimile of the deadly Pennsylvania rifle. But this latter achievement, while an effective "widow and orphan maker," as proved in the bloody Battle of New Orleans, was never the thing of beauty and fine inlays achieved by the "Dutch" gunsmiths.

The forefathers of our mountaineers left Europe before even the foundations for universal education had been laid. For the masses, the printed page was a mystery as deep as the Delphic Oracle. It is probable that the great majority of the men and women who were destined to become the forebears of the Southern highlander lacked the ability even to subscribe their names. Since they were brought to the New World to labor, it is unthinkable that they received instruction in reading and writing arts on the tobacco coasts; and once removed to the Blue Ridge, they were in a world in which the printed page had never existed. On the brawling frontier the cabins were too far apart, the struggle for existence too intense, to permit time and effort to be devoted to such learning; and besides, there was no one who could teach. Those few who possessed a rudimentary skill at reading and writing doubtless attempted to pass it on to their offspring and perhaps to their neighbors, but their efforts were swallowed up in the sea of illiteracy around them.

Thus the mountaineer who reached Kentucky about 1800 was in most instances already removed from literacy by two or three generations — assuming that his forefathers had been among the handful who had learned to read and write in the British Isles. For most of them, literacy had never existed.

These forces had been at work long before the mountaineer's ancestors reached these shores, and for three or four generations before he had reached Kentucky. By 1840 they had accomplished their work. The twig had been bent. The tree had grown. The course of the mountaineer's development was determined. Consider then these forces in synopsis: The illiterate son of illiterate ancestors, cast loose in an immense wilderness without basic mechanical or agricultural skills, without the refining, comforting and disciplining influence of an organized religious order, in a vast land wholly unrestrained by social organization or effective laws, compelled to acquire skills quickly in order to survive, and with a Stone Age savage as his principal teacher.

From these forces emerged the mountaineer as he is to an astonishing degree even to this day.

PART II

A Land Divided

CHAPTER THREE

The War

TOWARD the end of this first quarter of the nineteenth century the people in the fast-filling Bluegrass region began to take interest in one part of the plateau's great tangible wealth — its trees. The rolling hillocks of central Kentucky were originally dotted with splendid hardwoods, but these were too few to meet the needs of the growing towns and cities and at the same time to provide fuel against the cold winters. Besides, these trees, growing in relatively open country, were not the pencil-straight giants found in the mountains, and carpenters preferred the matured tulip poplar above all others. These were rare in the Bluegrass.

So timber buyers began to reach the tiny, widely scattered county seat villages on the edge of the plateau, looking for the best of the trees and tempting the mountaineer with the glint of gold. The mountaineer responded by chopping down some of the great yellow poplars and white oaks growing close to his creek banks. During spring "tides" or freshets he rolled them into the stream and let them ride the flood crests to the downriver markets. They were caught, most of them at Frankfort, in booms stretched across the river. Each mountaineer marked his logs with a distinguishing brand so they could be identified.

Sometimes the great logs were bound together in rafts and the mountaineer, with his sons and sons-in-law, rode them down to Frankfort or Louisville to revel in the fleshpots of those roaring towns.

Usually such rafts carried a cargo of hides and whiskey to be sold, and when the mountaineer returned to his lonely cabin he brought a small pouchful of gold and silver coins. Thus began the break with the ancient frontier agricultural and hunting life, and the people embarked falteringly upon the road to a cash economy.

Prices paid for these great trees were pitifully small. A poplar log measuring sixty or seventy inches in diameter at the butt was likely to bring no more than a dollar and a half or two dollars at Frankfort and a forty-gallon charred white-oak barrel filled with whiskey could be bought by one of the big-name distilleries for as little as twenty-five dollars.

Nevertheless the demand for such products was not great, and the supply was apparently unlimited, so the number of mountaineers who made these trips remained relatively small. For most of them the isolation and the loneliness continued nearly complete. However, here and there a farmer began to prosper by the standards of the time. The number of slaves in the plateau slowly increased and some of the farmers owned a dozen or more such chattels. For the most part the Negroes were owned by those fortunate landowners who lived at the mouths of the larger streams on the broad bottoms, while their kinsmen farther up the streams, on the narrower and less desirable lands, being unable to amass the money to buy them, were without slaves.

The rich, densely wooded land could become valuable only as the labor was available to develop it. Trees had to be felled and burned or floated down stream for sale. The fields must be plowed, planted and harvested and fenced with split rails against the inroads of wild hogs. If whiskey was to be sold to the burgeoning distilling industry in the "settlements" the stills must be set up and operated and the barrels hewed out and fitted together by hand.

These tasks required immense amounts of hard, grueling labor — labor in such quantities as to be wholly beyond the capacity of the mountaineer and his family. But if from the initial sale of timber and whiskey, and perhaps hides, the mountaineer could acquire enough money to buy himself a sturdy black slave or two, then new possibilities lay before him. With the help of such unpaid laborers he and

his family could cut more "sticks"* and make more whiskey to be
floated down to the markets for the acquisition of additional slaves.
So it was that here and there across the Cumberlands there came
to be a prosperous farmer whom his neighbors on less productive
lands referred to as a "good liver," whose log house was bigger than
most, sometimes containing four or five rooms. This mountaineer
had barns filled with corn and his crop lands were fenced. He owned
two or three hundred wild hogs, their ears cut with identifying
"marks," roaming on lands which he vaguely thought of as his own.
And in lesser cabins near his own there lived a small company of
Negro men and women who labored for him without compensation
save for the rough clothes upon their backs and the coarse food
which they ate. These hapless souls reproduced new slaves whose
numbers slowly swelled and whose value increased year by year.
Though the number of slaves in the plateau was never large, amounting perhaps to no more than thirty-five hundred all told, their
presence in the fateful years before the Civil War had the effect of
dividing the mountaineers into two fairly distinct groups — the
comparatively few who owned slaves, and their following of close
relatives and friends, and, on the other hand, the greater mass of
the people living in lesser cabins on inferior lands who could afford
no slaves or who were too shiftless to work hard enough to acquire
them.

However, it is doubtless true that in a vague way some of these
poorer mountaineers, fiercely independent as they were, found something abhorrent in the ownership of one person by another. And this
uneasy conviction added to their economic resentment against and
envy of their wealthier neighbors. Sometimes, perhaps, when those
who "have not" live in association with those who "have," antagonisms develop which, when they come into the open, are likely to be
justified on lofty moral grounds.

Now the social fabric woven on the cruel and democratic frontier
was rent. The coming of slaves had for the first time made it possi-

* The mountaineer from the earliest times applied this term to the trunks of
his great trees. Settlers on a stream in what is now Leslie County found hundreds
of ancient trees which had died of old age. There were so many of them that it
was called the "Thousand Sticks Creek," by which name it is still known to this
day.

ble for one group of men to become significantly and obviously more prosperous than the others amid whom they dwelt.

In the early months after Fort Sumter, the conviction crystallized in the mountaineer's mind that he must fight for his slaves or lose them. As a highland slaveholder recruiting troops for the Confederacy once told a group of his fellow mountaineers: "We've got to jine and fight, 'cause if they can take our niggers away from us they can take our cows and hosses, and everything else we've got!" Though the slaveowners did not make up a large portion of the population, each of them could count a few kinsmen or friends who resented the idea that property earned by hard toil — even when that property consisted of fellow human beings — should be wrested from the owner. Many of these sympathizers were willing to support the Confederate cause and even to join its army with the sons of their wealthier neighbors.

But the great majority of the highlanders were, from the outset, sympathetic with the Union. Their reasons were not so simple or so easily defined as were those of their Rebel fellows. The inevitable and very human element of envy and resentment against their more successful neighbors was important and, in many instances, the real cause for their enmity to slavery. Nevertheless there is no doubt that Chad, the hero of John Fox's *Little Shepherd of Kingdom Come*, was not the only mountaineer to risk or endure death on the battlefields because of a sincere desire to see the shackles stricken from millions of men and women.

Perhaps the most important factor causing the mountaineer to enter the army, regardless of the side to which he gave his fealty, was boredom with his monotonous and innately melancholy existence. He and his forefathers had dwelt amid the primeval quiet of a great forest for generations. Life had flowed on in the same primitive routine for so long that a subconscious and deeply felt yearning for a break with his environment had come to beset him. As rumors began to filter in about the great events transpiring in the "outside world," they brought a craving to burst through the forest walls and to escape into the adventure and color of a realm which most of them had never seen and had sensed only from an almost impassable distance.

Too, these were not men who, in the modern sense, had to be trained and inured to the privations and bloodletting of warfare. They had known the discomforts of cold and heat, and sometimes of hunger and thirst, since boyhood. They could walk tirelessly for many miles and the use of the rifle came almost by instinct to their hands and eyes. No great bridge between their life and the hardship of camp and battlefield had to be crossed, and it was with ever-quickening excitement that they heard tales of "the War."

For whatever reason individuals chose to enter military service, there was a great outpouring of men and boys into the recruitments of the two contending armies. The world may not see again the match for these men as soldiers. Indefatigable afoot or in the saddle, they fought on practically every battleground, ignoring the legislature of their state — which solemnly declared Kentucky to be neutral in the great struggle. The fierce cry that became famous as the blood curdling "Rebel Yell" had been learned by their forefathers from Indian warriors, and was now carried North and South by soldiers from the Southern mountains. But to their soldierly virtues was added a grave defect — an unrelenting hatred of discipline and order. The highland soldier wore the collar of military discipline with poor grace, frequently deserting when an officer "got too big for his britches." The Confederates generally elected their officers — a democratic but perilous practice — and at least one soldier refused to vote at all, explaining his stand with, "God damn it, I'm ag'in *all* officers."

From every valley went forth Confederate and Union men. Cousins took opposite sides, and sometimes brothers and even fathers and sons split on the issue. Such partings in the early stages of the war were relatively friendly, but it could not remain so for long. As the months passed wounded and crippled men began to return, and they brought reports of the deaths of others. When the occupants of a mountain cabin learned that a son, brother or father had died at the hands of Union or Rebel troops on some distant battlefield, they fixed their resentment, not against the far-off armies but against the known and near neighbors, relatives or former friends who had put on the uniform of the army at whose hands the loved one had perished. These were simple people lacking complexity in emotional or mental makeup. They were quick to anger and quick to carry that anger into effective action against the offender. And within a short time there grew up within the confines of these valleys a war in miniature, fought by the people back home, neighbor against neighbor, kinsman against kinsman. By the end of 1863 practically every household was involved in the struggle, at home or on the great battlefields of Virginia.

At first the two camps simply drew sullenly apart from each other; but, in an atmosphere charged with the electricity of ever-deepening hatred, outbreaks of violence were inevitable. They were not long in coming.

Sometimes the immediate cause was some trifling local incident. A man might find one of his hogs dead and jump to the conclusion that his neighbor of the opposite camp had killed it. Or a mountaineer might conclude that his former friend across the ridge had shot his missing hound. Such trifling sparks set fire to emotional powder kegs, and the battlefield in the mountains came to be almost as tragic as the ones developing before Vicksburg and Gettysburg. Men were killed from ambush when they left their cabins in the early dawn. They were ambushed on the trails and shot from the sheltering forests. Sometimes a cabin was attacked under cover of darkness and set afire, and the family shot as they fled the flames. Still children of the frontier, with traditions of warfare acquired in the cruel border struggles, they fought each other now with the same brutality and disregard of chivalrous restraints with which their grandsires had fought the hated Cherokee, Shawnee and Choctaw.

When men were killed in this harsh land women were left to till the land and raise children. They must plow and plant and harvest without help except for the small hands of those whom they toiled to feed. And all too frequently, when a crop had been raised and when a widow had butchered and salted her hogs with her own hands, partisans of the hated enemy swooped down and carried away her treasures. Sometimes the longest-lasting hatreds were planted in the bosoms of these bereaved women and of the children whom they sought to rear. Thus the land was sowed with bitterness, from which crops of bloodshed were to be harvested for generations to come.

As a child I heard my paternal grandmother tell countless tales of her wartime childhood. She was eleven when the conflict began, and when her Confederate father rode away to join General Lee in "Old Virginny." In 1864 he came home on a "crop leave" — to plant corn and vegetables for his family. One day while he was at work in his field a half-dozen pro-Union guerillas swept down on him. Seeing that escape was impossible and resistance futile, he attempted to surrender. But the guerillas were implacable and riddled him with bullets. His teen-age daughter held his shattered head while his brains ran out onto her aproned lap. To the day of her death she was an unreconstructed Rebel, and her eyes glinted and her lips tightened into a thin line at the merest mention of even the grandchildren of her father's killers.

The "war tales" still remembered and retold by the old bring into focus a vivid tableau from this most bitter of battlefields. In generations of retelling they have lost little of the hatred and vengefulness which flamed so intensely a century ago.

In 1941 a ninety-year-old mountaineer led me and my father to a "sinkhole" on a hillside near his family cemetery and pointed to the spot where, nearly eighty years before, he and his fifteen-year-old brother had buried the body of a Yankee cavalryman. It was a still, droning day in July, and in the rich bottom beyond his house his grandchildren were dutifully "hoeing out grandpap's corn patch." We sat on a fallen log while he recollected the details.

Pap warn't no nigger lover and on t'other hand he didn't hate 'em. But he thought hit was right to own 'em because they are skasely human accordin' to th' Bible. So when the war started pap got ready and went off to fight fer the South.

Me and my brother was left at home to take keer of things. He was five years older than me and he sort of run things about the place. Ma and the girls worked, too, and we got along all right till the damned Yankees started stealin' everything a body could raise.

Well, about two years after the war started, about this time of year, a gang of Union soldiers come through this here country. They was camped at the Cumberland Gap and had to just take things to eat away from folks. They went through the country robbin' widders and orphans, and payin' 'em with greenbacks if they was on the Union side and nothin' atall if they was Democrats. They was about fifty in this gang and they was ridin' horses. They had a herd of cattle they had stole and was drivin' 'em to the Cumberland Gap. They called their robb'ry "foragin'."

They camped right thar in that bottom and cooked supper. They eat up all our ham meat and about ten fat hens. The next morning they left afore daylight and took all our cattle and work stock with 'em. Their captain said he didn't have to pay us a cent fer nothin' because pap was a traitor.

Well, ma cried and begged him to leave us a mule to plow with but the captain said, "No, let yore old man quit fightin' his country and come home and work fer ye." So just afore they rode off one of them sons-of-bitches went to the creek and got water and poured it in our bee gums and drownded our bees. All them other rascals just stood around and laughed.

As soon as they got gone brother Oliver grabbed pap's old hog-rifle and went to the mountain, and me right after him. He took a nigh cut and got ahead of them Yankees, so we could see 'em come in sight. Oliver put in a good smooth ball and a heavy charge of powder and waited. Pretty soon we seed 'em a-comin' and just waited real still till they was all out of sight except the last one. Then Oliver took good aim and shot him right betwixt his galluses. He yelled and fell out of his saddle and me and Oliver took off back to the house. We stopped just long enough to clean the gun, then hung it up over the fireboard and started hoein' corn just like nothin' had happened.

In about twenty minutes here come them Yankees with their dead buddy. They was awful mad and threatened to kill us fer shore. But the captain said we hadn't done hit and made his men leave us alone. He went up to the graveyard and had his men dig a grave and bury the dead Yankee. Then he come down to the house and all the men got a drink from our well afore they left. The old captain sort of softened up and give us back a plow mule and warned me and Oliver to stay out of trouble. He said he had two young-'uns about like us back home.

When they got plumb gone ma tol' me and Ol to go dig up that Yankee and git him outen our graveyard. So we uncovered him and pulled him up the hill and buried him in a sinkhole where a big tree had turned up by the roots. We didn't git him very deep though, 'cause a hog rooted him up and carried off his head. Ma said that proved that hogs and other Yankees was the only things that could stomach a Yankee, dead or alive!

Before the war ended conditions in the mountains defied description. Death, robbery, rapine and starvation were rampant and both civil and military authorities were helpless to restore order. At last the "Federals" established camps on the fringes of the mountains and urged victims of the war within a war to find refuge in them. One such camp was established at Stevenson, Alabama, and sheltered refugees from many parts of the Southern highlands. A young private in the Union Army, Frank Wilkeson, a New Yorker, has left us a vivid description of these unfortunate mountaineers. His book, *The Recollections of a Private Soldier,** is one of the finest commentaries on the War Between the States. He wrote:

At Stevenson there was a large refugee camp, where many women and children and a few crippled or age-enfeebled men had sought refuge from attacks by murderous bands of guerrillas. . . . These pretended soldiers, it mattered not which uniform they disgraced by wearing, were, almost without exception, robbers and murderers, who sought to enrich themselves by plundering their defenceless neighbors. They rode through the Southern highlands, killing men, burning houses, stealing cattle and horses. To-day a band of guerrillas, alleged Unionists, ravaged a mountain district. They killed their personal enemies, whom they said were Confederate sympathizers, and destroyed their property. Tomorrow other guerillas burned Union men's houses, and shot so-called Union men to death. This relentless, mountain warfare was exceedingly hard on women and children. Agriculture was suspended in the highlands. No man dared to till his lean fields for fear that some hidden enemy might kill him. No stack of unthrashed grain or garner of corn was safe from the torch. The defenseless women and children were starved out of their homes, and they sought safety and food within the Union lines. Our government established extensive camps for these war-stricken Southerners.

Curious to see these people I spent a day in camp at Stevenson. I saw hundreds of tall, gaunt, frouzy-headed, snuff-dipping, pipe-smoking, unclean women. Some were clad in homespun stuffs, others in calico, others in bagging. Many of them were unshod. There were hundreds and hundreds of vermin-infested and supremely dirty children in the camp. Some families lived in tents, some in flimsy barracks. All lived in discomfort. All drew rations from the government. All were utterly poor. It seemed that they were too poor to ever again get a start in life. Haggard, wind- and sun- and storm-burnt women, their gaunt forms showing plainly through their rags, sat, or lolled, or stood in groups, talking drawlingly. Their features were as expressionless as wood, their eyes lustreless. I talked to many of these women. All told stories of murder, of arson, of blood-curdling scenes. One, gray-eyed, bony, square-jawed, barefooted, forty years old, clad in a dirty, ragged, homespun dress, sat on a log outside of a tent sucking a corncob pipe. Her tow-headed children played around her. She told me that before the war she and her husband owned a mountain farm, where they lived in comfort; that they owned horses,

* G. P. Putnam's Sons, 1886.

cattle, and pigs, and raised plenty of corn and tobacco. One day her husband, who was a Union man, was shot dead as he stood by her side in the door of their house. She buried him in a grave she dug herself. She and her children tended the crops. These were burned shortly after they gathered them. Then her swine were stolen, and her cows and horse driven off. Finally her oldest son, a boy of fourteen, was shot dead at the spring, and her house and barn were burned in broad daylight, and she and her children were left homeless and without food on a desolate mountain side. Many of her neighbors had been burned out the same day. They joined forces and wandered down the mountain, hungry, cold, with little children tugging at women's dresses, to a Union camp. From there they had been sent to Stevenson. Long before this woman had finished her story she rose to her feet, her face was white with intense passion, her eyes blazed with fire, and her gaunt form quivered with excitement as she gesticulated savagely. She said that if she lived, and her boys lived, she would have vengeance on the men who had murdered her husband and son, and destroyed her home. As she talked so talked all. These women were saturating their children's minds with the stories of the wrongs they had endured. I heard them repeat over and over to their children the names of men which they were never to forget, and whom they were to kill when they had sufficient strength to hold a rifle. The stolid manners, the wooden faces, the lustreless eyes, the drawling speech of these people, concealed the volcanoes of fire and wrath which burned within their breasts. . . . It was easy to foresee the years of bloodshed, of assassination, of family feuds, that would spring from the recollections of the war, handed from widowed mothers to savage-tempered sons, in the mountain recesses of Georgia, Tennessee, Alabama, and Kentucky. And long after the war closed rifles continued to crack in remote mountain glens, as the open accounts between families were settled.

Here the mountains were like the walls of a great jail which shut in the combatants. After Appomattox it was as though mortal enemies had been locked in the same prison without taking away the deadly weapons they knew so well how to use.

Perhaps in no other region of the United States except the Southern mountains were the lives and property of a great number of pro-Union civilians lost in the war. In Pennsylvania, Kansas and a few other border areas the people were subjected to occasional Confederate forays, but those areas were comparatively rich and the losses were soon restored. But in the highlands much of the modest and slowly-built-up accumulations of three generations were destroyed, impoverishing virtually the entire population.

Thus the curtain rose upon one of the most fantastic dramas in American History — the ferocious Kentucky mountain feuds. Their story has gone largely unchronicled, but in savagery and stark horror they dwarf the cattle wars of the Great Plains and, by contrast, make the vendettas of Sicily look like children's parlor games.

CHAPTER FOUR

The Wars

THE KENTUCKY mountain feuds commenced a few years after the Civil War and continued with unchecked ferocity until about 1915, an interval of nearly half a century. These dreadful interfamily wars constitute a truly astounding chapter in American history. A few statistics from the region will reveal the stark outline of their horror. During the half-century mentioned, the nineteen counties of the plateau achieved a maximum average population of about fifteen thousand people. Careful research in the files of the Circuit Court Clerk's office in one of the counties disclosed that between 1865 and 1915 nearly one thousand murder indictments were returned by the local grand juries. Thus we know that twenty homicides per year occurred, and inevitably many killings must have taken place in which for one reason or another no indictments were made.

Some of the feuds involved whole armies. A wandering Presbyterian preacher arrived in Hazard, the county seat of Perry County, to find the town in the midst of a roaring battle. This feud, then called the "French-Eversole War," eventually caused an almost complete suspension of the law courts within the county. The preacher arrived at a time when the two factions were locked in mortal combat for the courthouse and its records. The Eversole clan had holed up in the structure, while the more numerous French faction fired at them from doors and windows of neighboring buildings. This siege lasted until the approach of a company of militiamen forced the besiegers to flee.

Probably the most famous of the feuds was the "Hatfield-McCoy War." This great struggle eventually involved, directly or indirectly, practically every inhabitant of Pike County, Kentucky and Logan County, West Virginia — and resulted in at least sixty-five deaths. This epic clan war was fought out to its grim conclusion with all the characteristic savagery and tenacity the borderers had displayed a century before in struggles with the Indians. The vendetta brought the governments of the two states to the brink of war, and the correspondence between the governors on the matter reveals a situation so fantastic as to defy belief.

During the war, according to a letter from West Virginia's governor, E. W. Wilson, the families fought on different sides and relations between them became unfriendly. In those days before voter-registration, the Hatfields habitually crossed the border to vote in Kentucky elections. This unlawful franchise was resented by the McCoys and one of them, Tolbert by name, stabbed "Big Ellison" Hatfield to death at a voting precinct in 1882. Tolbert McCoy and his brothers Hurmer and Randolf were arrested for the slaying, and law officers undertook to deliver them to the jailer at Pikeville. A dozen or more mounted men armed with Winchester rifles and Colt revolvers crossed the Tug river and, at gunpoint, took the prisoners from the custody of the officers. They were taken out into the mountains, tied to pawpaw bushes and shot. Their killers were led by Anderson Hatfield, a brother of "Big Ellison."

The McCoys retaliated with murderous raids into West Virginia after the killers of their kinsmen. Jim Vance and William Dempsey, Hatfield warriors, were killed on one of these raids and six captured Hatfields were carried back to Pikeville under guard. Eyewitnesses reported that two of the surviving McCoy brothers shook hands in self-congratulation over the dead bodies of their enemies, and "crowed like roosters," while their father, Randall McCoy, vowed he would not rest until he had slain Anderson Hatfield with his own hands and had "cut a slice of meat from his body and broiled it and eat it."

In due course, the Hatfields returned the raid. They surrounded Randall McCoy's cabin at night and set it afire. Another son, Calvin, was slain in the gunfire that followed. The vengeance seekers this time turned their guns on women and children when they fled the cabin.

But old Randall escaped to continue the feud. Four of his sons died in the long vicious struggle. Both counties were occupied by militiamen time after time, and civil authorities were helpless and hopeless. Legend has it, however, that the feud at last ended happily in the marriage of two of the few survivors — a Hatfield youth to a McCoy girl.

Knott County was riven by the terrible "Knott County War," which raged for many years between the followers of "Cap" Hays and Clabe Jones. Hays had been a cavalry captain in the Confederate army and Jones a pro-Union, guerilla leader. When these two strong-willed men resumed the war in Knott County most of the population enlisted in one faction or the other and in a pitched battle at McPherson Post Office (which later became Hindman, the county seat) a half-dozen men were shot to death. Old Clabe Jones was renowned in song as a "booger," little less evil than the devil himself. When he was not feuding with the followers of "Cap" Hays he warred with "Bad John" Wright, his neighbor in Letcher County. This mountain baron was an ex-Confederate who was captured during the war and imprisoned in Ohio. He escaped and thereafter acquired a small fortune by repeatedly enlisting in the Union Army for the bounties which were paid. With his roll of "Yankee greenbacks" he returned to his Rebel unit, where he remained until the war ended. He and Hays were eventually able to decimate the Jones crowd and bring this war, at least, to a close.

One dreadful feud began when a family which had given its support to the Union buried the body of a little girl on land which a family of ex-Confederates claimed as its own. The latter unhesitatingly dug into the grave and pitched the coffined body across the fence onto land recognized as belonging to the offenders. This hideous act elicited murderous retaliation and plunged the county into a war that lasted more than two decades and cost unnumbered lives.

In 1888 conditions became so tumultuous in feud-riven Rowan County that a special committee of the Legislature was appointed to investigate the situation. It recommended that the act establishing the county be repealed, and that the territory be thenceforth governed by martial law. The committee found no disposition on the part of the officials to enforce the law or on the part of the populace to obey it. Twenty "open murders and secret assassinations" had been committed in the county without a single conviction having been secured in the courts. In addition, sixteen other persons had been wounded in shooting affrays. And this in a county shown by the census of 1890 to have a population of 6129!

But hardly a county was without its "war," and some had a whole series. The "troubles" in Breathitt won for that county the somber sobriquet of "Bloody Breathitt" and gained for its populace the shocked attention of the world. An eighty-year-old lawyer once related to me the unique manner in which court adjournments were occasionally obtained in its Circuit Court. A murder case was docketed for trial and numerous friends of the defendant appeared at the courthouse heavily armed and in a belligerent mood. When the judge called the case for trial, the defendant's father, a man of about fifty with huge handle-bar whiskers and two immense pistols, rose and walked to the judicial bench. Wringing the gavel from the fingers of the startled judge, the feudist rapped the bench and announced, "Court's over and ever'body can go. We ain't agoin' to have any court here this term, folks." The red-faced judge hastily acquiesced in this extraordinary order and promptly left town. When court convened at the next term the court and sheriff were bolstered by sixty militiamen, but by then the defendant was not available for trial. He had been slain from ambush.

Nor was this incident the only one of its kind. Sometimes, though, the feudists were not satisfied with seeing a trial delayed or a judge run out of town. At least four men have been shot to death on the lawn or within the walls of the crumbling, ancient Breathitt County Courthouse at Jackson. And at Hillsville, Virginia, not far from the state line, feudists in the "Allen-Edwards Wars," enraged by the outcome of a trial, entered the circuit courtroom and shot to death the circuit judge, commonwealth attorney, sheriff and three of the jurors.

Clay County was the scene of the "White-Baker War," that terrible and prolonged war of attrition in which countless participants died in grim gun battles, some of them on the streets of Manchester, the dusty little county seat.

Immediately after the Civil War, a struggle for political power was waged within each county. Union and Rebel forces fought for ascendancy by seeking to capture local offices. In no more than four counties were the discredited ex-Confederates able to succeed. Elsewhere the "good old Union boys" elected their former comrades to fill the log courthouses and to run the counties. These backwoods politicians promptly set out to harass their old foes with indictments for wartime crimes. Long dockets accumulated in the Circuit Courts as Republican grand jurors charged defeated rebels with every imaginable crime — murder, arson, rape, grand and petty larceny, treason against the Commonwealth, unlawful assembly, conspiracy to commit unlawful acts and "obtaining property by false tokens." This last offense referred to purchases made with Confederate currency. So formidable were the assaults made on them through the courts that the unregenerate Confederates were in grave peril.

Their reaction was deadly. Jurors learned quickly that to convict a man was to risk prompt and certain death. Not all rebels could be imprisoned, and once court was over and the juror was at home his back became a target for rifles hidden on the hillsides that overlooked his cabin. Even rabid, vengeance-thirsty "Yankees" became slow to convict.

The courtroom perpetuation of war and feud, though it imprisoned few people, added fuel to the fires of hatred and kindled new violence on every hand. Nor did conviction by a court and jury mean the sentences would be carried out. When officers attempted to convey prisoners to the state penitentiary at Frankfort they had to traverse the baronies of many heavily armed feudal lords. Often, indeed, these mountain chiefs "took pity" on the prisoners and, supported by small armies of retainers, demanded that the officers surrender their charges. Knott County's Clabe Jones acted as a one-man appellate court and freed many malefactors whose crimes were no greater than his own. He stirred up no little trouble by entering the bailiwicks of other war lords and rescuing men whose sad plight touched his tender heart. During the feuds such a friend was infinitely more valuable to a defendant than any number of skilled lawyers.

In at least one county, officials resorted to a unique device in an effort to preserve the life of the trial judge: sheets of steel were bolted together around the judicial bench to form a protective box or canopy. By this means it was sought to lessen the danger of having the judge shot by an irate spectator or, perhaps, with a high-powered rifle from a wooded hillside. Mountain judges during these years risked their lives daily, and some died in an effort to bring respect for law to a grim and savage people.

So diabolical did the feuds become and so long did they persist that they sparked a considerable exodus from the region. Thoughtful men who had no interest in the wars which so engrossed the energies of their kinsmen began "moving west." The disorders in Kansas, Texas and New Mexico were as teapot tempests compared to those raging in their own mountains. Today countless mountaineers have distant relatives residing half a continent westward.

A terrible quality of these monstrous adventures in homicide was that they were virtually self-perpetuating. Without distractions from the larger "outside world" to attract the highlanders' attention and hold their interests, each personal affront or injury was remembered and recounted. The ties of blood kinship were exceedingly important and an injury, real or imagined, even to a "third or fourth cousin" was likely to instill indignant umbrage. Their thoughts tended to dwell on the accumulating grievances of the decades and frequently hatreds came to center on an entire family because of some act of one of its long-dead ancestors. Sometimes such hatreds persisted even after the name of the original offender was only dimly remembered and the offensive act itself was forgotten. Thus the mountaineer came to inherit the hatreds of his father along with his name. Corn liquor copiously consumed to induce relief from boredom often fired vengeful excursions against the foe. The mountaineers' hatreds became so many-layered, so deeply ingrained and so tenaciously remembered that they were subconscious, and as such they have, to a remarkable degree, been transmitted to his present-day descendants. This accounts largely for the remarkably personal turn which politics always takes in the highlands even now — a fact which will be discussed at length in later chapters. Even today a mountain officeseeker is likely to find it impossible to win by taking a stand on public issues. His electorate is far more likely to vote for or against him because of something his uncle or grandfather did, perhaps before the candidate's birth, than because he proposes to improve schools or construct new roads.

———•———

CHAPTER FIVE

The Things That Are More Excellent

BUT THE feud years, bloody and hideous though they were, were not given over entirely to mayhem and murder. In this era the first faltering steps were taken toward a public school system and a few gaunt, graceless "meetinghouses" were built for public worship.

Kentucky as a whole has lagged behind the rest of the nation in almost every field of government and public service, primarily because the fiercely independent and uncooperative mentality of the frontier hunter-farmer has remained so deeply and tenaciously embedded in the mass psyche. And the frontier modes have endured in no other part of the state to such a marked degree as in the isolated and land-locked valleys of the plateau.

An essential element of the frontier mind was a jesting abhorrence of the intellectual. Thoroughly content with the uncouth frontier world about him, the pioneer tended offhandedly to reject all discussion and consideration of ideas in the abstract. Things and people — food, whiskey, heat, cold, shelter, enmities, sexual gratification, birth and death — were the ingredients of his life. These he could understand and appreciate. Beyond them he seldom allowed his thoughts or aspirations to stray. It is not remarkable, then, that the state was nearly a century old when the first hesitant efforts were made in the direction of Thomas Jefferson's great dream of a broadly based, free system of public schools.

This stark and popular anti-intellectualism has manifested itself throughout the history of Kentucky whenever reform groups have undertaken to expand or improve the public schools. For nearly seventy-five years after the state was established, most of Kentucky lacked a school system even in name. Not until 1864 did the state levy a tax for the support of its schools. This niggardly effort was so inadequate as to be grotesque. In that year the generous lawmakers required that the owners of dogs should pay a tax of a dollar a head, and that the money thus collected from each owner, *after the second dog*, should go into the school fund. The state also permitted one half of the fines collected from violators of the antigambling laws to go for the same purpose. Somewhat later the General Assembly imposed a tax of five cents per one hundred dollars of assessed property for the support of schools. These trifling sums were all the sovereign people were willing to devote to the education of their children, and at the next session sober second thoughts moved the Legislature to require that the paupers in each county should first be supported out of the school fund and only the residue devoted to education! And this was in a state where most people simply ignored the dog-tax law and where few gamblers were ever apprehended or fined.

In this same hesitant manner the state government stumbled ahead in other areas of governmental activity. Uninspired and uninspiring men followed each other in the governor's office and Legislature. The great battles which engrossed their attention centered around such momentous issues as the pardoning of convicts and the granting of commissions to officers of the militia. Office was sought as an end in itself and rarely indeed because its power afforded the candidate an opportunity to render an obviously needed public service. In these years, so eventful in the conquered Confederacy, the ancient dearth of leadership persisted in Kentucky — a dearth made inevitable, perhaps, by a society whose every member was so individualistic that he would follow his impulses alone, and rarely anything or anyone else. In the prostrate states farther south a transfusion of new, radical and generally effective thinking was poured into the capitals by the "carpetbaggers" from Yankeedom. These political adventurers have received mountains of abuse from generations of historians, but they could hardly have been inferior to the platoons of lily-white politicians whom the people had duly elected as their predecessors. They sought, at least, to rebuild what the folly and wickedness of others had ruined. Nor were their "black and tan" legislators greatly more capricious or selfish than the gatherings of Southern manhood who had voted for secession. Such impetus as the Southern states have enjoyed in such fields as public education, wage and hour regulation, child labor and health and welfare legislation received its initial inspiration in these hectic times. And, unlikely as it may seem, it is probable that one of Kentucky's historic misfortunes lies in the fact that it did not share in the process of reconstruction at the hands of the carpetbaggers. Certainly some explanation must be found to account for the manner in which this great state, rich in minerals, timber, fertile bluegrass farmland and a virile people, drifted far behind the modest achievements of her drastically poorer neighbors farther south until at last her unofficial motto became "Thank God for Arkansas!" — the only state beneath her in public achievement and aspiration.

In a state so indifferent to the mental development of its children it is not surprising that schooling of even the simplest sort remained practically nonexistent in the mountains until after the Civil War. In a few widely dispersed communities mountaineers made some effort to teach the 3 R's to their children, and perhaps an occasional one-room schoolhouse was built. These, however, were too few to have any real effect on the ocean of illiteracy which was the plateau country. Almost without exception the people remained oblivious of the knowledge to be gleaned from the printed page and no more than a scant 5 or 10 per cent of the adults possessed more than the bare ability to scrawl their names.

But in the years after the Civil War — in the years of Southern Reconstruction — some trifling progress began to be made in this vital field. Men who had seen the outside world, with its industry and activity, came back to their narrow valleys with a slight new desire to have their children "know something." By then most of the counties had been organized and the law required that a superintendent of schools be elected. This official, all too often, was virtually without schools to superintend, but his efforts resulted, inevitably, in the organization of an occasional "common" school. County real-estate taxes and the trifling support from the state enabled these early institutions to operate only two or three months each year. These "blab schools" were almost entirely without books. If the teacher or county could provide a slate the children were fortunate. Few of the teachers had been to school for more than twelve to fifteen months all told, and they knew little more than the taxpayers who supported them. Most such schools were conducted in a fairly large log cabin with a puncheon floor and a huge wood-burning fireplace. The hickory limb was seldom idle and scholars of both sexes were whipped for the slightest infraction. The blessings of such an institution were meager, but in them some of the new generation learned to write their names and to read passably well. Looked at in the abstract they were wretched indeed, but considered against their background they constituted great progress. The teachers were miserably paid, sometimes drawing as little as ten dollars per month, but they brought the first crumbs of learning to the Cumberlands and, deficient though they were, they were heroic in many respects. In a time and land in which the principal business was endless feuding and fighting, these harsh pedagogues exemplified the hope, at least, of something better.

But even their blessings were restricted to the white majority. Some 3 or 4 per cent of the plateau dwellers were Negroes, but neither state nor counties made any effort to teach their children. The Legislature established a policy of "white taxes for white schools and nigger taxes for nigger schools." Under this plan schools were segregated and could exist for Negroes only if sufficient taxable property was owned by their race to support them. Since the newly emancipated blacks owned virtually nothing, there was no possibility of their children acquiring any "book learnin'."

Amid the welter of bloodletting of the feud era a yearning for peace came to beset a great many people. Most of the news which rumor brought to them, for there were no newspapers, was of ambuscades and killings. Inevitably, reaction against such violence and its accompanying grief and unhappiness made its appearance. Though the feuds raged on until the railroads pierced the plateau, there came to be a strong countertide of sentiment for peace and calm; and in this undertow the Church took root and began to grow.

This term, Church, is applied in its broadest sense, to religion as an organized entity. The plateau, as we have seen, was practically without churches for fifty or seventy-five years after the arrival of the first settlers. There simply were no preachers or ministers, few Bibles and little religious knowledge. The atmosphere among these rugged pioneers was inimical to the development of any organized religion. Here and there a few men and women got together in the 1830s and 1840s to organize a "meeting" and to hold religious services when a preacher could be found. But these were few, and some counties had only a single such establishment when the Civil War came. Many of these first churches were nondenominational, their sponsors being willing to hear the sermon of any preacher who might come along. Others were inspired by the religious revival which occurred in central Kentucky early in the century and from which ideas and influences slowly filtered into the fastnesses of the plateau. But amid the tensions and anxieties of the war and postwar years many people came to yearn for spiritual guidance and solace, and groups of them came together to organize primitive churches. A people whose only experience for generations had been with a world of hard realities unadorned by the arts, eloquence or imagination, it was inevitable that their folk churches should be founded upon fundamentalism of the starkest sort. The King James Bible was their pillar and rock and all other religious authority or inspiration was summarily rejected. A precise, literal, matter-of-fact meaning was accorded to each word and sentence in this book. Hell was a place filled with fire such as any mountaineer could kindle on his own hearth, and heaven was a place vague in its nature but extremely pleasant for all who should have the good fortune to attain it. The world had been created in six days, exactly as related in Genesis, and all man's troubles stemmed from the eating of an apple by the first woman. Satan was an "evil spirit" whose unseen hand constantly enticed the mountaineer to sin. The Son of God had been sent into the world to give men a second chance, and all who failed to conform with what the mountain preachers said were his Commandments would be thrown into an everlasting hell. There they could never die but would fry eternally in much the same manner as a piece of bacon is broiled. Salvation from this dreadful hell was granted by the grace of God, but only to those who in genuine contrition begged the forgiveness of their Creator.

The preachers, true to the frontier instinct, were self-proclaimed. In the welter of ignorance, superstition and overwrought emotions a troubled man could hear a summons from the divine lips; and be persuaded that he possessed the fluency to preach and the power to convince. Education was not needed, because God would give knowledge. Many preachers were illiterate and knew nothing more of the Bible than the passages read to them by a schoolteacher on an occasional evening spent in the preacher's cabin. It is not surprising, then, that the Scriptures preached in these early churches were a garble of unrelated and misquoted snatches, or that the doctrines which emerged were sometimes bizarre.

For many years and, indeed, to this day, there were "hard-shell" preachers, so named because their doctrine was so harsh. They preached, among other things, the cruel doctrine of infant damnation. To their fanatical minds it was apparent that if a man could not enter the kingdom of heaven until he had been spiritually "born again," even a little child was shut out of the Celestial Kingdom if death came prior to an age when awareness of sin had brought repentance and rebirth. And it followed that if failure to be born again excluded the soul from heaven, that soul must certainly go to hell. This fantastic nonsense anguished generations of mountain parents, nearly all of whom had seen more than one infant die.

The wellspring of these folk churches was a stern Calvinism which the Scotch element of the population had carried with it from the dour highlands. Without competition from other religious ideas or doctrines it slowly pervaded the whole populace, and eventually became deeply rooted in their mores, so widely and unquestionably accepted as to constitute unwritten law. And while its adherents might split into a myriad of disputing minor sects, they were to remain steadfastly loyal to its basic tenets. One of these was a hatred for the Roman Catholic Church and the Pope as nothing less than arms of Satan. Another was confession of sins "before men," and a third was the requirement of baptism. Still another was an immutable principle that no preacher or minister be compensated in any way for his time or work. Their Biblical hero was John the Baptist, and each church was fiercely proud to call itself "Baptist," the members insisting that they alone were true followers of the methods and doctrines of the prophet. Each group, also, claimed to trace its origins back through the ages to this forerunner of Christ. This curious idea, now a folk notion throughout the region, resulted in the use of such church names as "Regular," "Old Regular," "Bed-Rock," and "Primitive" Baptists. These groups in subsequent years were to split again and again, like endlessly dividing amoebae, in fierce wrangles over the very meaning of the word "baptism." Their irreligious neighbors captioned them according to the amount of water their doctrines made mandatory for a proper baptism. Some, a steadily shrinking minority, adhered to a mere symbolic sprinkling of the head and were called "half-pint" Baptists. Others believed the body must be thoroughly wetted, and were denominated "five-gallon" or "ten-gallon" Baptists. Others, and their notion eventually achieved virtually unanimous acceptance, would accept nothing less than total immersion. These were called "forty-gallon" Baptists.

But while these Baptist sects were to labor prodigiously and gain a nearly unanimous acceptance of their basic preachments, their appeals for church membership were to fall, generally, on deaf ears. A Presbyterian survey group found in 1906 that only 6 per cent of the mountaineers "belonged to or were affiliated with" any church. Today, more than a half century later, the mountaineer's remarkable indifference to the church and its works remains little diminished. Not more than 12 to 15 percent now have church membership or affiliation, though countless dedicated evangelists have worn themselves out in proselytizing labors. Today the plateau probably contains the lowest percentage of actual church membership to be found in any other region of Christendom. And, as we shall see later, the lack of order, solace and restraint, and the absence of a sense of continuity, afforded to most societies by a religion and its priesthood, are among the cardinal reasons for the discouragement which so generally marks the mountaineer in our own times.

PART III

The Coming of the Coal Men

———•———

CHAPTER SIX

Trees

FOR MORE than forty years their timber had been a source of income to the mountaineers, but in the 1870s the selling of the great trees took a new and highly important turn. Prior to those years the mountaineer had been compelled to deliver his trees via the spring river "tides" to the markets at Frankfort and Catlettsburg, but now amid the tumult of the feuds appeared a market for the uncut and still living trees. Speculators in Cincinnati, Philadelphia, New York and other northern cities had become aware of the immense stands of still virgin forest, and exploring geologists had begun to report the existence of vast beds of bituminous coal underlying the timbered hills. In financial and industrial circles occasional talk was heard that railroads should be built into the region and its great wealth of raw materials made available to the nation's rapidly swelling industrial complex. And while the vicissitudes of commerce were to prevent such railroads from becoming realities until just before the First World War, such discussions were sufficient to set off anticipatory tremors among capitalists in a half-dozen states. Their agents were soon traversing the narrow, winding mountain trails to seek out boundaries of the best trees and to buy them cheaply against the day when the coming of the iron road would automatically multiply their value many fold.

Corporations were organized for the express purposes of buying and speculating in eastern Kentucky timber, and a number of established lumber companies with operations elsewhere began now to turn an attentive eye toward the plateau. Some firms sent lawyers to scout the region and appraise the condition of land titles. Some contracted with businessmen in Lexington, Louisville and Ashland and sent them riding through the mountains to view timber stands. Few attorneys resided in the hills, and most of the corporations found it necessary to import lawyers to make title abstracts.

But, however the sales were negotiated, huge numbers of the virgin trees began to pass into the hands of the Eastern and Northern corporations. To the mountaineer a few hundred dollars had always heretofore been a great fortune. Never had there been any means of acquiring substantial sums of cash, and since his appetite for material things had never been whetted by contact with them, his wants remained few and simple. A rifle and a pistol, a good horse or two and some "factory" clothes for his wife, were about all he had ever yearned for beyond the shelter of his cabin and the rough food which his fields and livestock afforded him. In short, the mountaineer was without perspective and lacked the ability to comprehend the value of his possessions or to negotiate for their sale.

The eyes of the "furrin" timber hunters must have popped with amazement as they rode the treacherous trails and creek banks of the plateau. On hundreds of such tucked-away places as Frozen Creek, the Bear Pen and Ball's Fork he found a sparse population strung out along the banks of streams which still ran clear as crystal. Two generations had occasionally felled trees and floated their logs down to the "settlements," but their inroads into the mighty forest had been puny. Most of the bottoms had been cleared and here and there a cove had had its timber cut down and the soil planted in corn or allowed to grow up in wild grass for pasture, but generally the timber began at the "foot" of the hills and extended upward over the "spurs" and "points" and through the rich coves to the tops of the ridges. The great poplars and whiteoaks grew, for the most part, near the base of the hills and in the coves, while the lesser oaks and chestnuts predominated on the sharper points and near the hilltops. Countless walnuts dotted the forest, thousands of them without blemish and a yard or more in diameter. The Goliaths were the superb, pencil-straight poplars, some of them towering one hundred and seventy-five feet and achieving a diameter of seven or eight feet. Next to these in value, if not in size, were the whiteoaks, which sometimes reached a thickness in excess of five feet. There were also the sturdy red, black and chestnut oaks and whole armies of tremendous hickories, huge but lovely beeches, "sugar trees" and maples, basswoods, an occasional ash, persimmon or black-gum, and, lining the creek banks, the poetically graceful sycamores, birches and willows. And everywhere among the others were the mysterious, moody evergreens — the huge cedars, pines and hemlocks. These found refuge, particularly, on the points and in the hollows of the cloud-capped Pine and Big Black Mountains and on the ridges which overlook the fairyland beauty of the gorge of the Red River. No region in earth's temperate zone boasts a larger variety of forest trees than the Cumberland Plateau, and in these years they abounded in natural profusion, little damaged by the avarice or caprice of men. The tree blights of the Old World had not yet infested this forest, and many specimens were centuries old and had withstood the fleeting decades without impairment. Tens of thousands of acres of such timber fell to the exploiters, from a people who, though they might fight each other with medieval brutality, at a business negotiation were as guileless as infants.

From time to time, however, a mountaineer was wilier than his neighbors and suspected that the sea of trees possessed a value greater than the timber prospectors were willing to admit. Such a mistrustful one was likely to drive a harder bargain than the purchaser had offered. In response to this situation the companies began to operate through county-seat merchants and courthouse officials whom they took into their confidence and employed to buy timber tracts on a commission basis. These men spoke the language of the mountaineer and were more likely to be believed when they assured him that his trees were of little value and that he and his descendants might never again have an opportunity to trade them for cash. Too, they could appear to buy the trees for themselves without disclosing their agency. Since the mountaineer had no newspapers or other sources of information except rumor, it was not a difficult task to convince him that his timber was practically worthless and that the merchant or politician was doing him a favor in offering to buy it all.

At an ever-rising tempo this valuable portion of the mountaineer's legacy was transferred to men who lived far away. The price was rarely little more than nominal but so naïve was the seller that in most cases he congratulated himself for having driven a sharp bargain.

Thousands of trees were sold for as little as forty to seventy-five cents each. Few of them brought more than a dollar. One deed, executed in 1889, exemplifies the type of transaction by which the greater stands were sold. It recites, "that for and in consideration of the sum of $20,000, the grantor hereby bargains, sells, grants and conveys unto the grantee 40,000 poplar and whiteoak trees, each of said trees to measure not less than 30 inches in diameter under the bark, stump high, measuring three feet above the ground, without fire damage or blemish; and the grantee shall have two years after the date hereof to mark said trees with its brand."

The grantee was permitted to leave the trees growing upon the land so long as it or its assigns should deem necessary or desirable.

Practically every courthouse in eastern and southeastern Kentucky contains scores of such timber deeds, though few of them involve such large numbers of trees or such sizable sums of money.

The magnitude of the wealth thus acquired by the speculators is difficult to convey to the reader who has never seen virgin stands of timber or the great stumps which endured until recent times. Senator Doug Hays represented his native county of Floyd in the Kentucky Legislature for more than a decade, and he used to regale his colleagues with accounts of his logging activities. He had operated a sawmill in the mountains for many years and thereby earned the nick-name of "Saw-loggin' Doug." On one occasion he told how he had been given a contract to procure "square sticks" for an English shipbuilding company in 1912. These were huge timbers used in the building of wooden vessels and only the finest whiteoak was acceptable to the British shipwrights. The trees were selected and cut down and then squared with broadaxes at the little end. Each of them was hewed to the largest dimension possible and these dimensions were continued along its four sides for the entire length of the timber. The object was to obtain a square beam measuring as wide as possible on each of its four sides and as long as the trunk would allow. "Saw-loggin' Doug" avowed that he had cut and delivered onto the flat cars at Pikeville one such monster thirty-six inches on the side and forty-two feet long!

In 1937 newspapers related that the largest tree known to have grown in Kentucky within historic times had just been felled on Big

Leatherwood Creek in Perry County. This poplar colossus measured no less than eleven feet and seven inches in diameter.

Most of the timber bought by the Eastern tycoons remained standing until after the railroads came into the plateau. Thereafter great amounts were cut and used in the housing boom which came during and after the First World War. With the coming of the railroads the buying speeded up, and exploitation of the forests continued until the onset of the Great Depression.

Some of the magnificent trees survived until the close of the Second World War. Fordson Coal Company, a subsidiary of Ford Motor Company, bought both land and timber and acquired between 1915 and 1924 more than half of Leslie County. Timber companies usually bought only the trees, but a number of corporations purchased both the timber and the underlying minerals.

When the agents of the timber corporations investigated the land titles, it was discovered that many of the highlanders were claiming lands to which they held no legal title, or title claims tenuous in the extreme. Therefore, the companies sent teams of surveyors to survey lands which had not been formally patented in previous years. These "wildcat" surveys usually started at the mouth of the stream and embraced immense areas, including farm lands obviously covered by prior patents. These "junior" patents were void as to lands within their compass which had been previously granted by the state, but subsequently the courts held them to be valid as to all intervening lands the mountaineers had neglected to appropriate. Occasionally an angry mountaineer shot a surveyor or ran his party out of the territory, but bit by bit great areas were surveyed and patented by the wildcatters. Thus, much of the plateau came to be blanketed by conflicting and overlapping land titles. From them were to emerge generations of litigation between coal and timber companies and the mountaineers; and, as we shall see, the companies were to "reach the ears of the Courts" and win a long series of law suits which eventually stripped away from the highlander much of the land which had supported his rugged independence for so long. These legal actions were fought out, on the one hand, between batteries of able attorneys imported by the companies, and, on

the other, by such lesser lawyers as were available to the mountaineers in the county seats or who "rode circuit" with the judges. The
companies possessed the capital to support their expensive advocates while the costly suits wended their leisurely way through courts
of appeal. The mountaineer, by contrast, was frequently to impoverish himself in the struggle, even when he managed to save his land.
In this era of protracted title litigation we find the major factors
which were to make the mountaineers one of the most litigious
people in the world and which effectually contributed to their permanent indigence.

Even in the rare instance when the mountaineer acquired substantial sums for his timber, it was to bring him few lasting benefits. He
lacked a sense of values and was unprepared to spend his money
wisely. He knew nothing about corporate stocks and in many counties
there were no banks in which to deposit his hoard. The feuds raged
on and much of his new cash was spent for firearms and in de-
fending criminal prosecutions brought against himself or his kinsmen,
or in hiring counsel to assist in the prosecution of enemies. Some
of the money was invested in improved houses, and here and yonder
a log cabin was given a facing of clapboards or was replaced by a
gaunt two-story frame building roofed with tin. Additional sums were
spent for "factory" beds and chairs and an occasional Hamilton or
Waltham watch. But the mountaineer and his sons had retained their
impetuosity and their weakness for firewater, and these weaknesses
amid the welter of lawsuits resulting from the wildcatters and the
feuds were to dissipate most of his new wealth without lasting benefit to him or his family. Indeed, when most of his timber had found
its way into the hands of absentee owners he found himself in drastically worse circumstances than before, for then a great feature of his
environment — a principal source of food for his livestock and money
for his pockets — was gone insofar as title was concerned, and, before
many more decades had passed, was to be gone in fact, leaving him
a poorer, sadder, and perhaps a wiser man.

A sustained logging boom accompanied the drive of the timber
companies to buy up the best of the trees. For some forty years
after 1870 thousands of mountaineers toiled a large part of each year

to produce logs for the downriver markets. Occasionally the timber companies hired mountaineers to fell trees on company lands and haul them to the streams. Most of the splendid logs that left the plateau in those years, however, were cut by the highlanders on unsold lands, or were somewhat inferior trees for which the companies were unwilling to pay.

Huge cuts were made on the trunk with the keen, long-handled axes. Generally two men faced each other on opposite sides of the huge column and swung their double-bitted axes in a measured tempo which filled the air with flying chips and caused the assaulted giant to lean in the direction of their cut. When approximately one third of the trunk had been chopped away, the axes were laid aside and a long cross-cut saw was laid to the opposite side. For an hour or two the droning teeth gnawed their way into the vitals of the centuries-old titan. Suddenly, when the unsevered wood was only inches thick, the dying monster swayed and crashed to earth. Its descent was terrific, its ancient branches tearing a mighty swath through lesser timber on the hillside below. The mountains and valleys echoed and re-echoed the thunder of its fall. Wild creatures fled the area in fright; then, a moment later, the thunder was replaced by a curious stillness as though the forest and all its creatures had paused to mourn the passing of one of its patriarchs.

Next the men chopped off the limbs close to the trunk, leaving immense heaps of discarded "laps." The saws sliced the trunks into lengths ranging from eight to sixteen feet. The tree was then ready for the "snakers" with their teams of moaning oxen. Sometimes a dozen yoked pairs were required to pull a single "butt cut" from the woods. The cattle dragged or "snaked" the heavy mass of wood down the hillside to the creek, and along its rocky bank to a collecting point. There it was left, with hundreds of others like it, to await the log run.

To add to the stream's volume the mountaineers worked together to build "splash dams" at intervals along the creek. These obstructions were made of long slender tree trunks staked to one another and sealed with rocks and mud. Each dam backed up acres of water to a depth of six or eight feet. The branded logs were piled in the stream bed in the stretches between the dams. When a heavy spring rain filled the rivers and sent torrents flowing over the crests of the dams, the mountaineers were ready to follow their logs to the great mills at Jackson, Catlettsburg, Ashland, Beattyville, Frankfort, Louisville and other points "down the river."

A charge of explosives ripped out the dam nearest the head of the creek and the unleashed flood surged down in a bubbling wall onto the thousands of "sticks" cluttering the channel. These were picked up and flung along on the roaring tide to the next dam. As the "splash" thundered onto this empoundment it, too, was blasted. Like rising thunder the water and its cargo rushed downstream, gathering momentum and freight with each succeeding mile. The loggers followed it afoot with cant hooks and hand spikes, rolling back into the stream those logs that had escaped the clutch of the flood. At last, with a boom like the massed cannons at Gettysburg, the boiling tide roared into the river and rushed furiously down its watery thoroughfare. So violent were the splash tides that they sometimes shattered tough oak logs.

During the next week or so small armies of lanky, mustached and grimy mountaineers followed their logs to the great steel booms near the giant sawmills. There the logs were caught, measured and paid for by the lumber corporations. Each logger had a registered, identifying mark or brand which he hammered into the ends of his logs and the companies maintained a separate account for each brand.

The perils of the "log woods" and runs were fantastic, and death stalked the logger's every step. Sometimes a falling tree unexpectedly turned on its splintering stump and toppled onto its fleeing assailant. Sometimes a log escaped from the haul road, crushing oxen and men. The treacherous tides drowned "log rollers" who lost their footing on the slippery banks. Gangs of rascally and heavily armed "log pirates" sometimes caught logs at river bends and hacked away the rightful brands for replacement with their own. The mountaineers who followed their timber to market went heavily armed with pistols, rifles and shotguns, and many fierce and bloody battles erupted between the robbers and their intended victims.

The log runs and timber sales provided nearly all the region's money, but they left in their wake legions of maimed men and widows and orphans. My maternal grandfather and my father's brother

died in logging operations, and countless other present-day mountaineers have similar family memories.

The runs made deep inroads into the vast forest, and commenced
its reduction to the pitiful remnant of cull and second-growth
timber which cloaks the plateau today.

CHAPTER SEVEN

Coal

ITS LORDLY trees were not the plateau's only wealth to attract the interest of distant speculators. In fact, by the middle Nineties interest in them had become secondary and emphasis had shifted to the numerous thick seams of high-grade bituminous coal striating the hillsides and underlying mountain and valley floor alike.

Christopher Gist, one of the earliest explorers of the region, had reported the finding of "fine coal" nearly a century and a half earlier, and in the intervening generations geologists had been able to form a comprehensive picture of its extent and quality. Some geological explorers had been sent into the area by the state as early as 1836 and thereafter others came in the employ of the United States or as spies for prospective railroad builders. While knowledge of their mineral riches was commonplace enough in scientific and industrial circles, most of the mountaineers had remained blissfully ignorant of their significance and, frequently, of their very existence. Few of them had ever burned anything but wood in the huge fireplaces of their cabins, though in some areas, notably in Perry County, mountaineers had occasionally dug a hundred bushels or so of coal and floated it on rafts or flatboats down the Kentucky River for sale at Richmond or Frankfort. Bell County, too, had been the scene of considerable small-scale mining. But such operations were primitive and minuscule and such knowledge of his coal as the plateau dweller may have possessed had, more often than not, come to him quite by accident rather than through curiosity and investigation. It should not surprise us that when, a dozen years after Appomattox, a forest fire ignited a coal seam on Kings Creek in Letcher County, astounded mountaineers gathered from miles around "to see the earth afire," and to marvel at it.

Then, in the gigantic industrial growth which occurred throughout the Western World in the last half of the nineteenth century, coal came to its throne and reigned with a despotism as black as its own dusty lumps. Ships, locomotives, factories and newly built electric power plants were driven by coal and millions of people warmed by its sooty flame. Steel and coal production were the yardsticks by which the Victorian world measured its increasing power, and it was inevitable that the confident overlords of the nation's industrial empires should turn covetous eyes upon the mineral-rich highlands.

As early as 1851 a railroad company was incorporated for the purpose of building a line from Winchester, Kentucky to Abingdon, Virginia. But sufficient capital was never subscribed and the corporation languished without construction's ever getting under way, and eventually expired during the Civil War. After the war, however, interest in railroad building revived, and in addition to the timber speculators, coal buyers began to penetrate the mountains.

Like the timber companies, most of the coal corporations were organized by Northern and Eastern speculators, though not a few of the stockholders lived in England and other foreign countries. Sensing that the world was in the throes of a gigantic industrial growth whose power was likely to be derived from coal for generations to come, they converged on the highlands to garner their mineral riches before the mountaineer was able to learn the meaning of his black gold.

The mountaineer had jealously guarded his domain but had seldom bothered to obtain formal title to more than a small portion of the lands which he claimed and used. Vast areas had lain unpatented, their title reposing in the state and available under the law to any person willing to lay claim to it, survey it, and pay a nominal fee to the state treasury. Land was still "dirt cheap," so that in 1875 huge tracts of it were selling for no more than 26½ cents per acre.

Though many of the first speculators bought only the standing timber, some of the corporations were capitalized for the purpose of acquiring the land *in toto*. By purchase and by grants from the state, some of these companies in the quarter-century before 1900 acquired huge expanses ranging up to ninety-five thousand acres.

But other profiteers entered the mountains for the purpose of acquiring title to only the minerals underlying the land and the appurtenant right to mine and remove them. By limiting their purchases to the minerals they were able to minimize tax liabilities. They foresaw that many years might pass before railroads could pierce the region and bring a market for the minerals, and during all this period taxes upon the surface would be annually required. As time passed, the feverish buying of land caused prices to rise steadily, so that in some areas the cost had risen to five or six dollars an acre. Since the "furriners" had no intention of utilizing the surface, it suited their purpose admirably to restrict their purchases to the "mineral estate."

In the summer of 1885 gentlemen arrived in the county-seat towns for the purpose of buying tracts of minerals, leaving the surface of the land in the ownership of the mountaineers who resided on it. The Eastern and Northern capitalists selected for this mission men of great guile and charm. They were courteous, pleasant and wonderful storytellers. Their goal was to buy the minerals on a grand scale as cheaply as possible and on terms so favorable to the purchasers as to grant them every desirable exploitive privilege, while simultaneously leaving to the mountaineer an illusion of ownership and the continuing responsibility for practically all the taxes which might be thereafter levied against the land.

The mountaineer still lived in a manner not strikingly different from that of his forefathers forty years after the first settlements. It was most likely that he still dwelt in a log cabin, though perhaps it had been sheathed in clapboards, and an occasional "good liver" had erected a "plank house." His life was a melancholy and monotonous round of plowing, planting, hoeing and harvesting, interspersed with hunting and fishing and shadowed by the ever-present specter of death. Because of his close family ties and his limited number of acquaintances, death was a far grimmer and sadder experience than to people living in a wider and more complex social order. The latter might find other interests and diversions to blunt their grief when loved ones were inevitably borne away, but to the hill man, with almost unlimited time in which to brood, the demise of a cherished friend or relative brought despair and melancholia which not infrequently persisted for the remainder of a lifetime. And death from disease, logging accidents and the feuds was never far from his community.

To such people the affable mineral buyer was a Godsend. With his stock of stories and friendly willingness to "set down and rest and talk a spell," he brought a pleasant interlude in the tedium of a dull and ungracious life. The aged residents of the plateau recall with pleasure W. J. Horsley, T. P. Trigg, E. B. Moon, John C. C. Mayo and a score of others, and nostalgically reminisce about their tours of the isolated backcountry.

These representatives of the new day were great raconteurs. Their collections of interesting stories were almost limitless. They brought with them in lavish measure a quality which is almost never encountered in the highlands to this day: a willingness to commend a person openly for a favor done or for some desirable skill or trait. In a sense the mountaineer was literally starved for compliments and for some outward show of appreciation.

With every convincing appearance of complete sincerity the coal buyer would spend hours admiring the mountaineer's horse and gazing over a worm-rail fence in rapt approbation of his razorback hogs while compliments were dropped on every phase of his host's accomplishments. He marveled at the ample contents of the mountaineer's smokehouse and savored the rich flavor of the good woman's apple butter and other preserved delicacies, while he assured her that no dainty to be found in the big city confectionaries was half so tasty. He ate the rough "grub" she prepared for him, and happily slept in the softest featherbed the cabin afforded. After such a visit he and "the man of the house" would get down to business and before long the deed or option was signed with the uncertain signatures of the mountaineer and his wife, or, more probably, with their duly witnessed marks.

When the highland couple sat down at the kitchen table to sign the deed their guest had brought to them they were at an astounding disadvantage. On one side of the rude table sat an astute trader, more often than not a graduate of a fine college and a man experienced in the larger business world. He was thoroughly aware of the implications of the transaction and of the immense wealth which he

was in the process of acquiring. Across the table on a puncheon
bench sat a man and woman out of a different age. Still remarkably
close to the frontier of a century before, neither of them possessed
more than the rudiments of an education. Hardly more than 25 per
cent of such mineral deeds were signed by grantors who could so
much as scrawl their names. Most of them "touched the pen and
made their mark," in the form of a spidery X, in the presence of
witnesses whom the agent had thoughtfully brought along. Usually
the agent was the notary public, but sometimes he brought one from
the county seat. Unable to read the instrument or able to read it only
with much uncertainty, the sellers relied upon the agent for an explanation of its contents — contents which were to prove deadly to
the welfare of generations of the mountaineer's descendants.

Sometimes the instrument was what lawyers in later years called
"the short-form deed," merely passing title to the minerals underlying the land "together with all the usual and ordinary mining rights
and privileges thereunto appertaining." But the great majority of
these deeds were the "broad-form" and, in addition to the minerals,
conveyed a great number of specific contractual privileges and immunities.

The broad-form deeds passed to the coal companies title to all
coal, oil and gas and all "mineral and metallic substances and all
combinations of the same." They authorized the grantees to excavate for the minerals, to build roads and structures on the land
and to use the surface for any purpose "convenient or necessary" to
the company and its successors in title. Their wordy covenants passed
to the coal men the right to utilize as mining props the timber growing on the land, to divert and pollute the water and to cover the surface with toxic mining refuse. The landowner's estate was made perpetually "servient" to the superior or "dominant" rights of the owner
of the minerals. And, for good measure, a final clause absolved the
mining company from all liability to the landowner for such damages as might be caused "directly or indirectly" by mining operations
on his land.

Beneath the feet of the highlander lay quantities of minerals,
the magnitude of which would have dumfounded him. In practically every ridge a vein of coal was to be found near the top of the hill,
sometimes with as little as forty feet of overburden on it. Other

seams ran through the mountains at intervals all the way to the base of the hill. Some hillsides contained five or six seams. In addition, at depths of a hundred and fifty feet or more under the creek beds lay other great coal veins. Wholly unsuspected by the mountaineer, his land also contained quantities of oil and gas — which are only to-day beginning to be extracted on an appreciable scale. These had done the Cumberlander no good in the past. The agents assured him that the coal would not be mined for many years and then only under circumstances harmless to him and to his children. So the deeds were signed and duly recorded in the clerks' offices of the county courts, and then the coal buyers, or most of them, departed.

We have seen that the mountaineer sold his great trees for a consideration little more than nominal, but if his timber brought him a small financial reward, his minerals were virtually given away. The going price in the early years was fifty cents per acre, and though the price rose, little by little, over the next three decades, it rarely surpassed five dollars. Under ordinary mining methods prevailing throughout the region during the years after 1913, the operating coal companies were able to recover from one thousand to fifteen hundred tons of coal per acre foot. This means that a seam of coal five feet thick produced a minimum of five thousand tons per acre! Where more than one seam was mined, a single acre sometimes yielded fifteen or twenty thousand tons! Even this prodigious re-covery left thousands of tons underground — plus the oil, gas and other minerals. For this vast mineral wealth the mountaineer in most instances received a single half-dollar.

So immense was the coalfield and so roadless and rugged its terrain that the process of buying up the region's wealth necessarily con-sumed considerable time. Commencing about 1875 with the first roving timber buyers and their wildcat surveys, the task was not sub-stantially complete until about 1910. By that year a major portion of the land was owned in fee simple by nonresidents. Perhaps three fourths of the remaining salable timber was held by absentee in-vestors and at least 85 per cent of the minerals had passed out of the hands of the plateau dwellers. Thus the stage was set for the most momentous single occurrence in the history of the Cumberlands — the building of the railroads. After years of rumor and speculation, the iron horse was to intrude upon the ancient solitudes of this beautiful land.

The mountaineer's imagination was fired by this event as by nothing else that has befallen him in his long sojourn in the Southern highlands. He hoped that the much-touted railroads would bring many benefits. The income from the sale of his timber and coal, small though it was, had caused him to acquire a taste for things he could not make and which money alone could provide. His quickened appetite for "factory goods" remained, but his money was soon gone. Hence the boom promised by industrial development offered hope for more such desirable things. Perhaps he and his sons could find jobs at high wages at sawmills or in mines. More and better schools might be built so his children could "larn somethin'," the tempo of life would quicken and his drab existence would take on new color and sparkle. The mountaineer had come to look forward to the new era for many reasons, but most ardently because he knew that his long isolation would be broken and the monotony of his ancient mode of living would be interrupted by new experiences. He was confident of his ability to profit from this new and startling event. Though he had known many hardships and his folk memories groped back through eras of toil, tears and blood, he had never known failure. His life, like those of his ancestors from the Piedmont and the Blue Ridge, had been lived in fiercely free independence, and when the gangs of track layers first poked into the long valleys of the Kentucky, the Big Sandy and the Cumberland, they found the essential physical environment of the plateau remarkably unaltered. Though millions of logs had been sent down the river and many coves were now growing corn instead of tulip poplars, the changes wrought by such labors were not large and thousands of acres of still virgin timber persisted on every hand. But these outward appearances were deceptive. Now the trees that shaded him were no longer his property, and he was little more than a trespasser upon the soil beneath his feet.

CHAPTER EIGHT

———•———

The Frontier a Century After

MANY OF THE little swarm of teachers, missionaries and school and church organizers who followed the railroads into the plateau were so impressed by the surviving frontier modes and methods that they saw the mountaineer as a sort of latter-day border pioneer, summed up in the expression "our contemporary ancestors." To a remarkable degree this concept was accurate — but its accuracy was limited, and it fell far short of describing the mind and manners of the mountaineer. True, an astounding number of his habits, tastes and outlooks had come down to him little diluted from his pioneer fathers of the eighteenth century, but in the meantime he had acquired serious defects which had not plagued his forebears.

A terrific population explosion had multiplied the highlanders at a breathtaking rate in the half-century since 1860. In that year the Federal census revealed a total population, including slaves, of 84,028 in the plateau counties. Despite the distractions of war, feuds, reconstruction and exodus the total climbed to 98,150 in 1870. Twenty years later it was 173,927. In 1910 the enumerators found 294,193 residents! This incredible upsurge of nearly 400 per cent reflected a very slight influx and occurred not withstanding a substantial outflow.

To be sure, the plateau had experienced its first great boom in the Eighties and Nineties when English steel interests had sought to build a great iron and coal empire in Bell County. The ridges full of coal and the millions of tons of low-grade iron ore in the surrounding area touched off a frantic era of coal buying and town building.

The town of Middlesboro was built along the new tracks of the Louisville and Nashville Railroad Company complete with blast furnaces, coke ovens and luxurious hotels. Prophetic of events in later years, ten or fifteen thousand people poured into the county from Europe and other parts of the United States. Their presence accounts in large measure for the population growth in that county but had little effect elsewhere. In fact many of its new residents were drawn from other counties of the plateau.

By 1894 the Bell County bubble had burst. The Bessemer process of steelmaking had made its appearance, and had deflated the boom in the wilderness. The roaring new communities subsided into still ghost towns. The frantic activity in that area had caused little of the population rise mirrored in the census reports.

The old fertility of the frontier held sway in every cabin. Childless women were practically unknown. Midwives, "granny women" to the mountaineers, toiled incessantly. One- and two-room log cabins sheltered from a half-dozen to a score of children. Though the infant mortality rate hovered between 30 and 40 per cent, the birth rate was fabulous. In the plateau the white woman proved her ability to produce children in numbers unsurpassed anywhere in the world.

Generally parents were extremely indulgent, allowing their children to grow up under few inhibitions and restrictions. They reached maturity with the impetuosity of young Indian braves. However, as a matter of economic necessity parents had to insist on hard work from an early age. At six or seven years girls and boys went to the cornfields and did their share of the labor. Failure to "be smart" at assigned tasks brought severe whippings. Children worked, stayed out of the way and "minded" the few instructions they received from "ma" and the "old man."

Hospitality was the mountaineer's noblest virtue. Whatever his degree of wealth it was a point of honor and courtesy to offer food, drink and shelter to any caller. Perhaps this trait originated in the Scottish Highlands, where it still prevails, but whatever its source it became a folk habit on the frontier. When a friend or stranger appeared at a cabin door he could enjoy the best the household afforded. "Come in and eat with us, and take a drink" was a sincere invitation and failure to accept the invitation was deemed an insult.

Sexually the mountaineer enjoyed many of the free and easy habits that have made the Tahitians famous. He and his womenfolk were far less inhibited than the ritualistic Indians who had once camped on his creek banks. The land abounded with "woods colts" or "come-by-chance" children. The children of unwed mothers grew up with those of the marriage she soon contracted, and little attention was paid to such episodes. The young man who "destroyed" a girl in this manner usually married her, but if he did not other men failed to regard her blemish as disqualifying or fatal.

Whiskey was absent from few households. If a mountaineer could not enjoy its stimulation because of religious convictions he consumed it as a medicine. It was believed to benefit every ailment from snakebite to arthritis. Its fiery influence bared knives and pistols upon slight provocation. The land was without milder beverages, save for an occasional cask of "methiglum." This ecstatic drink was the fabled "honey wine" of Wales, and was said to "kiss like a woman and kick like a mule."

The fights and brawls which erupted with such frequency and deadliness were fought with the savagery and ruthlessness of the North Carolina frontier of the 1750s. There were no rules, and no holds or blows were barred. When men grappled they fought like savage beasts. Ears and cheeks were often bitten off. A favorite tactic consisted of "gouging" an adversary's eyes from his head. The horrified Legislature forbade such practices under heavy penalties, but to little avail.

A story is told of a mountaineer who was walking through the woods in the years of settlement. He was suddenly attacked by a large and angry female bear. So quick was her onslaught that he had no time to use his rifle or draw his knife. The monster hugged him in her immense forepaws and undertook to bite away his face. But the mountaineer was determined to die hard. He seized the end of the bear's nose between his sturdy teeth and plunged his thumbs deep into bruin's eyes. With a roar the bear flung him aside and fled, leaving the tip of her nose in his mouth. The victor proudly displayed her nose, explaining that "bars can't stand bitin' and gougin'." Whether true or not, the tale illustrates the vital savagery which the mountaineer perpetuated so long.

When death came it was met with resignation if it came from natural or accidental causes and with vows of vengeance if inflicted by an enemy. So many people had died of violence that when a report of death reached a mountaineer he generally asked who-or-what had done the killing. Burial in a homemade coffin took place the day after the demise, and, since there were few preachers, often without religious services. When a leisurely interval occurred and a Baptist lay preacher was handy, a funeral service was performed. Thus the funeral sometimes came months or years after the mourned one's death. This practice gave rise to the "memorial funerals" which still occur, sometimes even a decade after interment. The hysterical grave-side grief so often seen in the region today was then only beginning to make its appearance as the people, without religious moorings, sensed a deepening helplessness and futility.

But it was in the faces and hearts of the women that the land's tragedy, folly and failure were most deeply etched. In their world the man was a tyrant who ruled his house with medieval unconcern for his wife's feelings or opinions. She rarely sat down to eat a meal with him, it being her duty to "wait on" him. When a stranger was present she stayed discreetly out of sight. As a girl she saw her broth-ers and father "laid away," the victims of feuds, quarrels, logging ac-cidents or disease. Her girlhood was spent in graceless toil and crowned by an early marriage. Wasted by a quarter-century of child-bearing, she saw a row of graves dug for her children. Often she survived as a widow to fend for the remainder of her brood. She could rarely influence the impetuous decisions of her husband and sons, and, never far from the family graveyard, mourned through long years the results of their errors.

By 1910 this society had been stratified into the usual layers of the poor, the reasonably well off and those who, by the standards of their environment, were wealthy. Though there was no substantial wealth in the region when measured by the standards of the nation gen-erally, there were men here and there who were able to live by the labor of others without having to toil long and hard themselves. In short, the rough equality of the frontier had vanished. As a result of coal and timber sales, considerable sums of money had filtered into the plateau. Within a few years county-seat merchants and some of the shrewder farmers managed to accumulate most of these sums. The merchants stocked goods, from Louisville and Cincinnati wholesalers, which tempted the mountaineer and his wife to part with their easily-come-by dollars. Once the mountaineer's timber and coal money was exhausted he was, frequently, willing to sell parts of his land for more money. Some of the more clever and ambitious farmers hastily took advantage of the opportunity afforded to buy tracts of land from their neighbors. Usually the lands thus accumulated were river bottoms and the larger coves. These coves and bottoms could be plowed and planted with corn to feed the livestock of the prospering farmer.

Little by little the landholdings of some of the mountaineers grew larger and embraced more and more rich lands, while the estates of others dwindled and shrank and came to consist of the poorer spurs and knobby ridges. These, once cleared, were so infertile that they could produce passably well only one or two crops of corn before the thin topsoil was washed away or depleted. Land was still the basic wealth of the region and though the underlying minerals and the remaining stands of good timber were, in most instances, now owned by absentee corporations, the expanding farmers and the land traders among the county seat merchants were able to prosper from their real-estate transactions. It must be remembered that while the absentee corporations held legal title to most of the coal and timber, little was done to utilize them until after the railroads arrived. Those farmers who saw fit to buy the lands of their neighbors could do so in an agricultural society still practically untouched by the displacements of industrial development.

Slowly over the years men who were "well fixed" accumulated long stretches of fertile bottomland along the banks of the larger creeks, together with the deeper and more gently sloping hillside coves. When his neighbor had exhausted the funds derived from the sale of his land, when, in short, the money for his "surface land" had been frittered away along with that derived from his minerals and his trees, he had no choice except sharecropping. He possessed no skill or knowledge which would enable him to make a living except by the rude system of agriculture that, with few refinements, had come down to him from his early pioneer forefathers. He must have pork, milk, butter, corn, beans, squash, cushaws, onions, Irish and sweet potatoes and tobacco, and these could be derived only from the soil. His ancestors had obtained them successfully from his lands for more than four generations and, when title to the land departed, reliance upon it remained. The mountaineer must cultivate the earth to survive. Once his fields were exhausted he had no means of replenishing them. There were no industries to afford him wages and while an occasional day of work might be obtained from the wealthier farmers, the wages were always shockingly low.

So, quite rapidly indeed, the system of sharecropping grew up. The farmer-purchaser simply permitted the seller to return to his ancestral land and to cultivate his fields as he had previously, but now the tiller of the soil did not harvest the crops as his own. Instead he delivered one third to one half of his corn and other crops to the landowner, and hauled the rest away in his sled or wagon to his own smaller cribs. This process had been under way for twenty-five years or more before the arrival of the railroads, circa 1910, and the railroaders found perhaps a third of the people living upon and cultivating the lands of others.

The new class of landlords was not made up of bloated barons who lived without toil but of men who still went into the fields at croptime and labored beside their tenant farmers and sharecroppers. But they did not labor so many days, and as their barns filled with corn and their smokehouses with meat they toiled less. As their sons grew to manhood some of them became dandies who rode handsome horses and spent much time with local belles and little time in the cornfields and logging woods. Since the prevailing mode of agriculture could produce only a simple living at best it effectually pauperized the tenant because, labor though he might, he could extract from his neighbor's land only enough corn, meat and potatoes to feed his family and livestock from one year to the next. He found himself in a vicious cycle from which there was no escape by any agricultural means known to him. As his sons came to manhood they perforce followed in his footsteps — and the ranks of the sharecroppers steadily swelled.

The agriculture of the region had remained incredibly primitive. The bottoms had long since been cleared and thousands of acres of corn were annually planted on hillside clearings. The mountaineer knew nothing about fertilizer or cover crops. He knew nothing about soil conservation, and about land use practically nothing which the Indian squaws had not known more than a century before. His system of plowing and planting, hoeing and harvesting was extremely exhausting to the soil, and the winter rains fell year after year upon crop lands unprotected by winter cover. Tremendous amounts of corn were required to feed milk cows, hogs, saddle and draft horses and the teams of oxen which dragged the mighty logs down to the splash dams. Constricted bottomlands, even when cultivated to the uttermost, could not supply enough of this indispensable grain, so that the hillsides were increasingly resorted to. When the timber had been cut from a cove it was either plowed with a "bull tongue" or "dug in" with a hoe for corn planting. Such a crop was hoed two or three times in order to keep down weeds and young tree shoots. While the coves were on the gentlest slopes to be found on the hillsides, they were, notwithstanding, steeply angled and when summer thunderstorms smote them with sudden downpours mold was washed away, sometimes as much as two inches at a time. When the autumn rains and the winter snows and thaws followed the summer storms the precious humus accumulations of millenia vanished leaving semi-sterile, yellow sub-soil whose fertility was low and which annually declined in productivity. Since landlords and tenants alike required such fields for their continued existence, they moved on from cove to cove until the landlord had cleared the last one he owned. Out of necessity he then authorized the clearing of even steeper and higher lands so that more "new grounds" could be had. These fields were less fertile initially and, lying at a steeper angle, washed even more quickly. Thousands of such acres were cleared though rarely could more than a single successful crop be expected. Sometimes the second year did not produce more than ten or fifteen bushels of corn per acre!

Consequently the railroads found splotches of hillside land wholly cleared of timber and eroded down to the yellow subsoil.

This vastly wasteful system of land exploitation was accompanied by the rise of the tenant class. The tenant lived in a cabin of hewed logs, or had reverted to the less elaborate pole cabin of the earliest settlers. Most of the landlords also occupied log houses but they had become "double-log" structures and were two stories high. At a convenient distance stood the kitchen, with a "dogtrot" connecting the two buildings. Some of the more substantial farmers had abandoned their log houses entirely and had hired rudely skilled local carpenters to saw out planks by hand and build for them gaunt, graceless two story weather-boarded houses with a tall chimney at each end. This was the mountain version of the plantation house.

While practically all the tenants and most of the poorer sort of landowning farmers still ate meals their wives had cooked in pots and frying pans over the huge wood-burning fireplace, the wealthier farmers had acquired "step-stoves," and these inelegant contrivances were the pride and joy of their womenfolk.

The feuds had by no means ceased, but in many areas raged on with great intensity. Scores of men were shot down annually for little or no provocation and practically every Circuit Court clerk's office recorded a long and congested docket of murder, manslaughter, mayhem and other cases involving crimes of violence. Most of the leaders of the warring faction had by this time come to be landlord farmers who were supported in their squabbles by small legions of relatives and tenants.

By this time, also, the long years of violence had caused hundreds of the more peaceable sort of men to leave the country and to migrate in all directions. This exodus, coupled with more than a generation of slaughter of its most virile men, had to a degree weakened the mental and physical fiber of the population.

The feuds had narrowed still further the limited social contacts of the people. The interests and experiences of the mountaineer were centered close to his cabin door and rarely did he seek a woman from another county or district. The animosities of the feuds shut a prospective bridegroom off from adversary clans, so that he tended to turn to the womenfolk of his own blood-line or of others friendly to the faction to which he gave his allegiance. Frequently he paid courtship to cousins of the second or third degree, and eventually marriages between first cousins became commonplace. As the process of "marrying close to home" continued over the decades, the mountaineer came to be fantastically inbred. To this day "double first cousins" are frequently encountered in the mountains, and occasionally a person is found whose duly married parents bore this consanguine kinship to each other. On practically every creek and stream the inhabitants are a tangle of cousins, aunts, uncles, nieces, nephews, parents and grandparents. In some communities the blood lines are so few and so intermixed that the most patient genealogist might lose his wits in attempting to unravel them. The inbreeding with its attendant genetic pitfalls contributed much in later years to the erosion of the highlander's self-reliance.

However, it should not be inferred that inbreeding, sharecropping, the feuds and the out-migration had destroyed the independence and virility of the Cumberlander. These were weakening influences, whose effects were then beginning to be discernible to a keen-eyed observer, but the mountaineer with all his shortcomings was still a remarkably strong human type. Though his land was thinning he was still well fed on simple but nutritious foods. His life had been spent in the outdoors and he was able to endure, without even a realization of discomfort, circumstances which our modern city dweller would consider grievous hardships. Because of his feuds and his multitude of personal antagonisms the mountaineer was seldom without his long blue-barreled, walnut-handled Colt revolver. He still slept on a bed made of shucks or feathers and, except for the more prosperous of the landlord farmers, wore clothes made of homespun cloth, with perhaps a single factory suit which he reserved for the courthouse or other great occasions. In summer he spent much of his time barefoot, his soles as tough as those of a modern Congolese. More than one newcomer to the region in the years after the turn of the century reported finding farmers and loggers barefoot, their feet apparently impervious to the sharp mountain rocks.

Though the greater game had long since been eradicated the hunting of raccoon, possum and squirrel remained the mountaineer's principal pleasure. The yellowing streams still abounded with catfish and trout and he loved to catch them with a pronged gig or kill them by gunfire. On Saturday, nights the young men "went a-courtin'," and the most popular gatherings were the square dances. A large floor space was cleared by carrying the furniture into an adjoining room. Then the couples "ran sets" to the music of a fiddle and a five-stringed banjo. Sometimes these instruments were homemade, of large seasoned hollow gourds, and the favorite tunes bore such unromantic names as "Soapsuds over the Fence," "Sugar in the

Gourd" and "Grandpappy's Sledge." Sometimes when the dancers began to tire the musicians would play and sing such ancient, sad ballads as "Barbara Allen" and "King Henry's Wife," or other songs which had "been brought from over the waters." The most widely loved instrument, however, was the "dulcimore," or dulcimer. This plaintive harp had a place in most houses and to its accompaniment were sung tales of love, war and death.

In the forty-five years since "the War" the public schools had slowly but steadily multiplied. Most communities had a log schoolhouse within "walking distance of the scholars" (this phrase was applied to an area within a radius of four or five miles). Though statutes required all children to attend school for at least eight years, few bothered to do so and it is doubtful whether more than half the children had ever darkened a schoolhouse door. The school term continued to be three or four months; many of the teachers were coarse near-illiterates who sought to instill knowledge into the child's head by constant application of a stick to his back. Though many children were reluctant to go to school at all, others attended the same school term after term long after they had completed its entire course of instruction. Such children felt a natural aptitude for learning, and there were no other institutions to which they could advance. If other tasks were not pressing they completed the course of instruction and then returned each July when "school took up" to repeat the process at the highest grade for several additional years. These students became extremely well grounded in the few subjects taught, and in later years were remarkably apt at remembering dates from American history, diagramming sentences and ciphering.

The highly emotional, bedrock fundamentalist preachers strove mightily with Satan for the souls of men, but most of the mountaineers blissfully ignored their efforts. Membership in the scattered churches remained small, and though good and honest men and women were to be found on every creek and in every community, religion in the conventional sense played little part in the lives of most of the people. The few who were religious at all were narrow, dogmatic and argumentative. Occasionally a "revival" preacher would stir a wave of hysterical repentance, but like Omar Khayam's, their fire of repentance was usually short-lived. Judging from court records, nearly as many people attended church services to harass the preachers as to benefit from their sermons. Gangs of rowdies habitually converged upon the little churches firing off their pistols and yelling like wild Choctaws.

The story is told about a burly mountaineer named George Johnson who had been a great rough-and-tumble fighter before he "got religion." Thereafter he was in faithful attendance at the small weatherbeaten church house on Grapevine Creek, and was a great comfort to his preachers. One warm Sunday morning, while religious services were under way, a half-dozen drunken roughs appeared outside the open door and, after listening awhile to the exhortations of the preacher, began to mimick him loudly. The preacher could hear his every word repeated from beyond the door, and the interference so confused him that he was unable to proceed. At last he asked all his flock to bow their heads in "a moment of silent prayer, after which we will adjourn the services for a few minutes while Brother George Johnson knocks hell out of 'em fer God!"

The herb doctors persisted, but college-trained medical men of a sort were beginning to reach the hills. Standards for training physicians were low and some of the doctors who held themselves out as college-educated had attended medical school for as little as one year. For many years the state had no mandatory requirements for the education of doctors, and anyone could practice medicine who could find patients willing to risk his treatments. An enterprising would-be doctor simply ordered a "doctor book," studied it awhile, bought a quantity of pills, salves and tonics, and went to work. As medical knowledge increased, doctors in northern and central Kentucky became competent enough by the standards of the day, but the mountains were practically without real physicians. In time, however, young men began to leave the plateau to study. Few of them could boast more than seven or eight years' schooling, substantially less than the equivalent of today's junior high school, but they were able to struggle through the two- or three-year course offered by the medical schools. When they returned home their services were eagerly sought, and most of them were looked up to by their fellow men as paragons of wisdom. Notwithstanding the confidence of their patients, it is probable that quite as many people died from their ministrations as were cured thereby, and most of the sick throughout the plateau still relied largely upon a potpourri of Indian medicines, folk brews and superstition.

Few people who traveled through the mountains in these years before the railroads have favored us with accounts of the mountaineer and of the primitive society in which he lived. The striking beauty of the mountains and the stark lives of their people must have impressed them, but rarely did a surveyor, coal buyer or drummer go to the trouble to preserve his observations. Happily, though, at least one gentleman and his daughter traveled widely in the hills and wrote numerous letters about their experiences and observations. Dr. E. O. Guerrant of Lexington, Kentucky, was a Presbyterian minister who undertook to establish a presbytery in southeastern Kentucky. In 1892 Dr. Guerrant rode from Jackson in Breathitt County some forty miles up the North Fork of the Kentucky River to Hazard. In a letter he described what was probably a typical county-seat town:

Hazard, the only town in Perry County, consists of a Courthouse, a jail, four stores and seventeen families. There is no church or schoolhouse. I am trying to preach in the Courthouse.

Four years later Dr. Guerrant came back to the mountains and this time he brought his daughter, Grace, a sensitive and keenly observant teen-ager. A logging railroad had been extended to Jackson and they were able to travel that far by train. In two letters to her sister, Anne, at Lexington, Grace Guerrant has bequeathed us a fresh and remarkably clear word picture of the mountaineers, their wives and children as seen through the honest eyes of this impressionable young woman. Because of their clarity and sincerity I have reproduced parts of them:

We went one hundred miles to Jackson, in Breathitt County. The road went up the Red River, where the big cliffs stand up on both sides of the road, hundreds of feet high. Many of the mountains have rocks on top like domes, bigger than a church. They are grand. The river was lined with beautiful flowers of ivy and laurel.

I saw some men cutting oats with a big scythe, with fingers on it. Papa told me they were cradling. That was curious to me. One big tree was growing on top of a big rock. About six in the evening, we reached Jackson, on the North Fork of the Kentucky River. It is a very nice town, and we have a church and a college there, where a few years ago we had none. On Wednesday morning we started for the mountains in Perry County.

We went up the Kentucky River ten miles to the mouth of Troublesome Creek. Here we got into trouble enough. We had to get out and help the buggy down the rocky stairsteps in the road. We went up Troublesome a mile, then up Lost Creek ten miles, then the man there said there were ten thousand big saw logs in the creek. I never saw the like. The little houses all had martin boxes, but no yard or shade.

Down on Troublesome, we saw some ladies barefooted, and one old lady had on shoes, but no stockings, and one had on a dress shorter than mine. I guess she must have been an old maid.

The mountains were very steep, but had corn growing on their sides nearly to the top. They can't plow them up and down, but crossways. We saw coal mines all along the road, just sticking out of the mountains. Sometimes we rode over solid coal beds, and the biggest trees I ever saw grow along the creeks and rivers. They are awfully big. We saw a big boy, who had only a shirt on, and most of the men were barefooted, but they were very clever.*

When we went ten miles up Lost Creek, we turned up a creek called "Ten-Mile" Creek. Well, it was awful. I thought we had passed bad roads, but we were just beginning them. Three men went along to cut trees and roll rocks out of the road. And such a road! Over big rocks and logs and steep banks and deep holes and around splash-dams. I thought our buggy would be smashed all to pieces. The horse pulled our trace in two, and a big rock broke a spoke out of the buggy. Sometimes I bumped Papa, and sometimes he bumped me. It was too funny. Papa got a man to lead the horse around a big tree on the mountain while he and another man held the buggy. The horse got strangled and the man cried out, "Here's a dead horse," and scared me nearly to death. But they got the horses up and we went over a mountain to the Grapevine Creek. Here we had a time getting down the mountain, the path was so steep and sidelong. Mr. Little's horse went over the mountainside and he jerked him back and he fell down, with the buggy on him. Papa and some men helped to take him out, then the buggy got away and ran down the mountain and broke the shaft. They all took our horse out and got the buggy down to the foot of the mountain by the hardest work.

The road down the Grapevine was no road at all. Mr. Little and Papa had to walk and lead and roll logs out of the way. It took us five hours to go seven miles.

* This word, as used here, is synonymous with "hospitable" or "generous."

Mr. Sawyers, our missionary, was there. Papa is preaching in the little schoolhouse, on the bank of the river, and it is crowded at 10:00 A.M. and 4:00 P.M. Miss Kate Patrick and I play the little organ, the first one ever played in this county for worship. Emma Johnson has the only one in the county. The people are very clever and attentive, and most of them walk to church. About twenty-five have joined, and Mr. Johnson was the first one, and an old man nearly seventy, and a real pretty girl named Dora Duff. Mr. Johnson is the leading man in the county, and lives in the only brick house.

Your sister,

GRACE

DEAR ANNE:

My last letter brought you to the mouth of Grapevine Creek. Well, we had a big meeting there Sunday from 10:00 A.M. til 5:00 P.M., two hours for dinner. There was a crowd — the schoolhouse was packed — and it was so hot I could hardly get my breath. Papa preached morning and evening; thirty-five joined, and he had to baptize most of them, as they had never been baptized. Some people had to stand out in the rain. We passed a little schoolhouse and all the children ran out to see the buggies. They were curiosities to them. One little boy said he lived up a creek, but didn't know its name. He saw big rattlesnakes up there too. One funny man was riding an ox, and he had a bed quilt for a saddle and bark for a girth. Another man had an ox geared up like a horse and it was plowing for him. An old lady was carrying her baby and a little pig was following her like a dog. When she stopped, it lay down at her feet. One little house had a pole put up in the front yard, and three bottles hung up on top for ornaments. There were no trees in the yard. One lady had a naked tree in her yard, covered with egg shells, like a snowball bush. It was funny to me.

Well, after a hard journey over mountains and more creeks we reached Big Creek. Papa had been there before, and the good people came walking up the road to meet us. I never saw cleverer people, though they are not rich or proud. Papa preached in the schoolhouse for four days, and twenty-seven joined the church.

On Friday evening we crossed the mountain, and went to Hazard, the county seat. It is a little town of about one hundred people. It used to have a bad name, because so many people were killed there. It is better now. They never had a church here before. Papa preached in the Courthouse. Many people came, and twenty-three joined. He preached in the jail one day, and three poor prisoners joined. It was an awful place, and I felt sorry for them. The doors were iron bars, with big locks and bolts to hold them safe. A mountain preacher came to church, and he had been shot in the ear by some bad men. They said he killed their hogs. A big freshet came down the river and carried away hundreds of saw logs. They said a water spout broke on a creek called "Kingdom Come."

Near the turn of the century John Fox, Jr., of Paris, Kentucky, came into the mountains and began to gather material for his novels and short stories. Out of this research came *The Little Shepherd of Kingdom Come, The Trail of the Lonesome Pine*, and numerous short stories including "Christmas Eve on Lonesome," "A Knight of the Cumberland," "The Army of the Callahan," "The Pardon of Becky Day," "A Mountain Vendetta," "Christmas Night with Satan," "Courtin' on Cutshin," and "The Passing of Abraham Shivers." Fox was an incurable romanticist and he dealt with the mountaineer with a tenderness and sympathy which no other writer, perhaps, was ever willing to accord him. His mountaineers were ignorant and frequently bloodstained but they possessed a certain dignity and honor which was comical at times but was always genuine. On the whole his descriptions and character sketches of Devil Judd Tolliver, Abraham Shivers, the Preacher of Kingdom Come, Polly Ann Sturgill, Becky Day, Mace Day, Daws Dillon and the many other men and women who move through his pages were accurate. Most of them were taken from life and described clearly people identifiable by a generation of contemporaneous mountain readers. If he found romance among these rough-hewn folk where others saw none perhaps it was because his eye and ear sought more eagerly for it. His descriptions of the mountains and streams are remarkably good and in themselves justify the reading. Any person interested in the life and times of the plateau dwellers before the coming of the railroads will do well to read the works of this nearly forgotten author.

The mountaineer was ardently patriotic, and in the war of 1898 and again in 1917 thousands of men and boys eagerly "jined the army." Volunteers walked to Lexingon, Kentucky — for some a distance of one hundred and seventy miles — when the war with Spain broke out, and nineteen years later Breathitt County provided so many volunteers that it was the only county in the United States in which the draft never became operative. Willie Sandlin of Leslie County won a Congressional Medal of Honor because his mountain-learned skill with pistol and rifle and his intrepidity with the bayonet enabled him to single-handedly destroy a series of German machine-gun positions and their gunners. These hardy, uninhibited, aggressive highland men made particularly fine infantrymen and, together with their kinsmen from other regions in the Southern mountains, were in no small measure responsible for the renown for deadly accuracy with the rifle so long enjoyed by the American soldier.

_____•_____

CHAPTER NINE

The Alabaster Cities

THE HEART OF the eastern Kentucky coalfield lies in a group of eleven counties near the headwaters of three of Kentucky's major streams. These counties are Johnson, Floyd, Magoffin, Pike, Knott, Letcher, Harlan, Perry, Leslie, Clay and Bell. To pierce the coalfield on the broadest practical front the railroad builders followed the valleys of the Poor Fork of the Cumberland River, the North Fork of the Kentucky and the Levisa Fork of the Big Sandy. In two or three years the track layers drove through the vitals of the plateau until, in the spring of 1912, the Lexington and Eastern Railroad reached McRoberts near the source spring of the Kentucky's North Fork. Within a short time thereafter the Louisville and Nashville reached the shabby village of Poor Fork in Harlan County, and the Baltimore and Ohio arrived within the shadow of the Breaks of the Big Sandy, a breathtakingly beautiful canyon later renowned as the "Grand Canyon of the South." When the construction gangs laid down their tools at these points on the eve of the First World War, the vast, backward Cumberland Plateau was tied inseparably to the colossal industrial complex centering in Pittsburgh, and a dynamic new phase in the region's history had begun.

The railroads were built by a small army of contractors, each of whom was assigned a stretch of two to five miles of line, and the work progressed remarkably fast in view of the difficult terrain and the primitive methods employed. Fleets of "section" cars followed the workmen and were parked on the side tracks for occupancy by the laborers, their wives and other "camp women."

Most of the contractors were from the Deep South, primarily Alabama and Mississippi. They used thousands of mules and mule-drawn scrapers, and hordes of Negroes from the cotton fields. Practically the entire length of the line was blasted out of the mountain sandstone, and countless blast-holes had to be drilled. These were filled with explosives and the rock was dynamited away. Surely the legendary John Henry, that immortal hero of Negro folklore, must have had his counterpart on every sweat-stained mile of winding roadbed.

In some communities stay-at-home mountaineers, particularly the womenfolk, had never seen a Negro, and people flocked from miles around to see the gangs of burly workmen driving steel and laying track. Their bare black backs glistened in the hot sunshine as the powerful arms swung giant nine-pound "sheep-nose" sledgehammers. One man hammered the steel while another, his "shaker," loosened the drill in the stone after each blow. When the hammered drill had penetrated the rock about four feet, the steel driver laid down his hammer and three or four men went to work with giant "churn" drills. These long, pointed steel shafts were so heavy that from two to four men were required to lift them. They were raised a foot or two from the bottom of the hole and then allowed to drop of their own weight. These were no match for the steam drill which eventually defeated the mighty John Henry, but they accomplished their purpose and the holes were drilled.

Once the rock was loosened by blasting, other gangs of Negroes hammered it to bits. Week by week this chanting, singing black army pushed the railroads deeper into the heart of the plateau country.

Freedom had not brought the good life which the emancipationists had promised, and the Southern Negro was willing to abandon the cotton rows for a chance to build railroads and mine coal. After six ten-hour workdays the railroad builder would yearn for love, and the softhearted contractors obligingly allowed him to bring his woman along. The contractors were unable to provide living quarters for enough women, however, so not every "hand" was permitted to bring his favorite. Those who came were expected to share their favors rather widely.

The generous contractors also provided rolling commissaries stocked with groceries and work clothes, and with ample supplies of cheap whiskey, gin and wine. These head-splitting beverages were withheld from sale until Saturday afternoon when work was ended until Monday morning. Then the alcohol began to flow and the workmen carried from the commissary in food, clothing and intoxicants the entire earnings of his week's labor.

But the alcoholic beverages were not the only wares in whose use the laborers could find oblivion. The present strict Federal drug laws had not been enacted and such potent narcotics as cocaine, morphine and heroin were sold. On Sunday afternoons rows of black "dope fiends" could be seen lolling with open mouths and gaping eyes in the grass along the right-of-way, or, in winter, stretched on the pine floors around the coal-burning stoves in the house cars. Mammoth hangovers resulted from these week-end binges, and much stern persuasion was sometimes required to get recalcitrant Negroes to work on Monday mornings.

Enticed by the lofty wage of a dollar and a half a day, many mountaineers joined the work gangs, and men who did so and who survived the intervening years recall that "it was all a nigger's life was worth for him even to ask for any cash wages." It behooved him to pay the outrageously high commissary prices and to use up all his wages in this manner. Some of them did not do so, however, and "made trouble." There is no way to estimate with any accuracy just how many such hapless Negroes were shot to death on the slimmest pretexts by the contractors and their brutal foremen. But inquiry along the winding tracks among the elderly men and women who watched the railroads built has disclosed that the number must have been startlingly high. One contractor named Pat Logan acquired an almost legendary reputation; it is recounted of him that he "must have killed a nigger nearly every Monday morning."

The bodies of these poor wretches, whose bondage was little less than that from which "the War" had freed them, were buried on knolls overlooking the tracks they had worked so hard to lay, and occasionally the sunken graves in these weed-grown "nigger graveyards" can be found to this day.

But if many Negroes were slain by their white taskmasters, even more died at the hands of their black fellows. In their drunken orgies fights erupted every weekend, usually over the charms of the all-too-scarce women, and knives and razors went into action. By whatever means they died, homicides involving Negroes rarely attracted the attention of law enforcement officers in the county courthouses. These gentlemen took the lenient view that "niggers ought to be allowed to settle things between theirselves" and when a white man was reported to have killed a black, indictment was generally withheld because the white mountaineer grand jurors opined that "niggers have to be kept in their place" if they were to get any work done.

The manner in which the American railroads were built — the vast issues of watered stock and immense public subsidies on the one hand, and the driven armies of Negroes and imported Chinese coolies and Irishmen on the other — constitutes a disgrace to the nation as a whole, but in the remote and isolated valleys of the Kentucky mountains where public scrutiny was often nonexistent and always indifferent, the disgrace was vastly compounded.

The licentious and dope-infested railroad labor gangs were not to pass from the scene without leaving their lasting mark on at least some of the mountaineers who watched them toil. In many communities through which the railroads passed, men and women were tempted to try the drugs which so pleasantly overwhelmed the Negroes, and before long these were confirmed addicts. Though drug addiction in the plateau never became widespread, families here and there became enthralled to narcotics and were never able to free themselves. They were to share for years to come the misery of the black railroad builders who sometimes sang with deep pathos:

> Cocaine done drove me crazy,
> Morphine done kill'd my baby,
> An' I ain't a'goin' to be treated thisaway!

In the solid years before the foundations of civilization were shaken by the great spasm of 1914-1918, a mighty boom suddenly burst in upon the primitive population of the plateau. Miles of crumbling, rotting coal camps and the ruins of innumerable tipples still testify to the feverish activity of those years.

Coal and Steel were the reigning industrial royalty and their demands appeared insatiable. For three decades men had been buying the mineral riches of the highlands in anticipation, and now the time had arrived for gleaning the profits they had so long anticipated. As the railroads poked into the plateau from the front and two sides, the construction gangs frequently blasted into thick seams of glistening coal. In place after place the track layers had hardly passed from sight upstream when agents of the coal companies began the construction of coal "camps," tipples and other installations.

Many of the companies were newly organized, while others were Kentucky subsidiaries of "old-line" corporations in other states. All employed men who were experienced in coal mining and a substantial number of their engineers were from English pits. But whatever their qualifications and backgrounds, they faced an incredibly difficult task and it must be said to their credit that they attacked their problems with remarkable, if ruthless, efficiency.

The officials of the coal companies found little of value to them except the coal itself and the mining timbers growing on the earth above it. The native population was without even rudimentary experience in mining or any other industrial activity. Even worse, it lacked the dicipline so essential to industrial enterprise. Fiercely independent, its members looked with disdain and distrust at anything they did not understand.

The land was without towns in the accepted meaning of the word so that the incoming crowds of people could find little semblance of such elementary requirements as restaurants and hotels. In most counties the county seat was the only "town" and sometimes its population did not exceed one hundred and fifty persons living in a cluster of log cabins and frame houses about the courthouse and jail. Some counties lacked a bank or wholesale establishment of any kind. The few merchants operated on a small scale and were unprepared to supply the needs of a community in the throes of burgeoning growth. Outside Bell County the plateau lacked even a single mile of paved road and such roads as existed were rutted, narrow, muddy trails which followed the game and Indian "crossings" of a previous century. Only on the fringes of the plateau could a telephone be found. Perhaps a half-dozen hospitals existed in the entire plateau, and these were tattered frame buildings containing four or five rooms presided over by one or two semiskilled physicians.

The tax revenues of the coal counties were extremely limited and their officials were without the imagination and courage to meet the demands which the new circumstances were to bring. Government at the state level was a mire of ineptitude and disinterest without dedication or inspiration. In short, a vast, tangled sprawling industrial boom was about to fall upon a pristine region and people, under circumstances whose final results could scarcely be foreseen.

Before the advancing railroads reached a county, the coal barons had chosen the sites for their own towns. These were laid out on the narrow valley floors. They varied in size and quality of construction from community to community and from county to county. Some were poor drab villages, even by the standards of 1912, while others were quite good. In the better towns the center consisted of an administration building, a recreation hall, a hotel, a rooming house or two and the inevitable commissaries. The better camps also contained initially a hospital and clinic. Nearby were the machine shops and warehouses in which mining equipment and supplies were stored and repaired. Since this was an age still much dependent upon beasts of burden, barns for ponies, mules and horses were constructed near the camp. And nearby rose the inevitable grim, ugly coal tipple, a plant where the coal was sorted and loaded into railroad cars.

The larger corporations — such as Inland Steel Corporation, Consolidation Coal Company, International Harvester Corporation, Elkhorn Coal Corporation and United States Coal and Coke Company — imported skilled, experienced construction companies to build their camps. Under the direction of these builders coal towns rose in the valleys with amazing speed.

In some instances the companies brought in huge circular saws which reduced the trees on company-owned land to towering stacks of lumber. But this process required considerable time, because the lumber had to be cured by stack-drying for a year or more, or seasoned in heated kilns. This latter process produced usable lumber rapidly but the kilns could hardly be built in sufficient size and number to meet demands and trainloads of seasoned lumber were imported.

Gangs of carpenters, plasterers and masons were brought in from Baltimore, Cincinnati, Louisville and elsewhere. Swarms of mountaineers were employed as unskilled or "common" laborers, at wages to them fantastically high. For a dollar and a half a day the high-

THE ALABASTER CITIES · 99

lander dropped plow and hoe and turned to the tasks of the coal barons, and though he might revert upon occasion to his ancestral agriculture he would never again free himself from dependence upon his new overlords.

The architecture of the coal camps varied somewhat from town to town, but had one common trait—a deadening, monotonous similarity among the buildings. All the camps were built of wood, but in the better ones — those built by the more heavily capitalized corporations — the structures were weather-boarded with the interior walls plastered. The roofs were covered with tarred paper, and, in an effort to break up the deadening sameness, the buildings were painted a wide variety of colors — green, yellow, red, white, blue and brown.

Some of the houses were four-room cottages with open front porches and small rear stoops. Most, however, were duplexes designed to shelter two families, with a continuous interior wall separating them. A single apartment in such a building contained four or five rooms and each family enjoyed the use of half the front porch and the covered stoop to the rear. At convenient shoveling distance from the front street stood a coal house for the family fuel and a few yards behind each abode was a privy.

To the mountaineers in whose midst such houses sprang up they were palatial, and rumors spread with wildfire speed throughout the plateau that "fine houses" were being built by the hundreds. The mountaineer had never experienced such quality construction and few of them had ever so much as seen a plastered wall. Compared to his cabins and crudely built frame houses the residences constructed by the larger companies were indeed enticing.

But not all coal companies were able or willing to build houses so comfortable as these. Many then and in later years lacked the capital to build weather-boarded and plastered walls and settled upon a far less satisfactory mode of construction. In these camps, the homes were cheaply built of upright boards with narrow strips nailed over the cracks between them. The interiors were finished with a thin ceiling lumber and the floors consisted of a single layer of pine planking. These shoddy houses were built of poorly seasoned, rough lumber and within a few years began to sag and sway.

In all the camps the houses were warmed by open fireplaces upstairs and down, but it was to be proved in many stark winters that it was practically impossible to burn coal fast enough to keep even one room comfortably heated.

All the camps, large and small, had a commissary or camp store in a convenient central location, and in the larger camps numerous store buildings were constructed. The company anticipated that the Federal Government would obligingly establish a post office to serve the new community and the commissary was designed with an area to be rented to the postal authorities. This device served a double purpose. It produced a dependable rental income and enticed someone from practically every home into the commissary each day. Some camps were later provided with three or four separate post offices, one for each commissary.

In the larger camps concrete sidewalks were laid down, on either side of the graveled streets, but in the poorer coal towns there were only narrow paths running alongside streets whose mud was to be unalleviated except for cinders from the fireplaces.

The larger companies recognized that the backward counties could not provide school buildings for these huge new population centers and, as part of their overall plan, built a schoolhouse or houses adequate for schoolchildren through the eighth grade. In a few of the better camps brick or masonry high schools too were constructed in these early years. However, they were not donated to the overwhelmed counties, but were leased to them for monthly rentals sufficient to repay the cost of construction within a few years.

In the subsequent forty years some of these scraggly, weather-beaten buildings brought back to the companies their original investment many times over. Under state law, any community with three hundred children or more could form an "independent" school district. This small governmental unit could elect trustees and operate its own public school system within the hazy limits prescribed by state law. The companies quickly took advantage of the opportunity which this legislation afforded to keep their school tax dollars at home. Since the coal companies were to dominate every phase of life within their towns, the schools were to become instruments of the "big bosses," reflecting exactly their philosophy of management and business.

The larger corporations undertook to provide for the medical needs of the communities they were building, and by the standards of rural America in those years, built adequate hospitals of brick or stone construction. By the time these companies began the mining of coal, they had provided hospital and clinical services to treat the armies of sick and injured men who poured in such profusion from the pits. Some of the physicians whom the corporations brought into the coal field were men of genuine skill and learning with a real interest in the welfare of their patients, but unfortunately, many others were little better than quacks whose limited abilities would never have enabled them to succeed in more discerning and sophisticated communities. As we shall see later, most of these doctors were to become swamped by a multitude of poverty-ridden patients and, without time or inclination to keep abreast of developments in their profession, resorted increasingly to symptomatic medicine with little effort at genuine diagnosis and cure. It is unquestionably true, however, that in these coal-camp hospitals some physicians were to become by sheer experience expert orthopedists and surgeons, and not a few were to become extremely skilled in the treatment of gunshot wounds as well.

The task of filling their shiny new towns with people presented the coal corporations with a task almost as complex as that of building the houses. People must be brought together from many lands to provide these raw communities with all the human material which their profitable operation required. Without men with knowledge of how to utilize them, the veins of coal would be worthless and the long miles of new railroad track would bear away no creaking trains of black gold. A formidable assortment of competent personnel must not only be found but, more difficult still, must be enticed to come to this new frontier. The towns must have managers and clerks to stock and operate the new commissaries. There must be postal clerks to handle the bags of mail certain to pass over the new postal counters. Policemen must be found who could maintain order on streets whose lusty population was certain to be quick with gun and knife and fist. School teachers would be needed for the multitudes of children. Maintenance of the towns would require the continuing services of carpenters, painters and plasterers, and if plagues were to be prevented from ravaging the communities a small corps of sanitarians must be set to work. Each company must assemble experienced business managers, and the buying of maintenance and mining supplies and equipment could be done only by purchasing agents of dependable judgment. The mining of coal requires constant supervision by engineers, and each company must find a staff of mining engineers to plan and supervise the labyrinthine operations in the points and ridges and, finally, there must be found many thousands of strong, willing men to perform the hard labor which alone could move the coal.

The coal operators brought a cadre of supervisory technicians with them from the old coalfields in Pennsylvania, Virginia and West Virginia. Local surveyors who claimed some knowledge of civil engineering were enticed into the industry and were taught the principles of mapping, "setting spads," roofing, draining and bratticing. Mining engineers were never in sufficient supply because members of the profession were seldom willing to enter the gloomy, often deadly, coal mines. And the shortage of engineers was to plague the industry and be reflected in countless accident reports of explosions, fires and roof falls.

By the time the camps were finished the executives, engineers, clerks, timekeepers, accountants and doctors were pouring into the towns. The families of the executives, doctors, engineers and store managers lived in a row of larger and more comfortable houses above the camp on a commanding flat or mountain bench. This section lay somewhat apart from the rest of the town and care was taken to see that the yards were drained and sowed in grass. If skilled personnel was to be kept in these grim mountains some enticement must be offered to them beyond handsome salaries. These houses on "Silk Stocking Row" were supplied with bathrooms, running water and central heating. Since every community manages to manufacture for itself a social elite, it was here that the "society" of the coal camps was to gather, apart from the rabble in the valleys below.

The operators took quick advantage of the opportunity presented by the horde of Negro railroad workers and persuaded many of them to remain behind and mine coal. Their railroad building had left hardly a dollar in their pockets and many elected to stay in the new camps. To this day white-headed, stooped Negroes who "helped lay the track" and thereafter spent more than forty years digging coal can be found still residing in the same houses to which they were assigned so long ago. A separate section of each camp, usually known as "Nigger Town," was set aside for these Negroes. As reports of their new homes filtered south, scores and hundreds of other Negro families entrained for the coalfields.

From all over the plateau there trooped in motley gangs of raw-boned mountaineers with their bonneted wives and barefoot children, to seek jobs in the mines. Initially most of them were share-croppers whose lessening returns from the soil had brought them to a point only a few jumps ahead of starvation. Here was an opportunity to live in a comfortable home and earn cash for work vastly different from but little harder than the logging and farming which the mountaineer had always known. Then, too, he and his wife had been bewitched by the breathtaking things to be had so easily in the commissaries. There were bright dresses, skirts, hats and shoes in tantalizing array for his wife and children, and blue and black serge suits for himself, and the canned meats, fresh and canned vegetables and fruits, spices and tasty sausages such as wieners, bológna and salami offered the mountaineer relief from the limited diet on which he had so long fed. In the first few years after the railroads were built, thousands of mountaineers rushed into the coal camps and their glittering commissaries with all the abandon of a troop of six-year-olds loosed in a toy store.

Families also came to the camps from the bordering states of Virginia, Tennessee and West Virginia, and up from the worn-out cotton fields of the Deep South came the sons and daughters of dirt-poor tenant-farmers to seek a new start in this beckoning land of opportunity.

But even these multitudes were not enough, and the coal barons turned to Europe — where labor agents, employed by industrialists and shipping lines, were busily signing up millions of people for transportation to the New World. From Italy, Hungary, Poland, Rumania, Albania, and Greece came shipments of immigrants, few of whom could either speak or comprehend a word of English. Many of these new Americans had had their transportation paid by the coal and steel companies which owned the mines, and every precaution was taken to make certain they did not desert their benefactors in New York City. Once allowed to get his bearings in that amazing warren the would-be coal miner was unlikely to be found again, so when he and his family had passed through the immigration quarantines they were hastily loaded onto trains and carried to their destination in the Southern coalfield. These humble and bewildered wretches did not leave the cars between New York and the coal camp to which they were destined. Utterly mystified and astounded, smelling of garlic and carrying immense bundles of Old World shawls, dresses, petticoats, hats and accordions, they arrived in the middle of a brand-new town. These penniless "transportation men" stepped from their cars at Jenkins, McRoberts, Benham, Lynch, Middlesboro, Wayland, Wheelwright and numerous other wild coal towns, to jeers and hoots from crowds of mountaineers to whom they were more often than not simply "damn furrin' sons of bitches." Intently anxious to be good American citizens and find freedom and prosperity in the New World, they were to suffer much torment and ridicule at the hands of the native mountaineers, and not a few were to be callously slain. In these early years of the mining industry, "Wops," "Hunkies" and "Polacks" were regarded by the mountaineers, and by most of the camp overlords, as "only one notch better than the niggers" — and this notch was a narrow one.

The disillusioned and homesick Europeans clustered together in "Wop-towns" and "Hunky-towns" set aside for them by the operators, and the strange, sometimes guttural, sometimes melodious tongues of a score of Old World provinces were to be heard on coal camp streets mixed with the flat twang of the mountaineer's archaic English and the sometimes polished accents of the big bosses. The larger camps were turbulent Babels set in a wilderness.

Even when the long rows of houses were filled with people a dearth of shelter persisted. The companies flung up large frame boardinghouses of ten to twenty-five rooms each. Here single men and husbands who were unable to find houses for their families rented rooms. In addition, many families "took in boarders," renting one of their rooms to miners who could find no accommodation elsewhere.

The camps were endowed with a startling collection of incongruous names. The Elkhorn Coal Corporation named its towns — Haymond and Fleming — after two of its executives, Tom Haymond and Pat Fleming. Jenkins, Dunham, McRoberts, Lynch and Benham were similarly named for executives of the companies that built them. Not all the Big Bosses monopolized such honors for themselves, however. Some named their new communities after wives or lady friends. A coal operator named Craft was very fond of his wife. Her name was Belle, and forty-five years after his camp was completed a crumbling, dilapidated ghost town is still called Bellcraft. Another gentleman fell in love with a local damsel, and town and post office became Dalna, Kentucky. But his affections soon wandered to another woman; in due time the Dalna Coal Company became the Elsie Coal Company. Some raw new towns sported less prosaic or romantic titles. In rapid succession Kona, Allias, Happy, Scuddy, Apex, Acme, Carbon Glow, Sassafras, Mayking, Meta, Sharondale, Majestic, Coaldale, Coalville, Four Mile, High Splint, Diablock and Hardburley popped onto the maps. Others blossomed out with names distilled from the initials of the coal corporations. Virginia Iron, Coal and Coke Company built a town called Vicco, and Seco was headquarters for the South East Coal Company.

Teachers were imported from several states to preside over the new classrooms. Most of them were young men and women who were excited by the possibilities of teaching under such unique and challenging circumstances. Relatively high salaries were paid by the corporations, and the school districts which they fostered, and the "Caucasian" classrooms challenged the ingenuity of even the ablest and most dedicated teachers. The shy children of the highlanders with their primitive and limited background were difficult enough to draw out and inspire to learn, but the difficulty was vastly increased by the presence in many classrooms of children who understood neither English nor the Old World tongues of their fellows. These new teachers tackled their tasks so zealously that the best elementary schooling eastern Kentucky has ever known came to these years before the excitement and challenge gave way to the humdrum of life in gray, dull mining camps. The same cannot be said of the segregated "colored" schools because Negro teachers were often unavailable, and little effort was made to compel the children to attend. Many years were to pass before anything more than a token school system for black children was to be established.

Few newcomers had settled in the plateau in the preceding century. Four generations had gone by with the same human stock undiluted by other blood lines. As we have seen, this stock was primarily English with a rich dash of highland Scotch and enough Irish to give it flavor. And though the sprinkling of Negro slaves had been enough to cause social division in the years before the Civil War, their numbers relative to the whole population were never large, and some areas had never known them at all. But with the building of the coal towns the region received a massive injection of new blood which immensely benefited many communities adjacent to the camps. Men and women with such Old World names as Monjiardo, Codispoti, Palumbo, Wojchiehowski, Proko, Aleksandros, Farrah, Camaderi and Carrello were to marry Days, Andersons, Johnsons and Gilleys. Ironically the newly arrived black coal miners brought many surnames prominent in the self-created aristocracy of the plantation South — Thomas, Youngblood, Wellborn, Warmouth, Stephens, O'Haire, the names of families to whom their slave grandparents had belonged.

The vast population influx is difficult for us to comprehend. Many counties were, outwardly at least, almost completely transformed. In ten years some of them experienced a population increase of 200 per cent. Perry County had a total of 11,255 people in 1910 and 26,042 in 1920. The population of Harlan County rose even more dramatically in the same period from 10,564 to 31,546, and the pattern was the same elsewhere. The 900 new houses in Jenkins sheltered more than 8000 people on land which a few years earlier had served as "Bad" John Wright's corn and pasture fields, and twenty-five miles away in the shadows of the Big Black Mountain lay Lynch, the biggest coal town of them all, with a thousand buildings and nearly 10,000 inhabitants. In the inrush of new cultures, ideas, prejudices and ambitions, the mountaineer was bowled over and swept aside. Eventually, as we shall see, he lost his confidence in his own mores and moorings. That he never found new social foundations to which he might securely attach himself we shall also see, and the demoralization and helplessness which flowed from that failure.

The major camps were built within four or five years after the railroad penetrated the plateau, but the town building did not stop with them. The railroads had been enticed into the mountains in the first place by the most strongly capitalized corporations and these entities had carefully drawn plans for establishing communities, importing workers, opening mines and producing coal on a foreseeable schedule for a market which was anticipated, and in some instances, was wholly contracted for. In the case of the steel corporations, which established "captive" mines, an expanding market for their products necessitated new coal production and their mines were opened with a planned output adequate to supply their own furnaces. Hence the field's initial industry was tightly planned, and as human institutions run, was based on reasonable calculations. The planners needed additional quantities of fuel which they undertook to supply in an orderly manner. But in the uncontrolled market of those seething years the mechanism of Supply could not be restrained to fit precisely the specifications of Demand. There was too much coal in the region for a relative handful of corporations to acquire or control it all, so that town building and the opening of new mines spread until they became almost habitual in many counties.

The first towns built were the best ones. Attracted by the opening up of the immense mineral wealth, dozens of other opportunists flocked into the coalfield. Few of them possessed or were able to obtain sufficient capital to build towns on the scale undertaken by the giants. Many possessed little mining experience, and some had neither adequate funds nor knowledge of the industry. They hoped to shave their investments to the barest minimums, learn quickly and realize fast profits. They copied in the most shabby fashion the pattern laid down for them by the big, adequately financed corporations which built Jenkins, Hemphill, Haymond, Fleming, Lynch, Benham and Wheelwright.

The camps which these newcomers threw up varied considerably but none of them provided good housing even by the standards of that time. Neither state nor county possessed a building code or required homes to be built to minimum standards in any respect. The companies were entirely free to build any structure which greed might dictate. They climbed in rows helter-skelter around the sides of newly cleared hills — without streets, lighting or sanitary water supplies. Wells were drilled at intervals amongst the houses, and water was drawn from the same earth which the companies dotted with privies.

As time passed, native mountaineer merchants and professional men got into the business, leased or bought mineral tracts and constructed rows of rickety houses. In Letcher County alone, thirty-three camps were built and in Perry County thirty-seven were completed. In Pike, the state's largest county, no fewer than forty coal camps were constructed. Twenty-five were built in Harlan and nearly as many in Bell, Floyd and Johnson.

The orgy of coal-town building continued until 1927. By that time, the big boom had run its course and the coal market collapse smashed confidence in the industry.

As in the case of the larger camps, people had to be found to occupy the houses, to buy goods in the new commissaries and to mine coal for the scores of new tipples. The luring of men and women into the camps continued unabated with but a single significant change. The outbreak of the First World War cut off the supply of European immigrants so that thereafter only a handful of them trickled into the mountains. The great wave of foreigners reached the country before the end of 1914. After the war ended the flow was resumed but never again on the spectacular scale of the early years and in 1921 new immigration laws enacted by Congress stopped it entirely. Thereafter such transportation men as entered the region came from other parts of the United States.

Consequently the new camps, those poor and dowdy little towns so ill conceived and ill omened from the beginning, were filled largely with white mountaineers from the plateau counties and from adjoining highland areas of other Southern states. A considerable trickle of cotton-field Negroes continued to come in, but their numbers were small compared to the total absorbed by these new communities. At least 90 per cent of the people in these coal camps were mountaineers from the creeks and hollows of some twenty-seven Eastern Kentucky counties.

The process of town building was not monopolized entirely by the coal companies, however. At strategic points throughout the coalfields, entrepreneurs from near and far established stores to sell in competition with the commissaries. On the outskirts of a major coal camp or at a point near the center of a cluster of smaller mining communities the merchant would buy a lot and build a storehouse. Soon others followed suit, and the nucleus of a town was formed.

Jewish and Syrian pack peddlers had occasionally crossed the plateau since the end of the Civil War but none had resided in the mountains. Now, sensing profits, they appeared and energetically contributed to the growth of the little independent towns. Such names as Schine, Mazer, Max, Cury, Dawahare, Goldberg, Hazen and Abdoo blossomed on store windows, and the managers of the commissaries found themselves jolted by severe competition, especially in their clothing departments.

Quite without pattern or design, these trading centers spread outward; and by the middle twenties many of them had reached considerable size. These towns took unto themselves a variety of startling names — such as Neon, Blackey, Cumberland, Hellier, Hi-Hat, Garrett, Whitaker, Chevrolet and Jeff. By 1927 some of them boasted two thousand inhabitants. Their optimistic merchants and wholesalers petitioned for charters, and soon they were proudly displaying the paraphernalia of incorporated "cities." In addition to the stores and homes of merchants, they contained rows of cheap, shoddy little structures owned by local businessmen and rented to miners who worked in nearby camps. Some landlords built twenty or thirty such "shotgun" houses. These habitations, like the camp houses, stood on posts or piles at a distance of two to four feet above the ground. Most of them consisted of two or three rooms in a straight row without a dividing hall of any kind, with the first room opening into the second and thence into the third. The house invariably boasted that architectural feature so dear to the Southerner's heart, a small front porch. Not a dollar was spent on them beyond the limits of barest necessity; and these pitiful, hideous little shelters, with their occasional drilled well, rows of privies and narrow paths in lieu of sidewalks were slums as soon as they were occupied. But so massive was the movement of people into the coalfield that the houses were quickly snapped up by the coal miners and their families, and the exorbitant rents were happily paid. By using poorly seasoned, unplaned planks (some of which had been discarded by sawmill operators as unsalable "culls") and thin tarpaper roofing, such a three-room house could be "knocked together" for four to five hundred dollars. A rental of ten dollars a month could be easily collected; thus the entire investment could be recovered in four or five years. Between 1912 and 1927 scarcely an empty house could be found from one end of the coalfield to the other.

In none of these towns or camps were sewage disposal plants built or even considered. Such houses as possessed plumbing were served by septic tanks or cesspools. Eventually, waste of all kinds found its way into the streams, there to mingle with the inky "sump" water from the mines.

These years made up the Golden Age of the coal industry in the Cumberland Plateau. Its product was eagerly sought for the nation's fireplaces, furnaces and mills, and the black diamonds poured in endless torrents out of hundreds of great and small tipples. Serbian and Italian peasants, Alabama and Mississippi Negroes and one-time mountaineer feudists labored side by side in the depths of a thousand hills. The principal tools of the miner's trade were a manually operated breast auger, a pick, a No. 9 shovel, a carbide lamp, a miner's cap of soft canvas and leather, and a round tin dinner pail. Wages were not high but they did not linger appreciably behind earnings in industry generally across the nation.

But if the miner's wages were not high, neither were his wants many or expensive. Food, clothing and shelter were the things for which he gave most of his earnings, and his spending for these things was relatively lavish. The habit of vacationing was unknown to him, and he could live on a scale which he deemed highly prosperous but which, by the standards of our era, appears drab indeed.

The miner's wife acquired a new coal-burning cooking range and a wooden kitchen cabinet. Her house was filled with iron and brass bedsteads and dressers, and plush, mohair-covered living-room furniture from the commissary. Lace curtains fluttered in her windows, and brightly colored linoleums and flashy carpets covered her pine floors. With company scrip she was able to buy closetsful of clothing for herself and her children. The miner proclaimed his prosperity by clothing himself in silk underwear and shirts and expensive Stetson hats. Sometimes he went in debt to the extent of a month's wages to buy a fancy diamond-studded tie pin or a gold pocket watch and chain. All in all, his earnings were dissipated for household furnishings, clothing, food and a few personal effects, and rarely did the shovel wielder entertain the notion of saving some of his hard-earned dollars.

CHAPTER TEN

———•———

The Big Bosses

FROM THE beginning the coal operators exercised absolute dominion over the towns they had built. Whether the new community was Lynch, with its concrete streets, modern brick hospital and schools and a population of nearly ten thousand, or a cluster of thirty or forty grimy shacks centering about a rickety commissary and tipple, the pattern was the same. The Big Bosses possessed the craftiness and the will to impose their rule upon their communities — a rule which was to continue unweakened until the arrival of John L. Lewis's union organizers, and the coming of the New Deal.

The companies required their employees to live in their towns. Only when their last house sheltered an employee's family would they hire men who lived outside the camps. This requirement made it certain that within a few years the stockholders would receive back in rents from the houses and profits from the commissaries their whole investment in the mining operation. Assuming prosperity in the coal-fields for a few years, the rents alone assured that the operation would be a profitable one.

The bigger coal camps sought municipal charters and soon were organized as incorporated cities complete with mayor, town councils, schools and police and fire departments. By so doing, the operators were able to control most of the property-tax dollars which they paid. Judges, council members, mayors and all their underlings were hand-picked in the offices of the company, and their official hiring in the City Hall was nothing more than a ratification of decisions previously made.

Since the birth of the nation most of the population had lived generation after generation by farming. Over wide areas misuse of the land had wasted the soil, so that in 1912 millions of rural people were no longer able to derive more than a bare subsistence from agriculture. Their ancestral lands were exhausted and they lacked the knowledge of how to restore the earth by cover-cropping and fertilizing. Hence, they were anxious to forsake the land and seek wages in mines, mills and factories. And this was true, also, of the tatterdemalion Europeans who fled not only from poverty but from the threat of impending war as well. When these newcomers flocked into the coal camps, it was to receive wages handsome enough by their standards, and they looked upon their employers as genuine benefactors. Their confidence in the company officials had not yet been shattered by "hard times." Most of the coal barons took especial pains to be pleasant and helpful in their relations with their workmen, stopping sometimes to chat with groups of miners and, when necessity demanded, lending them money or advancing generous credit at the company stores. Many of the executives were from Pennsylvania and other Eastern states and brought with them a refinement of personality which charmed the rough-cut miners and their wives. Too, the miners had little interest in things outside their families and jobs, and generally were perfectly content to accept the opinions of the Big Bosses when it came to politics and management of community and municipal affairs. There were no labor unions, and when, once in a long while, a miner became difficult to handle nothing more was required than to pay him off and tell him to get his things out of the camp. While state law required that a tenant be given thirty days before being evicted from his home, the companies avoided the effects of this statute by compelling the miner, before occupying the house, to sign a contract whereby he obligated himself to remove from the premises immediately upon demand by the coal company. This contributed not only to social obedience in the towns but helped to promote discipline in the mines as well.

The companies brought with them the nefarious scrip system and promptly introduced it into the commissaries. This time-tested device was calculated to keep the greater part of each employee's wages safely within the camp. The company bought quantities of aluminum or brass coin-size discs stamped with its corporate name and with denominations paralleling the United States coinage, with the addition of two-dollar and five-dollar pieces. The miners were paid in cash at the end of each calendar month. Thus the coal digger could receive lawful money only once every four weeks. Since he more often than not spent a large part of his wages frivolously as soon as they were received and was likely to need a wide variety of groceries, clothing, and other necessities before the month expired, the infrequency of the paydays imposed a genuine hardship. Here the scrip came to his rescue and to the aid of his employer. The bookkeeper reported to the scrip cashier the amount of "time" for which the miner had wages due to him. Upon request of the miner or his wife, the "scrip office" would issue scrip in any amount up to the total sum of the wages earned by the miner to date. Most miners got into the habit of living almost entirely by scrip, and when they drew a few dollars in "real money" they hastily spent it in one of the nearby independent towns. The scrip system effectively stripped the miner of practically all financial resources and encouraged spendthrift habits of the most harmful kind. In effect, the company could turn him out of his house on a moment's notice, without any money in his pocket. This left him almost entirely at the mercy of the Big Bosses, and caused the growth of an astonishingly effective and far-reaching paternalism.

Because operation of the tipples, fans and other heavy machinery required large quantities of electricity, the power lines came early to the region. In the absence of other sources many companies installed their own electric generating plants. Consequently, the houses were electrically illuminated, usually by a single drop-socket and unshaded bulb suspended from the ceiling of each room. As the appliance industry developed, washing machines, vacuum cleaners, radios, refrigerators and other electric household aids were acquired from the commissaries. The coal company bought the electricity for the houses in bulk at reduced prices from the power companies, raised the price some 10 to 20 per cent, and passed the bill on to its tenants. Each miner had his monthly pay reduced by the amount of his electricity bill. The company sent its coal wagons on regular rounds through the camp. They kept the miner's coalhouse well stocked, and the price of his fuel, too, was deducted from his wages.

In the smaller camps water was obtained at manually operated pumps set on top of drilled wells and was carried in buckets into the houses. The cost of the water was included in the house rent. But in some of the larger towns organized as municipalities the company constructed a water system and sold it to the city government. The coal company then contracted with the municipality to withhold the household water bill from the miner's pay for remittance to the city clerk.

The company also undertook to look after the health needs of its employees. In the bigger camps staffs of physicians were installed in the company hospitals and in the less pretentious towns a contract doctor kept office hours at regularly scheduled intervals through the week. In the event of an emergency, he could be called at other times. The company withheld a small sum, usually two dollars a month, from the miner's pay and turned it over to the doctor. For this sum the miner and his family could receive medical treatment for run-of-the-mill ailments without additional cost. This charge did not, of course, cover surgery or treatment of major illnesses such as cancer, tuberculosis and diabetes.

Thus the miner came to be almost wholly insulated against the world outside his coal camp. In return for his labor his employers clothed his back, filled his belly, sheltered and lighted his household, and provided his family with medical treatment, fuel and water. The thoughtful operators even organized burial associations, withholding a couple of dollars each month from the workman's wages for payment to a favored undertaker, so that when death came the mortician's bill had been paid in advance. Needless to say, the company realized a profit on each of these endeavors. The miner found himself on a treadmill from which he lacked the knowledge and self-discipline to escape.

But it must be said in defense of the system that at this period most of the miners and the members of their families were content with it, and few cries of disenchantment were heard until the onset of the Great Depression.

Few safety laws had been enacted, and each company operated its mine generally as it saw fit. The perennial dearth of engineers and foremen made close supervision impossible and the coal miner, once he was "under the hill," was to a remarkable extent on his own.

Dressed in dirty denim jacket and overalls, long cotton underwear, yarn socks and high rubber boots, with his dinner pail filled with a quantity of fresh drinking water and sandwiches, or bacon, beans and corn bread, his way lighted by an open-flame carbide lamp fastened to the front of his soft-canvas-and-leather miner's cap, the coal digger reached the driftmouth about five in the morning. In an empty coal car on the "mantrip," he rode along the "main heading" to the place where his working room turned off to left or right. In the early years these cars were more often than not drawn by horses and mules, though the mine locomotive soon made its appearance. Leaving the cars, the miner walked along the dripping corridors to his working place. In many mines in this virgin coalfield the roof was more than six feet high and a man could walk without stooping, but in some, even then, the roof was not more than four feet high, compelling the miner to move at a crouch. Arrived at the "face" he set safety timbers as close as possible to the coal. These timbers were upright jack-props five or six inches thick. To insure a tight fit that would not allow loose bands of rock to sag, "cap" wedges were driven between the roof and the ends of the props. This done, the miner and his helper began to "cut the coal."

The more progressive mines, even then, employed primitive electrically powered cutting machines to undercut the coal, but in most operations the undercutting was done with picks. The miner strapped thick rubber kneepads to his knees, and, kneeling, began to peck at the coal in a strip of some eight inches above the slate floor. He and his helper thus removed all the coal for a width of twelve or fifteen feet and as far back as the pick handle would allow. The fine coal from the "cut-line" was raked out, and the massive block of black mineral was left suspended from the ceiling and the two sides. The workmen were then ready to drill and shoot the coal. A heavy breastplate was strapped to each miner's chest and the end of a long auger two inches in diameter was placed against the coal. Pressing heavily with his chest and turning the auger handle, the miner drove the shaft deep into the coal. A line of such holes was drilled. Then charges of black powder were affixed to fuses and shoved far back into the holes. The holes were tamped with "dead men" — tightly rolled paper cylinders filled with earth. The miners then removed themselves and their tools to a safe place and waited for the "shot firer." When this foreman arrived and had inspected the preparations and was sure all other workmen were out of danger, the flame of a carbide lamp was applied to the ends of the fuses and the hissing trail of fire went blazing into the powder charges. With a roar that shook the tunnels, the shots exploded and the coal was thrown in a glittering heap onto the floor of the mine.

After an interval had passed for the circulating air to blow away the acrid powder fumes, the men returned to the working place. With lengths of steel rails and wooden ties they extended the track to within convenient shoveling distance of the huge pile of coal. They received cars from the underground trains and pushed them as close as possible to the coal. This marked the halfway in their day's work, and they leaned their backs against the moist tunnel side — the coal "rib," as they termed it — and ate their cold lunch and rested for a half-hour. Then, with one man on each side of the car, the huge shovels quickly filled it "and rounded it over." The loaded car was pushed to the entryway, where it could be hauled to the outside, and another empty car was brought forward. The shovels rose and fell rhythmically, sweat dripping from the brows and noses of their wielders, until the pile of coal had vanished. As the coal was loaded the slate and other refuse was thrown aside. When the coal was gone this worthless "gob" was loaded onto a car. This done, the room was restored to essentially the same condition in which it had been found that morning, with the exception that now the working place was extended about six feet farther into the hill. The picks and shovels were leaned against the rib of the coal and, wet with sweat and bone-tired, the miners walked to the main heading to catch a "man-car" for the outside. Having completed another day of cutting and drilling, shooting and loading, the miner was free till another dawn.

The ten-hour day was routine during these years and the miner paid for his own carbide, tools and the blacksmithing which kept his picks and augers sharp. In some mines "company men" did the drilling and shooting, leaving to the loader only the duty of shoveling the coal into the cars. Twenty-five or thirty tons were likely to be lifted into the cars by a full-time loader in a single day.

The years between 1912 and 1927 constituted the longest boom in the region's history. The towns were built and filled with people. Long ridges were hollowed out and mountains of discarded slate grew up near every tipple. If coal mining can be said to have had a happy era, this was it. But it was not a happy era, because this immense labor was not accomplished without a gargantuan sacrifice in death and in mangled flesh and bone.

It was not a safety-conscious age, and in industry everywhere workmen were mangled and killed in large numbers, even in cities and states where a developing social conscience had forced the enactment of laws calculated to prevent accidents. But in the Kentucky mountains, state regulatory legislation was nonexistent, or, at best, feebly ineffective, and industrial managers operated their empires as they could and would. Competent supervisory personnel in every category was in short supply. The operators clamored for ever higher production, because the expanding market absorbed all the coal the miners could dig. And the strangely diverse character of their workmen made strict supervision quite difficult. Often the immigrant workmen could not understand the foremen's English, and if instructions were intricate the Negroes and mountaineers were just as unlikely to comprehend them. The result was a shockingly high number of industrial accidents which killed or maimed men by the hundreds.

Fortunately, most Kentucky coal seams contained little methane gas, the deadly colorless and odorless "black damp" so dreaded by miners. Occasionally, however, it was found in the Big Black Mountain, and there some of the biggest coal operations were under way. Thousands of men labored in this huge hill and sometimes blundering miners wandered into pockets of the gas. If exposed to it long enough they lost consciousness or died. Others breathed low concentrations of the gaseous hydrocarbons and after a time their nervous systems degenerated from the effects. Their limbs twitched convulsively and their faces drew in ugly masks. This permanent affliction made it impossible for the miner to continue to dig coal.

Another monstrous peril of frequent occurrence in the Big Black Mountain and other large ridges was the coal "bump." If engineers or foremen miscalculated and removed too much coal in a given area, or left coal pillars of inadequate size, the descending mountain shattered the mineral and flung it by the hundreds of tons into adjacent tunnels and working places. Unwary workmen were sometimes buried alive by coal from a thick, solid seam which suddenly roared lion-like and flung itself upon them.

Great amounts of finely powdered coal collected on the coal ribs and elsewhere throughout the mines. This substance is highly volatile and when conditions are right can explode with a power approaching that of dynamite. Occasionally when coal was shot from the face in a particularly dry working place the air was left saturated with millions of dancing particles of this deadly dust. When a spark from an electric wire or the flame from a lamp ignited a quantity of the particles, the flame surged with a mighty roar throughout the dust-filled air, and to the collections of dust lying on coal ribs, timbers and other surfaces. Flashing like lightning and booming like massed cannons, the explosion raced down headings, entryways and working places until the fuel was exhausted. Such chainlike explosions might last for several seconds as the fire rushed from one area to another. When the fiery tornado reached the long straight underground corridor leading to the driftmouth, the effect was like that achieved in a gun barrel when the powder has been fired. Sometimes the swiftly advancing fire reached the driftmouth and belched out an immense yellow tongue.

The power of such an explosion was incredible. Picks, shovels, sledgehammers, rocks, lumps of coal, empty coal-cars and human bodies were flung down the tunnels like pellets in the barrel of a shotgun. The electric power was snuffed out and the fans which pushed air into the mines were bent and put out of action. Not infrequently fires were started in the coal seams and the sulphurous fumes contaminated the whole area. Men who had escaped the vengeance of the explosion might then die from suffocation.

In the gloomy half-darkness of the mines men were sometimes caught between moving cars and the supporting timbers, and their bodies and limbs mangled horribly. Sometimes a hapless miner was caught between the top of a loaded coal-car and the periodic collar-poles which supported the roof. The space between the top of the car and the bottom of the horizontal collar-poles was rarely more than six or eight inches. As the car was pulled along the track the miner's body was "rolled" very much as a pencil may be rolled between one's hands, crushing ribs, pelvis and shoulder bones to bits.

Within a few years after the mines were opened electric locomotives began to replace the horses and mules which pulled the underground trains of coal. Power for these machines came from naked cables suspended from the tunnel roofs. The wire was never more than a foot or so above the motorman's head; many motor operators accidentally touched it and were electrocuted. Other miners straightened up at an unfortunate moment, or stumbled over cross-ties, and touched the deadly cable. The consequence was always death or serious injury.

But the most frequent accidents were the roof falls. Most of the coal in the plateau has a slate bottom with a layer of sandstone on top. This overlying sandstone is separated from the coal by a shield of slate, sometimes two or three feet thick. This soft slate adheres weakly to the sandstone. It could be held up only by numerous stout timbers or, in more recent years, by steel roof bolts. With startling frequency huge slabs of the slate broke loose from the sandstone and, splintering oak collar-poles and hickory jack props, crashed onto the heads of the miners, crushing their bodies against the muddy floor. Many miners who worked through this era used crowbars and jacks to raise tons of fallen rock from the flattened bodies of their fellow workmen. An aged Negro once related to me how he and two of his "buddies" loaded the pancake-flat remains of a foreman and two miners into a coal car for removal to the outside. Their bodies, he said, were ground into the floor and the miners scraped them loose with their huge coal shovels. As he put it, "We had to jest shovel 'em up." But such slate falls were not always fatal. Often they crushed spines, arms and legs and left the miners grotesquely mangled and twisted.

The black powder used in the mines was another dreadful breaker of men. The fire-train fuse so widely employed before the electric fuse replaced it was not always reliable, and the spitting trail of fire sometimes diminished to a slow smoulder inside the tamped hole. After waiting a long interval for the fire to eat its way to the charge and thinking the shot had failed, the disappointed miner approached his working place "to pull the charge." All too many times he arrived just as the fire ate its way into the charge of powder, and with a roar tons of coal were blasted at him. Men were slain in this way and others were reduced to lifelong cripples. Still others were blinded by particles of powder and fine coal which were thrown into their unprotected eyes.

By accidents of these types and by others so varied as to be past count, the industry took its toll in the ranks of its workmen. It is difficult to estimate with any accuracy the number of men killed or seriously injured in the eastern Kentucky coalfields in these neophyte years, but thousands of widows and orphans were left in the camps, and multitudes of ruined, broken miners were cast out to loaf before their dreary hearths and on the porches of commissaries.

Most of the laborers who moved into the camps were little better than paupers, and disability or death rarely found their situation substantially improved. The companies made no provision for their care aside from payment of the small sum required by the Workmen's Compensation statute. This Kentucky law was patterned after the English model and required the company to buy insurance for protection of the miner and his family. The benefits were payable on a rigid schedule prescribed by the Legislature. Death of the breadwinner brought the widow four thousand dollars, while total and permanent disability caused payment to the miner of forty-four hundred dollars. Loss of an arm, leg or eye was treated as a 50 per cent permanent partial disability to the body as a whole, and was compensated with twenty-two hundred dollars. However, these meager benefits were not paid in a lump sum, but in as many as four hundred weekly installments.

The pathetic helplessness of the workman of these years and his childish confidence in his employer was brought home to me in a conversation with an aged miner who lost a leg in a mining accident in 1919. After a man was killed or disabled, the company, as a matter of policy, always demanded removal from the house which the family occupied, so it could be turned over to a new recruit. This man still remembered the kindness of the Big Boss. On the day after he left the hospital with his crutches and new cork leg, he was told by the superintendent that he could remain in the house for a whole month, rent free, as a donation from the company, "but be sure to get out by the end of the month."

Since the families of the dead and disabled miners were expelled from the camps to make way for able-bodied new arrivals, the hollows in the outlying rural areas and the marginal "rat rows" of the independent towns filled rapidly with widows, orphans and cripples. With their trifling checks from the insurance companies and produce from vegetable gardens planted on the eroding hillsides, they could hardly do more than subsist even in these boom years of the industry. The habitual slaying and crushing of men was an accepted commonplace in the coalfield, as it had been earlier in the logging industry and in the hideous feuds.

Soldiers who have experienced combat and who expect to return to the battle lines are rarely paragons of thrifty virtue. They spend their pay in poker games, and for wine, women and song, on the practical ground that there is no need to save for a tomorrow that may never come. For precisely the same reason miners adopted the same outlook. They spent their small wages on things they coveted and could enjoy and became a generation of spendthrifts. Miners, as a class, became wastrels who spent their money as quickly as it was acquired or even before, and in this habit and attitude they were wholeheartedly joined by their wives.

The prosperity was not limited to the coal companies and their employees, but spread its blessings into the countryside surrounding the camps. The mountaineers who remained on the land now had an opportunity to raise large quantities of corn, potatoes and other foodstuffs for sale. The concentrations of people in the camps and in the growing county seats and independent towns constituted a market which could absorb thousands of bushels of truck produce and immense quantities of milk, butter and eggs each year. The mountaineers had always grown these things for their own tables and now they endeavored to widen their fields and to increase their flocks and herds. Practically every day in the week saw mountaineers hauling mule and wagon loads of farm produce along the rutted county roads to the camps. Though stores and commissaries bought much of their produce many farmers peddled their wares from door to door throughout the camps and towns.

But foodstuffs were not the only merchandise they sold in the mining communities. Large new stills sprang up all over the coalfield and "stillers" bootlegged their "white mule" inside the camps and towns. Those who were reputed to manufacture the best whiskey rarely needed to carry it to market because customers came regularly to their doors. A bushel of corn was worth about a dollar but could be converted into thirty or forty dollars worth of whiskey when sold at retail. The temptation of illegal riches was too great for many hillmen to resist, and the stills multiplied endlessly despite determined efforts on the part of state and Federal revenue agents. With the adoption in 1919 of the Prohibition Amendment to the United States Constitution, the Federal Government launched a full-scale crusade against the moonshiners which plunged the entire region into bloody and violent warfare. As we shall see later, the best efforts of the government were insufficient to suppress the industry but they did, at least, succeed in making it largely unprofitable.

During these years the shabby little county seats expanded rapidly, and villages containing no more than a couple of dozen cabins and frame cottages in 1912 were able within fifteen years to boast a population growth of several hundred per cent. Substantial numbers of attorneys, physicians and other professional men took up permanent residence in the plateau and hung their shingles from windows in the new two- and three-story brick buildings. The thriving towns began the Herculean task of pulling themselves out of the mud, and concrete streets, the first hard-surfaced roads ever to be seen in the highlands, were laid down — at least on the inevitable Main Streets.

Under relentless prodding from the coal operators the state government began for the first time to take some notice of developments in the region. Soon after 1920 the Department of Highways was established and its engineers hesitantly began the planning of paved roads to lead from the edge of the Bluegrass throughout the plateau. Under statutes then in effect it was anticipated that the counties would bear the cost of the roads, with the state providing only the surveying, engineering and other necessary supervision to make sure the construction would satisfy minimum standards set by the department.

The building of these traffic arteries was to prove both a blessing and a curse to the rugged, roadless plateau. In the automobile age these thoroughfares would be absolutely essential, but the manner of their financing imposed a monstrous burden which some counties still carry and which was to impede every phase of development for more than thirty years to come.

We have seen that the coal company was able to impose its political will upon the inhabitants of its camp. Associations of coal companies were to control with equal effectiveness the politics of the counties and of the two Congressional districts which lay largely within the highlands. Most of the mountain counties were predominantly Republican and had been so since the close of the Civil War, though some counties, particularly Knott, Breathitt and Wolfe, had strong Democratic leanings. Heavy doses of Federal pension money doled out to Union veterans and their widows had strongly bolstered the Grand Old Party at precinct, county and congressional district level.

Nearly all the coal operators shared enthusiasm for the party of Lincoln. A majority of the Kentucky and West Virginia mountaineers who came into the camps were members of this party, but nearly all those from farther south, from Virginia, Tennessee and Alabama, were deep-dyed Democrats. The Negroes, of course, had never voted anywhere, but thought of themselves as "Abraham Lincoln Republicans." The mass of the European immigrants sympathized with the Democratic party, but were willing to acquiesce to the wishes of their employers in an effort to curry favor.

At election time the companies sometimes sponsored mammoth parties at which beef carcasses were barbecued and dispensed with barrels of beer among the voters. Candidates favored by the companies were brought into the camps and introduced by company "big shots" at gatherings of miners. At the political "speakin's" which followed, spokesmen for the operators were careful to point out that the continued prosperity of the new towns depended upon the election of Republican officials. By such cozenage and intimidation the companies managed to elect to the United States House of Representatives lawyers who had represented them in title suits and who were known to be safely conservative. They sent to the state Legislature nonentities who advocated little or nothing for the improvement of the region and whose sole purpose was to serve as apologists for the coal interests, expounding the thesis that the operators had brought a bright new day to the mountains and that the state government ought to leave the industry and all its activities strictly alone.

But the interest of the coal companies in politics was not directed primarily to the election of Congressmen or state legislators. Their first and most important interest lay in the election of county judges, sheriffs and tax commissioners, because in the control of these offices the companies were to find the power to police their camps and to limit taxation of their property to rates approved as reasonable by their general managers. Under the archaic Kentucky Constitution immense power is vested in a swarm of county officials, each of whom is elected for a four-year term. They possess the power to assess and tax property and the coal barons were determined to keep both assessments and tax rates low.

The first goal to be sought was the election of friendly politicians as tax commissioners. The commissioner or "assessor" was (and still is) charged with the duty of listing all the property a given taxpayer owns and setting upon it an evaluation which represents, in the commissioner's opinion, its fair market value.

If a taxpayer had reason to believe that the assessment of his property was unjustly high, he could appeal to the County Board of Tax Supervisors for a downward adjustment. This board consisted of three "reputable" taxpayers appointed by the county judge. Hence it was absolutely essential to the coal companies that they secure the offices of tax commissioner and county judge for trusted friends if they were to minimize their property taxes.

At informal meetings of company executives, candidates for these offices were chosen. Usually they were indigenous mountaineers who had worked as surveyors, store clerks or bookkeepers for the companies. They were men whom the operators had sized up as being safe, docile and absolutely unradical, and who could be trusted to heed the advice of the Big Bosses. Local men enjoyed the advantage of being related by blood to many mountaineers and by marriage to others. We have seen that it was not a difficult matter for the coal companies to manipulate the votes of their armies of employees. In addition to their gentler tactics, which have already been mentioned, the operators sometimes informed their workmen that, if people hostile to the companies were elected to these important offices, taxes would rise to such high levels that the companies would be compelled to suspend operation, thus idling their numerous employees and causing a first-rate crisis. While to enlightened minds such pretenses were absurd, they were generally accepted by the credulous miners — who dutifully turned out to vote for "friends of the coal industry."

While the tax commissioners and county judges were the key taxing officials, members of the fiscal court could not be neglected. At least three and sometimes as many as eight of these minor officials were elected in each county and it was their duty to determine the rate at which each one hundred dollars worth of assessed property would be taxed.

Once the election of their friends had been secured the company executives could safely relax. Each year the tax commissioner or his deputy came to the office of the general manager and received a list of the company's properties and their estimated values. Rarely indeed did the commissioner find fault with either the number of chattels or tracts of land, or with their suggested value. If, despite their precautions, the tax commissioner "got out of line" and set a higher value on the property or demanded an official survey of a large boundary of coal or land, an appeal could be taken to the Board of Tax Supervisors. Escape was almost certain to be found there.

The chairman of the Board of Tax Supervisors was likely to be a local attorney who was employed by the major coal companies in the county, and who was paid a regular salary by each of them. Sometimes he was an accountant for one of the companies. Occasionally an out-of-office politician whose trustworthiness had been previously proved was chosen. The county judges unhesitatingly appointed to the board servants of the coal industry, appointees who brazenly accepted monthly salary checks from coal corporations whom it was their sworn duty to tax according to law and without fear or favor.

The results of these developments soon became painfully apparent. Hardly a county in the plateau contained property with a total assessment of one million dollars when the railroads arrived, and while houses, tipples, stores, warehouses, shops and machines multiplied apace, assessments for tax purposes failed to rise proportionately, and within a few years fell far behind. Population might increase sixfold and the demand for schools, roads and health services a dozen times over, while assessments were slowly doubling or tripling. The same public officials who staunchly shielded their coal operator friends were driven by rank necessity to find large sums for public improvements. If reasonable contributions could not be exacted from the holdings of the coal corporations the levies upon the meager properties of individual citizens must be raised to unconscionable heights. So taxes on surface land and other possessions of the individual citizens spiraled upward, while duties on minerals and other corporate properties remained nominal.

In those years hardly any of the vast mineral wealth was valued for tax purposes at more than six dollars an acre. Land surface owned by companies was given an official worth of no more than five dollars to the acre while such realty owned by individuals was, unaccountably, much more valuable, bearing listings of fifteen or twenty dollars. The houses in the camps were uniformly assessed at twenty-five dollars per room so that even the most comfortable and spacious residences on Silk Stocking Row were rarely valued at more than two hundred dollars each. It not infrequently occurred that one of these structures, well built as the home of the general manager, had a fair market value, in the opinion of the commissioner, of two hundred, while a farmer's house of similar size but of inferior construction carried an assessment tag of a thousand dollars.

But no matter how high assessments might be raised on the property of the mountaineers they could not produce sufficient revenue to meet the barest needs of the communities. The streets swarmed with children to be educated, but the school system lacked funds decently to house them. Teachers' salaries, adequate at the beginning, could not rise and as the children of miners increased in number the educators could not build the classrooms and hire the new teachers so urgently needed.

In the stark region in which the mining towns had sprung up there were few of the governmental services and facilities which are generally taken for granted in a civilized society. The courts, aided by sheriffs and their deputies, tried with little success to maintain order. Such roads as the counties had so far established were mere Indian trails and game tracks which had been but little improved by the occasional gangs of mountaineers who turned out for free "road workin's." These meager roads, dismal schools and ineffective courts and officials constituted the sum and substance of governmental aid to the people. And the independent highlanders rarely asked or expected more.

The coming of the coal industry changed this. Survival demanded the creation of public health systems, with sanitarians to test the water supplies of the camps and to give immunization shots to multitudes of schoolchildren. Few counties had established schools past the eighth-grade level and, if executive personnel were to be kept in the coalfields, high schools for their children had to be promptly staffed and housed. These must have faculties of a higher competence than the plateau had ever known. Teachers and principals must be imported and paid larger salaries than the old "normal" school graduates had expected. Then, too, highways were needed because the single-track railroads could not carry all the people and merchandise that the area required. Communication and travel between the scores of new camps and towns and the county seats made all-weather roads imperative.

The coal counties found themselves in a deadly squeeze between irreconcilable forces. Their finances were thrown into an unbearable strain. The companies had made certain that their taxes would remain low, and in a few years political pressure from wrathful noncorporate taxpayers compelled the officials to lower their levies also. Since the corporations owned tens of thousands of acres of land and practically all the minerals, and since these lands and minerals were the region's real wealth, the counties were starved for revenues. The powerful overlords in the company administration buildings would not yield. In desperation their pawns in the courthouses turned to the only avenue open to them. Since they could not tax they were compelled to borrow. In the tragedy of the huge bond issues that followed lies one of the causes for the region's prolonged destitution in later years.

The fiscal courts first authorized the sale of bonds to finance the building of arterial highways. State officials planned a continuous highway from Frankfort, near the center of the state, to Pound Gap on the Virginia line in Letcher County. Nearly a hundred and fifty miles of this road lay in the Cumberland Plateau. Another highway was to run from Madison County southward, through the great "laurel patch" to Bell County, and thence up the Poor Fork of the Cumberland River to Harlan. Still another would leave Ashland near the mouth of the Big Sandy River and push upstream through the coalfields to Pound Gap. These automobile roads would follow the basic routes of the railways of a dozen years before. But the state Constitution flatly prohibited the state from building highways; the statesmen who wrote that ruinous document had supposed that only counties should have such authority, and not until 1922, when the electorate finally approved an amendment striking out the restrictive section, was the state government able to get construction under way. Even then, for all practical purposes, its contribution was limited to planning. Each county was compelled to finance the stretch of roads within its borders.

The mine operators and their minions in the courthouses assured the voters that the roads would bring new wealth to the area, adding to the value of each man's property and fetching hundreds of new jobs in other industries. It was asserted that the wealth of the region would be so hugely magnified under the beneficent influence of the roads that their cost could be repaid in a few years without the money being missed by anyone. So ignorant were the people and so powerful were the industrialists that the bond issues were given voter approval by wide margins. In those plateau counties which lay beyond the rim of the coalfield but whose sons had gone to labor in the mines, the road-building fever which came with the Model T Ford fired almost equal enthusiasm for the bond issues, and they were unfailingly approved by the voters. Road bonds were sold at intervals from 1914 to 1929. The amount of bonded indebtedness varied from a half million dollars in the smaller counties to more than a million in the larger ones. Considering the almost boundless natural wealth and the industrial activity of the region, these debts were not large and with even a moderate tax base could have been retired in a few years. But with the wholly inadequate taxation the coal operators had decreed, it soon proved impossible to reduce the principal. The counties, burdened and straitjacketed, were barely able to pay even the annual interest.

And, predictably, public borrowing did not stop with the road building. The harassed school superintendents placed their dilemmas squarely upon the shoulders of the members of the fiscal courts, and those stalwarts promptly voted to sell more bonds for school construction.

In the middle and late 1920s contractors built the roads and bridges which the Department of Highways had planned. As the graveled roads crept through the hills the mountaineers were delighted. To people who had spent lifetimes walking, riding mules or driving teams along ribbons of bottomless mud the new highways were marvelous indeed. The miners and the coal operators, the merchants and the moonshiner-farmers, could now turn their horses out to graze and replace them with the versatile Model T Fords. Swarms of these black beetles were soon sputtering along the new roads, nor were they deterred by the abominable county roads which served as feeders for the highways. In dry weather, especially, they went sputtering along creek banks and over narrow trails around the sides of mountains, clambering protestingly over huge boulders and deep "chug"-holes. And wherever these marvels of mechanical efficiency appeared on the remoter creeks and hollows they fired the heart of every beholder to own one and to drive it home. These taxpayers and voters quickly brought pressure on their servants in the courthouses, and more bonds were sold to pay for "farm-to-market" roads leading to the "main highways" or to the county seats.

Nor did the new consolidated grade schools which rose in the big coal towns, the county seats and some of the new independent towns satisfy the needs. Their twelve to sixteen rooms were filled to overflowing on the first day after they were opened and the parents of children who were required to remain in the drab little log and frame structures pressed for similar schools for their own precincts.

Deepening the tragedy was the fact that the "fine" schools and roads which so captivated the hearts of the highlanders were actually poor by national standards. By the time the arterial highways had taken on their first coat of macadam they were obsolete, even for the automobiles of 1929 or 1930. Their pavement was narrow, and they wound in and out along the riverbanks and around the sides of hills and mountains in an amazing tangle of horseshoe bends and blind curves. They were dangerous avenues of transportation long before the Model T was supplanted by the peppy new Model A of 1929.

and countless homicidal accidents had been caused by their steeply crowned crests, treacherous curves and unfenced shoulders.

Nor were the new school buildings less out of date. The outside walls were of brick but practically all the interiors were of wood. Heavy timbers supported the pine floor joists on which was laid the pine tongue-and-groove planking. They were all of a similar design: two stories high, with a coal-burning furnace in the basement. Invariably within a few years the oil-soaked floors began to sag and the crumbly plaster to peel from the wooden lathing. These tinderboxes had been little better than "firetraps" since the beginning, but a merciful providence had spared the coalfield the catastrophe of major school conflagrations which could snuff out hundreds of lives.

During those early years, when a school system in the modern sense was being organized and given its initial impetus, the overwhelming majority of the people possessed little concept of the role of learning in the building and nurturing of civilization. A parent prided himself on having done "a good part" for his children if he kept them in school until they had completed the eighth grade. Some, of course, particularly the people in the towns and bigger camps, wanted a high school diploma for their offspring; and in the swollen population with its numerous imported managerial personnel there were enough students to fill the few high schools as soon as they were built. But viewed against the background of the whole population, those families who planned a high school education for their children remained severely limited. In 1928, for example, one county with a population of slightly more than 35,000 persons produced fewer than 100 high school graduates. Such ambitions for their children as most people entertained were reserved for their sons, because it was assumed that the "girls will get married and won't need to know much anyway."

In these circumstances such new schools as the bond issues provided fell prey to athletics to an extent that is difficult to overstate. The miner learned quickly to escape from the dreary routines of camp life and coal digging into the exhilaration of a basketball gymnasium or a football stadium, and was far more interested in the hoopla of school sports than in the riddles of grammar and mathematics. His enthusiasm went to the sterile playing fields and his children, imbued with his infectious zeal, sought to emulate his heroes on grid and court.

The prospering merchants and professional men on the Main Streets of the county seats and trading towns, like Babbitts everywhere, gave enthusiastic support to the ball teams, and organized musical bands directed by imported musicians to "support and stir up" the athletes. Thus the emerging school system fostered institutions oriented toward entertaining the communities rather than toward the teaching of the children. A pattern was established whereby vocal community leaders gave unsparing support to teams and bands but ignored laboratories, libraries and classrooms.

The academic pall that began to fall upon the new schools was resisted valiantly for a good many years by the new teachers who came into the area with the camps. But as time passed their zeal waned and gave way to disappointment, disillusionment and bitterness. A hundred dollars a month was enough for a third-grade teacher with several years experience, an excellent reputation for effective teaching and a degree from the University of Tennessee. By contrast, a football or basketball coach on his first assignment could generally anticipate twice that sum. One by one the new teachers who had arrived with such high hopes began to slip away. By the early 1930s most of them were gone. As they departed their places in the classrooms were taken by sons and daughters of mountaineers — young men and women who had managed to get through one of the new high schools and to complete a semester or two at a state teacher's college. Once embarked upon a teaching career such a teacher sometimes required twenty years in occasional summer terms and correspondence courses to accumulate enough college credits to acquire a Bachelor of Science degree in Education. Having drunk but shallow drafts from the Springs of Learning they could hardly inspire a thirst for knowledge in the minds of their pupils.

Other factors, too, were at work to prevent the counties from establishing quality schools or preserving the headway they had already made. The most destructive of these factors lay in the political nature of the Kentucky school administrative structure, a structure which has kept the region's schools in deep political involvement for many years.

Under the law each county or independent school district was divided into small subdistricts, each of which contained from thirty to a hundred pupils. The people of such a district elected a trustee, whose duty it was to select and employ the teachers. Once the teachers were appointed, an elective superintendent managed the schools and "took care that the laws be faithfully executed."

Thus by law the trustees and superintendents were creatures of public political whim and early came to be sordid local politicians of the most pernicious type.

As time passed, the coal barons were no longer content to control such offices as the fiscal court, tax commissioner and county judge. Success in securing these nerve centers tempted them to take over the entire political management of the counties.

Recruiters for the United Mine Workers of America and the International Workers of the World began to seek members in the coalfield before 1917, and continued their efforts for six or seven years. Their arguments were logical and persuasive, but they were premature. The miners were riding the crest of full employment and high wages. They thought of themselves as prosperous, and most of them simply ignored the organizers' promises of even better days to come under union leadership. A good many thousand laborers joined the unions, but they did so more in quest of social fellowship than out of a conviction that they were enlisting in a just cause. Their attitude was not unlike that of the bored citizen who seeks membership in the Order of Free and Accepted Masons or the Independent Order of Odd Fellows. Without strong roots, unionism could hardly flourish. But the presence of the organizers did not go unnoticed by the operators. They let it be known that any man who joined a union would be fired. Nor did they stop there, for each operator contributed to an industry-wide "black list" of suspected unionists. The operators obligated themselves to give no employment anywhere within the coalfield to any man who was ever so proscribed.

Nevertheless, fear of the labor organizers moved the operators to capture the office of county sheriff. This official could appoint badge-wearing gunmen to "protect company property" and to incarcerate as "loiterers" any suspected organizers who might venture within their domain.

To the end of the 1920s, many operators were in almost constant litigation. Some of the lawsuits were between coal companies, but most were with landowners who claimed the companies had invaded their premises. These title suits were of supreme interest to the companies and they made every effort to have "sensible" men on the benches of the Circuit Courts. We have seen that the operators held the esteem of their employees and could effectively direct their voting, but in the rapidly filling creeks and hollows outside the camps their influence was weak and the votes of the mountaineers had to be captured by other means. The operators simply undertook to purchase enough of these nonminer votes to assure a favorable outcome in otherwise doubtful elections.

The companies appropriated generous "slush funds" to be dispensed by their representatives. The Big Bosses worked through precinct politicians chosen by their friends within the courthouses. These petty politicians knew the individual voters, their weaknesses and their strengths. They compiled lists of voters whose franchise could be purchased, and on election day or the night before they were sought out and bribed. Many thousands of dollars were habitually spent in this manner. Some mountaineers had a granite integrity which could not be corrupted. Such a man might kill his neighbor for slight provocation and he might have spent a year or two in the penitentiary for moonshining, but vote selling was abhorrent to him. The politicians must know and scrupulously avoid his like. But there were multitudes of others who had little interest in political contests. Like their forest-dwelling ancestors before them, they chafed at the restraints of all laws and had little intention of complying with court orders, whoever might be judge, clerk or sheriff. These citizens were habitually willing to sell their votes for a few dollars and a little whiskey. The slush funds amassed by the companies controlled this element of the electorate with tight efficiency.

In 1913 a particularly vicious campaign for circuit judge occurred in the judicial district composed of Letcher and Pike Counties. A suit alleging violation of the state's Corrupt Practices Act reached

the Court of Appeals.* That court's opinion is a startling commen
tary on the political methods and morals of the coalfield. The
court found that hundreds of "floaters" had been rounded up and
paid. At Lick Precinct in Pike County fifty men received money for
their votes. At Peters Precinct three times that many were paid two
dollars each to induce them to support the favored candidate. At
Forks Precinct twenty votes were sold for six dollars each. In North
Pikeville, Caney, Upper Elkhorn, Fords Branch, Linefork and other
precincts scores of voters were openly bribed. In Brushy Precinct
floaters brazenly auctioned their votes to the highest bidder.

And if political offices and votes could be thus bought and sold, it
was unthinkable that the elective school officials could remain un-
contaminated. In the welter of vote buying and selling, the school
trustees and superintendents were caught up as allies to the political
factions, with teaching positions treated as so many patronage
plums. In short, the mine operators financed a political machine
whose toils extended throughout each county and into every office
in its courthouse. The local elective offices in the school system
were simply incorporated into the machine.

The trifling but coveted office of school trustee inspired many battles which went beyond the ballot box and voting booth. At election
after election, armed partisans gathered at polling places to support
their candidates and gunfights erupted in which men were crippled
and slain. Such "school fights" blackened the name of the state
wherever reports of their occurrence were heard. The bloodiest
episode of this kind took place at Clayhole on Troublesome Creek
in Breathitt County on November 8, 1921. The right of "Aunt"
Liza Sizemore to vote in the election was challenged and within a
few moments nine men were slain and six others were seriously
wounded. Scarcely a county is without its memory of such dreadful affrays — though, fortunately, none of them was so deadly as
the Battle of Clayhole.

The political school trustees discovered that many teaching positions were occupied by men and women from other parts of Kentucky and from other states. Their qualifications might be excellent;
an illiterate trustee was unlikely to know what these qualifications

* *Butler* vs. *Roberson*, 164 S. W. 240.

were. But he could appreciate that these "fotched-on" instructors were without local relatives who could vote for him, the superintendent and his other allies, while there were other applicants for the job who could point to dozens of first and second cousins and a small army of uncles and aunts. The politicians could not long resist the temptation to profit from this situation. One by one the competent teachers from outside the plateau were dropped from the rosters and the sons and daughters of local citizens assumed their duties. These children of the plateau were long conditioned to mountain politics in all its nefarious aspects. They were willing to see their employment as a political job rather than as a high and honored professional calling. A good many of these political teachers were undoubtedly competent, and inspired their pupils to look beyond the dingy limits of the coal towns and the narrow hollows. But too many performed their work simply as tasks to be gotten through with no great outlay of effort. If a teacher had obtained his position because his numerous clan had pressured the trustee, the same political influences which secured his job for him could be depended upon to preserve it.

Nor did these teachers, principals and superintendents bring inventiveness to their tasks. They found only the basic framework of an educational system and it does not appear to have occurred to them seriously to improve the schools. There were no facilities for teaching the mentally retarded, the blind and physically handicapped, and there was no instruction in the manual skills for those who desired to become carpenters, electricians, masons or mechanics. If educators within the coalfield ever thought of adding these indispensable parts of an effective school system, they quietly put such thoughts out of their minds.

Thus, in the fateful years between 1912 and 1927 which so strongly influenced the whole future of the coalfield, that which it needed most was aborted and lost. Its foremost need was for a comprehensive and effective system of public education, to gather up this rich human material from a dozen states and many countries and convert it into a wise and virtuous citizenry. But this foremost requirement was denied it. The schools were robbed of adequate financing. The best teachers, those with the richest gifts of inspiration and experience, drifted away, and a vicious system of intellectual inbreeding was established which has never been broken. At best, its instruction was not good. And as the school population grew, in counties without funds to build new schoolhouses and hire additional teachers many thousands of children did not go to school at all.

PART IV

Boom and Bust

CHAPTER ELEVEN

The Big Boom

If the coal industry in the plateau may be said to have enjoyed a Golden Age, these years of the Big Boom were surely it. The companies which established operations early realized enormous profits on their investments. Since the mines employed many men and few machines, the rows of houses poured torrents of rent into company coffers. The tipples stood on the edge of huge tracts of virgin coal and the working rooms were never far from the driftmouths. Thus the cost of underground transportation was minimal. Scores of "coal drags" containing sixty to a hundred railroad gondolas each ran daily from the field, and during most of these years the only factor which limited production was a shortage of cars. Sometimes the railroad companies were unable to provide the "empties" which the billing clerks requested, and idle tipples were more often caused by this failure than by lack of orders.

I do not mean to imply that the boom was wholly without interruption. Between 1920 and 1922 a recession struck the nation and its impact was felt severely in the coalfield. Production declined for a year or two and the miners ran up substantial debts in the company stores and much of the confidence oozed out of the operators. But the recession was not prolonged, and after a year or so the downturn was reversed and the volume of orders began to swell. Confidence flowed back, and the old game of organizing coal corporations and building camps was resumed with new zeal.

But at intervals during the ensuing years tremors of uncertainty ran through the region's economy. From time to time the market be-

came briefly saturated and "demurrage" charges were levied by the
railroads for use of their un-emptied cars, but always, after a week or
two, new orders came from the middlemen dealers in Cincinnati,
Columbus and Chicago and the men went back to work.

Throughout the Golden Age the wage scale climbed bit by bit.
When the field opened, pick-and-shovel men could expect to receive
$1.50 for a ten-hour day. By 1927 they were earning $4.00 for 8 hours.
This represents a dramatic rise in income but it did not greatly
exceed the equally sharp rise in prices charged by the commissaries.
Since the miners were captive customers the commissaries were the
left hand which took back what the right hand bestowed. The prices
of beans, bacon, lard, meal and other staples of the miner's diet
doubled. Nevertheless, toward the end of the 1920s, the miners
were accumulating small sums beyond the absolute requirements for
rent, clothing and food and rows of canvas-topped, black Model T
Fords began to appear before the commissaries and administration
buildings, and conversation turned from more mundane subjects to
the family "touring car" and its flat tires, gasoline and spare parts.
The washing machine, the icebox and then the refrigerator could be
seen in the kitchens and on the back porches of camp houses.

This steady but gradual lifting of wages and living standards from
1912 to 1927 did not culminate at the end of the period. To the
contrary, a spectacular peak was reached near the middle of the years
which miners would always remember as "the good times" — during
the years of America's participation in the Great War. In those years
of crisis the nation lacked an effective program of wage and price
controls. Many of the young miners volunteered and others were
drafted. This exodus of labor occurred precisely when war orders
were demanding huge new increases in coal production. Even when
many older mountaineers came in from the creeks and hollows labor
remained in short supply and the companies bid against each other
for workmen. The corporations streamlined their labor schedules,
hiring company men to cut and shoot the coal while the loaders retained the task of shoveling it into the cars. Under this system of
"piecework" the men were paid according to the units of work performed rather than for the number of hours spent at the working
face. Hence a coal cutter was paid a given sum for each ton that he

undercut, and the loader was paid similarly for each ton he lifted onto the cars. This system encouraged the men to remain under the hill far longer each day than otherwise could have been expected of them. During these critical months when America's industrial might was being brought to the rescue of her embattled allies many men habitually worked twelve hours a day and sometimes six or even seven days per week. For this almost suicidal toil they earned fabulous wages ranging up to ten dollars a day. The money flowed in torrents into the commissaries, the new movie theaters which the companies had recently built and the poolrooms and restaurants of the recreation buildings.

But such exertion could not be long sustained, no matter how high the inducement. The excitement and sloganeering of the war acted as an emotional stimulus which inspired Herculean labors for unbelievably long hours, but the miners were glad when the war ended and they could loaf on Saturday and leave the pits two or three hours earlier in the day.

The miners did not consume the whole loaf of wartime prosperity. Indeed, their portion amounted scarcely to the crumbs from the loaf. The lion's share was gobbled up by their employers. So vast were the wartime demands on the industry that prices, too, soared to stratospheric levels, in some instances reaching twenty dollars per ton F. O. B. the cars. So high did the price ascend that many mountaineers who had retained small boundaries began to mine it as "wagon miners." These midget operators dug a tunnel into the coal, shot the coal "from the solid" — that is, without undercutting it — and hauled it in wagons to the nearest railroad siding. There they loaded it with shovels into the cars which the railroad companies obligingly set for them.

When the camps were new and stood glistening in their coats of fresh paint, the Big Bosses formed high resolves to keep their towns orderly and clean. For a good many years staunch efforts were made to preserve the camps as pleasant places for the executives who ran them and for the people who inhabited them. The houses were repainted every two or three years, and rows of shade trees were planted between the houses and along the streets. Most companies gave free grass seed to their tenants and urged them to sow plots of lawn around their houses. Prizes were offered to the women who grew the loveliest flower beds and for the best potted house-plants. The wives of company executives judged these events, and they, too, worked hard to keep the towns as tidy and pleasant as the physical circumstances would permit.

The better companies promoted the organizing of sewing and quilting circles and persuaded the housewives to form groups to study better ways of cooking and housekeeping. Some of the most progressive companies imported professional home economists and nurses who visited the homes and encouraged the women to higher standards in their domestic activities. All in all, the companies were proud of the towns which they had brought to this Southern wilderness.

From the beginning the struggle to keep the coal towns orderly and to maintain the brisk morale of cleanliness was an uneven one and in the nature of things was probably doomed to failure. Wherever coal has been mined a blight has fallen upon the land and upon the habitations of men. It is doubtful that any effort or amount of zeal on the part of the coal barons could have maintained for their employees standards of living even remotely near those of the nation generally. Perhaps nothing the Big Bosses could have attempted would have preserved their communities as wholesome and secure places in which families could be begotten, educated and instilled with the dynamics of good citizenship.

Certainly the family is the indestructible cornerstone of social organization, and within its confines must be nurtured, if they are to arise at all, those magnificent qualities we call honor, integrity and pride. Under the parental roof the child first gains experience of the world and acquires almost instinctively the passions and prejudices, the teachings and the inertias which largely shape his life. And in the camps it became increasingly difficult, even in the Golden Age, for the homes to be places of inspiration and refuge.

In the tipples near the "head houses" the output of the mines was cleaned and loaded for shipment. In the best tipples the coal was washed, but in most of them this phase of preparation was omitted. Powerful "shaker screens" vibrated the coal as it moved along conveyors. These agitated screens separated the coal into various sizes — "nut and slack," "egg" and "block." The slate and "bone" that had escaped the miners was picked out and cast aside by sharp-eyed "slate pickers." Much coal was broken in the process, and clouds of the pulverized stuff rose from the screens and "loading booms" which lowered it into the railroad cars.

Over the tipple there reared a monstrous coaldust genie which, as the ascending sun warmed the air, grew to immense proportions. Silent itself it emanated endlessly from the rumbling machinery, and twisted and bent and soared in the changing winds. Sometimes it rose mountain high, straight up in the August sunlight. Again it reclined against the soggy earth under the pelting of a November rain. But always its gritty fingers tapped silently against the houses and crept into every nook and cranny in the town. Its pervasive and unescapable presence gave rise to that saying so common among men and women who were born in the camps, "I was born with coaldust in my blood."

Near every tipple there grew up mountainous piles of discarded slate and low-grade coal. As the years advanced these refuse heaps reached heights of hundreds of feet and extended for hundreds of yards in length. As they grew higher chemical processes deep within them caused a spontaneous combustion which set fire to the coal. This fire spread, broke out in other places and burned inexorably, day and night. These monstrous "slate dumps" grew to mountains of living fire which blazed without intermission and daily received carloads of new fuel. The fires cast off clouds of oily black smoke which settled in the valleys and enveloped the homes of boss and miner alike, immersing them in a gray dinginess and in nauseous fumes heavy-laden with sulphur. Rain could not quench these fires and efforts by the companies to do so were wholly ineffective. Men might be set to work to cover the fire lines with dirt or cinders and all traces of the fire might disappear, but within days or weeks new fires always sprang up and the hideous pall came back to the valleys.

Every house within the camps was heated by coal-burning stoves, furnaces or fireplaces, and long rows of chimneys belched sooty smoke around the clock in the cold season and in the summer whenever the cooking of meals was in progress. This powdery waste mingled with the oily vapors from the slate dumps.

The polluted atmosphere peeled paint from walls and turned

them an ashen gray. The pollutants caused throats and eyes to smart and sting. Bed linens and furniture came to smell of them and clothes took on a yellowish-gray tint which no amount of bleach could remove. No matter how tireless the efforts of the housewife with her dustcloth, mops and brooms, she could make no headway against the clouds of smut. The communities gradually took on that sickly hue which miners called "coal-camp gray."

To this oppressive mixture of coaldust, smoke and soot was added the faint, vile stench from tons of decaying excrement in the open-pit privies. Once or twice yearly this revolting smell was stirred to stomach-turning nausea by visits from the "honey wagon." Men with long-handled shovels and scoops dipped out the contents of the pits and loaded them into a huge mule-drawn tank. The revolting cargo was hauled away to a large trench called the "honey hole," where it was buried. Sometimes a drunken wag would set up a mock tombstone to mark such a reeking grave.

Many women fought the dirt-and-grime battle through the best years of their lives and surrendered to it only in old age, long after the Big Boom and the Great Depression were history. Some never surrendered and today at seventy-five or eighty still war with the forces of their environment. But most of them surrendered bit by bit. Realizing that the contest could not be won, they slowly capitulated to the unremitting clouds and allowed their homes to lose the sparkle and shine which had characterized the new towns. The spick-and-span gave way to the dull and disordered, and the women sat down on the front-porch swings and in chairs before the fireplaces and allowed the victorious enemy to run riot through the towns. There appeared the first symptoms of the vacuity, resignation and passivity which so marks the camp dwellers today, traits which could only deepen as the years brought new defeats and new tragedies.

In discussing the Big Boom I have said little about the people who remained on the scrubby farms along the creeks and hollows. Though thousands of mountaineers forsook the land for the camps and mines, far greater numbers remained behind. These rangy, narrow-minded, stubborn, clannish men and women continued to multiply with all the astounding efficiency which has marked their history in the Southern hills. Marrying early and having a child with almost annual regularity, they produced frontier-style families of six to twenty children.

The skill of the new doctors who came with the industry saved the lives of many sick and injured persons whose deaths would have been assured only a few years before. And before the Big Boom ran its course one county after another hired a public health doctor, some on a part-time basis only, and his assistants, the public health nurse and sanitarian. These County Health Departments were pathetically understaffed and inadequately financed, but their benefits were marked. Deaths from diphtheria, scarlet fever, whooping cough, measles and smallpox declined dramatically as programs of immunization got under way in the schools. As these public healers preached sanitation to schoolchildren and their parents the ravages of typhoid were abated. All in all, the "creek and holler folks" bred a new and vastly heightened population surge during the same years the industry was importing trainloads of new families. These men and women of the native stock who continued to till the land produced sons and daughters of their own who built homes in the dwindling spaces along the narrow bottoms and up the hollows. Within the surprisingly short interval of twenty years, houses were within "hollerin' distance" of each other on most of the region's creeks from one end of the streams to the other.

Great numbers of these mountaineers worked for the coal companies. Some of them walked four or five miles to the pits and back again at night. Others rode mules or horses and left them in enclosures provided by the companies until the day's work was done. As the versatile Ford invaded the plateau still others bought cars and commuted over the dreadful roads.

Others, a majority, simply persisted in the ancient agriculture and lived by raising corn and cornfed livestock. They ate the same vegetables and grains that had nourished their ancestors for so long. But now these foods were supplemented by copious quantities of white flour and buckets of colorless corn syrup bought at the commissaries or "country stores" which endlessly multiplied throughout the countryside.

These farmer mountaineers abandoned the log cabins of their forebears and built nondescript cottages for their families. Without other architectural examples to pattern from, they copied the simple styles of the camp houses. Thousands upon thousands of four- or five-room "boxed" and weather-boarded houses sprang up. Like their models in the coal towns, they stood on posts above the ground. Shaky wooden steps led up to the indispensable porches. At each house the "box" which covered the hand-dug well stood a few steps from the back door. From this door a narrow path ran around the back of the vegetable garden to the outdoor toilet. Here were the "four rooms and a path" which became standard housing for the region.

Such "poor land" farmers might struggle to retain the old agricultural modes, but they were in the grip of forces which were soon to make those modes impossible. The sins and omissions of their methods of farming could lead only to disaster. The camps and towns had pre-empted a large portion of the narrow bottomlands. The mountaineer had traditionally built his cabin along these ribbons of fertile earth and his descendants now insisted on using the remainder of their tillable soil for house sites. They reversed the practice of the Italian peasants who build homes on the mountain slopes and preserve the valleys for cultivation. The Kentuckians built their homes on the meager bottomland and then attempted to farm the hillsides. Only when the bottoms were thickly dotted with habitations did the succeeding generations move to higher land. The shrinking acres of cultivable valley land had long been inadequate for the region's sustenance, even with a much smaller population. Now the mountaineers fell upon their hillsides with redoubled savagery. They were moved to do so by three considerations.

The first of these factors was habit. For generations highlanders had simply cleared new grounds when old ones had worn out.

The second factor was the demand for saw logs and mining timbers. The Big Bosses set gangs of men to work on company-owned lands sawing jack props and collar-poles. But these workmen could not supply the millions of timbers which the industry required and the mountaineer found that by clearing his lands for crops he could produce a valuable by-product. The rare mountaineer who had retained title to his trees was now willing to sell them to the "cruisers" whom the lumber companies sent around from time to time. So the larger trees on the farmer's land were cut down and hauled to the timber yards of the mining corporations. The demand for props was insatiable, and thousands of acres were cleared to provide the pine, poplar, hickory and oak timbers upon which the lives of the miners depended.

The third factor was the mushroom growth of the illicit moonshine whiskey industry. Though the mountaineer eventually fell into the habit of making "sugar top" instead of "straight corn" whiskey, his operations continued to require great amounts of grain. And with the advent of national Prohibition the underground distilling industry grew to mammoth proportions, and in addition to corn for his table and livestock he must grow it for his multiplying mash barrels.

So the yellow splotches of eroded hillside which had caught the eyes of the railroad builders spread mile upon mile across the corrugated terrain, through rich coves, along the skinny points to the tops of the jagged ridges. Each spring armies of mountaineers went forth with hoes and plows to scratch the surface and to plant it with millions of hills of corn. And once the crops were "laid by" the ring of axes and buzz of cross-cut saws echoed in other coves and on other points as new stacks of logs and mining timbers were made ready for the loading-skids. The wood smoke from burning brush heaps was as symbolic of the plateau as the coal smoke from the slate dumps.

The yellowing hillsides lost their humus to the swollen streams. Year after year, the mustard-colored blight widened its realm. Then, in 1927, the year when economic forces were to break the back of the Big Boom, outraged Nature struck back at the despoilers who had so long violated her laws.

Flash floods — those abrupt, vicious downpours — were never strangers to the highlands. The hills were too steeply sloped for even the primeval mold to absorb all the water, and the run-off was terrific. But on the night of May 30, 1927, the plateau was battered by a cloudburst more calamitous than any other single event in its history. The hillside crops had been planted and the multitudes of men, women, boys and girls had hoed them out, thoroughly loosening the soil and killing every bit of intervening vegetation their sharp eyes could detect. In about two weeks they would hoe the corn again, then, to use the mountaineer's expression, it would be "laid by": nothing more would be done to it until it was harvested and carried away in sacks or hauled on crude sleds to the cribs or mash barrels. But providence had ordained that this crop would never be gathered.

At dusk immense black clouds began boiling up on the eastern horizon and rumbles of low thunder sounded from their depths. Lightning flashed and the sullen rumbling grew louder. As the night came on the stars were obliterated and the cumulus piled ever more massively above the mountains. About 8:30 the downpour began. Immediately the cascade of water was terrific, but its volume steadily swelled. By midnight the rain had long since surpassed anything within the recollection of living men, and it pounded rooftops and cornfields with the concentrated power of millions of fire hoses. Water ran down the hillsides in sheets two or three inches deep in places. Hollows, dry a few hours before, roared like Niagaras. Log houses that had withstood the ravages of a hundred years were carried away. Scores of frame houses were washed off their foundations and whirled out onto the bosoms of surging rivers which lapped angrily where gangs of workmen had hoed corn during the afternoon before.

Highway and railroad bridges broke beneath the onslaught. Rows of camp houses were flooded, and people took refuge on rooftops or on the second floors of two-story houses. With hollow roars, mountains of slate crashed into streams, forming dams which restrained the water for a few moments and then released it with even greater violence. On the hillsides great landslides discharged tons of mud and rock down the slopes into the raging streams.

When dawn came nearly a hundred mountaineers lay dead under the swirling waters or along the muddy banks. Scores of highway and railroad bridges had been swept away. Automobiles had vanished, and thousands of head of livestock had been drowned. Weeks were required before the railroad companies could repair the tracks and bridges enough to haul away the cars of coal which had been loaded on the eve of the disaster. But the greatest calamity befell the land itself. Inches of soil vanished from each cleared acre. The crop of new corn disappeared. The yellow hillsides now lay bleak and dead in a state of sterility from which they have not recovered to this day.

This great flood marks one of the major milestones which the mountaineers have passed on the road to ruin.

The plateau dwellers emerged from their soggy homes to gaze dumfounded and bewildered at the blasted land. So overwhelming was the catastrophe that days passed before the weight of it could lift enough for the broken people to begin to clean their homes and to clear away the mountainous mud bars and refuse heaps which the deluge had brought down upon them. Most of the reconstruction which followed was performed spontaneously by the mountaineers with little assistance from the state or the Federal Government, and with only minimum leadership from any source.

Mr. Herbert Hoover, then Secretary of Commerce, traveled through the area, and considerable assistance was extended by the American Red Cross. But, however generous the gifts of food, clothing and medicines which were funneled in from other areas, the contributions were insignificant when measured against the overall need. They constituted but a drop of aid in a bucket of want. The entire plateau lay desolate.

The destruction was not restricted to the homes and lands of the people but fell with equal fury on the coal corporations. In many areas the drenched mountains poured such vast quantities of water into the mines that it rose over the laboring pumps to the roofs and drained out of the driftmouths in huge rivers. Tipples were damaged. Many commissaries were inundated and the grocery stocks destroyed.

At the insistence of their Congressmen, delegations of county officials went to Washington to seek Federal assistance in restoring ruined public facilities and institutions. But the government was in the hands of a President and Congress who believed that local communities should be ruggedly independent, and little aid was forthcoming.

So the people turned to and cleaned up the mess the best they could. There was no possibility of state or county providing funds for workmen. The magnitude of the damage precluded this. Farmers and miners turned out with shovels, picks, wheelbarrows and their own teams of horses and mules to dredge out the roads and build back retaining walls to confine the creeks. In gangs they shoveled mud from coal camps, yards and streets, and up the creeks every woman and girl was busy over steaming wash tubs and kettles sterilizing bedding and clothing. By degrees order came back into the chaos. The section gangs repaired the washed out tracks and train-loads of groceries crept slowly along the shaky road beds for un-loading at the wholesale houses and commissaries.

At least one permanent benefit came to the region as a result of the flood. Before the disaster, as we have seen, a few counties had established Public Health services and each of the major companies supported a Public Health program of sorts in its camp. Though some of these private programs were quite good, they were all limited in scope. But as a result of Mr. Hoover's tour most of the remaining counties were persuaded to create rudimentary Depart-ments of Health. Thousands of people had to be immunized against water-borne contagions. And when the crisis passed, the health depart-ments remained. Though their gifts to their communities have been priceless in terms of human life and improved health, the support given them by the county governments has remained niggardly in the extreme.

Now the absurdity of low taxes and high debts fell with crushing weight upon the county governments. Their limited incomes had prevented the accumulation of reserves for emergencies, and most of them had borrowed to the hilt. Few counties could sell another bond for any purpose. It was apparent that the pauperized people could tolerate no tax increases. To the contrary, many taxpayers were unable to pay their levies at all during the ensuing year or two, and the collectors were loath to attempt to compel payment. Most of the bridges which the bond issues had paid for were gone with the flood and miles of the new roads had been undermined and weakened. The debt-ridden schoolhouses remained, but some of them had been severely damaged. Many of the benefits which the huge debts had purchased had been swept away, but the bondholders remained to be dealt with.

CHAPTER TWELVE

Moonshine and Mayhem

AFTER 1920, the Federal Government's war against the "stillers" rose to an ever higher crescendo. In this Prohibition era the moun-taineers could manufacture whiskey for the great nationwide under-ground market as well as for the local "fruitjar trade" in the towns and camps. In each of the major cities, hooch gangs grew rich deal-ing in illicit alcohol — and one of the big sources of supply was the Cumberland Plateau.

A dependable and well-managed transportation system was re-quired to get the whiskey out of the narrow valleys of the highlands and into the big city markets. After the building of the arterial high-ways trucks were increasingly relied upon, but most barrels of "white mule" were carried out in freightcars where they were hidden with the connivance of railroad crewmen. Kegs were buried under the coal in the gondolas, to be dug out again at some pre-arranged stop-ping point in Ohio or Illinois. The business of smuggling whiskey out of the mountains became scandalously big and complex.

The Federal Government hired gangs of new special agents to assist in tracking down the stills and "stillers," and in some counties the sheriffs became fired with the "Prohibition fever" and assigned gangs of deputies to assist the agents. These heavily armed teams of local and national peace officers traversed hill and mountain in a never-ending campaign to destroy the stills and to arrest their opera-tors.

Thousands of mountaineers were arrested, tried and convicted in the Federal courts, and hundreds of them were sent in chartered railroad cars to the Federal penitentiaries at Atlanta and Leavenworth. So great was the number that the United States District Judges were compelled to probate most of them, lest the national penal system be overcome by a flood of prisoners which it could not possibly cope with. On the opening day of a term of the United States District Court at Jackson, Catlettsburg and London, it was not uncommon to see several hundred men and women lined up in front of the courthouse waiting for their cases to be called. Sometimes the long lines of defendants stretched from the door at the rear of the courtroom down the stairs, along the hall, out the door and onto the courthouse square. First offenders were nearly always probated, but prison sentences of one, two and five years were dealt out wholesale.

The government did not win all its battles with the moonshiners. The agents were dealing with a hardy and vicious race of men whose ancestors for six or eight generations had been accustomed to the spilling of human blood, and every raid against a suspected still site was fraught with deadly peril.

After the flash flood of 1927 the impoverished mountaineers were driven to "stilling" on an even larger scale. So devastated were their fields that the old system of agriculture was permanently disrupted. They were no longer able to produce huge quantities of white corn for their livestock and meal barrels, but the need to eat survived undiminished. Possessing no other skill by which they could survive in their homeland, a very large segment of the population turned to whiskey making.

In the years that followed the diminished corn crops were insufficient to meet the requirements, so the stillers turned to sugar and the sugar-top whiskey which is now identified in the public mind with moonshine. To a bushel of cooked corn meal and a peck of sprouted corn grains was added twelve or fifteen pounds of white, granulated sugar. This mixture fermented much more rapidly than did the crushed grain alone, thus lessening the danger of having the operation detected before the "run off." By using a "thumping keg," the moonshiner could "double-distill" his mash, greatly increasing the ratio of whiskey produced to grain used. The resulting "bust-head" was an extremely potent liquor which left a savage hangover in its wake. Under pressure from enforcement officers and the growing shortage of corn, the old talent of making a high quality, carefully distilled whiskey gave way to the hurried making of an increasingly wretched product which killed, maimed or blinded hundreds of people.

The more unscrupulous of the moonshiners resorted to fantastic practices to make the mash barrels ferment faster and to give to their product the all-important "bead" by which its quality was superficially judged. One of these unspeakable practices consisted of dropping carbide into the meal barrels. The heat which it generated effectively cooked the crushed corn, but the chemicals it released could be deadly. Others threw crushed buckeyes (inedible mountain nuts) and lye into the barrels and these were reputed to make a low grade "rotgut" bead like straight corn.

The moonshiners became increasingly cunning in the location of their stills. The barrels were carried far up the hidden hollows and some were secreted in deep caverns which time and long-dry streams had carved under the mountains. Other "stillers" set up their plants inside abandoned mines, allowing the smoke from their fires to be dissipated in the underground chasms. Still others went modern and cooked with electricity, making the stuff in cellars under their homes.

There was a continual contest of courage and brains between the law officers and the lawbreakers, and to a degree never surpassed in the great feuds the land again ran red in homicidal blood. The mountaineers developed effective systems of lookouts and signals and many times the lawmen approached a still only to find that its owners had seized the more valuable parts of their equipment and fled. Sometimes the agents arrived so stealthily that the still operators found themselves looking into the muzzles of cocked pistols and could neither flee nor fight. But all too often heavily armed moonshiners learned of the approach of the agents and truculently decided to fight for the family enterprise. Some of the gun battles that followed were bloody in the extreme.

Winchester rifles and large-caliber pistols were favorite weapons of the moonshiners and were never far from their hands. But another firearm occupied the position of highest esteem in the hearts of these rugged manufacturers whose product was so formally loathed and so informally prized by the American public. This death-dealer was a lineal descendant of the slug-loaded musket which the

borderer had once used with such murderous effectiveness against
Indian war parties.

Many stillers acquired double-barreled and magazine-loading re-
peater shotguns of twelve, ten and even eight gauge. These murderous arms were invariably loaded with buckshot or with slugs of a
far more deadly character. Sometimes a mountaineer would use a
cold chisel and hammer to cut the heads off a number of twenty-
penny nails, leaving a quarter of an inch of the spike attached to
each nailhead. The cartridge then had its load of slugs withdrawn
and replaced with a handful of these chopped-off nailheads. Other
mountaineers loaded their shotgun shells with screws. An angry and
resolute mountaineer firing such a weapon from behind a well-con-
cealed barricade could wreak fearful havoc in the ranks of Uncle
Sam's Prohibition agents.

As in any account of the great feuds of an earlier era, any attempt
to detail the bloodletting of the "moonshine wars" or to bolster
them with statistics is a baffling enterprise. The Federal Prohibition
Director for the state employed a small army of agents, most of whom
were native mountaineers with previous experience as sheriffs or
their deputies. Many of them were ex-soldiers. There can be little
doubt that the men who directed the struggle to make Prohibition a
reality rather than a dream were earnestly dedicated to their cause.
A crusade to drive drunkenness from the land had been preached by
many sincere people for decades, and the people who were given the
task of barring alcohol from the nation were convinced they were
laboring in a righteous enterprise. On the other hand, some of the
agents were highly cynical about their mission and were perfectly
willing to drink up a portion of the whiskey they captured on each
raid.

The county sheriffs adopted differing attitudes toward the demon
drink, but many of them were sincere in their desire to banish stills
from their jurisdictions. Such officials were willing to deputize huge
numbers of men to help track down the moonshiners. Time after
time such deputies rode with the Prohibition agents and wholeheartedly supported their efforts. Other sheriffs took an intolerant
view toward the antiliquor campaign and refused to co-operate with

the Federal officers. Though the state Legislature had made the manufacture, sale, or possession of intoxicants unlawful under severe penalties, these sheriffs were little moved and were suspected by the Prohibition agents of giving aid and comfort to the moonshiners, and even of giving them advance warning of contemplated raids. In such counties the agents had to be careful to prevent knowledge of their plans and activities from reaching the sheriff's office, and this, of course, imposed severe limitations upon their effectiveness.

All this was part of the national schizophrenia which had produced the Volstead Act in the first place. A madness had seized the nation, and the plateau was caught up in the violent convulsions it induced. In the cities men and women attended meetings at which they applauded speakers who demanded unqualified enforcement of the Prohibition laws and afterward, on their way home, stopped off at speakeasies for a round of drinks. Jurors who kept bottles of moonshine hidden in their homes found moonshiners guilty and sentenced them to long prison terms. District Attorneys famed for their eloquent courtroom denunciations of the still operators sometimes whispered to a special agent to inquire whether he had any whiskey in his hotel room. People drank alcohol for the same reasons others consumed it before and after that era — to escape the tensions and frustrations of their lives — and then, by supporting efforts to ban the stuff, sought atonement for their sense of guilt and wrongdoing.

This wide divergence between the forms and the facts of Prohibition was not lost on the mountaineers whose family stills provided bread and butter for their households. Similar stills had been in most families for too many decades for them to be quietly surrendered. The plateau dweller was likely to believe that he had the same right to make his apples into brandy that his wife had to make hers into jelly. I have heard old ex-moonshiners remark, "If it's my corn I've got a right to eat it and I've got a right to drink it, and damn the man that says I can't sell it if somebody wants to buy it."

Stilling had long since become a part of the mountaineer's ingrained habits. Many of his folkways and mores centered around the still. For generations the accepted tenets of hospitality required that whiskey be offered to every guest. Mountain preachers, fostered and conditioned on the frontier or in the surviving frontier atmosphere of later years, had not hated whiskey as a vicious social evil. More than one of such "old-time" preachers had risen before a congregation to find that his appreciative auditors had set a fruit jar of "spirits" by the water bucket for his occasional refreshment as the long sermon progressed. These mountaineers, then, saw whiskey and whiskey making as a fundamental part of their lives in no wise wicked, and an economic prop which supported many of their families. To them a despotic government was sending gangs of "revenuers" to destroy their property and imprison them unjustly. Many of these men resolved to fight for the family stills with the same ardor they would have displayed in defense of the family hearth.

Consequently, between 1920 and 1934 the mountains and the rhododendron thickets which draped them resounded to the clatter of horses' hoofs as the raiders ferreted out the violators of their sacred law and, frequently, with gunfire when they were found. From the bloody groves of little Menifee County to the cloud-capped crags of the Big Black Mountain in Harlan and Bell Counties, the moonshiners and the state and the Federal officers fought out the issue.

Creeks whose white discoverers had called them by such picturesque frontier names as Wolf Pen, Broke Leg, Marrowbone, Little Ruby and Squabble, became battlegrounds as men fought tenaciously for their mash barrels, thumping kegs, cooling worms and — convictions. The magnitude of the struggle is difficult to grasp. Hundreds of thousands of dollars' worth of illegal property was seized and destroyed. The diary of one agent, John D. W. Collins, of Blackey, Kentucky, reveals that in 1921 he and his band of agents destroyed 365 stills, an average of one a day for the year. And that year, he says, was not the best. In later years, "we beat that record considerably!"

No fewer than thirty-five such agents were slain in Kentucky during the "moonshine wars." This should be contrasted with populous England which passed twenty years after the First World War without a single peace officer being slain while performing his official duties. This remarkable achievement on the part of our law-abiding British brethren may be even more starkly compared with the record in Letcher County, which, during the four-year term of a single sheriff, saw sixteen deputies shot to death. And this in a county generally reputed throughout the mountains to be "peaceful"!

Nor did all the fighting which shook the mountains during the Prohibition years occur around the hidden stills on the remote hollows. Even more people were slain in the camps and independent towns where an intransigent and ill-assorted population had been brought together without adequate law enforcement or recreational facilities. The heterogeneous populace of each such community was composed of three, four or five relatively distinct groups with markedly different backgrounds. To each group the others appeared strange, outlandish, inferior and perhaps dangerous. In any event they were to be resented. Pistols and knives were never in short supply and moonshine and applejack from the back country stills flowed in abundance. It was impossible for the sheriffs, constables and police to maintain order in these rows of look-alike houses over which a brooding air of violence seemed to lie. Fist, gun and knife battles between men frequently occurred and it was not unusual for harridans to fight each other in screaming, hair-pulling affrays. The amount of mayhem, murder and manslaughter spawned out of this background is as astonishing in its magnitude as was the violence of the great feuds.

The Hazard *Herald* has been published in Perry County weekly since 1911. Turning the crumbling, yellowed pages of its issues in the Prohibition era is a startling experience. But the events its columns have preserved for us were not dissimilar to those transpiring in all the counties of the plateau.

In those years Perry County was the home of some 40,000 people. Many of its hollows were filled with coal camps and in others camps were under construction. The editorial drums sounded an untiring tocsin for community improvement and happily prophesied an ever-brightening future. A month before the Volstead Act became the law of the land, the editor happily proclaimed the death and burial of "Old John Barleycorn." But his triumphant blast was sounded too early. Five years later the editor was still pounding away for the Prohibitionist cause, but Old John Barleycorn was far from dead. In fact a large percentage of the subscriptions must have been paid for with "moonshine money."

I have chosen a period of eight weeks in the life of this remarkable weekly journal and have reproduced verbatim some of its shockingly typical headlines.

February 13, 1925:

YOUNG DOCTOR KILLED BY ANGRY MINER AT ALLAIS

FRANK SPENCER, "KING OF THE MOONSHINERS," KILLED BY DEPUTY SHERIFF

MAYOR OF HAZARD ASSAULTED ON MAIN STREET

February 20, 1925:

NEGRO WOMAN KILLS MAN ON LOTTS CREEK

MAN SHOT RESISTING ARREST AT LOTHAIR

POLICE CAPTURE STILL IN HAZARD

February 27, 1925:

The front page in this issue is without news of a single moonshine raid, killing or wounding.

March 6, 1925:

THREE PISTOL BATTLES IN COUNTY, ONE KILLED, SEVERAL WOUNDED

SEVEN STILLS, THREE MEN CAPTURED IN COUNTY

This story reports that in the preceding eleven months a Perry County man, Federal Prohibition Officer Bill Turner, and his assistants had destroyed 175 stills and captured 350 stillers.

March 13, 1925:

LESLIE COUNTY HAS THREE SHERIFFS IN ONE WEEK

Leslie County adjoins Perry, and this news item relates that the elected sheriff had resigned, apparently because conditions were so lawless. The Governor appointed a successor but he was driven out of Hyden, the county seat, by a large gang of armed men who invaded the town and fired more than a thousand shots around the courthouse. The Governor had appointed a third sheriff just before the paper went to press.

March 20, 1925:
> EVERETT BRASHEARS KILLED BY MITCHELL SMITH

March 27, 1925:
> WARD COMBS SLAIN, $500 REWARD OFFERED FOR SLAYER

> SEVEN MEN AND EIGHT STILLS IN TWO DAYS

This headline alluded to the capture of stills and their operators. No deaths occurred in these raids.

April 3, 1925:
Again there is no news of murder, mayhem or moonshine raids.

April 10, 1925:
> TWELVE MORE STILLS GO

> FUGATE KILLS NOBLE

> THOMAS BERRY, LOTHAIR, KILLED, SON WOUNDED

> WILL WARD ARRESTED FOR SHOOTING DAVE RIDDLE

> VICCO MAN DIES, SHOT BY MAGISTRATE

From this headline tally we know that in a small county of no more than eighteen or twenty thousand adult persons nine homicides occurred in eight weeks, and at least twenty-eight stills were destroyed in raids. Yet there was no editorial mention of a crime wave or any expression of indignation at such a state of affairs. And the period covered was not taken from the worst years of the moonshine wars. These were to come after the great flood. Altogether hundreds, indeed thousands, of men lost their lives in the moonshine wars and in the tumultuous camps and towns. Grand juries frequently returned more than one hundred and fifty indictments and it was not unusual for the criminal docket in a single county to record from ten to thirty murder indictments awaiting trial before the harassed circuit judges. Cases involving wounding and attempting to kill were proportionately numerous. A few lives were taken in defense of life, home or property, but most occurred in what Kentucky law terms "sudden heat of passion." Such cases arise in "sudden affray," when the killer is aroused by such provocation on the part of the person slain as "is reasonably calculated to arouse the passions of an ordinarily prudent person beyond his control." When such a killing occurs, Kentucky law permits the jury to reduce the homicide from murder to manslaughter and to impose a relatively lenient prison sentence. This is precisely what occurred in most cases. The Hazard *Herald* in its May 8, 1925 issue reported that five men had been tried for murder in the county's Circuit Court, and that in all the sentences together a total of only twenty-two years' imprisonment was meted out! To the jurors, human life was cheap, even as it was to the defendants whose cases they heard. One issue of the Hazard *Herald* reported that a thief was given two years for stealing a turkey, while at the same term of court another man was sentenced to two years in the State Reformatory for killing his neighbor.

Nor were the governors who augustly presided over the affairs of the state any more strongly inclined to law enforcement. They made lavish use of the pardon power and commuted or voided the sentences of hundreds of prisoners. It may be said in their defense that so numerous were the crimes of violence no prison system of reasonable size and cost could have contained the convicts, and since the Legislature persistently failed to build new prisons the governors had no choice but to pardon many of the inmates. Pardons were extended on the slimmest pretexts, without any kind of post-parole supervision and without any systematic effort to grant clemency to persons with a demonstrated capacity for rehabilitation. Most pardons were inspired by political considerations. If a convict had a numerous clan of politically active persons, His Excellency was likely to hear his pardon plea with compassion, but if a prisoner was friendless his prospects were bleak.

Illustrative of the public and official attitudes toward crime in this Golden Age of prosperity, illicit whiskey, murder and mayhem is a story once told me by a man who had sojourned for three months in the State Penitentiary at Frankfort. Elderly when he told the story, he was perhaps thirty years old when the incidents occurred. His narrative in his own words follows:

In them days I lived about four miles from the camp and I peddled a whole lot of garden truck over there among the miners. I got up one morning early-like and loaded my mule with fresh corn and beans and took off fer the camp. I never had no gun, and shore warn't a-lookin' fer trouble. Well, sir, I got over to the camp and hitched up my mule and started down the railroad track to the fust row of houses. I was a-walkin' along a-mindin' my own business when I seed a man a-comin' toward me. I walked up to him polite as any man you ever seed and I said "Howdy." I seed that he was a big red-faced Hunky and was drunk. Well when I spoke to him it seemed to make him awful mad and he started a-cussin' and a-swearin' and called me ever' kind of bad name he could lay his tongue to. He was about twice as big as I was and I just had to take it. And right then it didn't make me much mad. After he finally quit cussin' and threatenin' me I went on and sold my vegitables and started back home, and the furder I went the madder I got as I thought about what that old Hunky son-of-a-bitch had said to me and me not a-botherin' him. Well, I got back home and I couldn't eat nary bite of supper I was so mad and all night long I just rolled around thinkin' about hit and a-gettin' madder all the time.

Well, the next mornin' I got up and I sot down to eat breakfast and I told my wife what had happened the day afore and I said, "I never will have no peace as long as this is on my mind and I am a-goin' over and kill that Hunky if hits the last thing I do." So I got my pistol and loaded it with good fresh shells and took off across the hill fer the camp. When I got to the camp I axed several people if they knowed the man and described him and finally one woman said, Yes, she knowed him, and told me what his name was. I axed her if she knowed where he was at and she said he was down at the lower end of the camp. So I started a-walkin' down that way.

After I walked maybe 200 yards I seed him a-comin' and I recognized him as soon as I laid eyes on him. I walked right up to him and he started right on by like he didn't know me so I stopped and I says, "Do you know me?" and he looked all shifty-eyed and said hit seemed like he remembered talking to me the day afore and I says, "Yes, by God, you talked to me yesterday and I remember very well what you said, too." I had my hand right on my gun all the time. He said, "Well, I was dronk. Doan-ah pay 'tention to what a man says when he's dronk," and he kind of smiled-like. But I was a-gittin' madder ever' minute a-thinkin' about what he had said to me so I jest drawed my pistol and let him have it.

Well, I was arrested and put in jail but I got out on bail, and after I was indicted and the case come on fer trial in the Circuit Court I told my story to the jury jest exactly like it happened and the jury couldn't agree because some of them wanted to turn me loose and some of them wanted to give me about ten years. Well, at the retrial in the next term of court the Commonwealth attorney got up and made a turrible speech agin me and told the jury hit wouldn't be safe to walk the roads as long as men like me was free, so I'll be damned if the jury didn't give me twenty-one years.

Well, sir, my lawyer come around to me when I was a-gittin' ready to go off to the penitentiar', and he says, "Don't you worry now, I'll take this up with the Guv'ner and see if we can't git you a pardon." So I went on to the penitentiar' and in about three months my lawyer went down to Frankfort to see the Guv'ner. He explained to him that I was out of a good family and that all my kinfolks had been fer him when he was a-runnin' fer Guv'ner and that we was all fer his man in the United States Senate race that was a-comin' up. And then he explained how the man I killed was jest a old Hunky that nobody didn't like anyway because he was so overbearin' and hateful to get along with. So the Guv'ner sot there a minute and thought it over and called in his clerk and wrote me out a full pardon, and I come on back home with my lawyer.

When I got back home and the Commonwealth attorney that had prosecuted me so hard found out that I was pardoned, it made him so God-damn mad he shore like to have died!

The double standards of the Prohibition era had a profound impact on the mind and character of the mountaineer. Realizing that he was being pilloried by society for manufacturing a product which that same society demanded and highly prized, he developed an abiding distrust of officials at all levels. He became deeply suspicious of the motives of government, both state and Federal, and cynical of its purposes in every field. The notion sank into his mind that the men who preside over our public affairs are dishonest and hypocritical; that they may be too powerful to checkmate in a contest of strength between government and citizens, so that a man is justified in beating them by any trick, guile or deception. The mountaineer developed the deep-seated conviction that he is governed not by just laws but by corrupt and venal men — men who would betray him when it was to their purpose and reward him when it was to their gain.

He was to carry this attitude unshaken into the Great Depression and into the humanitarian "Welfare state" which was to come with the New Deal. And by reason of it the mountaineer was to view government largesse in a light wholly different from that in which it was seen by millions of suffering Americans in other states.

CHAPTER THIRTEEN

The Great Depression

IN 1927, when spring came, the Big Bosses prepared for the seasonal flurry of coal orders generally referred to as "the lake trade." This business resulted from the increase in steel production when the melting ice on the Great Lakes made it possible for the ore boats to carry iron southward from the Mesabi Range. But in this fateful spring, the same season which saw the plateau hammered by the great flood, the operators were bewildered by a drastic falling-off of orders. As in past years, preparations had been made for the men to work extra hours and some of the mines had planned an extra shift for a few weeks, but the season for the lake trade came and only a trickle of orders reached the offices of the coal companies. The larger companies operating in the thick, high-quality seams of coal received the lion's share of the business and after a week or two of uncertainty began production at a rate approaching the normal level of previous years, but the smaller companies, producing from the inferior seams, found themselves short of orders. After their managers had sent a rash of futile telegrams and telephone calls to their coal brokers their operations began to lurch to a halt. A few of them were never to work again, but the greater number began to receive orders after a time and their tipples hummed once more.

But operations were never again at their old tempo. The high level of production which the fields had known with relatively brief interruptions for so long had ended. Beginning in the spring of 1927, the region's coal industry commenced to sag, sliding bit by bit into

the abyss of depression, blazing the road down which the entire nation was to roll in the mad autumn of 1929.

The rank and file of the miners had till now enjoyed at least the
illusion of prosperity. They had been "born poor," and their wages
were better than most of them had known before entering the mines.
But as the "Roaring Twenties" advanced there crept slowly into the
miner's mind a vague feeling that he was not receiving a fair share
of the industry's earnings. Watching the Big Bosses drive past in new
Packards and Cadillacs and being rarely able to afford even a sec
ondhand Model T for himself, he sensed that his slowly rising wages
were never high enough. Though the operators heartened him oc-
ocasionally with small new wage hikes, the notion persisted that the
increases were too infrequent and too little to allow him to share in
the good life which the National Administration constantly proclaimed. This hazy discontent was by no means crystallized. It was,
at most, an unease. But the same years had brought buoyant
confidence to Silk Stocking Row. Salaries, profits and hopes were
high and prospects for endless prosperity were taken for granted.

Labor was abundant. Innumerable hollows and creeks spawned
armies of new workmen, ever eager to fill the vacancies caused by
death, injury or discharge. The mechanical undercutting machine
and the electrically powered coal drill had become standard in virtually all mines. Electric mine locomotives had replaced most of the
ponies and mules on the underground trains. Nevertheless, the mining operation was still essentially manual. Low-wage workmen were
cheaper than machines, and applicants were available for every
working place, underground and topside.

But while optimism was still the order of the day, there were engineers and managers within the field who knew conditions were
changing and that the old pattern could not be indefinitely perpetuated. This was primarily because the main headings had been
pushed from the driftmouths far back into the mountains. In the
smaller camps the working places were a mile or a mile and a half
from the tipping scales, while in the larger ones the "main track
headings" had driven to the centers of the mountains and thence had
followed the ridges for distances of five, six, or even ten miles. These
lengthening underground distances imposed a growing burden on
the companies; the cost of transportation from working place to

tipple was growing steadily higher. This meant that the cost of coal must rise, or economies in operation must be effected, if the mines were to remain in competition with those farther north. One means by which such savings could be achieved lay in tearing down the tipples and moving them up the valleys closer to the working places, and then driving new shafts into the hillsides. But this would require considerable money. Some of the major companies, particularly the mammoth operations of Consolidation Coal Company at Jenkins, owned many tipples scattered here and there in strategic places. This one company operated fourteen such plants, and the task of relocating the tipples was an expensive one for any company, whether it turned out ten cars of coal a day or two hundred. To relocate and rebuild the tipples would necessitate a suspension of mining for weeks or months, and this the stockholders were little inclined to condone.

Since the companies had distributed their earnings in the form of huge executive salaries and fat dividends, they had neglected to accumulate any appreciable money reserves. Hence when the industry began to lurch crazily to a halt, they were nearly as poorly prepared for the new situation as were the miners. The miners and their wives were bewildered when the work whistles ceased to blow, but positive chagrin and consternation prevailed in the offices of the Big Bosses. There shock was mingled with a sense of betrayal. The managers had lived by the prevailing rules of business and most of them were indignant when disorders cropped up in the economic machine. The old friendship between the men and the bosses had continued with only a slight cooling over the years, and even when the wheels of industry began to slow and when the work week dwindled from five or six days to three and finally to one and, sometimes, to no days at all, for many weeks at a stretch, the feeling of mutuality of interests did not evaporate. At first each group deeply sympathized with the other. Trust and affection died with remarkable slowness, and only after they had been dealt many blows — blows impelled more often by desperation and a blind urge to survive than by malice or ill-will.

Depression had been deepening in the coalfields for two years before the stock market crisis of 1929. 1927 was a poor year and 1928 worse. In 1929 the situation was quite bad indeed. By that time the major companies were gobbling up the lion's share of the region's coal business and the smaller corporations were fighting for their lives.

The course of events since the first railroad spike was driven in the plateau had destined that this should be so. The railroad barons and coal kings who had opened the field had never visualized the colossal multiplication of mining companies which had occurred. They had financed the construction of the railroads for a relatively few large operations in the best seams. Scores of other would-be coal magnates had rushed into the field and had formed corporations of their own. These numerous companies of lesser magnitude had swelled the plateau's coal production far beyond all expectations, so that the railroad companies had sometimes been overwhelmed and unable to haul the coal away. The same process of multiplying coal operators had been under way to a lesser extent in other major coal-fields in the nation, so that the industry was vastly overexpanded. During the same interval the oil industry had grown to giant proportions and made huge inroads in the fuel market. A massive switch from coal to oil had occurred because of the latter's relative cleanliness. Ships, locomotives and countless factories now acquired fuel from refineries rather than tipples. Though coal still provided the bulk of the nation's energy needs, its tonnage output had grown far more rapidly than the country as a whole, and had outstripped its market. A surplus of coal had become available and this surplus had to go unsold. Since the Eastern Kentucky coalfield lay farther from the great industrial centers of Detroit and Pittsburgh than any of its competing fields, it was unavoidable that its coal should constitute the dispensable surplus. Consequently the stunning shock fell first on the scores of new mines in the Cumberland Plateau.

During much of the time since the inception of the coalfield, competition among the operators had been little more than nominal. Until a year or two after the First World War the demand was so great that each operator could sell his output to any one of several buyers. And after the postwar slump had given way to the big nationwide boom the demand had been again so continuous for the next five years that the operators were compelled to give little consideration to the nasty subject of competition. Rarely had they bid against

THE GREAT DEPRESSION · 169

each other for orders and usually when a rising business tempo increased the demand for coal it had been felt at all the pits almost simultaneously.

But as the spring of 1927 grew old and turned to summer the old pattern was not repeated. The greater corporations were still active, but at the other end of the ladder the latecomers who had established themselves in the thin, low-quality seams were without orders. The coal brokers offered little encouragement; and as the market dwindled more and more pits found themselves in the same plight.

Most of the newer corporations were in debt. They had borrowed from banks to make the investments in houses, commissaries, tipples and side tracks and, to use a coal-miner's expression, were "between a rock and a hard place." Impelled by the instinct of self-preservation, their Big Bosses telephoned and telegraphed customers of other operators, offering coal at reduced prices. They were often rewarded by having orders switched to their own billing clerks and the work whistles on their tipples sounded again.

Outraged by such treatment the companies so losing their orders retaliated by offering coal at still lower prices. Thus was set in motion a vicious price-cutting spiral which led ever downward until at last, in 1932, at some pits slack coal was offered for sale for the incredibly low price of ten cents a ton!

During the boom lump coal, those football-sized pieces so favored for domestic use in fireplaces, brought the best prices on the market and usually sold for approximately five dollars a ton. Egg-size coal was slightly cheaper and nut and slack ran considerably lower. Domestic and industrial stoker coal was not yet in substantial demand. The progressive price cuts in each category of the fuel were generally at the rate of three cents, five cents or ten cents per ton. But as the market glut worsened, the possibility of a price reversal vanished and the price sank down, down, down.

The operators absorbed the initial price cuts out of their profits, and executive salaries were not sacrosanct. In most organizations an honest effort was made to absorb the reductions by achieving greater efficiency, and by eliminating unessential personnel and wasteful overhead of all kinds. But even under the best of conditions and assuming a genuine desire to preserve the existing wage level, such efforts were inadequate. The technological progress within the industry did

HOMER BABBIDGE LIBRARY, STORRS, CT

not permit the replacement of men by more economical machines than were then in general vogue. If new price cuts were to be made to keep the company competitive in the sinking market, the Big Bosses must impose wage reductions. There was simply no other alternative. No feasible method existed for establishing a minimum price floor. Market conditions could reduce the price to the rock bottom and the miner must absorb most of the loss.

So the bulletin boards by the payroll windows blossomed with notices that, beginning with the forthcoming half, wages would be reduced by a given amount per day or per ton loaded. Such notices were accompanied by talks made by company executives to the assembled men, explaining to them the changing circumstances and that wage and price cuts could no longer be avoided.

There was no little grumbling on the commissary porches and on the man-cars as the men rode through the somber depths of the mines to their working places, but on the whole the initial wage cuts were accepted with remarkable composure. In the first place a majority of the miners were now well into middle age and had been in the mining communities so long that the camps and towns carried all the sentimental attachments of home. They were held to their jobs by inertia and a realization that they knew nothing except coal mining. As a Harlan County miner once said to me, "We had all got coaldust in our blood, and once a man gits coaldust in his blood he can't never do nothing else except mine coal." Some men left the smaller camps and sought employment in the big operations, particularly in the captive mines, but the MEN WANTED signs had been withdrawn and few jobs were to be found. So the wage cuts were accepted with the realization that the company was in distress and that miner and operator must sink or swim together.

A pitiless economic war was waged within the valleys, as the companies and their impoverished employees engaged in an ever more degrading cutthroat competition for the shrinking coal market. The miners' burden consisted not only of lower wages, but, as the years progressed and times grew harder, of increased hours underground. One company after another abandoned all pretense of paying its employees a flat daily wage and put them on a straight piecework basis. The men were permitted to spend as much time underground as they wanted and the work day stretched from eight hours to nine or ten and, ultimately, in many pits, to eleven or twelve. And all this increased effort at the coal face produced only more trouble, for the product swelled the glut and forced the prices still lower.

But the whole burden of the Depression did not consist of reduced earnings. It manifested itself also in mounting fatality and injury rates as the demoralized operators allowed their safety organizations to deteriorate. To lessen payrolls, safety foremen were discharged or reduced to the status of miners. The all-important mining engineers were reduced in number, and those remaining were kept underground for shorter periods of time. The already shockingly high casualty rates soared anew and the dead and maimed were borne daily from pits somewhere in the plateau.

The companies sought also to economize in the maintenance of their towns. It was recognized that "paint don't mine no coal," and the painters and maintenance crews visited the houses less frequently in some camps and ceased coming altogether in others. Within a few years the paint, always hard beset by sulphur fumes from the burning waste heaps, began to peel and blister.

In widening ripples economic ruin spread outward from the mines to the rural areas surrounding them. The orders for jack props and collar-poles were curtailed and the prices paid for them dropped precipitously. Here again was an area in which the operators could economize at the expense of their wholly dependent suppliers, and as the process of underbidding speeded up, the bottom dropped out of the timber market. The prop cutters were so numerous and had depended for so many years upon their work that they, too, were sucked into cutthroat competitive underbidding. By 1932 many men engaged in this hard and dangerous work were netting no more than fifty or seventy-five cents a day. Nor were these workdays frequent, since the lessened mine production and lowered safety standards demanded far fewer timbers.

In growing numbers camps suspended operation altogether. Orders for their coal simply ceased to come at all. The tipples rusted and rotted until at last receivers for the bankrupt companies dismantled them and sold the machinery for scrap iron. At some mines the receivers managed to withdraw from the tunnels the miles of

steel track for similar sale, but in others as the props rotted without
replacement huge roof falls trapped machinery, tracks and other
impedimenta of the industry which now lie buried beneath the
weight of mountains.

Bankruptcy became the rule across the plateau. One by one the
companies were liquidated, their puzzled and resentful stockholders
realizing little or nothing in the process. The miners who remained
behind in the towns could pay no rent and the houses fell into ruinous decay.

But not all bankrupt companies suspended operations. Court-
appointed receivers conducted the affairs of some of them with more
success than had been displayed by the operators themselves. Others
were reorganized and merged with neighboring companies in the
same valley. Sometimes a distant financier bought an entire company, to be held as an investment in anticipation of a revival of the
industry.

The National Government made half-hearted gestures toward providing relief for the stricken industry and people, but in the dead-
lock between a selfish Democratic Congress and an unimaginative
and ineffectual Republican President, nothing of consequence
emerged and by 1931 scores of coal operators had lost hope for their
operations.

Amid the welter of collapsing corporations the banks of the plateau
commenced to fold. When prosperity was rampant banking institutions had sprung up in profusion. Some counties had a half-dozen or
more, though only rarely did one accumulate total deposits in excess of a million dollars. The deposits came primarily from the small
savings of miners and the rural moonshiner-farmers, bolstered by deposits from the coal corporations and their officials. The merchants
in the small towns and along the creeks had placed their savings and
operating funds in these tiny banks. Doctors, merchants, lawyers,
farmers and coal operators held stock in them and served on their
boards of directors.

The principal business of these minuscule lending institutions had
consisted of financing the expanding and multiplying mining companies. As new camps were built money was lent to pay for the
houses, tipples, power plants, mining machines and power transmis-

sion lines. The loans were secured by mortgages on the mining properties and by the "accommodation endorsements" of company executives. Such investments had been made at a time of advancing
prices and the costs were immensely inflated. Such money reserves
as most small mining companies possessed were on deposit in these
local banks.

In a few instances the banks were virtually "company owned," like
the commissaries and motion picture theaters. Organized under the
loose provisions of state law, they were brought into being by groups
of company officials. Such a banking corporation rented a building
from the coal company and solicited deposits from all company executives and employees, and from the public generally. The stockholders could then organize a mining company and finance it with
loans from their own bank. The Big Bosses were thus enabled, in
these instances, to found and vastly multiply coal operations with the
funds of their trusting employees, and in this laissez-faire age and
state such operations were legal. For protection of depositors the
law made each stockholder liable to the bank for twice the par value
of his stock, but this would prove to be of little effect in those numerous situations where both banks and bankers were left penniless.

So in their own death spasms the coal corporations brought down
the banks. In rapid succession the institutions closed their doors.
When the new President, Franklin D. Roosevelt, proclaimed the National Bank Holiday in 1933, only three banks were operating in all
the plateau.

These bank failures carried away the savings of practically the entire population. On the Main Streets in the independent towns
and county seats and along rutted, winding creek roads, stores closed
their doors, and actions by wholesalers against the merchants multiplied in the Circuit Courts.

The vicious financial disaster had swept away the jerry-built economic structure of the whole plateau. Without orders and income
the coal companies could not pay the banks. Without wages the
miner could not buy merchandise. Without customers the stores could
not pay the wholesalers or the banks from whom they had borrowed.
The prop cutters could find no money with which to repay loans
from the banks, or even wages due their hired helpers. The money
supply dried up with magical speed. The companies for all practi-

cal purposes ceased to pay-wages in currency and the scrip disks became practically the only medium of exchange in many counties.
When a bank or other creditor brought a lawsuit to foreclose a
mortgage the effort was largely worthless. Installations which had
cost hundreds of thousands of dollars were sold by the sheriffs at
public auctions for a few thousands and sometimes no bidders were
found at all.

So with a ponderous sigh the Big Boom died. In a few short years
the coal-rich plateau had traveled from rags to riches, and back to
rags again.

The Great Depression is a nightmare in the memory of most
wage-earning Americans who carried the responsibility for supporting a household in those grim years. For all but the very wealthiest,
it was a time of hardship. For millions it was an era of hunger, cold,
indignity and, most searing of all, a feeling of deepening uselessness.
But, whatever its effects on Americans generally, the Great Depression was nowhere more appalling then in the coal counties of the
Cumberlands. There destitution came first and stayed longest. There,
for most, destitution still persists.

People who have never lived in mining communities cannot comprehend the feeling of captivity and helplessness which lay so heavy
in the coal camps through these years. In times of prosperity the
miner had been little better than a serf in his master's mine, and the
Depression was far advanced before union membership and the
apparent sympathy of a great national administration brought relief
to a situation which had become, by then, highly explosive.

We have seen that the miner was only a licensee of the company
in the occupancy of his camp house. He had always spent at least
three quarters of his pay in the company stores. He and his family
found recreation in the company-owned movie theaters and when he
managed to finance a secondhand automobile he bought tires and
gasoline for it at the company-owned service station. His children
were delivered by company doctors and if the birth occurred in a
hospital, the hospital was company-owned. If he was one of the relatively few miners who attended church services, he was likely to do
so in a building which the company had thoughtfully provided for

the congregation in return for a monthly rent. His school-age children climbed a muddy path up a rock-strewn bank to a company-owned schoolhouse. And, in many instances, when death came from a slate fall or explosion his mortal remains were laid to rest by a company undertaker in a plot of company-owned land. This paternalistic system had instilled a sense of dependency and a feeling of inadequacy which probably have never been surpassed anywhere else in our free society.

This system had given the coal corporations many years of the miners' arduous labor at low wages and under circumstances which had enabled the stockholders to recapture their investments very quickly. It had worked to the enrichment of the companies during years of prosperity; but it now served as a millstone about their necks in the lean Depression years.

The Big Bosses were confronted with a dilemma. In each office building the question was debated: Should the company discharge its miners and disclaim all further responsibility for their welfare? By so doing the company could rid itself of an incessant drain in the commissaries where the men accumulated ever-mounting debts for groceries and other necessities. On the other hand, if they were severed from the company and permitted to wander away the labor organization upon which coal production was dependent would be destroyed and a major effort would be required to recruit enough men to open the mine in the event of a brightening business picture. The managers had been able to winnow out their employees during the preceding years and to acquire relatively stable and dependable work crews. Much experience had been required to accomplish this, and the Big Bosses dreaded the task of going into the labor market and attempting to assemble other such crews.

Too, the long years of prosperity died hard with them. Optimism for the future withered slowly and hopes persisted, even into bankruptcy, that a business upturn would send envelopes full of coal orders to their desks. Such optimism is a very human and commendable trait and, without it, it is scarcely likely that man would have left the caves to take up the trail toward civilization. It is not surprising that this hope continued to linger in the hearts of the hard-pressed operators.

So the company officials almost invariably gambled that business would improve within the near future, and even when coal orders reached the vanishing point the men were kept on the payroll. Their small earnings were quickly consumed by grocery, light, water, coal and rent bills and even then were rarely enough to enable the miner and his family to survive. More groceries and clothing had to be bought than could be paid for with the wages for an occasional day of digging at the coal face, so the company advanced small sums of credit to its employees. These pittances added one to another until, at the end of a year or two, the miner owed his employer several hundred dollars. This the sinking company could ill afford, and some corporations which otherwise could have remained solvent were forced into bankruptcy by mounting bills owed to wholesale houses.

The swarms of miners whose cheap labor and strong backs had powered the Big Boom simply ate the companies into bankruptcy during the Great Depression.

As months and years dragged by without the long-anticipated business upswing, the companies which managed to survive gradually changed their attitude toward their legions of idle workmen. By scarcely discernible degrees they came to regard the miners in much the same manner one views an unwanted guest who lingers under the family roof long after the WELCOME mat has been withdrawn. The man who came to the payroll window to inquire whether any work was in sight or who shuffled to the scrip window to request a dollar or so in "flickers" ceased to be seen as a valuable part of the company's organization. He became a sort of enemy within the gates who had somehow helped to cause the company's distress and who was now adding to its burdens. This attitude could not be long concealed and the operators gradually cut themselves off from their employees. A deepening void spread between the two groups, and resentment against the burdensome workmen replaced the old friendship of many years. The coal digger detected the change of attitude and was deeply distressed and offended by it. His loss of status in the eyes of the most important men he knew brought him shame and degradation. He knew that he was blamed, subconsciously at least, for the whole region's misfortune — a misfortune he had not brought about and could in no way mend. In long days of idleness when his mind had little else to reflect upon, he brooded over his loss of dignity and importance in the eyes of the Big Bosses whose approval he had once enjoyed. And he developed a counter-resentment. He began to feel a hostility toward his old bosses and toward the company as he pondered the facts: the company had brought him into its camp, had worked him hard for a good many years without substantial advantage to himself, and now spurned him when it could no longer use him. The Great Depression pushed boss and miner apart and created an enduring enmity between them.

The enmity persisted through the Depression, deepening during the union-membership drives in the 1930s and hardening still further during the bitter struggle for decent wages of the war and postwar years.

So low were his wages that the miner could not survive on the earnings of an eight-hour shift and was compelled to "double back" and put in an extra half or full shift. He knew from experience what it meant to spend sixteen hours at a stretch underground. Even such a prodigious workday was unlikely to net him more than two dollars. When he sat down under a creaking propped-up mountain to eat his cold lunch, his dinner pail contained an incredible assortment of miserable food. Sometimes he directed his wife to peel the few potatoes the house afforded, reserving the vegetables for herself and the children with the peels being washed and fried for his own nourishment. Sometimes he carried only sandwiches of bread or biscuits smeared with white lard. And when his day's work ended he emerged from the dark mine into the darkness of another night.

The terrible suffering in the coalfield provokes the query why the miner did not leave the camps and seek a better life in other parts of America. It will be supposed that circumstances could hardly have been worse for him elsewhere, while the possibility of improvement was always present. This question is an important one and deserves consideration.

The indigenous mountaineer coal miner was so deeply rooted to the country that he felt a powerful attachment to the familiar hills, valleys and institutions surrounding him. This in itself was a powerful factor inducing him to remain where he was.

Most of the white and Negro miners from other Southern states had come from worn-out farms. They remembered land so exhausted it would scarcely sprout cotton seeds without generous applications of guano. Most of their fathers were indigent sharecroppers who could recall decades of grinding poverty. To leave the coal camps and return to such environment offered little prospect for improvement and might be only a jump from the frying pan into the fire. But any inclination to leave the plateau for employment in the big cities was soon dispelled by the appearance of small swarms of work-hunting men from those parts of the nation. These newcomers came from every area in the United States from which the inhabitants of the camps had derived. Some were Southern Negroes and some were Southern white men, starved out by a decade of falling cotton prices. Some were unemployed factory hands from Northern and Eastern cities, and, of course, there were the ever-present job-seekers from the backcountry areas of the plateau. All were on the road seeking work of any kind.

Few of the miners were literate enough to maintain much of a correspondence with the "folks back home," but during the Big Boom the camp-dwellers had written glowing letters to kinsmen and friends describing the spectacular developments in the coalfield. Some of these relatives and friends had visited in the camps. When the numbing paralysis clutched the country after the 1929 stock market collapse, these things were recalled and a multitude of would-be miners poured into the coal counties.

As coal trains clattered along with strings of empty cars toward the upriver tipples, groups of ragged men clung to the rods under the cars or sat slumped inside the gondolas. These hopefuls besieged the company offices and then, disappointed, climbed aboard the next coal drag to be hauled out. The railroad companies abandoned all pretense of combating these free riders, and eventually attached an empty box car to each train for their convenience. Its floor was covered with straw and its doors were left open so the cold and hungry men could at least ride with minimum danger to their lives. These penniless job-seekers brought tales of woe from the very places the discouraged coal miners were considering moving into, and convinced the miner his prospects were as good in the familiar here as they were likely to be in the unfamiliar there.

Nevertheless, it would be erroneous to suppose there was no significant out-migration during these years. A substantial number of the more aggressive and better-educated sort managed to move away. Their lives were grim and hard as they built W. P. A. roads and drew Relief rations in Michigan, Indiana and Ohio, but many of them stuck it out and never returned to the coalfields. The most important part of the exodus, however, lay in the departure of the foreign-born. A surprisingly high percentage of the Italians, Hungarians, Poles, Serbs and Russians whose outlandish tongues had once so startled the camps had relatives who had accompanied them to the United States but had settled in the bigger population centers, principally New York. In mounting numbers the foreign-born coal miners forsook the plateau and took their families aboard trains, headed for their kinsmen in the cities. Rarely did one of them return. At least three quarters of the "foreigners" gave up coal mining and today they are found in sizable numbers in only a few plateau communities.

Among the rural population outside the camps, the collapse of the coal industry spread consternation almost as deep as that experienced by the miners and the Big Bosses. These communities had become inextricably tied to the camps. The old practice of living on home-grown corn and pork had been irrevocably shattered by a shift to a cash economy. The rural mountaineer still kept a milk cow and a drove of hogs, and annually he planted a "patch" of corn, but his dependence upon them was fast decreasing. He had come to rely heavily upon the dollars the industrial communities poured into his pockets and when the dollars ceased to come he experienced very real hardship. This loss frequently meant he could not buy sugar and coffee for his table or shoes and clothing for his children. It necessitated a drastically lower standard of living and reversion to the subsistence-type agriculture of his fathers.

And this is precisely what he attempted to do. With corn and hogs and a few other barnyard animals and fowls the creek farmer could keep body and soul together, and a majority of Americans were doing little more during these same years. His greatest difficulty lay in the fact that his land had not recovered from the ravages of the Big Flood. The cornfields that had been stripped of their topsoil on that memorable night were now expanses of brown broom sage.

This tenacious grass could nourish cattle passably well in the spring when its shoots were young and tender, but as the season advanced it toughened and became inedible. And the barren, acid land would support nothing else. No matter how long it lay fallow the fertility did not return, and today, more than three decades after they were damaged, thousands of acres of sage-covered hillsides can be seen throughout the plateau.

The burdens of the creek farmer were increased by his brothers and cousins who, having moved into the camps during the prosperous years, now sought to return to the ancestral farm, bringing wives and children with them. Because of the deaths of landowning parents many farms were now held jointly by brothers and sisters who had inherited in equal shares, and the miner who held such a divided interest in a mountain farm was tempted to forsake the hungry camps for the slightly less certain prospect of hunger on an eroded farm. When he did forsake the camp, and he did in countless instances, each household had to "get by" on fewer acres and, in most instances, on acres that had long since ceased to be really productive.

So again the mountaineer attacked his dwindling forests to clear new grounds for cornfields and cattle pastures. Though County Agricultural Agents had begun to labor among them in the middle Twenties, the poor land farmers were still essentially the unskilled tillers of the soil that their forefathers had been. The young men from the agricultural colleges worked hard, but acceptance of their ideas came slowly and on a small scale. The conservatism and traditionalism of the mountaineers were little weakened by two decades of association with the world to which the railroads had bound them. When a farm agent pleaded with a farmer to spread crushed limestone on his land and to abandon hillside corn raising in favor of grass and clover fields, his words usually fell on deaf ears. The farm agent then pointed out that the worn hillsides were now scarcely able to produce more than twelve to sixteen bushels of corn to the acre. If the same land received a heavy application of crushed limestone and a proper seeding with lespedeza it could support numerous cattle without further soil wastage. He argued that it was better to sow the grass and let the cow do the leisurely work of gathering it and converting it to milk than for the farmer to toil prodigiously to plant, cultivate and harvest a crop of corn which was rarely more than adequate to feed the plow mule through the winter. Logical though his entreaties were, they were largely rejected by the older farmers.

The attitude of the mountain farmer toward the college-trained agricultural teacher was pretty well summed up by an exchange which occurred between agent and farmer on a creek in Johnson County. The farm agent had argued eloquently for a change in method and the farmer had listened with mounting skepticism. To him his youthful visitor was a boy whose college education had not allowed much time for practical experience. Finally he concluded: "I don't see how you know so much about farming. After. all, I've wore out two good farms on this creek since you was borned and I bet you ain't even wore out one yit!"

The agricultural reformers were doomed to frustration and despair. For approximately sixteen years in most counties — from 1925 to 1941 — the agents worked zealously to break the old and ruinous pattern of land use and abuse. Stony silence and contempt were often their reward. Sometimes they were openly ridiculed and and at least one was beaten by a farmer who "already knowed how to farm." But by slow degrees a change of attitude began to assert itself. Some farmers bought purebred swine to replace the inefficient frontier razorbacks, and the nondescript brindle cow gave way in a few stalls to purebred Jerseys and Holsteins. Hillsides began to turn green with clover and vetch, and fields of soybeans and alfalfa made their appearance. By 1941 progress was apparent; County Agricultural Agents were optimistically foreseeing huge improvements in the plateau's standard of living. However, the progress came too late. The seed of reform had sprouted but it was not to flower. After Pearl Harbor the coal industry revived and mounted another gigantic boom which, as we shall see, took a wholly unexpected turn and diverted the mountaineer from farming to mining again.

So despite the zeal of the "college farmers" agriculture continued generally in the old pattern. New crop lands were constantly cleared and in the spring burning brush piles remained a symbol of the plateau. Most of the flood-washed lands had been abandoned and the farmers cleared and planted new acres as though nothing had ever happened.

The Depression had largely stifled the sawmilling industry and stacks of lumber remained unsold in every yard. The smaller trees were no longer needed in such great numbers by the coal companies, and much undergrowth was simply burned. Too, by this time practically all the timber lands had been cut over at least once and the best trees removed, leaving only inferior timber. While W. M. Ritter Lumber Company and Fordson Coal Company still held large tracts of virgin timber, few such primal trees survived elsewhere. The new-ground fields which the Depression farmers cleared for planting lay largely in cut-over tracts.

The process of clearing new croplands received two important boosts from other quarters in these hard years. The first of these was the great blight which destroyed the American chestnut trees in 1929 and 1930.

The chestnut sometimes reached a diameter in excess of four feet but its lumber had never been valuable. The lumber was decay-resistant and easily worked, but it was extremely coarse-grained and would split under slight pressure. As a consequence the chestnut trees comprised a very large part of the remaining timber. Their huge and abundant nuts were beloved by men and beasts, and had provided the bulk of the mast which had supported the highlander's hogs for so many generations. They were sweet, succulent and highly nutritious and as long as the chestnut survived the hunter could always kill a kettleful of gray or red squirrels. But in the summer of 1929 this noble plant fell prey to a deadly disease. A fungus blight spread inland from the Atlantic Coast, ruthlessly killing every chestnut tree and seedling. From ridge to ridge the brown death spread with incredible speed. The wind-borne spores sought out each spur and point, each creek and hollow, and no survivors were left alive. Forest giants centuries old turned brown and dry as if live steam had been applied to their roots and foliage. At least 17 per cent of the trees in the plateau died in those two years. The dry dead trees crashed down easily beneath the onslaught of saw and ax, and the ashes from the burning trunks assured at least one good crop year.

Another assist to the land clearing came from repeal of the Eighteenth Amendment and the Volstead Acts. The reopened distilleries were an industry whose affairs ran counter to the general downward trend. The long drought had to be overcome and the distilleries sought to relieve its pangs. The millions of gallons of new whiskey had to be stored in charred whiteoak barrels. Buyers for Seagram, Schenley and other rejuvenated whiskey manufacturers took rooms in the local hotels and scoured the countryside looking for good whiteoak trees. Mill operators with contracts from the distilleries established themselves at strategic points and large-scale manufacture of barrel staves got under way. In most of the plateau the timber companies had already removed the trees which bore their brands, and in such areas the mountaineers were able to sell their whiteoaks for desperately needed dollars. Untold thousands of superb trees were cut for this purpose. By the middle Thirties countless thousands of new acres had had the timber "skelped" off them and were growing corn.

Federal relief programs began to operate in the stricken counties during the latter part of the Hoover Administration, but soon after Roosevelt's inauguration they multiplied and expanded. Thousands of miners and farmers lined up before the "giveaway offices" to get free bags of potatoes, meat, flour, lard and other staples, and half the children in the plateau wore the shapeless gray cotton Relief sweaters to school. Just as they had given silent Calvin Coolidge credit for the glorious prosperity of other years, they poured out the vials of their wrath on Herbert Clark Hoover when the economic tide turned against them. To the miners certainly, and to the creek farmers to an almost equal degree, there was no ground for doubt that the Depression had been induced by the evil machinations of this one man. None of them could make it quite clear what Mr. Hoover expected to gain by bringing this singular tragedy down upon the millions of Americans who had honored him with their votes, but it was accepted as a verity that he had planned and executed these hard times for the benefit of the rich. Shortly after the famous First Hundred Days of the New Deal a group of miners in one camp disposed of the arch villain in what they deemed a fitting manner. Over one of the freshly filled honey-holes they set a wooden slab on which was printed Mr. Hoover's epitaph:

HERE LIES HOOVER,
DAMN HIS SOUL,
BURIED IN A HONEY-HOLE.
LET HIM LAY HERE TILL THE END,

POOR MAN'S ENEMY,
RICH MAN'S FRIEND.

During the first administration of Roosevelt the multiplying Fed eral agencies put thousands of mountaineers on their payrolls. Enor. mous gangs of men used wheelbarrows, picks, shovels and hand drills to carve out miles of W. P. A. roads. In the Civilian Conservation Corps hundreds of teen-age boys built observation towers for forest fire detection and pounded out other miles of rural roads. Under the auspices of the Public Works Administration imported contractors constructed consolidated schools and added wings to county court- houses. Hundreds of boys and girls were paid small sums by the National Youth Administration that they might continue in school until a high school diploma was earned. The free school lunch made its appearance and women whose own families were a single short jump ahead of starvation cooked hot food for school children who sometimes had little other nourishment.

So severe and abject was the region's poverty that three quarters of its inhabitants could lay claim to Federal assistance in one form or another.

The first objective of the new administration was to get enough food and clothing to the people to prevent further deterioration from cold and hunger. This was no small undertaking in itself. Though a surplus of food was one of the government's major prob- lems there was certainly no such surplus on the tables of the plateau dwellers. The idled mines and the failing, antiquated agriculture had brought half the people to malnutrition. Some of them simply had no food at all for days at a time and starving beggars made daily rounds in the county seats and towns abjectly imploring food. In more than one camp hungry miners went en masse to the commis- saries and forcibly carried off large bags of food, determined to give their families at least one decent meal before they all starved to death.

Bags of dried rice, dried beans, meal and flour and slabs of salt pork were the foods the agencies distributed most frequently. These foods the mountaineers could appreciate and relish but the results were sometimes comical when the relief trains brought foods with which they were not familiar. In a laudable effort to provide a measure of Vitamin C to the recipients and, at the same time, to bolster the citrus growers, the government distributed huge quantities of grapefruit. While some of the miners may have gotten acquainted with them in the commissaries, this fruit was totally unknown to most of the rural population. However, they were eagerly carried away in the supposition that they would taste like oranges. The mountaineers were astounded by their sourness and did not know how to eat them. Stories were widespread of the strange cookery in which they played a part. Some women squeezed out the juice and made "lemonade" with it. Others attempted to make the puzzling fruit edible by boiling it, and it is even related that some of the baffled women scooped out the pulp and fried it. Since the greater part of the mountaineer's food was fried in pork grease, this final resort is not improbable. But whatever he did to grapefruit the mountaineer was rarely able to make it fit his palate and the relief offices soon encountered much difficulty in distributing this nutritious food among the hungry people.

Boxes of processed cheese, canned milk, cartons of butter and tall cans of citrus juices were also distributed in trainload lots among the starving populace. Long lines queued up daily to carry away the doles of foodstuffs.

Here begins one of the most significant factors in the wholesale demoralization of the mountaineers. In most of the nation the dole was an emergency lifesaver until a job could be obtained and a relief job was seen as a temporary expedient good only until a respectable position could be found. But in the plateau the dole continued — as necessity dictated — for more than a decade. It continued so long it became a standard ingredient of life, and a generation grew up with it as their constant helpmeet and companion. To stand in the "giveaway lines" ceased to be shameful or irritating; it became merely the regular procedure for acquiring food and clothing. To a population becoming increasingly cynical in the rapacious clutches of the coal barons and their political hirelings in great and small offices, the relief offices afforded an opportunity to reacquire a portion of the livelihood which they sensed had somehow been wrongfully stripped from them by corrupt men and unjust laws. Nor was the dole ever dispensed with fully. When the distribution of free food and clothing was discontinued the issuing of numerous types of welfare checks supplanted it, and the scramble for relief as a matter of "right" went on with ever-increasing guile and determination. We shall see that this shameless struggle for "assistance" took many novel twists and turns after the official demise of the Great Depression, but in the Kentucky mountains it never really lessened.

The first symptoms of spreading demoralization appeared in physical rather than human terms. Whatever his other shortcomings, the rural mountaineer was traditionally clean in his personal habits. From early times the women kept their crude abodes swept, and disorder and "nastiness" had always been signs of "sorriness," the mountaineer's term for shiftlessness. There had been very little opportunity for trash to accumulate about his house. The relatively few cans and bottles which he acquired could be disposed of without too much of a problem or put to handy use about his house or barn. In the camps, on the other hand, the people had "lived out of paper bags" since the inception of the coal industry and in towns and cities everywhere the disposal of trash and garbage presented a major problem. During the Big Boom the coal companies employed wagoners to haul this waste away to a remote out-of-sight dumping ground where it was eventually covered with slate or dirt. But in their depression-born economy drives all the companies except the largest and most stable dispensed with this service and left to each family the task of rubbish disposal. One would suppose that men with little else to do would have carried the waste to the dump, and for a while this occurred. But as idleness continued and as pride and self-respect drained away, family dumps were established in back yards or on nearby creek banks. Heaps of ugly refuse began to dot the coal camps, stinking, breeding swarms of flies and nourishing whole armies of rats.

Throughout the countryside on the creek and hollow farms the same process was under way. For the first time in their history most of what the people consumed was being carried home in paper, glass and tin containers, and the problem of getting rid of them was becoming serious. Sometimes the boxes were piled up at a convenient place near the house and heaps of discarded containers blossomed out everywhere. Increasingly miner and farmer alike turned to the creeks and streams and disposed of trash and garbage by dumping them in these waterways.

The embryonic public health departments were unprepared to cope with this vast, adverse new development. The tiny staffs were scarcely able to immunize the hordes of schoolchildren whose health was entrusted to their care. They could warn of the danger and urge corrective measures but were powerless to do more. As usual, the state government was little aware of developments in these far-off hollows. The county governments were without funds to finance trash gathering systems and so thoroughly laissez-faire was their philosophy that it doubtless never occurred to most of their petty officials that compulsory sanitary disposal was even desirable. Amid ever-deepening disorder and social decay a huge, overgrown and ill-disciplined population was permitted to fall, wholly without interference, into the habit of making their silt-choked streams into frightful open sewers and dumps. The custom of getting rid of undesirable and useless things by "throwing them into the creek" was allowed to develop all the force and acceptance of a folk custom.

Thus pride commenced to die in the mining communities when the first camp wife discovered she could not work hard enough to keep up with the dust, grime, grit and smells coal mining fostered. It ebbed away little by little for many years. Its grave was marked by cairns of discarded trash.

When men and women became willing to live amid ever-mounting piles of debris without seriously attempting to rid themselves of it, their morale was already undermined; and, barring some accident, their path could lead only downward.

CHAPTER FOURTEEN

The Union Drives

THE DETERIORATION of the friendship between the Big Bosses and the miners was many-faceted. It was everywhere evidenced by an increasing harshness on the part of the bosses and by growing sullenness in the men.

Many, indeed a majority, of the original operators who are remembered so kindly by aged miners left the coalfield in the early Depression years. They had presided over the founding of the companies and the building of the camps. They read the handwriting on the wall and understood that the industry was so sick it was unlikely to recover in time to save the companies. They so informed the stockholders, then gathered up their families and left.

But rarely could the shareholders bring themselves to part so easily with their investments. They reorganized the companies and sent new executives into the field or raised lower echelon officials to the top positions. Such men came into the managerial offices with an impassioned determination to save their companies from ruin.

We have already seen the difficulties which beset these "New Bosses." In a coal market in which competition grew steadily more vicious at the expense of its pauperized laborers, the new managers could find no new solutions. They could only apply the old screws even more ruthlessly, demanding ever higher output for diminishing wages. In the mounting coal glut no amount of willingness to toil could suffice. The exertions eventually demanded of the men were so great that heart and hand could not perform them.

The New Bosses can, perhaps, be excused for a part of their misdeeds on the ground of desperation. They were indeed desperate, and charity will sometimes forgive drowning men for clutching at straws, even when those straws happen to be fellow beings in even deeper distress.

In the deteriorating situation the New Bosses were seldom tactful. An old mine worker, still angry thirty years after the event, once related to me the reaction of his boss when the miner informed him that he wanted to miss work the following day to attend his neighbor's funeral. With an oath the superintendent declared, "Well, if you think more of funerals than you do of your job, take your damn tools out of the mine and don't come back. You know there's a half-dozen men waiting for every job we've got, and if you won't work I'll get somebody who will!" It might be supposed that this is an extreme example which demonstrates nothing except the ill-temper and bad judgment of a single man. But this is not so. To the contrary, it is illustrative of an attitude which came to govern the officials in a great many of the camps during these tragic years.

Throughout the coalfield one may find thousands of miners who indignantly remember similar treatment. In places where the unprofitable stone or slate middleman in the seam made the extraction of coal practically impossible, the New Bosses gruffly demanded that the cut of coal together with the gob be removed in a single day. The only alternative offered the men was that they bring out their tools and make way for others willing to attempt even the impossible. Not infrequently did a miner spend twelve hours under the hill loading rock and slate without pay so that on the following day he could bring out a few cars of coal. And all too often twelve hours of such labor failed to produce more than the few cents necessary to buy even a small bag of white flour. Not even the goad of desperation could long maintain order under such circumstances.

But pressure was not brought to bear on the men at the coal face alone. Some miners lived outside the camps, where they could keep a milk cow, a pig and a few chickens. Where company-owned houses were available the New Bosses demanded that such a miner occupy one of them or at least pay the rent on it. Sometimes a coal digger found it to his advantage to continue to reside on the farm and pay the monthly house rent notwithstanding. The house rented perforce to a nonresident miner was not always allowed to remain empty, but if an occupant could be found, was let by the boss to another family, thus realizing a double rent. The New Bosses justified this on the ground that the company was "putting meat and bread on the miner's table" and was entitled to his aid in supporting its housing and other investments. Miners deeply resented the wringing of these hardwon dollars from their fingers for shelter they could not afford to utilize.

The New Bosses took note of the number of people in each miner's household and observed the size of his monthly store account. If he fell into the habit of economizing at the commissary and drawing a few dollars in money to spend at a chain store or others outside the camp he courted the danger of immediate discharge. He was likely to be informed brusquely that if he could not afford to spend all his earnings in the company store the company could not afford to employ him. And woe to the miner who was suspected of buying a tire or gasoline at any place except the company service station!

Commissary prices had always been higher than those charged by merchants in the county seats and independent towns, but the New Bosses now lifted them to stratospheric levels. While wages shriveled, prices soared; and in cold and helpless fury the captive customers commenced referring to the company stores as "robbissaries." White bread could be bought for five cents a loaf at an A & P store, but the robbissaries exacted a dime for the same loaf. Salt bacon, the staple of diet which store managers sometimes jokingly called "Cincinnati chicken," sold for seven cents a pound in the chain stores and fifteen cents a pound in the commissaries. Coffee, milk, canned fruit and vegetables, clothing, carbide and all other merchandise stocked for the "convenience" of the miner were similarly priced at levels approximately twice as high as those charged in the neighboring towns. Aggravating the resentment stirred by the unconscionable price gouging was the widespread knowledge that the managers were allowed to purchase the same wares at prices little if any above their wholesale cost.

The New Bosses discovered still more clever ways of making dollars for their companies. A system which became quite widespread was the company raffle. Immediately after each payday, a company perpetrating this fraud would buy a cheap secondhand car and park it in front of the commissary. Each miner was strongly pressured to buy for a dollar a "chance" on this ancient vehicle. If the company employed 600 men the $600 so raised would pay for the automobile with $400 or $500 left over. On payday morning a number was drawn from a hat and the lucky miner drove off in his rattling "junker."

Not all the company managers were so inhumane and not all were goaded so sharply by economic pressures. In a few camps where an especially high grade of coal continued to be sought after for its by-products or its metallurgical properties, wages remained at least bearable and the old bosses remained in the camps. Even there much of the old comradeship died, but the hatreds experienced in the less fortunate camps did not materialize.

Almost without exception the companies became rabidly fearful the union organizers would return. Having ridden a downward spiral of wages and prices to a rock bottom, they failed to see that a stabilization of wages could offer some hope to the miner while preventing further disastrous price cuts at the expense of starving families. They knew only that they had remained competitive by progressive wage cuts and each of the New Bosses anticipated that unionism and enforced wage hikes would destroy the company's ability to compete, guaranteeing utter bankruptcy and the loss of everything.

Thus, even before the union organizers began to reappear, they assumed a place in the imagination of the New Boss fully as sinister as Satan's. In his mind trade-unionism was synonymous with anarchy, Bolshevism, national and international revolution, the end of private property — with every nameless evil.

In the early days of the New Deal the National Industrial Recovery Act brought some measure of hope to both miners and operators, and for a time the specter of unionism was held at bay. Under the "fair codes" promulgated by the Federal Government the operators agreed to pay an improved wage and a higher price for mining timbers and other supplies. They were tempted to do so by similar pledges of higher prices from their coal customers. By this system of fair codes the New Deal brain trusters sought to end the deathly deflation and inspire a revival of business. The experiment was greeted with unqualified enthusiasm by the miners, and most of the operators entered into the scheme with equal hopefulness. The codes offered hope at a time when no hope was to be seen in any other quarter, and whatever their effects may have been in other sections of the nation, an improvement in the economy of the coalfield began to occur. Prices and wages commenced a slow ascent and the number of workdays increased. A surge of confidence and buoyancy became apparent in the pits and company offices. The darkness of despair descended upon the region when the Supreme Court shattered the Recovery Program by declaring the Congressional act unconstitutional. By the mandate of the court, the fair codes were dissolved and prices and wages plummeted to the old subterranean levels. In the gloom that followed the apparition of trade-unionism was replaced by the appearance of the genuine article. Organizers for the United Mine Workers of America entered the field under the determined direction of a battle-hardened warrior, John L. Lewis.

Few of the miners had had any real experience with the union movement. Drawn as they were from rural antecedents, they had been traditionally almost as conservative as the operators themselves. Any movement toward collective bargaining had been viewed as an infringement on the right of the individual to work for such employer, and at such wage, as the workman might choose. In the union membership drives of the early 1920s, most miners had spurned the entreaties of the "field workers."

But in the intervening years their outlook had changed radically. They were now willing to listen to any man who offered a possible solution for their problems. No longer were the advocates of unionism disdained. To the contrary, when rumor spread the word that a representative of the union was in the vicinity miners began to seek him out.

The organizing of local unions was bafflingly difficult. The operators knew each man in their respective camps. Any act or word indicating pro-union leanings came promptly to the attention of the New Bosses. The sheriffs and judges were little less than hirelings of the coal corporations, and the men who successively occupied the governor's office were wholeheartedly sympathetic with the operators' point of view. Sheriffs could be counted upon to arrest any union representative who "loitered" or "breached the peace," and the judges were certain to reform him with swift jail sentences. In a pinch, the governor could be relied on to send national guard units "to preserve the peace" in the coal towns. The majesty and power of the law were on the side of the operators.

Under statutes then in effect, "industrial peace officers" were employed by the coal companies. It was their duty to protect company property and preserve the peace. The larger coal companies and associations of the smaller ones hired little armies of such industrial policemen. The sheriffs appointed many of them deputies so they could act both as private and public peace officers, as occasions might require. In addition, little swarms of private sleuths were engaged from Pinkerton's Detective Agency and other similar firms. These latter sometimes masqueraded as miners, finding underground employment and ferreting out evidence of union activities among their fellow workmen.

"Bloody" Harlan County acquired its famous prefix during these years because there the Harlan County Coal Operators Association, marshaled by the United States Coal and Coke Company, fought a violent, years-long campaign to prevent their employees from taking the "obligation" required of United Mine Workers.

The baleful blacklists came back, and any man who was known to have joined the union or was suspected of being sympathetic to its objectives was summarily fired and his name added to the ban. Some companies publicly posted their blacklists by the payroll windows. Gangs of heavily armed "goons" were imported from Chicago and other crime-ridden cities to beat, murder and intimidate organizers and miners. In automobiles and on motorcycles, they patrolled the camps and highways of the county. They wore the uniforms of the iniquitous industrial police and were as arrogant as Nazi storm troopers. Their testimony was accepted by the courts in preference to that of any number of coal miners. The tactics of these desperadoes violated both state and Federal constitutions and can scarcely be conceived of in this later era of civil rights consciousness.

The company-directed law officers were unbelievably numerous, and were on constant lookout for union agents. If a stranger came into a coal camp he was accosted and his business and identity demanded. If he could offer no explanation for his presence that suited the company, he was told in no uncertain terms to get off company property and out of town. If he failed to depart with sufficient alacrity he was taken into custody on a charge of trespassing on privately owned land, or of loitering. These agents were unswervingly determined to prevent loitering and breaches of the peace by strangers.

I recall a trip I made with my parents and other relatives to the home of an aunt in Lynch. The year was 1934 and the organizing drives were in full swing. Harlan County had attracted nationwide attention by the violence which had accompanied the operators' efforts to forestall collective bargaining with their employees. But our party was wholly peaceful and none of us was connected in any way with the United Mine Workers.

When our automobile crossed the county line a heavily armed industrial policeman observed that our license plate did not bear a Harlan County number. He immediately followed the car, remaining at a discreet distance. When we parked on the street of the mining town our pursuer was with us. He made a note of our license number and the model of the automobile. He then demanded the name and age of each member of the group, including children. He insisted that we tell him what business we had in Harlan County and why we were in Lynch on company property. His skepticism was apparent when it was explained that we had come merely to visit relatives. He wrote down the names of my uncle and aunt and their house number and called the information by telephone to his superior. Still suspicious that we were agents of the United Mine Workers, he remained on watch in the vicinity. When, some four hours later, we left the house to return home, he escorted us to the county line. It is scarcely to be wondered at that, against such oppressive tactics exercised by an unscrupulous and numerous Gestapo, the organizers encountered difficulty in obtaining enough members to demand supervised elections under the new collective bargaining laws. Though such police agents were in violation of the New Deal enactments guaranteeing the right of workmen to join unions and bargain collectively, they continued to function under the guise of protecting private property which, the operators insisted with some justification, was in peril of being destroyed by dynamite or fire.

But the companies were sitting on an emotional powder keg the lid of which could not possibly be held in place. Their thousands of employees were too embittered to be kept longer in company straitjackets. They believed that unionism afforded a stairway by which they could climb out of their misery, and a majority of the men were fully determined to set their feet upon it.

Unionism came to the coal counties by varying ways. In a few, the operators capitulated rather quickly and, perhaps, with a sigh of relief. After all, when the first contracts were signed conditions had become so bad in the affairs of many companies that it was impossible for them to get appreciably worse. If unionism was to break the company, even that might be accepted as a welcome escape from a frightful and continuing dilemma. And a few operators came to adopt the hopeful attitude that stabilized wages might help the industry to recover.

At the other end of the scale were the embattled members of the Harlan County Coal Operators Association, who resolved to fight the menace so long as they had a shot to fire. From an understandable resolve to protect their corporate properties they proceeded step by step along the road to intimidation and coercion. Miners suspected of joining the union, harboring its agents or spreading its propaganda were summarily ordered out of company houses and off company property. The detailed leases covering the camp residences, as interpreted by the docile state courts, authorized such summary evictions. Many unfortunate coal diggers found their possessions and families thrust out of doors when they were practically without funds and with no place to go. If another miner took such a dangerous family into his own house for even the shortest period he risked the same fate.

Suspected organizers and miners who were believed to have joined the union were secretly slain and their bodies cast out, gangster-fashion, on creek banks or in alleys. The company-controlled sheriffs and state patrolmen were baffled by these mysterious happenings and found no clues as to the identity of their perpetrators.

Russell Briney, an able reporter for the *Courier-Journal* of Louisville, covered developments in that racked and tortured county during the union drives. From firsthand knowledge acquired on the scene he wrote:

In 1931, for all practical purposes, the only law for the miners of Harlan County was the mining companies' law as interpreted by deputies-sheriff selected and paid directly by the companies. . . . The system was simply law enforcement stripped of any pretense of impartiality, and it is difficult to imagine a more effective device for promoting violence and engendering resentful hatred among a people bred in the free air of the Kentucky hills.

To join the union a prospective member was required to take the oath or "obligation" required of the brotherhood. Clandestine meetings for the purpose occurred on remote hilltops, on railroad tracks, under highway bridges and in other unlikely spots. Hundreds of men became United Mine Workers late at night and in hidden places, knowing they were courting death or ruinous economic reprisals if such knowledge reached the company police. Since these latter worthies sometimes infiltrated the union membership, the decision to forego company approval and become a full-fledged United Mine Worker was a harrowing one and required no little courage.

But union membership swelled rapidly even under the most severe repression. The same fiery tempers that had sparked the great feuds and the moonshine wars flamed again, and armed miners became increasingly commonplace. When his wife packed the miner's dinner bucket she frequently reserved space for his .38-caliber revolver. And the armed and sullen men began to strike back with violence as deadly as any the companies meted out to them.

The spectacular Battle of Evarts was the first and bloodiest eruption of retaliation. Evarts was a mining town owned by Black Mountain Coal Company, and its industrial police had proved unusually reprehensible. Some small incident whose nature has never been made quite clear brought the miners' pistols into the open — and in a few moments, on May 5, 1931, one miner and three company policemen were slain. The rest of the company's police force fled for their lives and, for the moment at least, the jubilant miners were left in control of the situation.

But instead of softening the opposition of the operators or inducing them to gentler tactics, the bloody mutiny at Evarts and the vicious pistol battles which became commonplace throughout the county only made the bosses' antipathy more adamantine. Each camp became a guarded citadel whose laborers one by one joined the hostile fifth column. And camp by camp the citadels surrendered as the operators were confronted with demands for collective bargaining, backed by the requisite percentage of their employees. One by one lesser allies hauled down their colors, until at last only the beleaguered bosses at Lynch captained the last island of resistance.

And even at Lynch, as union miners increased in number their confidence and sense of power grew in proportion and the swarms of deputies-sheriff, state highway patrolmen, private detectives and industrial policemen felt control of the situation slipping through their fingers. In growing numbers pro-union miners displayed their arms openly and congregated in armies of pickets, to bring pressure on the managers of the huge subsidiary of United States Steel Corporation. The dwindling number of miners who remained loyal to the company were sometimes captured and whipped with thick, heavy-buckled mining belts. At other times roads leading to mines were blockaded, shutting off loads of timbers and other supplies. And the once omniscient and omnipotent company police were reduced to the status of powerless onlookers.

The operators now imported huge numbers of ignorant Southern Negroes whose cheap and willing labor was calculated to break the union drives. Even the low wages paid by the coal companies were better than what the Negroes had known on the Southern plantations, and they had little or no comprehension of the background that had spawned the miners' animosity for the bosses. Too, their loyalty had been courted with lavish store credit and other concessions. The miners resolved that their hard-won union would not die aborning at the hands of these hapless pawns. The Negroes must join the union, leave the country, quit working, or die; and in the bloody decade of the 1930s at least eleven of them were found shot to death on the sere hillsides overlooking Looney Creek and the Poor Fork of the Cumberland River.

Eventually, as darkening clouds of international conflict obscured the fires of domestic passion, the last of the embattled Harlan County operators was compelled to accept the inevitable and sign contracts with his arch-enemy. The triumphant chortle of John L. Lewis was as the turning of a dagger in the operators' vitals.

As experience had amply demonstrated in one world war, and was soon to confirm in another, the Harlan County coal miners were unswervingly patriotic. Nowhere in America did men and women love their country more simply or devotedly than did the inhabitants of the goon-ridden camps. But, predictably, the operators, their lawyers and a large segment of the press raised the hysterical cry that the unionists were Communists whose demands were written for them in the Kremlin. To the everlasting shame of every Kentuckian, Governor Flem D. Sampson repeated this slanderous nonsense. After the battle of Evarts, he had sent the militia into the county to "preserve order," asserting that Evarts was a "hotbed of Reds and Communists." On this occasion, and six years later when Governor A. B. Chandler dispatched the troops into the troubled county again, the miners hung out American flags in greeting. So far as I have been able to learn, no effort was made to harm any of the "tin-hatted play soldiers," as John L. Lewis scornfully termed them, though riflemen could have killed them with impunity from the tree-covered mountains. Time after time when miners were brought to trial in the company-dominated courts the charge of "Communist influence" was injected into the hearing. The "Red taint" bedeviled the organizers to the end of the Union drives — even while the real Communists, from their headquarters in New York City, scathingly belittled them as "lackeys of the nation's capitalist overlords."

The United Mine Workers always officially and unofficially denied that it had promoted or encouraged any counterviolence. And this is understandable because it had an important nationwide reputation to preserve. As captains of a major union which had launched the mighty Congress of Industrial Organizations, its officers were obliged to preserve the legend that their organization operated only peacefully under the provisions of the National Labor Relations Act. But such is only the legend. Nonviolence might never have organized the coalfield. Certainly, peaceful forbearance would not have sufficed within the foreseeable future. The new Winchester rifles and .38-caliber pistols which appeared in the hands of miners could scarcely have been bought by penniless laborers with little or no credit outside the company commissaries.

A unionist who had borne the brunt of the organizing battles in Harlan County once showed me a blue steel Smith and Wesson pistol which, with a twinkle, he referred to as a "John L. Lewis peacemaker." When I asked him if the union had issued the firearm to him he smiled slyly but made no reply except to puff on his pipe. He did explain, however, how he had helped to remove an offensive sign from the sidewalk in front of the general commissary at the camp where he worked. The news of a recent and bloody gunfight between miners and "the law" had left the whole county in turmoil and a huge crowd of pickets from Lynch and other camps had gathered in front of the store. A blustery oversized goon drove up in a company police car and, shooing the men aside, painted on the sidewalk a sign which read: COMPANY PROPERTY — No LOITERING. This little straw broke the camel's back and "the miners made a rush fer 'im. One man grabbed him by each arm and leg and another feller grabbed his pistol. We rubbed out that sign with the seat of his britches. Then we throwed him down the bank into Looney Creek and rolled his car down atter him. It was about as funny a sight as I ever seen to see that big fat son-of-a-bitch crawling out of Looney Creek."

But it should not be presumed that acts of violence occurred only in Harlan County. That county stood as a symbol of operator resistance and of union resolution and the battle there was pro-tracted longer than anywhere else. But in other counties, too, there were episodes of bloodshed and death.

In a few cases the operators found themselves face to face with mutinous crews who took charge of the operations, virtually at gun-point, and demanded a signed contract as the price of peace. One operator called the document he signed a "dynamite contract." His operation was in a poor seam with a huge layer of rock near the middle. The wages paid to his men had fallen to the disastrous level of 13 cents per ton. During the day before he signed the contract, his men had worked "from before daylight until after dark" and had produced an average of 6 1/2 tons each. The resulting 85 cents was not enough to sustain life, even if coffee was selling at 24 cents a pound and bread at 5 cents a loaf. The mine was working only two or three days a week.

After the men had completed the disastrous shift the work whistle signaled work for the following day. As if moved by a common im-pulse, the tired miners came together in a group near the tipple and agreed that "something" had to be done. On the following morning when they came to work they brought a case of dynamite which, to the amazement of the operator, they set in the midst of his tipple with fuse attached and a burning carbide lamp held nearby. The op-erator capitulated to the determined mob and signed the agreement in the half-dawn by the light of the same threatening lamp.

So, one by one, peacefully or otherwise, the operators came to terms with the hated foe. In the trough of history's most disastrous economic depression, the old relationship between miner and employer was destroyed forever. For nearly three decades the Big Bosses had ruled the plateau almost without restraint. As we have seen, they had chosen and elected public officials and, to a remarkable degree, had manipulated the votes of their workmen. They had fixed the prices at which the greater part of the merchandise in the coal counties was sold, and had set the wages their thousands of employees would draw. They had been landlords of whole communities and decreed the social and political order which would exist within them. Theirs was the nearest approach to dictatorship our free society has seen. But now all this was gone.

Under the new order of affairs they were compelled to meet their laborers as equals at the conference table and to bargain with them relative to the many matters affecting the welfare of the coal communities. An overwhelming majority of the miners were bound by a solemn oath to wage a united struggle for better wages and living conditions for themselves and their "brothers."

And once the first collective bargaining pact was wrung from the corporations an almost endless vista of contractual concessions was opened up. The first agreement was short and to the point; it recognized the United Mine Workers of America as the authorized representative of the miners, granted them a 9-hour day and assured a wage of at least $3.70 per day.

But from this humble beginning many other gains would flow, and as the years passed the humbled operators would be ever more generous with their miners. "Time and a half" for all hours per week over forty and "double time" on Saturdays would become an established fact. Much of their sovereignty over the camps would be surrendered to the union. Minimum wages would eventually rise to more than $24.00 a day and work time would shrink to only 6½ hours. "Portal to portal pay" would become a reality, and the miner would receive compensation for the long hours of "dead time" spent riding the cramped man-cars through underground passages to and from the working places. Safety committees sponsored by local unions would acquire the power to close down unsafe mines, and, hardest of all to swallow, a huge industry-financed Welfare and Retirement Fund would be created for the retirement of old miners and for the medical care and rehabilitation of the industrial cripples and their families. In the field of luxury the union would wring from the industry paid vacations, in which the miner could emulate his white-collar acquaintances and go fishing, or visit friends and relatives in Indiana, Ohio or Michigan. All these things would come, but few of them were foreseeable during the bleak years when the membership campaigns were under way.

The hatreds instilled in the union miners for their bosses and erstwhile friends were a new twisting and darkening influence in the whole society of the plateau. For a whole generation of workingmen such abhorrence became second nature and was directed indiscriminately at any thing or idea originating within the offices of the company officials. In later years, after the Second World War, the larger companies sent a new generation of youthful executives into the region for the purpose of ameliorating this deeply rooted animosity, but even their Rotary-learned jocularity and genial expansiveness could not soften the bias of men whose aversion had become hardcrusted in the heat of the bitter union drives.

But intense as the enmity between the union miner and his employer became it never equaled that arising between the union miner on the one hand and those of his fellows who joined the Progressive Mine Workers or who, because of convictions or idiosyncrasies, refused to join any union at all. The murderous passions separating these groups of coal diggers were such that their like has probably not been surpassed among any embattled people anywhere. Even in those miserable little communities where the men watched their children sicken and die with rickets, pellagra and other diseases of malnutrition the majority of miners who endorsed collective bargaining was seldom total. Almost always there was a handful of dissenters, some of whom believed the union would bring even worse times or feared it would dominate their lives so completely they would no longer be free men. A few were persuaded by company propaganda that John L. Lewis was an agent of Moscow and opposed the union on patriotic grounds. But whatever their reason the opposition of the minority was as unflinching as the support of the majority.

As the movement toward unionism and collective bargaining gained momentum its adherents became ever more tyrannical over the recalcitrant minority who persisted in opposition to their cause —a cause which was assuming an aura of holiness. This stubborn minority crossed picket lines when strikes were in progress and refused to take the oath required by the union brotherhood. In the eyes of the vast majority of their fellow miners they were traitors to their own class and were even more despicable than the operators whose cause they served.

In the invective of the mining towns they were "yallerbacks," "yaller dogs" and "scabs." They were ostracized by their neighbors, and even their children were scorned as "little scabs" and "little yaller dogs."

But even the holdouts in the end were forced to come to terms with the union. More than one miner who had borne the indignity of a beating with heavy mining belts was compelled to swallow his pride and take the obligation. Some of these stubborn resisters were inducted with mock religious services in which they were baptised in a creek "in the name of John L. Lewis." More than twenty years later these involuntary union members are still sometimes treated with scorn. For example, one of them paid his dues for two decades and came to think of himself as a loyal United Mine Worker. He even retired from the mines and drew a pension from the union's Welfare and Retirement Fund. But when he was bitten by political ambition and became a candidate for county jailer, the old story of his forced conversion was revived and he found himself branded as an "old yaller dog."

To forestall the inroads of the hated United Mine Workers some of the major operators would invite a competing union into their camps. This was the Progressive Mine Workers, a much smaller organization with its headquarters in Illinois. This organization was promptly denounced by the field workers for the United Mine Workers as a "company union," and every propaganda device conceivable was unloosed against it. Nevertheless its organizers made headway and at one time had pockets of membership in a good many camps. But they were too few to withstand the triumphant forces of John L. Lewis and after 1934 their organization withered and vanished from the plateau — with the exception of the town of Benham in Harlan County, where Progressives remained in control and became the bargaining agent for the miners. Friction between this union and the huge U. M. W. local at nearby Lynch was constant, erupting from time to time in gunfire.

By the end of 1934 most of the operators had either gone out of business or signed a union contract. Not all the companies were represented at the bargaining tables. More than half of them had disappeared as legal entities and their names today exist only as memories in the minds of older citizens.

In the main the corporations born in the later years of the Big Boom died early in the Great Depression. Ultimately their stockholders lost practically their entire investment. In most instances financiers bought the assets of the defunct corporations, forming huge nonoperating holding corporations. These concerns assumed that in a decade or so a business resurgence would revive the sick industry and make the properties valuable. In such event they could lease the coal to operators for a tonnage royalty, allowing the operator to assume all the risks inherent in the business. These holding companies were able to acquire vast boundaries of coal at low, Depression prices. The larger ones bought minerals in several counties and, of course, they acquired all the numerous mining rights and privileges which the original deeds had granted. Thus when the Depression ended the coal industry was radically altered. Instead of the minerals in a given county being owned by numerous operating corporations, they were concentrated in a few nonoperating real estate companies. In some instances the stock owners in the holding companies were little experienced in the coal business, some of them having never seen a mining area; one large holding company is controlled by a group of Americans who have spent practically their entire lives on the French Riviera.

Rarely did one of these holding companies attempt to find operators for their properties until after the Depression had ended. They bought the minerals and camps as a calculated risk and had no intention of spending good money on the maintenance of houses and other structures. Their interest lay primarily in the seams of coal and in the oil and gas. The burdensome camps were cast adrift and the inhabitants were abandoned to shift for themselves. The commissaries were closed and the clerks and bosses moved away. Much of the mining equipment and machinery was withdrawn and the towns were allowed to fall into rack and ruin. In some of them the entire population moved away. Some families returned to farms and others sought livelihoods in other camps. In all of them when company support evaporated a large part of the population fled. Dozens of coal camps became ghost towns rotting in melancholy silence through long years. Bit by bit the tar-paper roofing flaked away and the roofs began to leak. Vandals broke windows. Floors, walls and roofs collapsed. Houses lurched crazily on their pole underpinnings.

Hundreds of houses were torn down plank by plank and piece by piece by the remaining camp dwellers. The dried boards were chopped into kindling wood for the voracious fireplaces and cooking stoves. Sometimes the holding companies sent agents into the camps to sell the houses for demolition. A four-room structure could be bought at prices ranging from twenty-five to one hundred dollars. Countless houses were bought and torn down by rural plateau dwellers and rebuilt elsewhere. Rickety and unstable when first assembled, they made uncertain shelter indeed after the battered planks were nailed together a second time.

The decline and fall of these pathetic towns was almost as rapid as their rise. With spectacular speed camps disappeared, or surrendered all inhabitants except rats and owls.

To this day rows of rotting shacks can be found climbing snakily around brown, eroded hillsides, their walls and roofs sagging beneath a quarter-century of neglect and their vacant windows staring reproachfully at the heedless world. Here and there on the front of a decrepit commissary or office building a scarcely legible sign whispers the name of a long-defunct corporation.

The incredible growth and shrinkage of the industry was nowhere more extreme than in the area around the little town of Blackey. It was a trading center for a wide area in Letcher and Perry Counties. The town sprang up in the midst of a wilderness after 1912, and was nourished by no fewer than eleven small coal camps which ringed it on all sides. At the height of the boom approximately 1500 men worked underground in these mines. The little city wore all the essential municipal trappings. It was duly chartered and at municipal elections a mayor, councilmen and police judge were chosen. Three wholesale houses and rows of retail establishments did a thriving business. Profits and wages from several large sawmills supplemented the coal dollars and the optimistic merchants formed civic and fraternal organizations to promote the continued growth of the mushrooming community. A bank was organized and, in the words of the first mayor, "every businessman in Blackey did a land-office business."

But the story of its municipal life was short. Less than twenty-five years after its charter was hung in the city hall the dynamic little city was dead, a fate no amount of New Deal pump priming had sufficed to avert. Without exception the eleven coal camps were bankrupt, their lands in the hands of a single holding company. Most of the camps had vanished and many houses in those remaining were scarcely habitable. Only two of the tipples remained. The bank, too, was no more, and its wainscoted little building housed a halfhearted grocery. The wholesale houses were empty shells. People had long since ceased to run for the municipal offices and the city government had perished by abandonment. The bustling town of 1920 was a silent, shrunken village in 1937. Churches, schools and imposing cut stone foundations still testify to the thrilling life that once stirred in these cold ashes.

Less drastically, but similarly, the same process was repeated in community after community across the Cumberland Plateau.

CHAPTER FIFTEEN

The Legacy of the Thirties

THE MASSIVE passing of coal companies shut thousands of miners off from even the scanty benefit of two or three workdays per week and closed the doors of the commissaries and scrip windows on which they were dependent. Only a vast expansion of federal relief programs saved their families from starvation. The Works Progress Administration in particular endlessly multiplied projects to absorb the legions of marooned miners and the almost equally numerous starved-out hillside farmers.

The efforts of the Federal Relief Directors to find employment for these myriads of destitute, frightened men were sometimes comical. Sometimes worthwhile projects could not be organized rapidly enough and "gin work" or "little piddling jobs" were resorted to.

The clamoring workmen greatly outnumbered the available tools and on occasion this deficiency was circumvented by requesting the men to bring their own picks, mattocks, shovels and sledgehammers to the job. But sometimes, even when the tools were available, an interval had to pass before the fiscal courts and the federal agencies could give the projects the required clearance. During these red-tape delays the harassed local relief directors had to find something on which the men could work.

In the building of roads countless blast-holes were drilled in the rocky hillsides. Gangs of men drilled them along stretches of several miles at a time, and to prevent the holes from refilling with dirt and gravel they were plugged with wooden pegs. In some counties the relief directors set hundreds of men to work on the timbered hillsides hewing these pointed foot-long plugs. Other workmen carried them to convenient places near the rights of way. The armies of workmen piled up small mountains of these "stobs" in numbers dwarfing the actual need for them. So many were accumulated in some areas that long after the roads were completed families hauled them away by wagonloads for firewood.

Sometimes two dozen men could be seen raking loose stones off the yard surrounding a battered, dilapidated schoolhouse. Other crews laid stepping-stones across creeks. Still others laid up walls of uncemented stones to retain creeks that were prone to overflow their banks.

But despite the fantastic waste the circumstances unavoidably entailed, the relief projects brought a great amount of needed public improvement to the region. Since those years most high school graduates have studied in "W. P. A. buildings" and traveled to school over "Relief roads." A determined effort was made to raise health and living standards by improving rural water supplies and building sanitary privies. Hundreds of the latter were constructed in each county and it was hoped the mountaineers would appreciate their advantages and build others as a matter of course — a hope which has gone unrealized. Cased and sealed water wells were put down on many creeks, largely as demonstrations. Sanitarians tested the water supplies of thousands of residences and reported the startling fact that few of them were unpolluted.

It cannot be questioned that without the gigantic Federal Relief efforts many hundreds of people would have died for lack of food and utter anarchy would have reigned.

The Works Progress Administration was the Federal agency which employed most of the idle mountaineers, and during its early years there was little evidence that its purpose was any except to aid the suffering people. But in 1938 a new factor was injected into the Relief program, a factor destined to have a profound impact on the political structure of the plateau and on the future of the whole state.

The plateau had been overwhelmingly Republican in its politics since the Civil War, though a vigorous minority of Democrats had retained mastery in a few counties and had been loudly heard in all of them. But in the shock of the Depression hatred of Hoover and gratitude to the New Deal caused a sustained weakening of the traditional Republican strength. Legions of men and women who had never seriously considered voting otherwise than "straight" Republican now became equally rigid Democrats. These turncoats were warmly welcomed by the "old-line" Democrats who generally referred to them somewhat disdainfully as "New Deal" or "Roosevelt" Democrats. By whatever name they were known, their votes were effective and the large-scale shift of voting strength changed the political complexion of the region. The two Congressional districts had elected "Black" or "Radical" Republicans without interruption for nearly three quarters of a century; and now one of them, presently the sixth, experienced such a sharp repugnance for the Grand Old Party that it became safely Democratic. For thirty years after the first election of Franklin D. Roosevelt the seat was occupied by a Republican for only a single term.

The Relief directors made no effort to "play politics," though they were known to smile approvingly when they overheard one of their workmen say he had changed his registration to Democratic. Then came the incredible political campaign of 1938. Alben W. Barkley was the senior Senator from Kentucky and the Senate majority leader. He was one of the President's strongest legislative supporters, and his powerful oratory had been marshaled in many states in support of the New Deal's social and economic reforms. In the popular imagination he was more strongly identified with the New Deal than any other Congressman and it is understandable that the President was determined to have him continue at his post. His defeat would have constituted a serious rebuff to the entire philosophy of the New Deal at a time when it was beset by a rising chorus of conservative opposition.

The Governor of Kentucky, also a Democrat, was a brash young man named Albert Benjamin Chandler, known to his thousands of supporters as "Happy." In his rapid rise to the governorship he had never known defeat. His face was usually wreathed in the smiles that had inspired his nickname and his political opponents knew him to be a formidable vote-getter. Though Chandler gave lip service to New Dealism, he was essentially quite conservative. In the spring of 1938 he confidently set forth to topple Barkley from his throne and seize the Senate seat for himself.

The political war that followed was a savage, no-holds-barred affair. Chandler marshaled the formidable patronage power of the state behind his candidacy. Every state employee was pressured to support the Governor, and every job was dispensed so as to serve his cause. Influence was brought to bear on the county courthouses and rewards were dangled before the eyes of the powerful local politicians. Even more important, Chandler was — and is — a consummate politician with the ability to appeal powerfully to every element of the state's society. He was a master of the "common touch" by which mountaineers set such store, and it was apparent from the beginning of the campaign that Barkley was in grave peril.

In all species the instinct of self-preservation outweighs all other considerations — a truism as fully applicable to politicians and bureaucrats as to any other. Consequently when the "nonpolitical" Federal Relief agencies recognized the peril to their champion — and to themselves — they quite naturally reacted to the threat by striking back against their bold young foe. Silently and swiftly in the hungry plateau a subtle change came over the vast sprawling Works Progress Administration. In effect the gargantuan Relief program was transformed into a colossal and supremely effective political machine nourished by almost limitless patronage.

The transformation was effected with astonishing skill, but it did not go undetected by the sharp-eyed Chandler. Yet though he could denounce his new foe he was never able to prove its intervention against him. There was no breakdown anywhere in the smooth change-over from Relief to Relief politics.

Barkley's campaign managers selected in each mountain county a trustworthy, loyal and astute local politician whose dependability was undoubted. A spokesman for the state campaign headquarters called the politician by telephone or sought him out in person and asked him to come to the Senator's headquarters in Louisville. There his mission was explained to him and he was requested to visit the office of the state's Relief Director in the Federal Building. Behind closed doors, he enjoyed a long conversation with one or more of the top level administrators who were responsible for the far-flung, bloated Relief organization on which so many Kentuckians now depended for their daily bread.

In the following weeks the politician carried a heavy responsibility. It had become his duty to build a political army within the framework of the swollen W. P. A. He was the county field marshal, and his first task was to choose the lesser officers. These were selected from the county's precincts because of their influence and political acumen. Since everybody was "hard up," practically every citizen in the camps and rural areas was willing to accept a Relief job of one kind or another. To these little men of local leadership went positions as supervisors, foremen, "straw bosses" and timekeepers. Large and important precincts sprouted a profusion of such minor supervisory personnel.

The politician submitted the names of these men to the local Relief Director and they were hired as promptly as possible. Then came the task of recruiting and disciplining privates, those thousands of desperate men anxiously willing to wield a shovel or sledgehammer for eight hours for two dollars and fifty cents. The field marshal and his underlings compiled long lists of names for the ballooning payrolls.

Thereafter, the political campaign was primarily a competition in public works. Hordes of W. P. A. workmen built roads by day and said a good word for the Senator by night. Smaller but equally dedicated hordes of laborers toiled for the state and electioneered for the Governor both day and night. For a while practically everybody in the area had a job with one side or the other.

Besides being a contest in wholesale patronage this campaign degenerated into a sustained exercise in sheer nonsense, seldom relieved by a sensible word from the speaker's platform. Chandler zestfully opened the attack. Barkley, he charged in speeches to crowds of outraged mountaineers, had been in Washington so long he had lost interest in the people who had elected him. He no longer spent his days and nights with sensible people from Kentucky but wallowed in all the wickedness of Sodom and Gomorrah. "Happy" waved a newspaper photograph of the senator dining with visiting European dignitaries and charged that the table was covered with French wine and Russian caviar. Caviar, he thundered, is gravy made with fish eggs instead of ham! He demanded to know whether the interests of the great state of Kentucky could be well served by anyone so debauched that he would eat such unholy fare, and his delighted and indignant listeners agreed the question was an important one.

Too, Chandler confidentially explained, Barkley was a "yes man," whom the President sometimes voted by long-distance telephone calls. He had "no more backbone than a horse weed." Worst of all, Roosevelt had written Barkley a letter which he commenced with "Dear Alben." The Senator was the President's "dear and precious stooge," and to the end of the campaign Chandler rarely referred to his opponent otherwise than as "dear Alben."

But Chandler lived in a glass house himself, and drew many stones of sarcasm from his veteran antagonist. Before the votes were counted he was writhing under vicious counterassaults. Barkley learned that Chandler had caused a storage closet in the executive mansion to be converted into an additional bathroom, and the Senator promptly brought this bloodcurdling information to the attention of the electorate. He charged that the bathroom had cost the burdened taxpayers forty-five hundred dollars and that no one was allowed to use it except "Happy." He scandalized his listeners by assuring them that even Mrs. Chandler was denied access to that new and costly holy of holies. Besides, the commode lid was fashioned of "Bombay mahogany" instead of native Kentucky walnut or pine, a detail which had necessitated the sending of a ship halfway around the world for "this fragment of scented wood." Equally ruinous, it was disclosed that Chandler sometimes visited a masseur to "have his flesh rubbed with costly ointments."

Confronted with such formidable opposition the Chandler star waned. He was vastly outclassed in the field of patronage and he knew it. In his speeches he complained that he was fighting the entire Federal Treasury as well as dear Alben. To the surprise of nobody Barkley returned to Washington with a smashing victory.

In the ensuing year the demand for coal improved somewhat and many men left the Relief rolls for better-paying jobs in the unionized mines, but thousands of others stayed on the W. P. A. payrolls until Pearl Harbor. The supervisory force was sharply curtailed but few of the new bosses were angered by the loss of their jobs. They had not expected their new employment to last longer than the election in the first place.

But things were never the same again in the region's politics or in the Democratic party. The political machine financed by the W. P. A. and organized for the Barkley campaign became a relatively stable and enduring organization. In general it still effectively operates, though many of the original captains and organizers have passed from the scene. The tight-lipped secrecy imposed by the Hatch Act gave the organization the mystique of a clandestine brotherhood and instilled friendships and loyalties similar to those shared by old war comrades. Almost instinctively this "Barkley crowd" drew together in later years to help re-elect its hero, so that he remained in the Senate until his death, except for four years as Harry S. Truman's "Veep." It helped elect Earle Clements, Lawrence Weatherby and Bert T. Combs to the governor's office, and met defeat only at the hands of its old enemy, "Happy" Chandler, who snatched victory from its jaws in a bid for re-election as governor in 1955. The sons and converts of the politicians who organized the machine in 1938 are still loyal to it, and, when political squalls blow up, flock together with remarkable unanimity. It confirmed the Depression Era shift from Republican to Democratic and was largely responsible for preventing the countless new Democrats from reverting to their former allegiance in later years. In effect it made regular Democrats out of the New Deal Democrats, and gave their party vast new power and membership in the state.

The 1930s brought to the plateau a medium of mass culture capable of virtually eradicating important aspects of the deep-rooted cultural heritage of the mountaineer. His artistic expression had always been severely limited. In the creation of his house, his furniture and the other implements by which he lived, he had expended little conscious effort for the sake of beauty or inspiration.

There is no evidence that mountaineers ever attempted to portray in pictures anything which affected their lives, and in the field of sculptural art their record is equally blank. Though idle mountaineers were great whittlers it was a futile pastime and they never attempted serious woodcarving. The weaving and needlework of the women was repetitive and coarse. In effect artistic expression was confined to music, storytelling and dancing.

The ancient songs and ballads of England, Scotland and Ireland had survived oral transmission through many illiterate generations and with accretions and variations persisted in rich variety. The five-string banjo, fiddle and dulcimer had occupied places of honor in countless cabins and had been afforded all the care accorded to the family firearms. The sad tunes and plaintive verses of the hoary ballads had broken the stillness of many winter evenings. Lively fiddle tunes had set the pace for "hoe-downs" and square dances. The Saturday night square dance was a beloved folk institution. It was a regular occurrence on practically every creek, though one accompanied by serious trepidation in many minds. When large numbers of these boisterous people met for practically any reason whiskey was inevitably present, and at dances the combination of men, women, corn liquor and pistols often spelled trouble. Shootings and stabbings at these "frolics" were frequent, and while the mountaineers loved the dances, their willingness to "have a dance" was tempered by the fear that someone would be killed or injured before the entertainment ended. Today this remarkable frontier expression of dance and music is likely to be found only on such faraway and roadless creeks as Hell-for-Certain in Leslie County. The lapse of a few more decades will leave only a handful of people who are able to play the old songs or dance to them.

The radio has had a profound impact everywhere, but its effect was heightened and compounded in the isolated cabins and cottages of the Cumberlands. Radios began to appear in considerable numbers about 1930, and even the poorest of mountaineers managed to scrape together enough money for a receiver. With few interruptions the radio ran from "getting up time to bedtime." The day began with early morning sermons by evangelists of the most Fundamentalist character. These revivalist-style sermons were soaked up morning after morning by almost every household. As the day progressed the women — and, when they were not at work, the men as well — listened to long hours of tearful soap opera. In those woeful dramatizations attractive women and handsome men were always held apart by an unkind destiny though excruciating happiness dangled before them.

At night and in the late afternoons learned commentators dramatically related the news of the day and sagely advised their listeners how all the world's problems could be solved. Hillbilly music programs followed, and on Saturday nights the "Grand old Opry" at Nashville broadcast a regular orgy of such entertainment.

The mountaineer glued himself to his radio with fascinated attention. The broadcasters brought to dull, dreary lives a glint of the glamour and excitement they themselves could never hope to experience but which, like heaven, was assumed to exist somewhere. The old songs were dropped and the traditional musical instruments turned to unused junk. The square dance died because there was no one to attend it. When a dance-hungry mountaineer sent the word up and down the creek that a square dance was scheduled for the ensuing Saturday night, fewer and fewer people were willing to leave their radios to attend his party. The mountaineer's only significant forms of the aesthetic arts withered before the outpourings of this tireless box.

Nor was the preoccupation with radio listening the only factor inducing the mountaineer to forsake the dance floor and music making. The constant yammering of the radio evangelists brainwashed him and his wife into a guilty acceptance of the notion that dancing and music making were sinful, affording a certain pathway to hell. Curiously, the mountaineer could listen to radio frolickers without contaminating his spirit, but to attend a neighborhood dance in person was to court danger. The ether-borne exhortations of the fire and brimstone evangelists gained an acceptance which generations of hard- and soft-shell preachers had sought in vain.

Another factor which weakened the influence of the old habits and customs was the departure of the region's young men. From its beginning the Civilian Conservation Corps was highly popular with youthful mountaineers. Their enlistment in "the Three C's" was often encouraged by parents who could ill afford to support them and who needed a part of the twenty dollars a month a son could earn by enlisting. Camps dotted the plateau and, in addition, thousands of young mountaineers were shipped by the government into Western forests, where they planted trees, cut fire lanes and built roads. In mounting numbers they forsook homes, schools and all other interests and entered the camps. Letters to relatives and friends urged them to join, and enlistment quickened.

In a very large number of cases the C. C. C. was only a prelude to the Navy or regular Army. When an enlistment had been served in the Conservation Corps the youth was most likely to pull a hitch in the regulars. Graduation into the army became almost standard procedure. In that simple era before missiles and atomic bombs the mountaineers were remarkably well suited for infantry soldiering, and the recruiters strongly urged them to volunteer. Consequently, when the Second World War came each mountain county received the news with icy dread. Even before the Draft Act became operative some counties were substantially drained of young unmarried men. For example, more than two thousand Harlan County volunteers were already on active duty in the armed forces when the President signed the Selective Service Law in 1940.

This high incidence of volunteering brought shocking casualty reports to the plateau. The mountain counties sustained a casualty rate per thousand people nearly double that of the Bluegrass and Northern Kentucky counties, and this instilled a dread of war in the older men and women that persists to the present time. The mountaineer's fear of international bloodletting is roughly equivalent to that which might have arisen in the nation generally if World War II had continued another year with casualties approximately double those actually sustained.

PART V

The Second Boom

CHAPTER SIXTEEN

From Bust to Boom Again

WITH THE OUTBREAK of war in Europe and the placing of huge orders by the Allied governments in American markets, the moribund coal industry took a new lease on life. Surviving mining companies initiated programs to improve their operations and expand their output and *circa* 1937 automation in the modern sense began. When the mines were unionized the operators were prompted to find some means of reducing the climbing payrolls. The answer appeared in the form of the "duckbill" loader, a product of the Goodman Manufacturing Company of Toledo, Ohio. The machine was primitive by present-day standards, but it was startlingly efficient in 1937. It could propel itself into a heap of coal and load it in huge gulps onto a conveyor belt by which it was carried onto coal-cars. It proved a huge success and opened the door to a massive program of further automation in the industry.

The quickening industrial pulse focused new attention on the Cumberland Plateau. The reorganizing and consolidating of coal companies speeded up, and the new boom rose rapidly after the bombing of Pearl Harbor. In the remarkable manner so often experienced in the coalfields the plateau suddenly found itself in a situation wholly different from that of a short time before. Whereas its hotels had stood nearly empty during the long Depression they now filled with an assortment of coal brokers and their agents, would-be operators in quest of mineral tracts and lumber buyers seeking stands of timber for conversion into barracks and gun stocks. A land long deserted and ignored found itself swarming again with "outsiders" come to exploit or expropriate its wealth.

Early in the war a surprisingly vigorous minor boom occurred in the logging industry. Armed with contracts from Winchester, Remington and other rifle manufacturers, agents sought out most of the remaining walnut trees, and the sawmills worked at breakneck speed to reduce them to lengths suitable for the arms makers. Hundreds of thousands of military rifles and carbines were stocked with rich, dark, finely grained wood from the hollows of the plateau.

As at the beginning of the coal industry's first great boom the operators found themselves ensnarled in a multitude of grievous problems and shortages. Some of the tipples had stood idle so long expensive overhauls were required before they could operate again. Many driftmouths had caved in while some pits had become huge underground lakes. The work crews had shrunk to skeletal proportions which had to be immensely expanded. Thousands of workmen had to be transferred from W. P. A. jobs to the mines and the thorny task of assembling reliable labor crews had to be faced again and again, a task made maddeningly complex by the heavy drafting of the younger men.

Through 1940 and 1941 the industry had been gradually but surely tooling-up in preparation for the anticipated war orders. Loans from the Reconstruction Finance Corporation had financed new tipples and mining machines, and the company executives had come to terms with their miners and the triumphant United Mine Workers of America.

But noteworthy as its strides had been it was still a sick industry. Its investors had earned little or nothing in the preceding ten or twelve years and even after the wholesale liquidation of mining companies in the Depression it was still grossly overexpanded and could expect to make profits only in times of war or war-caused scarcity.

On the whole the industry awakened with startling speed and performed wartime production miracles. In a market in which heavy machinery of all kinds was extremely difficult to obtain, in which competition for labor was sometimes almost insane, the coal corporations managed to assemble the labor crews and find the essential equipment required to send the black rivers flowing from the hills.

Capital for the established mining enterprises came from loans or new stock issues and was generally ample. Financing for the new corporations was drawn from many sources and sometimes was wholly inadequate. Local doctors, lawyers, automobile dealers, merchants and other business and professional men founded corporations to exploit coal properties that had lain idle and neglected for a half-dozen years. Old men who had helped organize coal companies many years before came trooping back. Sometimes the sons of coal capitalists of another day came from Ohio, Illinois, Pennsylvania, West Virginia and other states to take up the threads their fathers had dropped years before.

And the creek and hollow mountaineers, and the multitudes of one-time miners employed on W. P. A. projects, turned eagerly to their old calling. Along countless streams there was a sound of hammering, sawing and clanging as men labored to reactivate rusty tipples. Dirt flew from caved-in driftmouths and where the old openings had collapsed new entries were driven. Empty camps filled again and the ghastly, paintless houses swarmed with new brigades of ragged, irrepressible children.

Rotten ties were withdrawn from scores of railway sidings and replaced with new black-oak beams. Fresh ballast was pounded under the rusty rails and the coal drags cautiously pushed empty coal-cars under tipples which had loaded no coal since the administration of Herbert Hoover. Eighteen months after American participation in the war began, the plateau was humming with powerful new industrial life. Growing numbers of coal trains clanked and clattered along the railroads and the men who stayed behind were toiling with Herculean determination to provide the fuel and weapons needed by their sons and brothers in the training camps. The industry was mounting the second, and in some respects the more dynamic, of its two vast booms. During the war years the production of "rail mines" (operations loading coal directly into railroad gondolas) soared nearly 500 per cent over the output of such mines in the last peace-time year.

The whole attention of the area's population fastened again on coal. The blossoming farmers among whom County Agricultural Agents had worked so hard discarded seed sowers and lime spreaders for picks and shovels. The small but growing herds of pure-bred livestock were turned into pork and beef. Here was an opportunity to work again and for cash wages far above the subsistence level of the Depression, and the hard work and comparatively low income of the mountain farmer paled by contrast. As the mines awakened other interests waned or vanished until at last it was difficult to detect that anyone in the coal counties was busy at anything except some aspect of mining.

Technological developments had advanced by long strides since the primitive wagon mines of the First World War. Motor trucks were no longer the high, gaunt, feeble vehicles of 1917. By 1943 conditions were ripe for the inception of the tremendous truck mining industry which for a time was almost to equal in magnitude the combined operations of the rail pits.

The mining corporations had found it uneconomic to withdraw the coal from the countless spurs which jut out from the long mountain ridges. Customarily a tunnel was driven along the center of a ridge with working places opening along either side and working toward the coal's outcrop. The spurs lay so far from the parent ridges that it was profitless to drive working places into them; yet each of these bony mountain fingers contained high quality coal. Thousands of bypassed acres had been lost to conventional mining methods because roof-falls in the long tunnels had made it impossible to approach them. The companies regarded these huge pockets of isolated coal as lost and had written them off as unrecoverable.

The legions of W. P. A. workers had pushed graveled roads into many hollows, and in some places the new arteries passed close by the jutting ends of these coal-filled spurs. Much thought was given by mining engineers to methods of recovering this lost mineral which lay so tantalizingly close to the processing tipples. The truck mine was born as the answer to this challenge.

Most of the truck-mine operators were indigenous mountaineers with years of experience as coal diggers behind them. If a man could get a half-dozen work hands together and a quantity of tough oak beams and planks from local saw mills he could build a loading bin. The holding company was willing to rent a bulldozer to cut out a haul road from the highway to the tipple site. The same bulldozer sheared off the layer of dirt covering the coal "bloom" or outcrop and the men could then commence driving a main entry and an "air course" into the seam. A short distance down the hill the wooden bin was built. This graceless structure could hold forty to sixty tons and stood on timbers high enough above the ground so that trucks could back under it for loading. The coal was conveyed down the hill from the driftmouth into the bin by a narrow steel-floored, wooden chute. Tracks were laid from the tipping horns at the top of the chute into the mine and small ponies hauled the coal in cars from the working places to the outside. The coal was universally "shot from the solid." Workmen simply drilled a series of holes into the coal, tamped them full of explosives and, without undercutting the seam, blasted the coal and its interlying strata of rock and slate from the face. The resulting "mine-run" or "bug-dust" was shoveled into cars and rushed to the loading bin, whence it was carried by trucks to the tipples.

Such a mine could be opened and put into operation for as little as a thousand to fifteen hundred dollars. Ponies were cheap and the "bank cars" and track rails abounded as little more than rusty junk. Heaps of them were owned by the same companies which held the mineral tracts and the owners were delighted to turn them to so profitable a purpose.

Other than the loading bin and chute, track rails and ties, the truck-mine operator needed few tools. The most complex of these was an electric coal drill. Electric power was essential for the operation of the rail mines and the lines could be cheaply extended to the new truck-mine openings. Two or three ponies, a half-dozen bank cars, picks, shovels, spike hammers and a quantity of explosives completed his requirements. With this modest outlay the operator and six to ten men could produce eighty to one hundred tons of coal daily. Even under the stringent price regulations imposed by the Office of Price Administration, he could clear at least fifty or sixty cents per ton. He hired an independent trucker to haul his output the short distance from his bin to the sizing tipple for as little as fifty to seventy-five cents per ton. If his haul bill was low and the coal seam thick and free of stone and slate, such a miniature operator could realize profits of close to a dollar on the ton.

The men who established these small mines had rarely earned more than seven or eight dollars a day, even in the best years and under the hard-won union contracts. The opportunity to get into business for oneself and to operate a mine, however small and crude, was a dazzling enticement. The possibility of netting more money in a day than one had previously earned in a week of strenuous labor was exciting indeed. The coal-rich spurs projected from every timbered ridge and the Office of War Mobilization urged increased production as the prime patriotic duty of every inhabitant of the coalfield. On huge posters in commissaries and post offices a stern-faced Uncle Sam pointed a reproving finger at the miner and declared: "Coal is power! Don't be a slacker!" The emotional stimulus of such propaganda strongly encouraged the bolder sort of miner to strike out for himself in an effort to profit both his country and his purse.

With rare exceptions, the miners who had entered the plateau from other areas were as poor as they had been on the day of their arrival. The Depression and their long servitude to commissary and scrip window had left their pockets empty. Their years of labor, disappointment and vexation in the pits had brought them little more than callused hands and worn bodies.

The indigenous coal miners were not quite so badly off. While many of them were sons of landless tenant farmers, a majority had inherited or bought small tracts of mountain land. They had left home as young men and in the later years their farm-owning parents had died, leaving them an undivided interest in two hundred or three hundred acres of surface realty. When this land was subdivided among brothers and sisters the miner acquired title to from thirty to fifty acres of his own. Such land was of little value, rarely selling for more than twenty dollars per acre. However, most such tracts boasted a camp-style house or two, and with the construction of W. P. A. roads up the creeks and hollows, their value rose as mountaineers moved in from still roadless areas seeking homes accessible by automobile. These small plots of rugged earth were the sole estates of thousands of coal-digging mountaineers and, inferior though they were, they constituted an all-important collateral. By mortgaging his inheritance to a local bank or to the holding company whose coal he proposed to mine, a would-be operator could borrow eight hundred to one thousand dollars. With such modest capital he could go into business for himself. From a mere handful at the beginning, the truck mines increased in number with unbelievable speed. More and still more mountaineers took the plunge, gambling every nickel between themselves and absolute poverty, on the hazard that they knew enough about mining to succeed.

The piles of rusty rails were swallowed up by the rapidly expanding new industry. During the war new mining equipment was never abundant but as the mammoth production program began to roll energetically the supply of industrial equipment increased. Steel production was dependent on coal, and despite reams of red tape the hives of bureaucratic agencies in Washington managed to funnel at least a minimum supply of motor trucks, track steel, spikes, fish plates, drills, hammers, picks, shovels and cars into the plateau. Old tools and machines were patched up and made to do. Abandoned mines were opened and long-forsaken steel rails were withdrawn at great peril from mushroom-encrusted tunnels whose ancient props had turned to pillars of mold.

This outmoded equipment, weakened by a decade of rust and rot, could no longer be used in the rail operations but could be satisfactorily employed in truck mines where smaller cars and lighter loads were satisfactory. As the war progressed the truck-mine industry took on an array of new and ancient mining equipment and presented the appearance of a burly giant clad in an undersized patchwork suit of new and rotten cloth. But while the government managed to divert thousands of new trucks and ample steel to the operators, it could do little about the even more urgent problem of man power. During the depression miners had become thoroughly disgusted with the industry and had instilled in their sons an aversion for coal digging. Few young men had been willing to take up the picks and shovels of their fathers. The aging miners of 1927 made up practically the entire labor force in 1941. The young men who reached maturity during the intervening years had gone into the army or the C. C. C., had drifted away to find work elsewhere or had simply loafed idly about. Those who were willing to become coal miners were a tiny majority.

The most important influence inducing this aversion in the younger men was the miner's loss of status. During the Big Boom, when the miner was honored as a brave man whose labor made the industry a reality, youths had been anxious to enlist, but in the gray Thirties this had changed and the young men felt the change even more keenly than their fathers. Thus when the war brought a tremendous demand for coal the operators, big and little, were stranded

with essentially the same workmen with whom the industry had
entered the Depression — minus deserters who had fled the plateau
and those who had in the meantime been maimed or killed in mining accidents. Although they were numerous enough during the first
year or two of the war, they were speedily absorbed, and by the end of
1943 an unemployed, experienced, able-bodied miner was practically
impossible to find.

The military and naval man-power requirements made heavy exactions among such younger miners as the industry possessed. Not
until the conflict was far advanced was the shortage of miners recognized by draft deferments. Eventually some servicemen were discharged to return to the pits.

The industry was compelled to launch an energetic recruiting program to entice into the mines such young men as remained in the
plateau. Nor were such young men few, for despite high enlistment
and heavy drafting surprisingly large numbers remained, most of
whom were rejectees who could not meet the requirements of the
armed services. The rejection rate for physical reasons was high from
the beginning. Years of poor diet — consisting in the main of salt
pork, corn bread, dried beans, potatoes, coffee and corn syrup — had
left a legacy of crumbly teeth and a high susceptibility to disease.
Those who had withstood the dietary and sanitary deficiencies of the
Depression-ridden camps and hollows were unusually sturdy individuals, but their less fortunate fellows who had fallen prey to diseases
caused by insanitation and malnutrition were legion. Illiteracy and
low mentality — the latter induced in part, perhaps, by generations of
inbreeding — also caused the rejection of hundreds of others. It was
to these young draft-rejected mountaineers that the industry resorted.

It was much easier to persuade them to enter the truck mines than
the rail operations. They were related by blood or marriage to the
truck-mine operators, and cousins, brothers, uncles and fathers persuaded them to shed their reluctance and enroll under the coal
miner's banner. Job hunters moved into the coal counties from the
fringes of the plateau. Patriarchs of sixty-five or seventy returned to
work in the small mines. Men with shortened legs, hunched backs
and a single eye — the industrial cripples of other years — found
employment in tiny pits whose bosses ignored the stricter safety and

physical standards of the rail mines. Beardless boys dropped out of school and, in defiance of child labor laws, took up picks and shovels.

Nor were the truck mines and the rejuvenated rail pits the only magnets attracting the mountaineer. For the first time in his history he was urged to leave his habitat for work in other areas of the nation. The giant shipyards in Baltimore were humming and Detroit and Chicago were vast mires which endlessly sucked men and women into their immense industrial complexes. Indiana was splotched with huge war-built manufacturing establishments and everywhere mills and factories begged for "work hands." The enticement of the cities was dual, because in them both the mountaineer and his wife could find employment at high wages while in the coalfield the man alone was desired. The highland girls and women had known the drudgery of the cornfield and of housekeeping, and a few had earned trifling wages as store clerks and waitresses. But in the labor-short war years, women were set to work as welders, riveters, assemblers and painters. If a man and his wife could finance the trip to Detroit or Baltimore they could expect sharp competition for their labor.

The plateau became a scene of seething. disorder — job-seekers arrived daily in the coalfield by bus or train from outlying plateau counties, while others, with wives and children in tow and most of their chattels packed in paper boxes and cheap suitcases, entrained for war plants in distant cities. Detroit and Baltimore were the beckoning meccas of most of these departing mountaineers. Thousands of families moved into the slum and near-slum areas of a dozen Northern and Midwestern cities. "I'm a-goin' to Dee-troyt!" was the parting shout of mountaineers from virtually every community.

Settled in a two- or three-room apartment in a rundown section of a strange city, with husband and wife employed at wages astronomical by the standards of previous experience, the mountaineer promptly took pen in hand to inform stay-at-home relatives of the delights of this new life. Enthusiastic letters urged cousins, brothers, sisters, uncles and aunts to forsake the narrow hollows and dusty coal camps for the boom in the big cities, and the outpouring of mountaineers became almost phenomenal. Each load of new arrivals promptly sought out acquaintances who had come before and rented living quarters as near them as possible. This process repeated over and over created "Little Kentuckys" — areas overrun with expatriate mountaineers who clannishly stuck together and perpetuated the ingrained habits to which they were accustomed back home. These vexatious newcomers heeded little advice and obeyed no more laws and regulations than were absolutely necessary. They outraged grocers by insisting on a fare of corn bread, salt pork and soup beans. Insofar as it could be managed, they lived a rural life in the midst of teeming cities. Their maddening insistence on living by the loose standards of their native hills added to the woes of a generation of municipal authorities and social workers.

When the war ended the returning veterans found a land vastly changed during their absence. Some of the developments left them bewildered. As one veteran described it, "When I left here in 1941 everybody was stone-broke and had just about run out of ambition to do anything except draw relief rations, piddle around on the W. P. A. and loaf. But when I got back home the mines was goin' full blast and a lot of men who didn't even have a job in 1941 was runnin' two or three truck mines and had seventy-five or a hundred thousand dollars in cash."

The camps received little maintenance during the wartime prosperity, aside from the patching of leaky roofs. The stockholders had lost interest in the company-owned communities which had so burdened them through the Depression, and they did not intend to plow their long-deferred profits back into them. The operators expected the nation promptly to revert to the prewar hard times as soon as the Axis surrendered; they were intent on accumulating cash reserves. Their employees had shared in the high wartime wage levels, especially after their successful strike against the inequitable "Little Steel" Wage Formula. They had earned ten or twelve dollars a day in years when there had been few things to spend their wages on. The stores and commissaries could stock only the essentials of food and clothing, and the rationing program had prevented an overindulgence in these. The miner had a few hundred dollars saved and he and his union were determined to share fully in any big new boom the postwar years might bring.

In 1946 the militant United Mine Workers of America began a series of paralyzing annual strikes calculated to break the spirit of the major coal barons and to bring the miner shorter working hours and higher wages. Of even greater importance was the establishment of the Health and Welfare Fund financed by industry contributions at the rate of 5 cents per ton of coal mined. Commencing with this modest levy in 1947, the union exactions rose year by year — first to 10 cents, then to 20 cents and eventually to 40 cents on the ton. The financial power of the trustees became enormous, administering more than a hundred million dollars in trust funds. From this rich treasury the coal industry was required for the first time to make restitution to the hosts of maimed and blinded men whom it had created and to the widows and orphans of its slain.

With the end of the war came a hysterical insistence that price controls be discarded. The National Association of Manufacturers and the American Chamber of Commerce did a superb job of persuading an unthinking public that the Office of Price Administration was Public Enemy Number One. Despite inevitable human failings, this agency had performed a near-miracle by holding inflation to a tight minimum. World War II had been the nation's best-managed war, and the terrific wage and price boosts of the First World War had been avoided. But millions of returned servicemen, factory hands, farmers and female riveters found themselves with money to spend and with little to spend it for. The spokesmen for American business seduced these impatient millions with assurances that oceans of low-priced, high-quality goods would miraculously appear if the iniquitous O. P. A. was abolished. When Congress dismantled the Office of Price Administration the effects were felt in few places so deeply or immediately as in the coalfields of the Cumberlands.

Since its beginning the O. P. A. had granted few price hikes to coal producers and these had been small. Twenty-one to twenty-five cents per ton had been treated as a fair profit. But now from one end of the nation to the other new factories were going up and old ones were being converted. Coal still provided the greater part of the nation's energy requirements and the coal brokers in Columbus, Cincinnati, Detroit and Chicago commenced bidding against each other for the output of the mines. While O. P. A. was operating it had made little difference who an operator sold his product to, since the price was practically the same everywhere. But with the lifting of price ceilings the brokers became antagonists, competing with each other at tipple and ramp. It became commonplace for an operator to receive a telephone call from a broker offering an increase of ten or fifteen cents per ton over the price paid by his present sales agency. If the operator diverted his output to the caller, he was likely to receive another message from the disgruntled loser offering to raise the price still further. Operators sometimes profited from five or six such price increases in a single month and within a year after O. P. A. was abolished the price of coal was up more than 50 per cent.

The industry expanded mightily under this heady stimulus but most of the growth was in the truck-mine segment. A few new rail mines were opened with immense tipples. They operated in virgin coalfields of thousands of acres and necessitated the building of stretches of new railroad. The largest of these developments was the Leatherwood field in Perry County where Jewel Ridge Coal Company and Blue Diamond Coal Company built modern tipples and washeries and employed several hundred men each. But the overwhelmingly greater part of the expansion was accomplished by the truck mines using techniques perfected during the preceding years.

Their first advantage lay in the fact that the small pits could recover coal the holding companies had previously treated as lost, thus allowing the land corporations to have their cake and eat it, too. In effect they could collect millions of dollars in royalties without diminishing their coal reserves. Where highways existed or where the state could be induced to build them, coal could be hauled by truck from the loading chutes to tipples much more cheaply than by the long underground haulways. A rail mine required many months to assemble tipple components, build the structure, drive the entries and arrive at a production of a thousand tons daily. Ten or twelve truck-mine operators could throw up the simple structures required of them, drive entries and arrive at that level of production within a matter of six or eight weeks. At a time when speed was the essence of moneymaking success, this all-important consideration weighed heavily with the men who controlled the region's mineral resources.

During the war years the midget operators had amassed sums of money which were large by their standards, making them rich men in the eyes of their neighbors. These men were ready to invest their capital in new mines, and countless veterans and returnees from the northern cities were itching to do likewise. In a land where practically every man claimed to be an experienced miner, with an apparently insatiable market and with rich seams of coal still abounding along thousands of miles of ridge-lines, almost limitless new output was possible.

And the production growth that followed was spectacular indeed. The tipples of the established companies were already running at full speed processing the coal of truck mines in addition to that of the workings they were designed to serve. It was impossible for them to handle more coal, so huge new loading "ramps" were built. Almost without exception the coal companies went into the truck mining business on a large scale, leasing or subleasing small tracts to many operators and buying back the output for their own tipples and ramps. Coal-hungry factories and mills did not insist on the carefully screened and washed coal of former years but perforce accepted the shattered mine-run from the new pits. The new ramps, therefore, were nothing more than loading docks, huge wooden structures onto which trucks could back for unloading directly into empty railroad gondolas.

The miles of winding railroad track afforded innumerable possible ramp sites and the established mining companies could not monopolize them all. Prospering truck-mine operators speedily diverted portions of their profits to the construction of ramps and entered the business of selling coal as well as digging it. The fantastic, unregulated, helter-skelter new industry operated along the following general lines:

The operator obtained a lease on fifteen or twenty acres of mineral from a holding company. The lessor provided an engineer who inspected the mine once a month to see that good recovery practices were being followed and to compute the tonnage of coal which the operator had removed. On the basis of the engineer's computations the holding company billed the operator for royalties. These payments ranged from twenty to thirty-five cents per ton.

The operator rarely employed fewer than eight men or more than fifteen. His workings extended only a few hundred yards into the hillside and a nimble-footed pony could haul out a ton of coal at a trip. Two or three ponies were employed in each mine and, under such favorable circumstances, the operator could maintain a daily output of ten tons per workman. His employees were union members, and during this period received a wage in the neighborhood of $14.00 a day. Labor costs amounted to approximately $1.40 per ton and were the largest item of cost. A trucker was paid 80 cents to a dollar per ton to transport the coal to the ramp. The cost of blasting supplies, tools, ponies, workmen's compensation insurance, unemployment compensation insurance and social security contributions required an additional dollar per ton. Thus total production costs hovered near $3.65. For his product the operator was paid as much as $5.00. In a successful day, he could realize profits ranging from one hundred to two hundred dollars. The cost of establishing such an enterprise had risen, but seldom to a sum in excess of $2500.

It is easy to understand why men ground by decades of poverty were quick to seize this opportunity to line their pockets.

The ramp operator invested forty to sixty thousand dollars in a rail side-track and a wooden dumping platform. He ordered empty cars from the railroad company and filled them daily with coal bought from truck-mine operators. He sold to long established brokers or "middlemen" in the Northern and Eastern cities, consigning the coal to consumers designated by the brokers. The ramp man carefully guarded his selling price, in order to buy as cheaply as possible; but in the years immediately after the war this price ranged from $5.75 to $6.50. A ramp of modest size was able to load twenty 50-ton cars per day (though more often than not they were overloaded with 55 to 60 tons), thus realizing a gross profit of $1000. A crew of four men could weigh and dump the coal, set and "pinch out" the gondolas, and run the ramp generally. At $15.00 each, they necessitated a payroll of $60.00 daily, to which was added the salary of a bookkeeper, telephone bills and other overhead — costing perhaps $50.00 per day. Thus a net profit of $900 per day was realized, and some ramps operated on a much larger scale, loading as many as 50 cars per shift and loading out twice daily. Profits of $3000 to $5000 daily were not uncommon on capital investments of $60,000 to $90,000.

The distant brokers operated coal companies that were such in name only. They worked from headquarters in Detroit, Chicago, Cincinnati and other Midwestern cities. They had no mines, and seldom possessed assets beyond an office, a couple of telephones and a bank account. They paid the ramp operator for his shipments and resold them to the consuming industry at a mark-up of fifteen to twenty-five cents on the ton. To be successful, they had to handle a large volume, and when ramp and mine operators flagged in their zeal or hesitated to make new investments in mines and ramps the brokers sent representatives to lend them money and to assure them of continuing markets.

On this base the new boom was built, but, in contrast to prior lush years, this time the huge profits were not limited to the relatively few Big Bosses in the company offices. This orgy of mining and profiting was powered largely by hundreds of small-scale operators who multiplied chutes, entries, trucks and loading docks in a frenzy of moneymaking.

As the truck-mining boom gathered momentum other adventurers entered the field. Local businessmen financed truck mines, sometimes taking experienced miners as partners. Miner-partners oversaw the functioning of the mines and received half the profits. Other businessmen opened pits and hired accredited mine foremen to supervise their operation. Clerks and timekeepers resigned their desks and invested their savings in truck mines. War veterans pooled their mustering out pay to become partners in the joint ownership of pits. At least one minister forsook the pulpit to become a mine operator. The energy and attention devoted to the new phase of the mining industry were enormous and for several years left little available for anything else.

For years the miners had known that operators would pay them on the basis of "short" weights unless prevented by strict supervision from the employees. This weight shaving had been accomplished by rigging the scale in such manner that a one-ton car of coal showed a weight on the scale considerably below that figure — perhaps 1850 pounds. Complaints from miners had caused the Legislature to authorize the workmen in each pit to hire a checkweighman to inspect the scales and watch the weighing of the coal. This precaution was absolutely essential where coal loaders were paid by the ton instead of by the hour. This same privilege was guaranteed by the earliest union contracts. When the ramp and tipple operators commenced the large-scale buying of coal, most of them promptly resorted to the old practice of short weights and the truckloads were shaved by skillful weighmen. Initially the trucks were rather small, usually with a rated capacity of one and a half tons, but capable of actually carrying loads of six or seven tons. From a load of this size the ramp operator was likely to pare a quarter of a ton. As the size of the trucks increased to a rated capacity of two tons and to an actual load of close to ten tons the weight stealing became more flagrant, amounting to nearly half a ton on the load. This robbery of the truck-mine operators was widely practiced despite state laws providing for periodic scale inspections by state employees and for the imposition of fines and jail sentences when violations were discovered. This law was of little effect, however, because such inspections were rarely made, and when short weights were discovered warrants were seldom sworn out. It was the custom for the inspector merely to mail the offending operator a letter telling him to correct the situation within the near future and pointing out the statutory sections which the inaccurate scale violated.

But few of the truck-mine operators were paragons of lamblike virtue in the clutches of wolfish ramp owners. Most of them were perfectly capable of playing the ramp man's game of tic-tac-toe, and they protected themselves to the best of their ability. The tare or empty weight of a truck was determined by weighing it without cargo on the ramp owner's scales. The latter recorded the tare weight and subtracted it from the weight of the truck each time it arrived loaded, thus determining the weight of the coal. It was this weight for which the operator was paid on the third and eighteenth days of each month. The mine operator arranged for the truck to be weighed when its gasoline tank was practically empty and when it was stripped of toolboxes, tire-changing equipment and all other dispensable hardware. Sometimes the spare tire was without air or even an inner tube. When the truck had been duly weighed the spare tire was inflated and the heavy tool kit and mud chains were stored under the seat. Just for good measure a heavy steel jack was stowed away in a safe place and, all in all, a couple of hundred pounds of extra weight was added. This amounted to a ton or more when the truck was weighed eight to twelve times daily.

In the apparently insatiable coal market the factory owners were willing to pay for practically anything that was black and would burn enough to give off smoke. Ramp operators made little effort to inspect the coal they purchased and huge quantities of worthless slate were mixed in almost every truckload. When this waste was wet it superficially resembled coal and weighed a great deal more. Besides, water too added weight, and the mine operators quickly discovered that water could hide a multitude of sins. If the coal came from wet working places it was rushed into trucks and away to the ramps, mingled with chunks of dripping slate. If a mine was dry the operator could overcome this shortcoming by rigging up a drainage pipe to carry water from the driftmouth into the loading-chute. A constant two-inch stream could thus be kept flowing into the bin and the coal could be hauled away in a properly saturated state.

Nor did some operators hesitate to load discarded slate directly into the loading bins. At some pits men were set to work shoveling slate from the waste heaps into truck beds. As one operator summed it up, "one man with a shovel on a slate dump can make me more money than three or four shoveling coal under the hill!" Nor were the truck mines the only offenders against the industry's customers. Between the autumn of 1945 and the summer of 1948, more than one rail mine operator mixed waste from slate dumps with his shipments and one operator, a West Virginian who had reopened a long-closed Kentucky mine, boasted that he had gotten rid of his old slate heap, leaving ample space for the making of a new one. Who his unfortunate customer was I have never been able to learn, but he set a power shovel to work loading discarded slate and low-grade coal directly into railroad "gons." It must be said to his credit, however, that he occasionally emptied a truckload of coal into this nearly inert waste — timing each truckload so that it was dumped on top of the carload.

The profits earned by the industry in these years were enormous at every level. Wages were high. Owners of trucks earned forty to sixty dollars a day, enabling a contract hauler to pay for his vehicle within a few months. Mine and ramp operators "got independent rich," and the prosperity spilled over into supporting industries — prop cutters, explosives and mine supply dealers, garages and service stations.

One disabled miner who invested four thousand dollars in a strategically situated service station in 1939 sold fifty thousand dollars' worth of truck tires in 1947. Thousands of men were deliriously intoxicated on the wine of new riches and the stuffed billfold became symbolic of the plateau. The tiny banks that had opened with minuscule capitalization and the support of the Federal Deposit Insurance Corporation in the middle and latter Thirties now increased their deposits by leaps and bounds. Typically a county-seat bank which had commenced doing business in 1935 with fifteen to twenty-five thousand dollars of paid-in capital and which had accumulated total deposits of one million dollars by 1941, found itself with increases of 600 per cent six or seven years later. But the new rich did not entrust all their money to the banks. Nearly as much was kept in currency in their homes or on their persons. The hardware stores stocked foot-long leather wallets equipped with two or three massive brass fasteners and with a tough leather belt or steel chain to be looped around the owner's waist belt. These outsize wallets were carried in hundreds of hip-pockets and became the badge of the ramp and truck-mine operators. Into them were stuffed countless necessary papers, including weight receipts from the ramps, bills for explosives and other supplies, and all the paper minutiae which an American businessman ordinarily collects in his desk or filing cabinet. But they also collected solid sums in cash. On one occasion a successful and at the moment a highly intoxicated ramp operator opened his hip-pocket treasury and allowed me to count sixty one-thousand-dollar bills.

There were several reasons for this widespread addiction to the carrying of cash. One was the fact that most of the newly prosperous had never known money in any appreciable quantities and they relished its presence upon their persons. A thick wad of bills was a solid reminder that the hard times were gone. Another, and the most important, consideration was the income tax collector.

An overwhelming majority of the mine operators were wholly without previous experience in the business world. Rarely had one of them drawn more in wages than was required for basic necessities, and the payment of income taxes had certainly never been a pressing problem. The industry had expanded so rapidly that the Treasury Department, hard pressed during the war by a shortage of investigators, had been unable to check the returns to insure that payment was made in accordance with the Revenue Acts. The mine operators and many of the ramp owners were semiliterate at best, and believed that if records were avoided the true size of their income could not be proved. Acting on this assumption they tended to operate on a cash basis, receiving checks for their product and paying in cash for most of their supplies. This practice caused operators much grief, and Treasury investigators many headaches.

There were few people in the coal country capable of the detailed and skilled accounting required in income-tax reporting. Few counties possessed a Certified Public Accountant. The major companies employed nearly all the qualified bookkeepers. The mine operator seldom possessed more than a fifth- or sixth-grade education and was unable to set up a system of records, or to make the daily entries required by the Internal Revenue Service. Few paid serious attention to the Federal statute requiring them to preserve comprehensive records of their income and expenses. Generally the operator failed to keep records of any sort, beyond the most rudimentary time books showing the hours worked by and wages paid to his employees; or else he innocently trusted in the complete honesty of Uncle Sam and kept a record comprehensible to himself, perhaps, but to no one else who might undertake to unravel its mysteries. For example, a miner-farmer whose possessions in 1941 consisted of a three-room "shotgun" style shack and a nine-year-old truck could point five years later to one hundred thousand dollars' worth of realty, bank deposits and cash. Yet his records available for examination by the income-tax investigator who called on him in 1948 consisted of a shoebox full of grocery bags on which he had undertaken to chronicle the rise of his estate.

In such sins of omission and commission the new fortunes were established, and most of them were raised on foundations of sand. They were so insecurely based that few of them were to endure longer than a few years.

The truck-mine boom left in its wake a vast amount of new housing. The money-laden operators built new houses or "fixed up" their existing homes with new rooms and other improvements. Plumbing, bathrooms and central heating were the first objectives and at every county seat plumbing and heating dealers materialized. Other operators diverted their coal dollars to the construction of "brick houses," long the symbol of real wealth in the mountaineer's mind. A great many of these new homes were artlessly designed by the operator-miners and were simply red brick versions of camp houses and creek cottages. Some, on the other hand, had the good judgment to obtain blueprints from a building materials firm. While such plans were never bold or imaginative, they were, at least, of basically sound design. Unfortunately, they were scattered about with little effort to fit them into the landscape, and in countless instances the attractiveness of an expensive new home was greatly impaired by the apparent fact that it was designed for an entirely different background. Nevertheless, the swarm of mine and ramp operators and their suppliers created scores of comparatively comfortable and well-built new houses in each of the coal counties.

But this segment of the region's new housing was minor. Hundreds of other structures of strikingly inferior quality were thrown up. On every hand operators, merchants and other newly prosperous businessmen constructed rows and clusters of cheap "rent houses." Like the rat rows of an earlier era they crept helter-skelter around the lean brown hillsides or along the edges of highways. As a rule they were built of unplaned, unseasoned, low-grade lumber from local sawmills. Their outer walls were covered with "brick siding," an asphalt composition calculated to bear a mild resemblance to brick and mortar. Their roofs were black tarred paper and their foundations were slender wooden posts or stacks of rocks. They were rented to the miners who toiled in the little pits. Within a year or two their walls and floors buckled and sagged as moisture was withdrawn from the sap-filled planks. The asphalt siding cracked and split under the strain. They promptly turned into abominable huts unfit for human occupancy. Their numbers were enhanced by similar structures built by miners struggling to feed and clothe enormous families and, at the same time, to acquire homes of their own. Built to no standards except the builders' whims they were of a quality whose like would not have been tolerated for an instant in most parts of the nation. Today these tattered, rickety boxes still shelter families and they and their occupants stare at motorists from every roadside — grim, disordered, primitive, dispirited and futureless.

Truck mines and ramps dotted the landscape everywhere. Over the ramps hung huge clouds of black dust as the trucks poured their cargoes endlessly into the waiting gondolas. And though the ramps were multiplied over and over again they were unable to keep abreast of the soaring output from the even more rapidly multiplying pits. A traveler courageous enough to drive his automobile along the truck-clogged roads found long lines of large Ford, Chevrolet, GMC, Dodge, Studebaker and International trucks lined up before the scale houses, their drivers impatiently awaiting the moment when their loads could be weighed and dumped. Such lines formed before dawn and were little diminished twelve or fourteen hours later. Strings of seventy-five to one hundred vehicles were by no means rare.

The winding, shoddily built highways were overwhelmed by the vast amounts of heavy traffic. They simply broke up and went to pieces. The state's inadequate tax base could not maintain the roads. With miners earning fifteen dollars a day the Department of Highways attempted to recruit maintenance laborers for less than half that sum. A competent foreman was worth five hundred dollars a month to a mine operator, but the Department of Highways could offer him only one hundred and eighty. The department's employees who were capable of operating heavy equipment resigned en masse to run bulldozers and other machinery for the operators. The numbers and effectiveness of the maintenance crews plummeted and long stretches of the roads on which the industry depended became little more than mires. Highways that had received their first applications of tar and gravel fifteen years before turned to expanses of muddy "chug-holes" over which it was scarcely possible for an ordinary automobile to pass. So numerous were the trucks that even skilled crews and competent foremen could have done little to preserve the roads. Strings of trucks swept over them bumper to bumper, and their drivers — their wages dependent on the number of loads delivered per day — would have put to shame the famed hell-drivers of the Burma Road.

The officials in the state's capitol beheld these tremendous developments with mild surprise when they were aware of them at all. None of them, from the Governor downward, comprehended that a tremendous revolutionary upheaval was in progress, an upheaval which had turned paupers into princes and brought cascades of wealth to one of the most poverty-ridden areas of the nation. If the notion entered the minds of governor or legislators that this opportunity should be seized to improve the state's antiquated school system and to finance other much needed and long-deferred public services and facilities, it was sternly suppressed.

The counties were no more inclined than the state to compel the industry to assume its responsibility to the communities it had created. For a generation their officials had functioned as little more than apologists for the coal interests. In an argument repeated over and over like a broken record, county judges, tax commissioners and members of fiscal courts had insisted that taxation of the industry in conformity with the clear import of state law would bankrupt the companies, thereby killing "the goose that laid the golden egg." For a good many years the industry was destitute and barely able to pay even the modest levies required by the local governments. But in this respect they were surely no worse off than other citizens of the plateau, and in the new boom that followed the Second World War money flowed in torrents and there was no valid reason why the corporations should not have contributed substantially to the shabby counties in which they functioned.

A majority of the plateau's schoolhouses dated from about 1910. Others were built in the years immediately following the opening of the region by the coal industry. Nearly all outside the county seats and larger camps were one-, two- or three-room affairs, heated by potbellied coal stoves. They were so poorly built that it was impossible to keep them warm in winter. Their water was drawn from wells drilled shockingly close to two stinking, fly-blown privies. By the end of the Second World War they were from twenty to thirty-five years of age. Aside from the W. P. A. structures — most of which were in county seats — few new units had been added. The children in the camps still learned the three R's in rickety, sagging structures whose floors and desks had been tortured by decades of wear. Along the creeks and hollows the buildings were in even worse condition, and generally older by nearly a score of years.

The teachers were dispirited and embittered by years of tormenting at the hands of politically motivated administrators and by crushingly low salaries. In the Depression a monthly salary of sixty to seventy-five dollars for a teacher with a college degree had been the rule, and salary rises in the postwar years were microscopic. In 1946 and again in 1948 the Kentucky Education Association asked the Legislature to guarantee a minimum monthly salary of one hundred dollars for a fully qualified teacher. This sum was, of course, too much for the lawmakers and several years passed before this modest goal was realized.

The county courthouses were crumbling, dilapidated structures which would have been condemned as threats to public safety in any of the nation's major cities. Some leaked like sieves and all of them were tobacco-stained and filthy. Year after year they crumbled and moldered without even rudimentary maintenance. Their custody was vested in elected jailers who saw little need for windows clean enough to permit the sun's rays to filter through. The jails were equally deplorable. With rare exceptions they were of cut stone construction and dated from the early years of the twentieth century. They had suffered innumerable jail breaks and their barred windows were crazy-quilts of welded patchwork repairs. Young and old, diseased and healthy, the prisoners were thrown together in huge "bull pens" without supervision and with scant efforts to preserve sanitation. The compensation of the jailer was dependent on a *per diem* payment of seventy-five cents for each prisoner "dieted." And most "jailbirds" agreed, after a stretch in the local "pokey" that they had indeed been on a diet, and a slimming one at that. Oatmeal and black coffee for breakfast and soup beans, fried bologna, corn bread and black coffee for lunch and supper were the rule.

There was not a county library anywhere within the plateau. Libraries in the public schools were rudimentary and few of the high schools possessed adequate collections of books, even by the low standards set by the State Department of Education. Facilities for public school lunches were primitive where they existed at all. Staffs of the Public Health Department consisted, in most instances, of a doctor, a nurse and a secretary, housed in some poor corner of the courthouse or other public building.

The steel bridges paid for by the bond issues of a quarter of a century before had gone unpainted for many years and were falling into rusty ruin. From time to time one of them broke beneath the weight of a coal truck. Others were spared this fate by huge timbers set under them as props.

The region's public facilities had always been poor, but during the Depression and war they had deteriorated to a level so low they could scarcely be imagined as existing in a civilized country.

The rise of the United Mine Workers broke the hegemony of the coal corporations over the region's voters. The operator's word was no longer law in the polling places. He lacked the respect and esteem to persuade his employees to vote in accordance with his wishes and the power to coerce them had been wrested away. Intolerable now was the old practice of notifying the men that unless the precinct voted for the candidate of the operator's choice the mine would be closed and reopened with a new work crew. In at least seven counties the center of political power had shifted from the offices of the Big Bosses to the halls of the local unions and to district headquarters in Harlan and Lexington.

But the transfer of naked political power did not mean that the companies were henceforth to be malleable clay in the hands of hostile politicians. While they could no longer fill the courthouses with their elected minions, guile and cunning could find means of controlling the officials whom the sovereign people elevated to public office.

Yet the old propaganda that equitable taxes would destroy the industry had taken deep root in the minds of miners, farmers and businessmen. Incredible as it may seem, it was taken for granted by practically the entire population that the industry would die if called upon to finance decent schools for the children who swarmed in the streets of its camps. The chairman of a County Board of Tax Supervisors summed up this nonsense a few years ago by confiding that "a coal company owns so many houses it would go broke if it had to pay a tax on each one at the same rate the ordinary citizen would pay on a similar house. They own so much property that it just don't stand to reason they could pay taxes on it at the same rate you or I pay on our houses and businesses!" This airy absurdity ignored the fact that these same companies owned nearly all of his county's income-pro-

ducing wealth and that each of the houses of which he was so solici-
tous was paying a hefty monthly rental to its owner.

Against such a ludicrous background it was not difficult for the
companies to retain domination over the county taxing officials. Some
of them were convinced by the smooth arguments of company lawyers. Many officials were honest in their attitudes, and their chief
sin was that they were too lazy or stupid to analyze the situation and
determine the facts relative to the industry's ability to pay. Other
officials — those with more intelligence and fewer scruples — were
influenced by more direct means. A favorite method of "handling"
the county judge consisted of leasing him a boundary of coal. His
Honor was then permitted to mine the coal on favorable terms
and sell it back to a company-owned tipple. Other judge-operators
were enabled to lease large tracts of coal and to sublease them in
smaller parcels and for higher royalties to truck-mine operators,
pocketing ten or fifteen cents on each ton for which they paid the
benevolent holding companies. Still other servants of the people
found profitable and easy jobs on company payrolls for brothers, sons
or daughters. Troublesome tax commissioners and members of fiscal
courts were dealt with similarly, but whatever means was employed,
the companies retained their grip on the local taxing power. In
practically every county the old practice of permitting the largest
coal company to choose the chairman of the three-man Board of Tax
Supervisors was continued in effect. Taxes on the industry's properties remained incredibly low and tax-supported institutions remained
incredibly poor.

For example, in one county a huge loading ramp was built at a
cost of $70,000. Its long tracks permitted the loading of 55 railroad
cars of coal per day, and in the boom years of 1946 and 1947 it
loaded that number of cars at least four times weekly. Its output was
limited only by the inability of the overtaxed railroad company
to provide cars more often. On this huge output its owners realized
a profit which stayed steady, in the neighborhood of $2.00 on the
ton. Yet this fantastically profitable installation was listed on the
records of the tax commissioner as having a fair market value of
$3500. The owners of the ramp paid annual real-estate taxes of
slightly more than $90.00 on property which produced an income
tax liability to the United States Treasury of $276,000 in 1947.

High quality seams of coal were valued for tax purposes at $5 to $15 per acre. Gas and oil were generally rated as having a combined value of 50 cents to one dollar per acre. A huge, modern coal tipple built at a cost of more than $1,000,000 wound up with an official valuation of $45,000. The miles of subterranean steel tracks were treated as only a little better than so much scrap iron and were taxed accordingly. This latter practice was justified by a county tax supervisor who remarked to his fellow members, "Now, men, we know that after track steel has been used awhile it's not much better than junk. We've got to figure on what the company could get out of it if it wanted to quit mining coal and just sell its equipment on the open market for scrap or salvage." The Board of Tax Supervisors concurred in his viewpoint without a single word of dissent.

Of all the factors that have affected the highlanders during their long sojourn in the plateau, none has had a more benevolent influence than the "G. I. Bill of Rights." This act, passed by Congress near the end of the Second World War, granted many benefits to returning war veterans, but in the hills its effects were felt most lastingly in its provisions for financial support to ex-servicemen who desired to go to college or to learn a skill. Thousands of young mountaineers who otherwise would never have seriously considered seeking a college education found the campus a strong temptation. After a visit at home they left every county and practically every community to attend the University of Kentucky, other colleges across the state and, in lesser numbers, institutions elsewhere. Sons of coal miners and poor land farmers became school teachers, doctors, lawyers, engineers, chemists, physicists, accountants, and, inevitably, football and basketball coaches. In countless instances these graduates have found successful niches for themselves in industry and the professions, thereby breaking the ancient chain of ignorance and poverty which had bound so many generations of their ancestors. The vast new crop of school teachers afforded a tremendous opportunity to improve the state's system of education at every level and, in some areas, the opportunity was seized upon. New and relatively well-qualified teachers brought fresh insights and forceful new patterns of thought to the classrooms. Unfortunately, in the boom-tossed plateau the opportunity was largely wasted, as we shall see.

On the one hand were hundreds of people dashing about with pockets full of money which they spent in the most irresponsible and profitless manner. They vulgarly proclaimed their new riches, boasted of their high incomes, proudly displayed rolls of cash and boasted that there was "plenty more where that came from." But the state levied no general sales tax, its income tax was low and efforts to enforce its payment amounted to little more than a gesture. Until about 1950 thousands of people blithely ignored its existence and failed to file annual returns. The chief source of revenue was the heavily taxed distilleries in central and northern Kentucky and they could not provide enough income to meet even the minimal requirements of a reasonably progressive society. Therefore public institutions were starved for funds and state and county employees worked for pitifully low wages. While many illiterate coal miners were earning seventy-five dollars a week and some illiterate or semiliterate operators boasted incomes of more than a thousand dollars a week, many schoolteachers were expected to survive on one hundred dollars per month, and in some instances on even less. Public Health doctors were promised salaries of around only four thousand dollars per year and their nurses as little as eighteen hundred dollars annually. This private gorge and public famine caused an immediate and sustained flight of the very people whom the plateau most desperately needed — its little cadre of educated men and women. Its few college-trained public servants were absolutely indispensable to the region's progress. They had been accumulated slowly and laboriously. Their degrees represented, in most instances, incredible sacrifice on the part of both graduates and parents. Young mountaineers had worked as waiters, laborers and at every conceivable menial task for dollars needed to supplement their meager support from home. It was unthinkable that the state that had fostered them and the counties which needed them so desperately would allow their departure into other areas already rich in skills and knowledge.

However, this is precisely what occurred. Principals and teachers by the hundreds resigned their posts and moved to Ohio, Indiana, Michigan and Florida. These and other states paid far more than the impoverished Kentucky school system could afford and the best teachers took advantage of the opportunity to earn a living wage for themselves and their dependents. Many of them stepped into positions with more than twice the pay they could have earned in any of the plateau counties. Because the states to which they migrated required comparatively high qualifications of its school personnel, the teachers who left Kentucky were the cream of the crop, the best of Kentucky's pedagogues, the finest products of her colleges and university. Those with inferior preparation could find little encouragement in other states. So the forces which drained away the plateau's teachers operated to skim off the top layer only, leaving the emergency teachers who had lacked the ambition and professional zeal to secure even a Bachelor's Degree in Education. In main they were the embittered, inferior, often politically minded products of a social order that had grown callous with prejudices, hatreds, and jealousies. Even when intermixed with numbers of dedicated and competent colleagues they were a serious handicap to the educational process. When left in almost undisputed control of the field they were disastrous.

Health Departments lost doctors and nurses to private practice. Sanitarians resigned to find more profitable employment elsewhere. Droves of teachers who did not follow their departing colleagues to other states left their profession to become mine operators or to earn many times a schoolmaster's pay as bookkeepers, accountants or business managers. Some even swapped textbook and blackboard for a miner's tools, shoveling coal by the ton. The competent engineers in the Department of Highways trickled away, leaving their desks to men willing to work for no more than three hundred dollars a month.

The flight of educated and trained citizens caused an abrupt plummeting to still lower levels in educational and other public institutions. Equally calamitous for the region's future was the failure of all but a handful of the new graduates sponsored by the G. I. Bill of Rights to take up residence in their native counties. With few exceptions they took their freshly embossed sheepskins and departed for other regions. Today every mountain county suffers from an agonizing lack of gifted leaders, while the nation's larger cities contain scores of physicians, teachers, ministers, surgeons, attorneys and corporate executives who bear highland names and whose voices betray traces of the highland accent.

Thus weak and venal leadership in courthouse and capitol combined to rob the plateau of that which it could least afford to lose. It forfeited its golden opportunity to augment immensely that tiny segment of its population which was educated and skilled, and having forfeited that opportunity there seems little likelihood that a similar one will come again in the foreseeable future.

While disaster was befalling the public sector of the economy the portents of ruin were making their appearance in the private sector also. The industry's consumers had patiently borne the burdens piled onto them by their suppliers. Their engineers had wrestled with furnaces choked with unburnable slate, and their purchasing agents had sworn in exasperation over the price gouges with which the producers and brokers afflicted them. Bit by bit a sizable segment of the nation's manufacturing industries shifted its dependence from the amoral, strike-plagued pits to oil and gas. Huge transmission lines had penetrated the East, bringing astronomical quantities of natural gas from the South and Southwest. Tanker loads of residual oil from Venezuela provided another cheap competitive fuel and the disgusted industrialists were determined to find reliable sources of fuel at reasonably stable prices. Scores of major industrial establishments began shifting from coal to oil and gas and by the middle of 1948 the consequences of this movement had become apparent to every coal broker.

Factories and mills which still relied on coal had stocked great stores of it. Millions of tons lay in mountainous heaps in their stockpiles. These reserves had been accumulated in anticipation of disruptive strikes in the mines and most such consumers possessed enough to keep their furnaces and power plants running for several weeks even if no additional coal was available.

In the three preceding years the nation had ridden an unprecedentedly vigorous boom, carried to ever higher altitudes by constantly rising wages, prices and profits. In 1948 came the first postwar recession. Mild in comparison to later ones, and when contrasted with the ruinous Depression of the prewar years, it nevertheless resulted in an appreciable dampening of the economy in the summer and fall of that year. Its effects, combined with the steady shift of customers from coal to competing fuels, dealt a severe blow to the truck mines in the eastern Kentucky coalfield.

Under the union contract then in effect a ten-day paid vacation was begun by the miners on July 1. Up to that time the pits had been operating at fever pitch. The railroads were congested with long lines of clattering gondolas and impatient ramp and mine operators cursed the engineers and conductors because they could not provide all the needed cars. When the vacation began it was taken for granted that at its expiration the frenzied digging of coal and counting of profits would resume unabated.

To the deadening amazement of the truck-mine operators and ramp owners, however, this happy prospect did not materialize. When the coal diggers returned to the pits the rail mines with their cleaning plants and washeries resumed all-out production, but dozens of ramps were left without orders or with orders for only a portion of the coal they were prepared to ship. When an explanation for this new circumstance was demanded, the brokers began sternly to insist on a markedly improved product, and soon were requiring coal wholly free of dirt, rock and other impurities. They declared their customers would no longer tolerate fuel mixed with wastes of any kind. Furthermore, the price trend was reversed and the operators found that "the shoe was on the other foot." The coal brokers now asserted they could handle truck-mine coal only if prices were cut. The incredulous ramp and mine owners suddenly realized that their market was collapsing and that to continue in business they must reform not only their operations but their attitudes.

PART VI

Waste and Welfare

CHAPTER SEVENTEEN

Darkening Horizons

ACCOMPANYING the new boom in coal there occurred a lesser but
equally significant boom in lumbering. Most of the huge sawmills
which had crept deep into the plateau prior to the Great Depression had suspended operations during the hard times. A few large
firms had worked on at a reduced tempo but between 1930 and 1940
the forests were generally left to the small "woodpecker" operations
of neighborhood sawmills.

The war brought a tremendous demand for lumber and the long
quiescent lumber corporations aroused themselves again. Despite the
mammoth logging operations of the three decades preceding the
"Hoover Depression," the timber companies still held thousands of
acres of high quality timber, some of it still untouched by ax or saw.
Perhaps the largest of these was Mineral Development Company
which owned broad areas in a half-dozen counties. W. M. Ritter
Lumber Company was a logging giant whose stack yards covered
river bottoms near the mouth of Leatherwood Creek in Perry County.
Fordson Coal Company owned more than half of Leslie County and
huge tracts in surrounding counties. Though most of this "company
land" had lost its great poplars to the splash dams and spring
tides many years before, other thousands of acres had escaped
practically untouched. On these huge boundaries tremendous oaks,
walnuts, beeches, hemlocks and poplars abounded along the still
crystalline streams.

The state had declined to set aside even a few acres of this magnificent forest heritage for the benefit of future generations. A few

stout-hearted people had crusaded tirelessly in an effort to persuade the state and Federal governments to conserve at least a tiny remnant of these majestic woodlands, but governors and legislators had scoffed at their requests. Then in a few years after Pearl Harbor the last of the plateau's magnificent virgin timber passed into history.

Huge absentee-owned lumber companies began mammoth logging operations, activities which, to be more nearly accurate, should be called "clearing" operations. In some areas so many trees were cut that the hills were virtually denuded. Almost overnight they were transformed from primeval and incredibly beautiful forests to desolate wastelands.

A wide range of methods were employed to get the timber to the highways where it could be loaded onto trucks and hauled to the sawmills. Some loggers fastened cables to the logs and powerful winches dragged them to loading booms near the highways. In other forests bulldozers slashed roads around the hillsides and caterpillars dragged strings of logs out of the coves. In still others, and this was most often the procedure, teams of sweating mules, successors to the mighty oxen of older times, pulled them from the hillsides. The swarms of coal trucks were mingled with log-laden vehicles. The monstrous sawmills whirred and screeched from early in the morning until after dusk as the logs ascended to the carriages and were reduced to planks of varying lengths and thickness. Mountains of sawdust rose nearby, some rivaling the hideous slate dumps in size.

And while the corporate giants were stripping the large timber stands and as much additional land as they could contract for, scores of lesser "saw-loggers" were active. They worked in relatively small stands of trees which they bought from individual citizens or leased from coal companies. Whether the lumbering concern was large or small the end results were the same. The big trees were cut down and in falling they crashed through the tops and branches of the smaller ones, stripping away their limbs and inflicting deep gashes on their trunks. Practically all the trees capable of producing a few reasonably good planks were cut down.

But the desolated hillsides were not yet to be given surcease. After the bulldozers had slashed deep cuts for haul roads and after the larger trees had been sawed up and carried away, armies of prop cutters attacked them. New millions of timbers were required for the mines and great amounts of the residue, the larger limbs and laps of the trees, were sawed into jack props and collar-poles. Then the cutters turned their attention to the surviving smaller trees, those twelve to fourteen inches or less in diameter, and the axes and crosscut saws reduced them to mining timbers.

Within a few years the results of these labors were startlingly apparent. By 1948 when the truck-mine boom received its first jolt, thousands of acres had been practically cleared of vegetation. They were dotted with big and little stumps and with heaps and piles of dry, inflammable waste. Unsalable logs, limbs, broken trunks, bark, twigs, splinters, dry leaves and chips from the woodchoppers' axes strewed the earth.

In addition it should be remarked that the larger companies employed a system of contracting which brought about enormous wastage. On the one hand they set crews of men to work felling trees and sawing their trunks into appropriate lengths. Company cruisers counted the logs and the men were paid at a prescribed rate for each one thousand lineal feet they contained. These workmen were under strong temptation to "work up" practically everything conveniently at hand, including sappy, immature trees and those so located in deep hollows or behind great boulders that they could not be recovered without splintering them.

Other crews contracted to remove the logs from the forest, placing them on loading booms near the highways. Since their pay depended on the amount of lumber in the logs handled by them, they seized upon the larger and most convenient ones and left the smaller and less easily accessible "sticks" behind. And despite the touted efficiency of private enterprise, little effort was made to discover why more logs were being cut than delivered. In any event many areas were left dotted with fine ten-, twelve- and fourteen-foot logs. They strewed the ruined hillsides, mixed with the broken residue of the trees.

Traditionally the state had taken little interest in its forests. A halfhearted effort had been made to create a fire-fighting system. A law permitted a county's fiscal court to levy a special tax on woodland, the proceeds to be used to prevent and extinguish forest fires. Some counties had levied the tax and others had not, but none could claim an efficient fire-detection and fire-fighting organization.

The thousands of acres of cutover forests were ripe for fire — and it came! Autumn after autumn saw miles of flame creeping along the earth, eating into the hearts of great logs and chewing into the trunks of standing trees. Sometimes when they fed on piles of dry tinder the flames reached high into the air. Again they smoldered for days leaving scarcely a trace of smoke. Countless acres were burned so thoroughly that no seedlings were left. The combined destruction of lumberers and conflagrations reduced the seed trees to columns of black char so that natural reforestation was extremely difficult or even impossible in many places. So fierce and vast were the fire that sometimes days passed in which the people were unable to see the sun or even to distinguish its location in the sky. Clouds of pallid wood smoke hung low in the valleys and the drifting ash settled in gray dust puffs everywhere.

And after ax and fire passed on the wintry rains pelted the unprotected hillsides, washing away inches of ash-covered humus and reducing thousands of new acres to grim barrens.

No county was so drastically changed by the coal and lumbering industries as Leslie. By all standards the most primitive in the plateau, and probably the most primitive political entity in the nation, this rugged expanse of hills and hollows had been little affected by the world beyond its borders. No railroads had reached it and it was traversed by only a single highway. A few miles of W. P. A. roads ran here and there, but essentially the county was a huge forest ruled by agents of Fordson and other coal and timber corporations. Its fifteen thousand people dwelt in cabins and crude houses along the larger creeks. Most of the original growth of tulip poplar had been removed, but other varieties abounded and one could walk for miles in woodlands which betokened no evidence of human intrusion. Greasy, Cutshin and Hell-for-Certain creeks ran clear and unsullied, and catfish and bass abounded in deep water-holes. The people were a preserved remnant of the frontier and rifles and pistols hung on the walls of every cabin. Hunting and fishing were passions with the men and the dinner tables were weighted with frontier foods. Fried pork was the mainstay, but cooked squirrel and corn bread "sopped" in the gravy were esteemed above all else. Strings of dried beans, onions, cushaws, pumpkins and "hands" of tobacco were stored in the lofts. The women made a skin-reddening soap out of hog fat and wood ashes. They still washed clothes on creek banks by pounding them with "battling" sticks. Generous and hospitable in the extreme, no visitor was allowed to leave a cabin without a sincere offer of food and a "dram."

Here John Shell and his numerous clan of brothers and sisters lived far past the century mark while flagrantly violating the sacred tenets of modern medicine. This leathery old mountaineer loved fat pork and its artery-clogging cholesterol. He smoked and chewed tobacco from daylight to dark, without incurring a trace of lung or throat cancer. He thrived on corn whiskey, draining off a full water glass at a draft. He lived in a drafty log cabin and bathed only when it suited him. Yet he managed to live to the ripe old age of a century and a quarter. Of his somewhat less fortunate brothers and sisters who shared his mode of living the shortest-lived of them reached only eighty-nine.

With dramatic suddenness the war changed this idyllic Al Capp-land. The loggers cut the trees by tens of thousands and the coal deposits were probed with hundreds of driftmouths. Without railroads to haul away the coal the operators trucked their product to railheads in adjoining Clay and Perry Counties. Truck mines blossomed along the highway and the stretches of W. P. A. road. The roads became black ribbons crawling with motorized beetles.

After the war, the trucks grew larger and the mines more complex. Monster vehicles carried twenty-two tons. Deep parallel grooves were worn on the traffic lanes used by the loaded trucks while the other lane traveled by the returning empties remained smooth. Because the operators had to absorb the large additional expense of transporting their coal thirty miles to the ramps, they sharply pared the wages of their miners. In a county so long isolated from the world this was not difficult to do, and while millions of other Americans drew high pay for comparatively light and easy work the Leslie County miners imagined themselves well off with wages of four to six dollars a day. Fiercely independent and savagely individualistic they brusquely repulsed all efforts of the United Mine Workers to organize them into local unions. While wages rose somewhat with rising postwar coal prices, the county lost its timber and a very large portion of its mineral wealth without its coal diggers and timber cutters ever being paid more than a subsistence hire.

After midsummer of 1948 truck mining fell into decline. There was no abrupt failure such as had occurred in 1927, but the "milk had been skimmed" and the operators who resolved to stay in business were forced to reform and overhaul their operations.

Clean coal required the elimination of the "middleman," the troublesome band of rock which often divides the strata into two parts. This could best be accomplished by clawing it out with a cutting machine, an expensive device which had hitherto been within the reach of rail operators only. It was practically impossible for the coal to be shot from the solid and freed of rock and slate fragments thereafter, and the operator was jarred into a realization that survival could be purchased only at the cost of mechanization.

Many of his colleagues rejected this viewpoint and continued operating without undercutting. Gangs of men — usually cripples — were set to work as "slate pickers." The added burden of their wages shortened the lives of scores of mines, causing the jack-in-the-box operators to fall as rapidly as they had risen. But the operator who had flourished so briskly in the days of the great fuel shortage rarely possessed the foresight to count up his gains and quit the business. A few did so and took their hoards and migrated to the Bluegrass or to Ohio and Indiana, where they acquired farms and took up new pursuits. These were a tiny minority, however, and their brethren persisted in the business. Some were successful and added new assets to their estates, but more failed, losing all they had gained in their rise from pauperdom.

And it is easy to see why they clung to mining. Few could comprehend the changes occurring in the nation's industry and commerce. The pathetic school system had given them little more than the rudiments of "learning." The better-educated had been in flight for years. Stock-market quotations and other business news was incomprehensible to them. With rare exceptions their lives had been spent within the coalfield and they were without beneficial experience elsewhere. They had accumulated thousands of dollars quickly and with little investment, and, like other operators of an earlier time, they optimistically believed "good runs" would be resumed. They swam against a tide of steadily rising costs and constantly dwindling coal prices.

Bewildered by the new turn of events, the truck-mine operator followed one of two possible courses — he mechanized or went broke. Most pursued the latter course. They continued to shoot their coal from the solid and to clean it by employing gangs of slate pickers. This system was ineffective and ramps continually exacted penalties from their pay. The prices paid for electric power, track steel, explosives, drills, trucks, gasoline and all the other supplies and paraphernalia essential to the industry crept ever upward. At the same time the price of coal shrank. By 1953 ramps were paying as little as $3.75 per ton F.O.B. the cars. This represented a price fall of close to a dollar on the ton.

Caught in the cruel pincers of cost inflation and price deflation the operator was driven to heavy losses, subsidizing his mine out of savings. Ramp owners and coal brokers, dependent on the small pits for their source of fuel, encouraged him, perhaps honestly, to believe that an upturn was near.

In deepening distress he poured out his accumulations from a happier time until, within a few years, he was as poor as at the beginning. When the "real cash," the shiny new automobiles, and the luxurious appliances and furniture had turned to memories he experienced a numbing demoralization.

And in these harrowing years the failing operator found a new nemesis dogging his trail. The Federal Income Tax collectors, their numbers swollen by numerous new recruits, began assembling information concerning the plateau's new-rich. One by one they sought out the operators and demanded to see their business records. All too often the books disclosed little except that the taxpayer had earned substantial sums of money for a good many years. Sometimes they revealed glaring tax evasions, disguising nothing from the eyes of trained accountants. The result was the filing of stacks of tax liens. These encumbrances gave the United States Government a mortgage upon all the property owned by the delinquent taxpayer. He was threatened with criminal prosecution unless his delinquencies were promptly paid, together with interest and heavy penalties. In most instances the revenue agents had no alternative except to "net-worth" the taxpayer. The value of his estate when he entered the coal business was computed. His present worth was then calculated. Allowance was made for his various exemptions over the years and his taxes were computed accordingly. Hundreds of operators found they owed more money than all their possessions would bring if offered for sale. When their tax liabilities were settled they sank back into pauperdom again.

The financial ruin of this multitude of small businessmen between 1948 and 1954 left thousands of miners without employment. They were thrown on the labor market to seek jobs wherever they could. By automobile and trainloads they moved away into the cities and farms of Ohio, Indiana and Michigan. There began a sustained flight of humanity which in the decade before 1960 curtailed the population of the plateau by 25 per cent. The exodus of these jobless miners marked the beginning of one of the most drastic population shifts in the nation's history.

However, many operators chose the alternative. They resolved to expand their mines and do as much of their work as possible with machines. Their undertaking was aided by developments in the rail mines.

For many years John L. Lewis had insisted there were too many mines, that coal digging should be done by machines and that their operators should be highly paid. He had ruthlessly demanded that this process of consolidation and modernization be carried through. This policy had brought him merited renown as the foremost labor statesman in the nation's history. Mr. Lewis believed the displaced miners could be absorbed by other industry and that automation would bring improved health, better housing and higher standards of living generally. He demanded for the families of the coal miners a mode of living closer to the national norm. In many respects his great dream was realized. In others it was tragically aborted.

A series of bitter strikes had driven many of coal's customers to other fuels. They were no longer in a mood to tolerate such protracted interruptions of their fuel supplies, a fact they made perfectly clear to the union and to the major operators. By 1951 the operators of the large rail pits had come to a realization that strikes must be avoided if the industry was to retain any sizable remnant of its traditional markets. The miners, as part of their modus operandi, had long insisted they would not work without a signed contract, and the annual work stoppage when the pact expired had become a rite.

Their position was summed up in the laconic ultimatum "No contract, no work." Fines, imprisonment and government seizure of the pits had failed to divert "John L.," as his followers affectionately called him, from his determination to require the industry to meet its responsibility to its employees and to its thousands of maimed and blinded victims. Year after year the Big Bosses capitulated in order to avoid the ruinous strikes which might deplete the stock piles near the factories, mills and electric generating plants.

In strike after strike the union humbled the operators until at last, to use Lewis's flamboyant language, he made them "come to Carnossa." This proud boast sent newspaper reporters and the public to reference books but steeled the operators to create, in so far as possible, a hedge against climbing wages and Welfare and Retirement Fund contributions.

In consequence the traditionally backward and hopelessly fragmented bituminous coal mines became, within a few years, one of the nation's most thoroughly mechanized industries. Miners could not be wholly dispensed with. Regardless of the tools employed, workmen and engineers must go underground and bring out the coal. But even the most conservative operators eventually realized that advancing technology had brought within their grasp efficient new devices capable of revolutionizing their ancient industry. Since the beginning of the industrial revolution the basic routines had remained essentially the same. The duckbill and its successor, the Joy loader, had only supplemented the human coal shoveler. The electric drill had supplanted the manual breast auger and the cutting machine had displaced the pick in all the rail mines. But the pick and shovel were still emblematic of the miner's trade, and the machines — electric drills and mechanical cutters and loaders — were only vastly more powerful versions of the simpler hand tools of early eras. They had, to a considerable degree, revolutionized coal mining. They had brought increased production with dwindling work crews and had freed thousands of men for the truck mines. Without the introduction of these machines laborers for the truck mines could not have been found and their millions of tons of coal would have been denied the nation at a crucial moment in its history. However, by 1947 these tools were obsolescent. Even in pits wholly equipped with them it was no longer possible to offset the endless demands of the union.

The big mines, like their little neighbors, were caught in a savage squeeze between the dwindling price of their product and the soaring costs of their labor and supplies. A new round of mechanization was seized upon as the only possible escape from this closing trap.

The giants of the industry — Pittsburgh-Consolidation Coal Corporation, Blue Diamond Coal Corporation, Island Creek Coal Company and the steel companies which held in fee the mammoth captive pits — had possessed the foresight to subsidize research in the design of radically new types of mining machinery, machines capable of swelling output by more than 100 per cent while simultaneously permitting the discharge of many underground workers. Out of this research came the superb "coal mole" or continuous miner. This marvelous mechanism can bore directly into the face, its teeth dragging out the entire stratum and loading it in enormous gulps into waiting cars or onto conveyor belts. It can mine coal more rapidly than it can be conveyed away. It completely eliminated the need for undercutting and for drilling and blasting. The use of explosives had necessitated a costly delay after each round of shots while the fans pushed enough air through the working places to carry away the sickening fumes. This drag on production was now a thing of the past.

Accompanying the coal mole came another magnificent contribution to mining efficiency — the endless conveyor belt. For centuries mules and ponies had dragged the coal from the working face to the tipping horns. In the preceding quarter-century the electric mine locomotive had replaced them in the big pits, clattering swiftly along the corridors with long strings of cars in tow. They were expensive and were frequently involved in accidents and costly breakdowns. In the progressive and more heavily capitalized mines they found their successor in the broad, fast-moving, conveyor belt. This device could be installed in the main entries and once in operation could deliver unceasing streams of coal to the tipples. Sometimes the mineral was brought in cars from the working rooms to the belt, but frequently a lesser belt was resorted to. Its receiving end was brought to the rear of the coal mole and the fuel was loaded directly onto its moving surface. Thence it was swiftly borne to the "main line" belt. In such mines the long lines of cars and their whirring locomotives were retired and the crews of track and motor men were handed discharge slips.

Another contraption also helped to free the engineers and miners from their trackbound regimen. The "shuttle buggy," a small, rubber-tired, electric car, was developed. It was affectionately called the "mining jeep" by crews who used it, and was almost as agile as the versatile vehicle after which it was named. It could carry away a ton or more of coal, and fleets of them dashed about in frantic efforts to keep the loading booms of the voracious moles freed for uninterrupted digging. They, too, hastened the disappearance of underground locomotives, cars and tracks, handling more coal at smaller investment and with fewer employees.

A fourth immensely important new contribution to the industry's efficiency was the roof-bolt. Since time immemorial miners had relied on wooden timbers to support sagging roofs and thousands of hunched backs and twisted limbs testified to their fallibility. Wood was expensive and increasingly difficult to obtain everywhere in the plateau. The roof-bolt is a thick, strong steel pin. A hole is drilled in the roof and the pin is inserted through the underlying soft ceiling slate with its tip imbedded in the hard stratum of sandstone above. The crumbling, deadly slate is thus bound to the rigid stratum and it cannot fall. It proved remarkably effective and is a splendid improvement over the old network of jack props and collar-poles. As the big operations swung to bolting the making of mining timbers became a dwindling business that relied increasingly on the vanishing truck mines.

These devices drastically lessened the number of workmen needed in the mining process. While skilled crews were required to keep the new machines functioning they were tiny indeed compared with the multitudes whom they displaced. In valley after valley the industry took on a radically new aspect. Gone were the gangs of timber cutters on the hillsides and the busy trucks which arrived day after day with stacks of pine, oak, locust and hickory timbers. Gone was the motorman, a personage of much importance a few years before. Gone were the gangs of track layers and timber setters. Vanished were the cutting machine operators and the blasting crews. Disappeared forever were the armies of black-faced shovelers on whose strength so much had for so long depended. The payrolls in the great mines dropped from thousands to hundreds while production stayed steady or rose.

The machinery thus displaced was little better than junk in the estimation of its owners and some of it met the ignominious fate reserved for scrap iron. But there were those in the coalfield who could utilize these obsolete "coal getters" and the shifting of them from large mines to the small rapidly grew into a major industry in itself. Used equipment dealers blossomed at strategic points. They bought the discarded machines at prices far below their original cost but substantially above the going price for scrap iron. They took the battered but still powerful drills, cutters, locomotives and cars to their shops where workmen overhauled their motors and sprayed them with fresh coats of yellow paint. Then new customers were sought out and the machines passed into the hands of truck-mine operators. To their new owners they generally meant the difference between profit and bankruptcy.

To the struggling truck-mine owner these hundreds of discarded machines were a treasure trove. A secondhand Joy loader operated by two men could easily replace ten coal loaders with shovels. A cutting machine could swell overall production and, by eliminating rock and slate before the coal was shot, eliminate the need for the costly slate pickers. The heavier track, larger cars and used locomotive made it possible for a single man to bring out more coal than a half dozen mules and as many drivers.

The dealer could afford to sell his property on reasonable terms. He could show a prospective customer a five- or six-acre field stacked high with obsolescent mining machinery of every imaginable character. If the mine operator could buy it and pay cash, well and good. A hefty mark-up was imposed and the profit was excellent. If the customer was "hard up" for cash, the dealer permitted him to sign a contract for payment at the rate of ten or fifteen cents per ton mined by him.

So the process of pit automation was double-barreled. The big mine went wholly modern with machinery of the latest design and the highest efficiency. The smaller workings inherited their cast-off equipment and became as efficient as their big brothers had been a short time before. In all the pits — big, middle-sized and small —

production capacity climbed while payrolls shriveled. The same industry which had required seven hundred thousand men to provide the nation's coal in 1910 was able to provide all of the same fuel required by a vastly larger nation in 1958 with fewer than two hundred thousand men.

The idled thousands of miners joined in the wholesale exodus out of the region. The canny businessmen who owned the larger camps did not, however, allow themselves to be stranded with numerous camp houses, commissaries and other facilities for which the streamlined industry could have no need. As early as 1945 they foresaw that the loading of coal by traditional methods would soon be passé, and began plans to unload their towns.

The first step in their program to "free" the camps lay in the making of blandly optimistic statements to their employees and to the general public. They gave the impression that the company anticipated twenty or thirty years of uninterrupted mining with their employees drawing high wages. No mention was made of mechanization or of reduced payrolls. While no specific promises were made, the miner and his wife were led to believe the inhabitants of the camps could expect continued employment at union-scale wages.

Next the company announced that it was going out of the real estate business so its executives could give their undivided attention to mining. Besides, said the benevolent bosses, they wanted the miners and their families to enjoy the feeling of independence and self-assurance that comes from home ownership. It was undemocratic, the Big Bosses now declared, for the company to dominate the affairs of the community. A new generation of stockholders and officials wanted the people to live proudly in their own homes and to govern their communities in conformity with the Great American Dream. The families who lived in the rows of company-owned houses on company-owned streets, who bought their groceries at company-owned stores and endured sickness in company-owned hospitals, felt their imaginations stirred. At war's end a majority of the miners were close to sixty years of age, but a new generation of younger men had come up among them. Old and young, they concluded that prudence dictated the purchase of a house.

Since constructing them more than thirty years before the company had recovered its investment in its houses many times. A house's floors were worn thin by decades of boots and the bare feet of multitudes of children. Its walls were scarred from the inevitable batterings that gangs of children inflict. Nevertheless such houses carried all the sentimental attachments of home to men and women who had known no other for more than a quarter of a century. The company established a real estate office at which arrangements for the purchase of a house could be made. Employees were favored in their sale and the occupant of a dwelling was afforded the first opportunity to purchase it. The prices asked were not high. Four-room cottages with front and rear porches, weather-boarded exterior walls and plastered interiors were sold for prices ranging in the neighborhood of sixteen hundred dollars. One half of a duplex house sold for a similar price. A parcel of land surrounding the building accompanied it. The buyer was allowed to pay in monthly installments which were deducted from his wages along with store accounts, union dues, Social Security contributions and taxes. Miners blithely signed the purchase agreements and entered into the joys of home ownership.

The process got under way soon after the end of the war and proceeded rapidly during the following three or four years. By 1950 nearly all the major corporations had disposed of their houses with the exception of a few retained for the top managerial staff. Of the biggest operations only Benham and Lynch in Harlan County and Wheelwright in Floyd County retained their towns. Wheelwright is still company-owned and is the cleanest and best-managed mining community in the plateau. In 1960 International Harvester began the process of "freeing" Benham. Lynch was soon being sold house by house for a few hundred dollars each, with the purchasers required to remove most of them from the company's land — sizable numbers of them being re-assembled farther south in the prosperous Tennessee Valley.

Thousands of houses in the bigger camps were sold between 1945 and 1948. The small, shoddily built towns of the smaller companies were not sold. They continued to rot over the heads of their occupants. Rarely were any of them given a coat of paint and most received none at all. Hundreds of such structures have now gone without paint for nearly thirty consecutive years. Some were treated with wood preservatives early in the Depression, an application which turned them a ghastly brown but effectively preserved them from decay.

The companies timed their sales remarkably well. The residences were sold and largely paid for when the great postwar wave of automation swept through the mines. Occasionally a miner found himself jobless before his home was cleared of debt, but most purchasers pridefully held a deed "free and clear of encumbrances" before the discharge notices were slipped into their pay envelopes. The impressive-looking title deeds, however, actually conveyed only half a title. The large print (which the purchaser had laboriously read) "granted, sold and conveyed" the premises, but two long pages of fine print (through which few miners could make their way with any real comprehension) excepted and reserved the underlying minerals. Paragraph after paragraph protected the right of the coal company to "drill for, excavate, dig, mine and remove" the coal, oil, gas and other minerals by any method or system deemed necessary or convenient by the company and its assigns.

I have said that during the war many miners managed to save a few hundred dollars. Some had deposits of as much as two or three thousand dollars in the local banks. Allotments from sons in military service had augmented their savings. More than a few had lost sons on the battle fields and had collected the proceeds of National Service Life Insurance policies on their lives. All or part of these savings were invested in company houses. The miner whose savings were ample paid for his home in cash, thereby profiting from a small discount. As soon as the house was paid for the new owner went to work to "fix it up." Generally he called in a contractor from the county seat and arranged to install a new roof of asphalt shingles, and the exterior walls were encased in asbestos siding or some other protective material. A concrete block foundation took the place of the slender props. A hot-air furnace supplanted the old fireplaces. Water was pumped into the house and a portion of one of the rooms was converted to a bathroom.

Such improvements added approximately three thousand dollars to the original cost, and when the repairs and alterations were finished and the interior stood shining in new paint and wallpaper the transformation was remarkable. The miner could take genuine pride in his climb up the ladder. He happily basked in a sense of well-being and achievement.

Before long, gleaming, monstrous machines of fantastic new designs began arriving at the mines. Engineers from the companies which manufactured them explained their operation to the crews of men who had been chosen to operate them. After a few weeks of uncertainty while the crews became familiar with their eccentricities coal production sky-rocketed. Simultaneously hundreds of men were informed that their services were no longer needed. They had been faithful and diligent workmen and the company would be happy to recommend them to any prospective employer. The company wished them the best of luck and bid them adieu. So the discharged miners from the automating rail pits were flung into the countryside to seek employment in the truck mines. And, to their dismay, they found that more than half the truck mines were being closed out by the price-cost squeeze and the income-tax collectors. Their laborers were on the road seeking work also, and as the discarded machines from the rail mines entered the still active small pits new multitudes of jobless miners poured out of them to seek employment wherever it could be found. Some of the unemployed attempted to establish truck mines of their own, and a few succeeded, but most failed — because even with the newly acquired machinery the truck mines were able to realize only a narrow profit. Those without experience in their operation and a keen eye for economics could not stay afloat.

The surviving mines began to operate near capacity and continued to do so generally until the spring of 1960. Profits were far below those of the three first years after the war, but the coal flowed steadily from the hillsides. The thousands of jobless men faced their situation with astonishment. Never before in the experience of the oldest miner had there been mass unemployment in the midst of booming coal production. The blight of idleness and poverty in the midst of all-out production was a phenomenon then peculiar to the coalfields but one which began to spread into every industry.

The first reaction of the idled miner was to "wait and see what happens." He hoped without cause that "something" would occur so that the discharged employees would be needed again. His unemployment checks "tided him over" the first six months Hundreds of men lined up week after week at the courthouses to sign application forms and to report that they were still unemployed. By hundreds and thousands their "unemployed" benefits expired without even the hope of a job. Within a few more months the last of their savings, too, were gone. Without money, without a job and without skills, the baffled miner was stranded on "the ragged edge of starvation." At this juncture, in 1956, the Federal Government came to his rescue by restoring the dole. Federal storage bins were bulging with surpluses and huge quantities of food were shipped to Kentucky for distribution to the indigent. Monthly rations of corn meal, rice, cheese, butter, dried milk solids, beans and other staples were issued. The state was required to establish administrative services for the distribution program, a responsibility which it promptly dumped into the lap of the county judges and fiscal courts. These petty officials could not afford to offend anyone regardless of his economic circumstances. The lines of hungry, pauperized miners were swollen by others who could afford to buy food but who saw no reason to do so when it could be acquired free. By the end of 1957 in some counties more than half the people were regularly eating Government relief commodities.

But when jobs still failed to materialize the exodus from the coal counties quickened. Since the end of the war there had been a steady trickling away of highland families. Miners and farmers "took off" for Ohio, Michigan, Indiana, Illinois, California and Florida. Most important of the emigrés, however, were the annual classes of high school graduates. Fully three quarters of each county's spring crop of brighter boys and girls left immediately in quest of jobs in other states.

They followed trails blazed by teachers and others of the region's scanty stock of educated men and women. They poured by the thousands into the "Little Kentuckys" in the Northern and Midwestern cities, then spread out across the country wherever rumor reported jobs to be available. Today there are few counties in the United States in which newcomers from the plateau have not sought jobs. Typically, today's mountaineer can count relatives in a half-dozen states. Harlan County, hardest hit of all, has seen its inhabitants dwindle from 75,000 to 51,000. Neighboring Bell County sank from 43,000 to 35,000. Letcher shrank from 40,000 to 30,000. Pike

County, the most stable and prosperous of the plateau counties, declined from 81,000 to 68,000.

The abrupt falling away of the people drastically altered every aspect of the region's life. Rows of camp houses were emptied almost overnight. The proud new homeowner of 1947 was dwelling in a rented apartment in Detroit or Cincinnati ten years later. His house stood empty or, if he had been fortunate, had been sold for a thousand dollars to some local businessman who was willing to gamble on finding a tenant. Along the creeks and hollows jobless miners moved away from their homes on the larger creeks and the people on the remoter hollows moved down to occupy the vacated homes. Such deserted houses were bought for a small fraction of their original cost or were rented for ten to fifteen dollars monthly. Along the better roads the houses remained filled. On such arterial roads as the plateau possesses one may travel for miles without seeing an empty dwelling, but this appearance is deceptive. The hinterland along the maze of hollows and lesser creeks is sown with vacant, desolate houses. On one mile-long stream I once counted sixteen such silent and deserted habitations. Weeds choked the lawns, the roofing had surrendered to the wind, and the floors sagged under the rains.

The truck-mining industry brought a terrific clamor for the construction of rural roads. Within a year or two after the war ended most of the bypassed spurs had been emptied, leaving only the narrow band of outcrop which cannot be recovered by underground mining. The overgrown new industry had to expand into new areas of untouched coal. Such mineral was available in large tracts. The companies which owned them had anticipated their exploitation by railroad pits, but now it was realized that the coal could be removed by truck mines without the expense of building railroads and huge, complex tipples. The chief drawback to this scheme was that such remaining mineral tracts were far removed from existing highways and roads, and a new network of rural roads was required if the coal was to be transported by motor trucks. The holding companies put pressure on county and state officials to build roads into the virgin tracts. They were powerfully supported by the people living along the creeks and hollows where the coal lay. The folk who lived on Kingdom Come, Big Clifty, and Jake's Creek were just as determined to possess a glittering sedan as were those delighted people depicted in the motor-car ads. They trooped to the county court-houses and in lesser delegations to Frankfort to coerce and wheedle officials to undertake the construction of backcountry roads.

The counties were broke and locally financed construction was out of the question. If roads were to be built they would have to be paid for out of state funds. From every part of Kentucky rural people demanded a system of all-weather highways — "farm-to-market roads," as they were called in western and central Kentucky. These pressures resulted in a rural program financed by a special levy of two cents per gallon of gasoline sold in the state. Passed in 1948, this new tax was designed to get the mountaineers and other rural Kentuck-ians "out of the mud."

Road building in the plateau has always presented many serious engineering problems. The bottoms are narrow and relatively valu-able. If highways are located on them juries in right-of-way condem-nation suits have always awarded generous sums to the dispossessed landowners. In a region where flat land is extremely scarce, this is understandable.

This factor necessitated their construction along the base of the mountains. Right of way could be obtained cheaply, but the grading required much blasting. Much of the roadway had to be carved out of soft shale or crumbly sandstone, and out of unstable, yellow clay the remainder of the distance. The myriad streams flowing into the greater creeks required bridges. In such terrain the construction of good roads required great outlays of labor and material.

These the Department of Highways could not afford. This agency of the state government — sometimes cynically called "the Depart-ment of Politics" or "the Department of Roads and Politics" — was hammered by influential county politicians and by the Governor and other state officials. Continued political dominance depended upon the construction of many roads in little time. The millions derived from the special levy were insufficient to provide quality construc-tion. The engineers would have to be content with quantity, allow-ing the future to cope with the built-in problems of maintenance.

For seven years after 1948 Kentucky was in the throes of its biggest rural road-building program. Miles and miles of new highways were cut out of the mountains. They were designed to provide at least sixteen feet of pavement and a drainage ditch. Long, snakelike yellow gashes appeared at the bases of innumerable ridges and concrete bridges jumped across streams. As rapidly as a mile of road could be completed by the hard-pressed contractor, mines sprang up along its right of way. In some instances the loading bins were so located that the trucks could be loaded while stopped on the highway itself.

The roads followed a uniform pattern. After a cut was made around the hillside the loose earth was piled in low places for fill material. It was rolled down and covered with a thin layer of white crushed limestone. At the base of the cut was a drainage ditch and the slope was left at an almost perpendicular angle.

The surface was "traffic bound." The passing vehicles were used to pound the limestone aggregate into the soft base. More gravel was applied from time to time and in turn was mauled into the foundation. In theory the roadbed would eventually become solid and hard. The settling caused by time, rainfall and traffic would make the base enduring and dependable.

But then came summer. The road dried out and the battered limestone gravel turned to dust. In places gray limestone lay fine as flour, dry as gun powder, and inches deep. Each passing vehicle stirred a hideous cloud which rolled for a mile behind its churning wheels. Cars and trucks were covered with ashen particles. No matter how tightly the windows were rolled up the dust crept inside and settled in upholstery, giving it a foul, gritty smell. It discolored trees and pastures and passed through the doorways and windows of houses like millions of tiny demons. Housewives added their complaints to the outcry of the truckers and automobile owners.

So the politicians were pursued by new mobs, who demanded that the roads be "blacktopped." This was the only means by which the unbearable dust could be stopped and the responsive politicians pressed the Department of Highways for surfacing contracts. The engineers argued with unassailable logic that the foundations were still too insecure to support a pavement and that it would disintegrate under the freezes and thaws of winter. But highway commissioner, governor and courthouse cronies could ill afford to heed such advice. The contractors were set to work and thin layers of tar and gravel, hardly more than "one gravel thick," were laid down on hundreds of miles of highly unstable roadbeds. In due course the roads went to pieces, but the process of building cheap roads and finishing them with dust-laying coats of tar and gravel went forward apace.

The new road projects broke the isolation of the mountaineer to a remarkable degree. They gave him access in his new or secondhand car to the stores and offices of the county seat. They shattered the ancient community-centered attitudes of thousands of plateau dwellers and hastened the exodus of the people out of the region. They made possible the mining of thousands of acres of coal, and the marketing of the remainder of the region's worthwhile timber. They made possible for the first time the consolidation of many of the plateau's schools. But the stretches of low-cost roads have proved almost impossible to maintain at a level anywhere near the standards generally expected of a paved, state-maintained highway. For mile upon mile, steep slopes rise almost sheer above them. Tons of rock and immeasurable quantities of loose dirt wash and slide into the drainage ditches, clogging them and saturating the roadbeds with water. In winter the soaked earth freezes and swells, bursting the pavement and leaving immense potholes. Every spring finds long stretches of vanished blacktop.

Lacking the funds to break up the pavement and start all over again with new applications of limestone, the Department patched and resurfaced. It cleaned out the ditches and shoved the debris over the lower shoulders of the road. From there it washed onto agricultural lands and into the streams. The Highway Department made no effort to stabilize either the slopes above or the banks below the roads with any kind of vegetation, an omission which facilitated soil erosion on a grand scale. This waste, combined with the soil loss caused by forest fires, hillside farming and mining, choked the streams with silt and mud. Huge water holes which as late as 1948 teemed with a dozen species of game fish were sinister yellow mud bars long before 1950.

But the greatest evil resulting from this large-scale construction of "political" roads was that it destroyed the state's ability to build more roads without massive borrowing. Within a few years the maintenance of each mile equaled its original cost. Their maintenance in 1962 consumed much of the department's revenues and has brought rural road construction to a virtual standstill. Since 1955 few new roads have been built in the plateau. Nor is there any real prospect that more will be built at any time now foreseeable. Though state officials, including Governor Bert T. Combs, have promised a network of superhighways for the mountains the promise is far from fulfillment. Funds for such roads are simply unavailable. In the last decade the state has gone in debt more than three hundred million dollars in order to keep its "road program" going, but this immense bonded indebtedness has deepened, rather than eased, its dilemma.

---◆---

CHAPTER EIGHTEEN

The Rise of the Welfare State

THE SHARP RISE in unemployment and the flight from the plateau of its hardier people were accompanied by the growth of "welfarism" on a scale unequaled elsewhere in North America and scarcely surpassed anywhere in the world. The "Welfare state," as it has developed in the highlands, is two-pronged. On the one hand are the public Welfare programs which were born in the Depression as part of the New Deal's efforts to shore up the nation's economy and stave off revolution. Mingled with these is the giant program of the United Mine Workers of America.

The public sector of the Welfare program consists of "State Aid" and Social Security. The former, often referred to by mountaineers simply as "the Welfare," draws most of its funds from the Federal Government but is administered by the state. It provides monthly checks to indigent citizens who are (a) blind, (b) dependent children, (c) more than sixty-five years old, or (d) totally disabled. The Social Security system is, of course, administered solely by the Federal Government; it provides checks for its beneficiaries who have reached retirement age or have become disabled so they cannot work, and to the widows and other dependents of deceased workmen.

The State Aid began with the Old Age Pension system. In the grimmest years of the Depression the "superannuated" were favored with tiny pensions. Initially these modest sums rarely exceeded six dollars a month and no old couple were able to live very "high on the hog" on twelve dollars every thirty days. As the nation climbed out of the abyss of depression the pensions grew larger and eligibility requirements were relaxed. By 1960 the payments averaged fifty-five dollars a month in Kentucky.

As the overseers of the Social Security system acquired assurance and funds, its benefits expanded. Congressmen ritualistically enlarged the payments and "improved" the program every two years just prior to the House elections. From its inception practically every industrial worker in the plateau was covered, and by 1950 thousands of miners had reached the retirement age. Since then Congress has added the program of benefits for the totally and permanently disabled.

There was also a steady expansion of State Aid. The Old Age Pension grants were augmented by grants to the blind. Next came assistance for dependent children whose parents had deserted them, died, or become disabled from disease or injury. This phase of the program also "benefited" illegitimate children whose fathers were unknown or could not be compelled to support them.

A "fourth category" (d) of public assistance extended monthly checks to persons "totally" disabled. The last addition was approved by the Legislature in 1960 and was a scheme to permit the state to pay a portion of the medical bills of Old Age pensioners and other needy persons.

These developments were part of a pattern which was repeated in a number of the world's civilized and industrialized states. They were inevitable in a society where the cohesion of the family was shattered by mass population movements and the social stability of farmer and peasant had been dissolved by the transformation of agriculture from its ancient patterns to a modern industrialized system of production and marketing. But in the politics-laden atmosphere of the Kentucky mountains, they worked wholly unforeseen results and contributed to the undermining on a mass scale of public morals and morale.

The aids and grants dispensed by the United Mine Workers were second only to the publicly financed Welfare programs in their effects, which were immediate and deep. Together, the two programs provided a vast treasury for whose benefits the population was unprepared by anything in its background and experience. Nothing in the history of the mountain people had conditioned them to receive such grants with gratitude or to use them with restraint. In a land in which huge corporations and their friends on judicial bench and in legislative hall had reduced the ordinary citizen to a status little better than that of a mere tenant-by-sufferance in his own home, the mountaineer had nurtured a cynicism toward government at all levels. The "handouts" were speedily recognized as a lode from which dollars could be mined more easily than from any coal seam.

The administration of any system of aids, gifts, grants or loans is fraught with peril to character and integrity. In the best of circumstances such programs must extend benefits to people who have performed no direct service to earn them. Granting the justice and logic of the argument that past service to society, for example, as a coal miner, obligates society to give the citizen a measure of its largesse when he is old or sick, the benefit nevertheless often appears as an unearned gift. It is unthinkable that a rich and enlightened society should permit its unfortunate members to starve in the midst of plenty; but once the justifications are admitted the difficulties still stand undiminished.

Since its inception a noble objective of our democracy has been to achieve government by just laws rather than by fallible and sometimes selfish men. But even when the laws are excellent the men and women who execute them are nearly always swayed by political considerations. When the public assistance programs were organized in the plateau it was scarcely possible to find persons capable of their administration who did not feel a keen interest in the outcome of pending political races, and in Kentucky there are elections twice each year. The ties of blood and marriage, the pressures of old animosities and new alliances tug at every citizen. Against such a setting not even the loftiest of leadership in the state capitol could have effected wholly honest and honorable administration of the Welfare program. And, of course, such loftiness rarely exists in public affairs. Practical considerations — the recurring need for votes and dependence upon allies — makes such nobility impossible if victory and political survival are to be achieved.

Initially the Old Age Pension program was modest in the extreme. Many of its beneficiaries were worn-out, crippled coal min ers. Others were farmers whose land was exhausted. Still others, and these were the most numerous, were widows. Nearly all had sons and daughters who had married and were struggling to keep bread and potatoes on their own tables. The small pensions were of inestimable comfort to aged people who otherwise would have lived out their days with less happiness and in deeper want.

Oldsters with sons and daughters wealthy enough to support them were not eligible for benefits. In the earlier years this reasonable limitation was taken for granted, and there were few protests against it, but as time passed there came a change of attitude. Instead of charity extended by government to its unfortunate citizens, the Old Age Pensions became grants whose recipients were "entitled" to them. This view was summed up in assertions that the pensioner "had a right to it" and "had earned it." With the general acceptance of this new point of view there came the feeling that *every* old person should have a monthly check. Some argued that the old people had paid taxes in their better years (these payments had been pitifully meager) and now in their old age they were entitled to receive their money back. Others argued that the contemporary generation of workers were paying taxes to support the government and that, *ipso facto*, the public treasury was obligated to support their parents. Some maintained that because an old man had produced coal when it was needed in past crises he should now be pensioned regardless of his financial standing or that of his children. But, on whatever ground, the mountaineer rationalized that his parents (or he himself, if he was past the magic age of sixty-five) should "draw a pension," and he resolutely set out to so weaken the legal barriers and administrative strictures as to permit them to do so.

Pressure was first brought to bear on the resident "Welfare workers." These men and women were local citizens, related by blood and marriage to countless people in the county. The staff grew larger as the program of benefits expanded. Theoretically they were impartial and interested only in serving suffering humanity. They were nonpolitical by the strict terms of the Hatch Act, but they could close neither their eyes nor their hearts to the fact that many of their friends and relatives held or ran for public office. They themselves had obtained their positions on the recommendations of influential county and state politicians. A sense of gratitude bound them to the groups whose efforts had secured their jobs for them. They could not turn deaf ears to the friends and relatives whose support had raised them to the positions they occupied. They could not be fired except for "cause." Political activity was cause, under the applicable statutes; but a century of "playing politics" had taught the mountaineer to be discreet when discretion is necessary — and politics can, of course, be played in such a manner that its occurrence could never be proved in a court of law.

The old man whose pension application was denied asked his friends — in and out of the courthouse — to intercede for him with the Welfare workers. These influential people requested that the claims be reconsidered and that new "studies" be made. They "talked to" the caseworkers, to the extent of expressing hope that the application could be reviewed and given the benefit of any reasonable doubts. The all-powerful courthouse coteries often interceded directly with the top officials at Frankfort, not hesitating to invade even the office of the governor for such purpose. Since the people in the top echelon hired the Welfare workers and were in turn elected by cliques of local politicians, the word filtered through channels — and concessions were made. Through such means the Welfare workers became, in the language of the mountaineers, "more accommodating." The lists of pensioners grew longer. Indeed, for a time practically everyone who applied for the Old Age grants received them.

The public's experience with the Old Age Pensions convinced thousands that other phases of the program could be successfully handled by the same tactics.

A. D. C. stands for Aid to Dependent Children, the "second category" (b) of public assistance. It provides help to indigent children whose parents cannot or will not support them. It is granted on condition that the child, if of school age, be in regular attendance. If the father is physically and mentally able to work, the child is ineligible. In the widespread unemployment that followed the decline of the truck mines and the automation of the pits, the specter of want began to haunt countless households. Most of the idled men were little better than illiterates. Few could read at better than the fourth-grade level and long failure to exercise their meager skill had diminished it still further. In their phrase they "had no learning," a fact which they painfully recognized and which, with the decline in importance of the manual laborer, left an overpowering feeling of inadequacy. They had spent their working lives in the mines, at a supremely hazardous occupation. Their eyes were dimmed by long use in the gloomy half-darkness of the pits, and were reddened by continuous irritation from particles of coal dust and rock dust. Their hearts were enlarged and weakened from years of arduous labor without sufficient quantities of oxygen. Hammers, picks and shovels had thickened their hands and made them large and clumsy. Strenuous exertion in cramped quarters, often on hands and knees or in a reclining position had made them stiff and awkward.

These circumstances curtailed their desirability as workmen in other industries. The young men on whom the mines had not yet set their ineradicable stamp could go to Detroit or other industrial cities with reasonable prospects of finding employment. But their older colleague, once his employment in the mines was ended, was generally helpless. The personnel directors concluded that he lacked the ability to be trained which the companies required. Another factor operating against him was the growing importance of industry-supported retirement plans. In all the major industries the labor contracts provided for a retirement pension at age sixty-five or younger. The personnel offices wanted men who could work for thirty or forty years before retirement pay commenced. A man of forty-five or fifty had too short a period of usefulness at the workbench or assembly line before the rocking chair of old age was reached. Besides, automation was under way in the industrial plants. They, like the mines, were beginning to replace men and the old-style machines they operated with far more efficient machines, and the personnel directors could choose their future employees with increasing care. The upshot was that the older sort of unemployed miners were driven into an increasingly desperate trap. Technology in the mines had made them obsolete, rendering unsalable the only skill they possessed. The factories and mills in distant cities would not employ them. While the young men and their families drained out of the plateau, the older miners — those in their early forties and upward — were stranded, and. as automation gathered momen-

tum in other industries, those who had "made the break" began to
return to the mountains.

The middle-aged unemployed miner and his wife were in a
dilemma of the sharpest character. They were among the world's
most fertile people. The 1950 census revealed that the people of
Leslie County had the highest birth rate in the nation, and pro-
created at a rate only a little higher than their kinsmen in surrounding counties. Children were numerous and the miner was stuck with
from three to a dozen of them to support. Food, clothing and shelter had to be provided. They could be acquired only by wages, and
there were no employers. Technically the miner was fit enough to
work if a job had been available. Had another vast coal boom occurred he and thousands of other such industrial rejects would have
flocked back into the pits and would have been invaluable workmen. Had a new W. P. A. program been instituted, they could have
graded countless miles of new roads and raised many new
bridges and schoolhouses. But no such projects existed or were even
visualized.
It will be supposed that the miners could have returned to the land,
becoming farmers with the assistance of the United States Department of Agriculture. The farm agents still labored among them,
seeking with little success to induce men to raise cattle, hogs, vegetables, fruits and berries for their tables and for sale. Generous financial aid was available for those willing to rehabilitate the land and
derive a livelihood from it, but the obstacles to such a shift were
formidable. Most of the land so situated that it could be cultivated
had long since been exhausted. Vast areas had been virtually steri-
lized by erosion and by mine wastes from driftmouth and slate
dump. The ancestral farms had been so many times subdivided
among succeeding generations of heirs that the portions were too
small for practical agricultural use. These difficulties were important
but the real hurdle was psychological. In the history of mankind
there have been no epochs in which an industrialized, wage-earning
population has voluntarily reverted to the soil. The trend of history
has been away from the land, rarely back to it.
So the jobless forty-five- or fifty-year-old miner with "a gang of

young-'uns" to support went through a demoralizing struggle. Bit by bit, his self-reliance and initiative deteriorated into self-pity. Seeing the hosts of pensioned old people and the swarms of dependent children whose parents were dead, fled or disabled, he came to the belief that he and his children ought to enjoy the same benefits. He reasoned that it was unfair for one child to eat because his father was crippled while another starved because his father was able-bodied. If disability and ill health were the magic keys that would open the Welfare portal he could, perhaps, find them.

He became, in countless cases, a Welfare malingerer. In a nation that was seeking to lead, liberate and protect the world, men were reduced to the tragic status of "symptom-hunters." If they could find enough symptoms of illness, they might convince the physicians they were "sick enough to draw." Like dispirited soldiers who hope to avoid combat, they besieged the doctors, complaining of a wide range of ailments. Their backs ached. They suffered from headaches. They could not sleep. They were short of breath and had chest pains. Their stomachs were upset and they could not eat. Above all, they were "nervous." To support their woeful histories they could point to scars on arms, legs and chest, mementos of old mining accidents. When lumped together and presented to a doctor, these things were supposed to indicate such disability as incapacitated the man from working. Then his children, as public charges, could draw enough money to feed the family.

Such people possessed little beyond their votes. Their ballots had helped to elect the men in the county courthouses. To offend one of them was to incur the wrath of many, perhaps enough to forfeit a precinct. The old pressures were brought to bear for the benefit of these new legions of "disabled" men, and the Welfare workers became ever more lenient and tolerant. But no matter how liberally the caseworker might view the claim of a robust-looking father of nine children, her hands were tied. Under the law an applicant could be certified as eligible only if the "Welfare doctor" certified him to be so physically disabled that he was unable to work at any gainful occupation. Doctors are a stubborn lot, and most of them take their duties and responsibilities seriously. As honorable men they are willing to give only honest appraisal of the patients who come to them. And they found that many of the disabled fathers were actually strong men driven to neurosis by circumstances with which they could not cope. The reports went out that the applicants had an accumulation of defects and illnesses but, on the whole, were able to labor.

Nearly all the plateau's physicians were native sons. They had grown up in the area and had gone away to medical school, generally at the University of Louisville. They had returned to practice medicine in their home counties. Most of them stood aloof from politics except to vote and to exercise the Kentuckian's usual prerogative to "cuss and discuss" the candidates. But here and there were doctors with keen political instincts. They had held public office themselves. Practically every county remembers when "Doc" So-and-so was county judge, justice of the peace, state senator or school board member. In rural areas the practice of medicine lends itself remarkably well to a political career. The physician can ingratiate himself with hundreds of people annually. He seldom has cause to offend anyone and if he is of a sympathetic nature he accumulates a great deal of gratitude in the procession of patients who pass through his doors. His plunge into politics is a lifelong step. He rarely manages to dissociate himself from the struggles which rage around him. If he no longer seeks public office he has friends and kinsmen who do. Such a doctor is likely to mix politics with his medicine. It was to physicians of their ilk that the symptom-nursers instinctively turned.

The political doctor found himself in a dilemma. His office was increasingly beset by men who said they were sick and unable to work. They brought a medical report for him to execute and sign. If he reported to the Welfare Department that the applicant was able-bodied, he would anger him and his family and friends. The doctor could reckon easily enough the extent of the applicant's influence and voting power. If too many such men were antagonized, the doctor and the candidates he favored would be in serious trouble. On the other hand acquiescence in obviously fraudulent claims would violate the basic ethics of his profession and bring down the contempt of his colleagues upon him. Consequently, the political doctor attempted to compromise. He gave the benefit of the doubt to the applicant and certified as sick those with reasonably convincing symptoms. Those who were rejected, however, returned undaunted and the eroding integrity of the physician soon washed away entirely. The stern demands of political necessity gave the applicants the coveted certificates of disability and, in return, the candidates whom the physicians promoted got their votes. The state paid a small fee for each such examination. The dominant coterie of local politicians called to the attention of the Welfare Department at Frankfort the doctor's professional qualifications. It was pointed out that he was friendly to all concerned and was able to recognize a sick man when he saw one. Almost invariably the department directed that the recommended physicians examine applicants from the county. Thus the "Welfare" or "State Aid" doctor became a powerful cog in the political machines which ran the plateau and dominated the state.

Not all doctors who examined applicants for the Department of Welfare were dishonest or lax. But the role of some physicians in manipulating public assistance for political ends became so blatant and widespread that it was a continuing scandal in many counties. But then, health or disease are matters peculiarly within the judgment of the physician, and whether they exist is a matter of opinion on which physicians of unquestioned integrity and competence may disagree. That great numbers of jobless men were added to the rolls and the Welfare doctor and his friends thereafter received their votes at election time might conceivably have been only coincidence. In any event, the program of State Aid, with its Welfare doctors, physical examinations and monthly checks, helped to build tremendously powerful political machines — organizations difficult to defeat in the counties of the plateau. In later years administrative and diagnostic procedures were tightened, and arrangements were made to have some applicants examined by physicians in adjoining or distant counties. But no safeguards yet devised have proved impregnable against determined Welfare seekers.

That segment of the Welfare program that provides assistance to the blind was also subject to abuses, and from the same quarter. But the number of people who could qualify for this category of aid was limited even under the loosest application of the law. Even so, a good many people were found to be technically sightless who could, to say the least, find their way about without a Seeing Eye dog. I shall never forget my astonishment when I visited the home of one of these unfortunates and found him reading a newspaper with his eyeglasses perched jauntily across the middle of his forehead.

After the "fourth category" of public assistance was provided by the Legislature of 1956, the desperate legions of jobless men sought lodgment on the rolls of the "totally disabled," using the same techniques that had worked so well relative to the Aid to Dependent Children program. The coal counties teemed with men who were able to qualify for this type of aid even under strict interpretation of the governing laws and administrative regulations. Commissary porches and camp streets were dotted with legless and armless men, for the mines had continued to take an awesome toll of life and limb. Yet there were also gangs of relatively sturdy men who were determined to "draw a check." When the word spread up the creeks and hollows and through the camps that anybody who was needy and "totally disabled" could receive monthly benefits, multitudes of men resolved to prove disability by hook or by crook. Like the symptom-nursers who sought support for their dependent children, they began to cultivate symptoms of disease or impairment. Stomach pains, chest pains, headaches and nervousness ran rampant. Men saw spots before their eyes. Their legs throbbed dreadfully upon the slightest exertion. Their heads swam dizzily and any effort to labor caused them to faint. When these miseries failed to convince the physicians they carried their woes to the local politicians. These, in countless cases, were able to persuade the doctors and the Welfare supervisors that the rejectees were indeed desperately ill. Half seriously, half in jest, some doctors referred to their malady as a "chronic, passive dependency-syndrome." The names of sick and well, halt, lame and strong crept onto the Welfare lists.

For several years, the chief objective in the lives of a great many plateau dwellers was simply to get their names added to the public assistance rolls, or, once there, to prevent their removal. Dejected and submissive from long unemployment, hopeless of ever again finding jobs, the Welfare grants became their only hope. Small though the monthly checks are, they usually permit a standard of living as high as the beneficiary and his family can hope to achieve even if the breadwinner eventually finds employment.

Let us consider the situation of a typical forty-five-year-old man who has long since ceased to support his household. He has a wife and five children ranging in age from four to sixteen. The Welfare doctor says he can never work again and his income from the state and Federal treasuries is one hundred and fifty-five dollars a month. He owns twelve acres of hillside land, and a four-room boxed house. His home is without plumbing — the water is drawn from a well in the back yard; the sanitary facility is a privy. His land was worn out by hillside farming years ago; most of it is covered by broom sage or scrubby cull trees. An acre or two, however, is growing up in young poplars and has a prospective value for some date far in the future. The property has a market value of perhaps a thousand dollars. The man dropped out of school when he was nine years old and in the fourth grade. His parents were practically illiterate and he found little or no encouragement for books and learning. His mother needed him at home to carry coal, chop kindling wood for the fireplaces and to help take care of the younger children. His wife went to school only a year or two longer than he.

They subscribe to no publications of any kind and neither of them can read or write except with difficulty. Such skills as they acquired in school have been largely lost by long disuse.

They live on a creek several miles from the county courthouse. Ten years ago the state built a rural highway near their home, but lack of maintenance has permitted it to so deteriorate that it now is scarcely passable. The children attend school in a two-room building nearly a mile away.

The woman has never held a job of any kind. Such work as she has done consisted of washing clothes, scrubbing floors, cooking and "pottering about the place." The man entered the coal mines when he was seventeen, working beside his father. He worked for various coal companies until five years ago. At that time he was "laid off" by the "dog hole" truck mine by which he was last employed. Since then he has sought work in Michigan, Indiana, Ohio and Illinois. At one time he found a job as a laborer with a construction firm for a few weeks but was discharged when cold weather came. No one else has been willing to hire him. After he lost his job in the truck mine he drew weekly unemployment insurance benefits for six months. Thereafter he had no income except the little he could earn from an occasional day of work for a local farmer or on some minor construction enterprise. For four years he has drawn rations of government surplus foods.

He is at a total loss to understand his predicament. Each evening he sits in his tattered living room and watches the television he bought in happier and more prosperous times. Glib-tongued commentators describe the tremendous economic and technical progress occurring elsewhere in the nation. He resents with increasing bitterness the combination of circumstances which has precluded him from participation in the progress of his country. He feels useless. He senses that his older children have already commenced to hold him in contempt.

When he finds an occasional day's work plowing and planting a vegetable garden, cultivating a field of corn, stacking lumber at one of the few remaining sawmills or helping someone to build a house, the pay is rarely more than six dollars. If despite the doctor's certificate of disability he feels inclined to do the work, he dares not do so, because such activity indicates recovery from his affliction and, if discovered by his Welfare worker, could cause the forfeiture of his precious check. If he could find enough odd jobs to keep him busy twenty days a month he could not earn as much as the state sends him. Hence, his check, small as it is, represents more money than experience has taught him he has any reasonable prospect of earning. On the public assistance rolls he can live as well without working as his neighbor with similar background and qualifications can earn by hard labor.

As hopelessness deepened general morality was undermined. The sexual mores of the mountaineer were never strict. While the highlanders were never "Tobacco Roaders" by any stretch of the imagination, they have, on the other hand, never been Victorians. They have taken a practical attitude toward sex and quite unashamedly behave as nature guides them. The illegitimate child — the mountaineer's term is "base-born" — was never viewed with the disdain accorded such unfortunates in other societies. The bastards were altogether too numerous for such treatment to be practical. The girl who bore a child before marriage was soon married to a tolerant husband, and the children born of her lawful union grew up with their unembarrassed elder brother or sister. Illegitimates made up a sizable percentage of the population and, though the circumstances of their birth sometimes called for off-color jokes, they were not seriously rejected or scorned.

This tolerant attitude toward the facts of life brought an amazing reaction when the public assistance program began to dispense hard cash for the support of illegitimate children. Before the advent of Welfare the "wronged" mother had been compelled to swear out a bastardy warrant charging the man with paternity of her child and requesting the court to require him to pay her a monthly sum for the child's support. Now, to draw welfare for the child, the woman had to report that the identity of the father was unknown or that she no longer knew his whereabouts. In the deepening destitution of the coal counties astonishing numbers of women resorted to illicit associations, illegitimate children and the certainty of welfare checks in preference to the uncertainty of the holy but penniless state of matrimony.

Incredible as this may seem, it was a wholly logical outgrowth of the social and economic setting. Each spring, with their new high school diplomas, the better-educated young women left the plateau, following their kinsmen North, East and West. Few ever returned. In the main those who remained were less ambitious and, frequently, of lesser mentality. Having grown up without jobs of any kind or the worthwhile activities generally available to the nation's adolescent girls, they suffered from a nearly complete absence of the teachings and disciplines which instill pride in members of their sex. In short, their shabby environments and the loose standards of their families and communities had made slatterns of many of them. Doubtless, their standards would have been higher if their sisters of stronger will and keener minds could have remained behind to set them a better example.

Fertile and amoral females resided in every camp and on every creek. Illegitimate pregnancies increased at an ominous rate. The new unwed mothers promptly appeared in the Welfare offices and applied for their monthly assistance checks. In due course, and in all too many instances, the first "mistake" was followed by another and the monthly stipend grew. Some of these uninhibited women have blessed the state with a half-dozen new citizens, all of them supported by the nation's taxpayers. One pair of sisters living in the same house began bearing children before their twentieth birthdays. As this is written one of them is the mother of five children and the other of four. These nine Kentuckians were born "without benefit of clergy," though their Welfare worker assured me that she rarely visited the house without seeing a man leave by the back door.

These "Welfare mothers" thus support their children and themselves and sometimes assist their parents as well. A check sent for support of the children buys food for the central table and all living under the same roof benefit from it. Usually the husbandless mother lives with her father and mother and perhaps a younger brother or sister. She and they and her children share the shelter of the house and the check supplements the foods from the surplus commodity distribution centers.

Such women cannot afford to marry. Matrimony stops the check, or at least precludes it for children subsequently born, unless the groom is so "disabled" he can work only on a mattress and is thereby eligible for assistance himself. Nearly every mountain woman yearns to have children and few live out their lives in sexual continence. For many pathetic mountaineer women babies and sex can be afforded only at the expense of the Aid to Dependent Children appropriations. In the poverty-ridden Cumberlands, the A. D. C. program has in great part been allowed to degenerate into a system of subsidies calculated to perpetuate and multiply immorality.

For example, I vividly recall a woman who came to my office and wanted a divorce. Her jobless husband was unable to support her and their child. Hesitantly she explained that if they were divorced the children she thereafter bore him would be eligible for state assistance. As she put it, "That's about the only way poor folks can afford to have young-'uns."

As the more intelligent and ambitious people moved out of the plateau the percentage of mental defectives relative to the total population rose sharply. Their low intelligence added to their employment woes, but their votes were as potent as those of the wealthiest

288 · WASTE AND WELFARE

merchants in the county seats. The doctors and Welfare workers
were sympathetic to them — and it is difficult for one to be otherwise. When a man and his wife are unemployed and unemployable,
public assistance is the only alternative to cold and starvation and
they inevitably wind up on the relief rolls.

But such disability as they may suffer does not prevent them from
procreating, and they beget great gangs of children who tend to inherit or soon to acquire the shortcomings of their parents and to
become Welfare beneficiaries as soon as they are born. Under present laws it is unlikely that their names will ever leave the relief
rolls. They will be supported as dependent children until they are
eighteen years of age. By then or soon thereafter many of the girls
will be pregnant and will draw public assistance for their offspring.
Others will receive grants because they are disabled by reason of low
mentality or diseases acquired in childhood from malnutrition and
insanitation. They will draw checks for that reason until they are
sixty-five years old, from which point their Old Age Pensions and
state-paid medical bills will finance them to the grave.

Only education with its accompanying sense of confidence and
purpose can break this deadly and ruinous sequence. Nevertheless,
the Congressmen who unhesitatingly appropriate generous millions
annually for the growing multitudes of Welfare recipients have declined to spend funds for schools. A small fraction of the money
now dispensed in relief checks would build attractive schoolhouses,
fill them with books and laboratories, and educate competent
teachers for their faculties. Until such schools are provided — for so
long as the present drab facilities are symbolic of learning, inspiration and hope — there will be no real alternative to the dry rot of
Welfarism.

Nor was the Social Security system invulnerable to abuses. The
mountaineers attacked certain phases of it with remarkable cunning
and persistence and found Welfare gold even where administrative
safeguards were strictest.

The Social Security Administration is staffed by civil servants who
work under the prohibitions of the Hatch Act. There is no reason to
believe they are not honest and capable. But again, they are subject
to human errors and pressures, and there is reason to believe they

sometimes yield to suggestions from Congressmen and issue decisions which fall somewhat short of the facts and the law.

The United States Old Age and Survivors Insurance Act was an enlightened piece of legislation. When Congress approved it, its forerunner had already been in effect in Germany for fifty years. However, the patient research and study of its authors could not have anticipated the abuses to which it would be subjected.

Fifteen years after the act became law many aged miners had retired. They had begun working in the pits more than thirty years before and were decrepit from age and hard labor. Their small monthly checks were well earned and they were grateful to a national administration which had prepared this hedge for them against poverty in their sunset years.

Some of the beneficiaries had taken grandchildren into their homes to raise. Generally they were the offspring of warm-blooded daughters who had worked awhile in one of the Northern cities and had come home "in the family way." Typically, in a few months the mother returned to Detroit or Hamilton, a bit sadder and somewhat wiser. The pampered child grew up with "grandpap and granny" and was their second family. He or she was a source of great joy to them in their declining years.

Then the old man learned that by formally adopting the child he could receive an additional monthly sum for its support, as the Social Security Act extended to all persons legally dependent upon the beneficiary. "Dependents" included his wife and minor children by blood or adoption. Legal dependency had to exist and it did not extend to grandchildren.

So the elderly couple retained an attorney to file an adoption petition in Circuit Court. The mother signed a written agreement by which she waived all objections to the adoption. Within three or four months a judgment was entered which declared the infant to be the heir of the grandparents and to be their own child for all lawful intents and purposes. From that month forward, the beneficiary drew approximately seventeen dollars extra. Payments continued until the child was eighteen years old and were unaffected by the death in the meantime of the grandfather, or if you prefer, the father.

In such an instance no injustice was done. The child was virtually deserted into the custody of the grandparents and they were bound to it by every tie of love and sympathy. But soon others in different circumstances profited from their example and mined more Welfare gold.

The adopting of grandchildren grew into an important business in the local courts. In growing numbers Social Security beneficiaries adopted their grandchildren even when the latter were living with their parents in a nearby house. In order to draw the additional money only a certified judgment of adoption was required — a document which could be obtained for a total cost of approximately one hundred and fifty dollars. The additional income was welcome whether or not the natural parents were employed. If the father was working the money could be deposited in a bank to defray the costs of a college education in later years. If the father's wages were too low to allow for the reasonable support of his children, part of the costs of their upbringing could thus be shifted onto the backs of the nation's employers and workmen.

This kind of pilfering has occurred on a considerable scale. If similarly resorted to over the nation as a whole, contributions at astronomical levels would be required to support the program. And, shockingly, this plundering of a splendid institution established for the benefit of old and disabled workers brought few protests from those who knew about it. The accepted attitude was that the old man, his wife and descendants had earned the money, were entitled to it and were "due" to receive it. Public opinion, instead of condemning such practices, condoned and approved them. An attorney in one of the coal counties recently called to my attention a flagrant example of this type of Social Security raiding. The wife of a successful truck-mine operator drives an expensive, late-model automobile and lives in a comfortable modern home. She is the mother of two children who, of course, reside with her. However, the children were quietly adopted by their grandparents. The checks are deposited in a special fund to the account of the children and already contains more than a thousand dollars. The children alone will draw a sum many times in excess of the grandfather's contributions.

As the Social Security program grew, Congress provided payments for all workmen covered who became "totally and permanently" disabled. This magic phrase again became the Open Sesame to

a measure of security for those who could prove sufficient impairment. Soon after the amendment was added swarms of men descended upon local doctors seeking certificates of disability for pres-
entation to the itinerant Social Security field agents. The same
tactics which had succeeded so brilliantly with the state-administered
public assistance programs produced the certificates for Social Security. However, this Federal agency evinced laudable skepticism
when confronted with stacks of letters stating strong-looking men to
be disabled. More extensive examinations by other physicians were
generally ordered. But the administrators commenced the practice of
making available to the applicant a copy of the examining physician's report and irate patients denounced those physicians who were
sturdy enough to declare that a hale and hearty man was still able to
work. In the face of such wrathful patients not a few general practitioners reconsidered and, out of pique with the agency, found more
ailments in the pension-hunters than had at first met their eyes.

If the people were merciless in their raiding of the Public Welfare
treasuries, they were equally pitiless in dealing with similar funds established by their labor union. In 1946 the United Mine Workers
commenced a prolonged strike against the operators. Their object
was to compel the industry to make provision for the support of
crippled miners and of the widows and children of those who had
perished. Health, sanitary and housing facilities in most camps in the
plateau had long since degenerated to a level more abominable than
in the worst city slums. With few exceptions the Big Bosses had
abandoned any real interest in their workmen or towns. At least
half the camps were scarcely habitable. Their water was drawn from
open springs and polluted wells. Diseases were rampant, and the
miner, notwithstanding his union scale wage, was living in an environment more reminiscent of the dark ages than of the twentieth
century.

The union also sought Federal inspection and safety regulation
of the mines. Their product was selling in interstate commerce and
there was every legitimate reason why the Department of the Interior
should have assumed responsibility for the lives and safety of the
laborers. Like coal mining states generally, Kentucky made little pretense of enforcing safety legislation. Its game wardens cost the state

four times as much as its mine safety inspectors. Mine fatalities and injuries occurred with blood-chilling frequency.

The plateau's worst postwar disaster occurred on Straight Creek in Bell County on December 26, 1945. Twenty-four men perished in a great underground fire and explosion. This was followed four months later by the hideous explosion at Centralia, Illinois, in which 111 men were incinerated. The union demanded protection against such needless calamities, and a Federal safety code with enforcement officers appeared to be the only solution. However, the Truman administration was determined to prevent an inflation-stirring strike. The mines were "seized" by the Federal Government, and the miners returned to their jobs. But their leaders wrung from the Department of the Interior an agreement that an impartial agency, the United States Navy, would be called upon to make a general survey of health conditions in the bituminous coal industry.

When in 1947 Captain N. H. Collison, Coal Mines Administrator, released the Navy's report it shocked the nation. Prepared by a careful and thoroughly competent team under the direction of Admiral Joel T. Boone, the "Boone Report" bolstered every contention the union had made and shattered the denials the industry had offered. The moderate and dispassionate language of the text was supported by a folio of stark photographs which any person acquainted with the industry knew to be fair and typical. Public sentiment shifted massively to the union side, and John L. Lewis found millions of new sympathizers for his Health and Welfare Fund.

The United Mine Workers' Welfare and Retirement Fund was born, with the Boone Report serving as midwife. Substitute proposals put forward by the operators were shunted aside and a union-management trusteeship was established by the 1947 contract. Even the small initial levy of five cents per ton mined by signatory operators poured millions of dollars into its treasury.

At first the fund's trustees were extremely cautious and supervised their money with the conservatism of bankers. Applications for retirement benefits were carefully scrutinized and pensions were approved only after solid evidence of eligibility. But as new millions poured into the coffers from the mounting levy, the trustees became increasingly generous.

The fund was calculated to benefit the United Mine Workers in three ways.

First, it provided retirement pensions of a hundred dollars a month for a union member who was employed in the mines when he reached his sixty-second birthday. He must have had behind him at least twenty years of work "in or around the mines."

Second, it financed disability pensions to members who had been crippled in the mines or had incurred the dread industrial "disease" of silicosis. Such benefits depended in part on the number of dependents the disabled miner could claim and, in part, upon the extent and nature of his disability. The Fund furnished wheel chairs, orthopedic beds, artificial limbs, and other aids and sought to rehabilitate the miners by teaching them new trades when feasible.

Third was the health phase of the program. The trustees planned a broad and comprehensive effort to raise the medical standards of the area, to attract additional doctors into the mining regions and to make available to miners and their families medical facilities near national norms. The principle behind the program was logical and just in every respect. It presupposed that the industry should assume a moral responsibility for the men it maimed and the children of those it slew and attempt to maintain the health of miners and their families as a "fringe benefit." During the years of his vigor and usefulness a fund should be accumulated for the worker from the wealth his labor created to retire him in his old age and to support his dependents in case of his death or disability. Surely, among enlightened men, fault cannot be found with this reasoning.

When the camps were new and bustled with thousands of wage earners, a considerable number of young men were inspired to become doctors. On borrowed money or on funds derived from the sale of mountain land, they attended medical school, usually at the University of Louisville, and as soon as their internship was completed, hung out their shingles in their native counties. Between 1912 and 1922 the coal counties produced a sizable crop of new doctors.

Then, too, the coal corporations imported physicians from other parts of the nation. The big companies built hospitals in anticipation of disease and industrial accidents and since there were no, or too few, local physicians they "brought on" staff members. In the ten or fifteen years after the railroads came, medical standards and facilities zoomed upward and, for the first time, the people in most areas could reach a doctor who had formally studied in an accredited school. Surgery became available for the first time in the mountaineer's history.

Sometimes several lesser companies joined to share the cost of a centrally located frame building to be used as a hospital. The miner paid his medical bill as he paid his house rent and other "company debts" and he visited his doctor as a matter of right whenever he chose.

The improvement in medical services was a concomitant of the Big Boom. But when the boom evaporated the enthusiasm died. The imported doctors, nurses and technicians followed the bankrupt company executives out of the land. In many camps the hospitals closed; in others the hospital was boarded up, its functions assumed after a fashion by a "clinic" staffed by a couple of doctors and sometimes by only one. The number of doctors subsided drastically and no new ones came on.

The young doctors of the Big Boom reached middle age and advanced toward old age. Beset by hundreds of sick and indigent people, the physician was hard pressed. He had little time for continuing study and fell far behind developments in his profession. The miners and their wives judged a doctor by his ability to produce immediate and dramatic relief for ailments. If a doctor was to hold their confidence he had to relieve their symptoms. In an effort to provide quick relief to his patients he handed out bags and bottles of medicine. Some of them were as harmless or benign as aspirin. Others were pain-masking sedatives. Jugs of vitamin "tonics" were doled out into quarter-pint bottles and dispensed by thousands. When penicillin became cheaply available it was injected on slight pretext and in treatment of the mildest infections.

Life in the Depression-ridden camps sunk lower and became more bleak and uninspiring with each succeeding year. Many of the hospitals and clinics went unpainted. Worse still, they went unwashed. They deteriorated into stinking shelters crammed with sick and injured people, without qualified, registered nurses and presided over by physicians whose knowledge of medicine was long since obsolescent. Their charges were minimal. A payroll "checkoff" of two or two-and-a-half dollars a month covered the cost of drugs and medicine for all "usual and ordinary" cases. Surgery and prolonged illnesses required additional payments. To make a profit the doctor had to buy his medicines in immense quantities. Each hospital and clinic had its medicine room in which were arranged stacks and rows of pill and tonic containers.

In the welter of misery, want and futility which was the Depression the people were deeply resentful of the circumstances which had reduced them to their low estate. Gradually this feeling gave way to bewilderment, then to self-pity, neuroses and imaginary ailments. The unfortunate women, in particular, had little to do except to cook three poor meals a day and loaf. Most of them had given up the struggle against the unceasing clouds of dirt and grime. They were starved for the milk of human kindness and, with rare exceptions, their husbands were not of sympathetic or communicative natures. Without time, inclination or knowledge to treat their deepening complexes and manias, the doctors simply dispensed handfuls of sedatives. These "nerve pills" calmed the jittery females and subdued them to a more tolerant acceptance of their lot.

The injured men who were borne daily from the mines also presented problems the physicians were little prepared to resolve. Perhaps a quarter of the doctors called themselves surgeons but lacked special training as such. Such skill with the scalpel as they had acquired was largely self-taught. A patient with a lung full of powdered sandstone or a shattered pelvis found little genuine relief at their hands.

The war and postwar years had brought more money into the hands of the doctors and to their hospitals and clinics but did little to improve the quality of their medicine. Indeed, in many respects it worsened, because the heightened industrial tempo brought more casualties to their treatment rooms and left even less time for study and diagnosis. Some counties had not attracted a new doctor in twenty years before 1948. In 1947 when the U. M. W. Welfare and Retirement Fund was established, the medical services and facilities available to the mountaineer in most communities were shockingly primitive.

It was to these doctors and to their hospitals and clinics that the trustees turned, and at first sought to raise standards simply by funneling huge sums into the dilapidated structures and into the pockets of the men who presided over them. The trustees were to learn that money alone will solve few of the problems that plague mankind.

Each union member was issued a "Welfare card" entitling him and his dependents to treatment by any doctor and in any hospital or clinic signatory to a contract with the fund. The doctor was to decide whether the patient was ill enough for hospitalization, surgery or other treatment. The fund paid at rates previously agreed upon for such services as were rendered. It paid ten dollars for each day a patient was hospitalized. This covered "bed rent" and meals only; medicines, nursing and other charges were paid for on separate monthly invoices.

Despite the bellowing of the American Medical Association that the fund was a venture in "socialized" medicine, many camp doctors promptly recognized the Welfare Fund as a gravy train. They climbed aboard with alacrity and plundered it with great skill. The empty rooms in their little hospitals were filled with beds and new cubicles were opened. Chronic ailments for which the patient had already taken bags of pills and gallons of tonics now required bed rest and hospitalization. Surgery was undertaken for trivial complaints. Bushels of tonsils, adenoids and appendices were removed. The "head nurse" at one of these establishments described the situation in her hospital in inelegant terms: "It's all a woman's sex life is worth to even walk through this place. It's got so the doctors spay every woman who comes in the door!" In their new-found prosperity the overworked physicians had to find assistants. They cast about and came up with a motley assortment of doctors from other states and from foreign countries.

The trustees eventually were driven to a realization that the fund was being robbed and that the multitudes of sick, injured and neurotic people were the levers by which the door to the treasury was pried open. In self-defense, they undertook to make certain that the fund paid for no unneeded and useless surgery. A regulation was adopted requiring the surgeon to forward to a laboratory designated by the fund the organ or tissue removed from the patient. This specimen was studied and if nothing of significance was found wrong with it, payment was refused.

No Kentucky agency set standards for operation of hospitals. In the major cities and in some county seats there were, of course, excellent hospitals, and the same could be said of the major coal camps — at Jenkins, Benham and Lynch, for example. From these high standards the quality of hospital service ranged downward through every conceivable degree of laxity and squalor. The worst were unspeakable. On one occasion, during an influenza epidemic, I saw a nurse take a six-hour-old baby into the "flu ward" and present it for approval to the feverish patients. On still another, a crippled, pauperized miner was hospitalized with bleeding from stomach ulcers. When I visited him on the following day he was in bed, still dressed in the denim overalls and shirt he was wearing when admitted. He was then receiving an intravenous feeding of glucose after declining to tackle a plateful of cooked turnips, corn bread and boiled pork. Quite often when surgeons attempted major surgery they admitted friends and relatives of the patient to the operating room to observe and admire the proceedings.

At last the fund was so thoroughly pillaged that the trustees gave up in disgust. No treasury, however ample, could endure such inroads. In 1952 some doctors with no training other than a thirty-year-old degree in medicine and with no postgraduate study netted incomes of more than twelve thousand dollars a month from the Fund. Hospitals converted from two or three camp houses joined together to form a single structure and, involving an investment in building and other equipment of from forty to fifty thousand dollars, were producing annual incomes of close to ten times that amount. The trustees quite logically concluded that if they were going to pay for good medicine they ought to receive it. They therefore undertook the design and construction of a chain of ten hospitals. The structures were large and magnificently planned. The architects incorporated into them the best that experience had taught. A 1954 issue of *Architectural Forum* magazine hailed the building scheduled for Whitesburg as one of the best designed facilities of its kind in the world. Others in Kentucky were built at McDowell in Floyd County, at Pikeville, Middlesboro, Hazard and Harlan. Dedicated as monuments to slain and disabled miners they were called Miners Memorial Hospitals.

The task of designing and building the hospitals was complex, but that of assembling staffs of physicians, surgeons, specialists, nurses and technicians was infinitely more so. The poor public schools and facilities frightened off many able people. The trustees sought administrators and staff members with a genuine interest in relieving human suffering and improving the social order. They wanted, in short, the ablest men in their field. It is extremely difficult to entice such men to move into a barren region such as the eastern Kentucky coalfields. The trustees met only a moderate degree of success, but they did contrive to bring together staffs of able men and women with a wide variety in experience and with medical knowledge of a newer vintage than was found elsewhere in the plateau. They came from many medical schools across the nation. They were keenly interested in developments within their profession and were tireless students of continuing medical progress. These newcomers from other parts of America were a refreshing addition to the towns in which they settled and helped arouse a revival of civic interest and activity in each of them. Accustomed to books and reading they sought to stir interest in the establishment of public libraries. Appalled by the poor schools they organized citizens committees to seek means of bettering the local institutions. And they brought to the coal counties a quality of medical service far above anything it had ever experienced before.

When the new hospitals opened the camp dwellers underwent treatment for the first time in their lives at the hands of painstaking people who required long histories and physical examinations in seeking to diagnose for effective cures. Patients who had "doctored" for more years than they could remember were cured. The neurotics and symptom-nursers poured in, in full flood, expecting the same symptomatic medication they had been so long accustomed to. When the "new doctors" opined there was nothing much the matter with them that a job or other engrossing interest would not cure, there was much grumbling that the doctors were hardhearted or ignorant. Many patients resorted to the hospitals when surgery was required but sought out the old camp doctors for run-of-the-mill doctoring.

As could have been expected many of the resident physicians deeply resented their new colleagues. Out of spite and envy they denounced the United Mine Workers' physicians as practitioners of "socialized" medicine, and in only one or two counties were they allowed to obtain membership in the county medical association.

The retirement phase of the union's program was almost as badly abused at first as the medical. The fund required the miner to prove that he had worked "in or around" the mines twenty years out of the thirty immediately prior to his sixty-second birthday. For those miners who had worked continuously for one or two large corporations proof of such employment was easy to obtain. The records of the company revealed when employment began and terminated, when checkoff of union dues began and all other pertinent data. However, most miners were much less fortunate. The corporations for which they had performed a large part of their labor had long since vanished, and their records no longer existed. To prove employment by them the miners were permitted to produce affidavits of fellow workmen, timekeepers, former superintendents and others who had knowledge of their periods of employment. That was the only proof available and the trustees were compelled to accept it or unjustly deny pensions to many deserving miners. Hence, a miner could show by affidavits that he worked for a certain coal company before its bankruptcy in the 1930s and by other records that he had worked for rail or truck mines in more recent years. On the basis of such evidence many work-worn old miners drew their retirement checks.

Some men with little service in the mines twisted the regulations to enrich themselves unjustly at the expense of the fund. The applicant induced relatives and friends to swear falsely that they had worked with him long ago when in fact he had never been employed by the company in question. Equally fraudulent means were used to prove employment in the mines immediately before the application was filed. One man worked five years at a truck mine between 1942 and 1948. He then found other employment and quit the mines. But his kindly son-in-law carried him on the payroll as a slate picker and reported his dues and other levies to the union regularly. In three years he did not once go to the mine. When he reached his sixty-second birthday, he produced the affidavits of his brother-in-

law and two first cousins to show he had been a muledriver between 1923 and 1934. His pension eligibility was promptly certified
and he received one hundred dollars monthly until his death.

Another man who gained a place on the pension rolls admitted
freely that he had never worked for a mining company in his life. He
laughingly justified the false affidavits by saying, "Well, I used to
cut trees in the log woods and they were not fer away from the mines,
so I guess I was working 'around' the mines."

The political doctors who labored so prodigiously for the public
assistance programs could resist the pretenses of few who sought
disability pensions from the union. The rolls of the disabled bal-
looned fantastically before the memorial hospitals were built and the
new doctors commenced screening the applicants. Nevertheless even
then the queues of men who claimed to be disabled from mining
accidents were so long that they eventually threatened the fund with
insolvency. Realizing that the sick, the lame and the lazy of the coal
counties were draining away the resources of the fund at a rate the
industry could never sustain, the trustees abolished that phase of the
program in 1952. They sought to justify their action by asserting
that responsibility for the sick and disabled rested primarily with the
communities, the states and the Federal government rather than
with the industry that had crippled them. This was a betrayal of one
of the fundamental purposes of the fund, but without it the whole
program would have been wrecked.

The physicians were not the only "professional" men to raid the
fund or to help others do so. The morticians managed to ladle large
sums from the gravy train. Under an early regulation, the trustees directed payment of one thousand dollars to the widow of a deceased
pensioner. The remittance was forwarded as soon as possible after
the death occurred and was intended to cover immediate requirements for food, fuel, medicines and other necessities, and the cost of
interment. The sum was ample in view of the likelihood that
monthly checks would commence soon thereafter. The general
population was so poor that four to six hundred dollars had been
deemed sufficient to pay for a "decent funeral," including coffin,
embalming and hearse. Nor, except in rare instances, could more
have been collected. Thus several hundred dollars were left to enable

the widow to pay debts and current expenses. However, most "funeral directors" promptly decided a miner could not be buried properly for a cent less than a thousand dollars. The grief-stricken women were pressured to buy coffins whose prices were suddenly raised, and the processors of the dead wound up with the entire grant. The trustees have attempted to combat this evil but to date their efforts have been without visible success.

PART VII

The Purple Mountain
Majesties

CHAPTER NINETEEN

The Rape of the Appalachians

The 1950s

THE SAME DECADE that saw the human resources of the plateau sapped and vitiated by Welfarism, idleness and defeat on the one hand and by sustained out-migration on the other, also brought the beginning of a terrible new emasculation of its physical resources. Strip mining, a branch of the industry which had previously been practiced in such flat coalfields as western Kentucky and southern Illinois, invaded the Cumberlands on a vast scale.

For nearly sixty years the greater part of the region's mineral wealth had lain in the iron clutch of absentee corporations. They had prospered and bankrupted and prospered again. But through their triumphs and tragedies, their successes and failures, the corporations had clung to all the old rights, privileges, immunities, powers and interests vested in them by their nineteenth-century land and mineral deeds. These relics from a laissez-faire century were construed to authorize the physical destruction of the land and the abject impoverishment of its inhabitants. With strip mining and its companion, the auger-mining process, the shades of darkness moved close indeed to the Cumberlands.

The courts have written strings of decisions which not only uphold the covenants and privileges enumerated in the ancient deeds and contracts but which, in the opinion of many lawyers, greatly enlarge them as well. We have seen that when the mountaineer's ancestor (for the seller is, in most instances, long since dead) sold his land he lived in an isolated backwater. Coal mining was a primitive in-dustry whose methods had changed little in a hundred years and which still depended entirely on picks and shovels. To the mountain-eer "mining" meant tunneling into a hillside and digging the coal for removal through the opening thus made. That the right to mine could authorize shaving off and destroying the surface of the land in order to arrive at the underlying minerals was undreamed of by buyers and sellers alike.

But technology advanced. The steam shovel grew into a mighty mechanism and was replaced by gasoline and diesel-powered succes-sors. "Dozers" and other efficient excavators were perfected. Ever cheaper and safer explosives came from the laboratories. These mar-velous new tools enabled men to change the earth, abolishing its natural features and reshaping them as whim or necessity might re-quire. And as these developments made possible a radically new application of the privileges granted in the yellowed mineral deeds, the courts kept pace. Year by year they subjected the mountaineer to each innovation in tools and techniques the technologists were able to dream up. First, it was decided that the purchase of coal automatically granted the "usual and ordinary" mining rights; and then that the usual mining rights included authority to cut down enough of the trees on the surface to supply props for the underground workings. This subjected thousands of acres to cutting for which the owners were uncompensated. It gave the companies an immensely valuable property right for which they had neither bar-gained nor paid.

Next came rulings which gave the companies the power to "di-vert and pollute" all water "in or on" the lands. With impunity they could kill the fish in the streams, render the water in the farmer's well unpotable and, by corrupting the stream from which his live-stock drank, compel him to get rid of his milk cows and other beasts. They were authorized to pile mining refuse wherever they desired, even if the chosen sites destroyed the homes of farmers and be-stowed no substantial advantage on the corporations. The companies which held "long-form" mineral deeds were empowered to withdraw subjacent supports, thereby causing the surface to subside and frac-ture. They could build roads wherever they desired, even through lawns and fertile vegetable gardens. They could sluice poisonous water from the pits onto crop lands. With impunity they could hurl out from their washeries clouds of coal grit which settled on fields of corn, alfalfa and clover and rendered them worthless as fodder. Fumes from burning slate dumps peeled paint from houses, but the companies were absolved from damages.

The state's highest court held in substance that a majority of the people had "dedicated" the region to the mining industry, and that the inhabitants were estopped to complain of the depredations of the coal corporations, so long as they were not motivated by malice. Since malice seldom existed and could never be proved, this afforded no safeguard at all. The companies, which had bought their coal rights at prices ranging from fifty cents to a few dollars per acre, were, in effect, left free to do as they saw fit, restrained only by the shallow consciences of their officials. When the bulldozer and power shovel made contour strip-mining feasible and profitable in mountainous terrain, the court promptly enforced the companies' right to remove the coal by this unusual and wholly unforeseen method.

The court spurned as unimportant the fact that competent engineers swore only 20 per cent of the coal in a virgin boundary could be recovered even when both strip and auger mining were employed in unison. It brushed aside proof that strip mining destroys the land and eradicates the economic base on which continued residence within the region is predicated. It substantially adjudicated away the rights of thousands of mountaineers to house and home. It bestowed upon the owner of a seam of coal the right to destroy totally the surface insofar as any known system of reclamation is concerned. It delivered into the hands of the coal corporations the present estate and future heritage in the land — in effect an option to preserve or ruin present and future generations. These fateful decisions of the state's highest court, decisions medieval in outlook and philosophy, are now buttressed by the hoary doctrine of *stare decisis* and can be dislodged only by social and political dynamite. And while there is strong reason to suppose that the court as presently constituted views these decisions with uneasiness and dismay, its relatively enlightened judges feel duty-bound to apply them in new appeals. This long line of judicial opinions opened the way for what may prove to be the final obliteration of the plateau's future as a vital part of the nation and its history.

It is probable that this process of judicially straitjacketing the mountaineers for the benefit of the coal companies reached its apogee in a decision handed down by the Court of Appeals on November 15, 1949. The appeal came up from the Circuit Court of Pike County. It involved one of the earliest stripping operations to be undertaken in eastern Kentucky. The Russell Fork Coal Company had cut the top off a mountain on Weddington Fork of Ferrells Creek, leaving ten acres of loose earth, mixed to a great depth with stones and fragments of trees. This vast mass of unstable rubble lay on the upper reaches of a narrow valley, on the floor of which several families made their homes. It was created in an area which had been battered by flash floods throughout its history, so that even the feeblest of minds could have anticipated their recurrence at almost any time. On the night of August 2, 1945, the calamity came in the form of a cloudburst and, foreseeably, thousands of tons of dirt, rocks and shattered tree trunks from the devastated mountain were flung down the hillside into the raging creek. Like a titanic scythe the rolling rubble swept downstream, working havoc among the houses, stores and farms. When the dazed inhabitants recovered sufficiently they sued the coal company for damages on the reasonable assumption that its digging had triggered a misfortune which nature, left undisturbed, would not have visited upon them. The appellate bench reversed the verdict of the jury and the judgment of the trial court. It ruled, in effect, that the rain was an Act of God which the coal operator could not have foreseen and that, had the rain not fallen, the rubble would have remained safely in place. Besides, the stripping had been done in the "same manner as was customary at all strip mines." Usurping the fact-finding prerogative of the jury, the judges, sitting as a self-appointed superjury, found the stripper innocent of wrongdoing and negligence.

In another case several years later, a mountaineer claimed that a company had plowed up his mountainsides, covered his bottomland with rubble, caused his well to go dry and, in his words, had "plumb broke" him. After he had heard all the evidence and arguments of counsel the trial judge dismissed the case. In doing so he told the mountaineer, "I deeply sympathize with you and sincerely wish I could rule for you. My hands are tied by the rulings of the Court of Appeals and under the law I must follow its decisions. The truth is

that about the only rights you have on your land is to breathe on it
and pay the taxes. For all practical purposes the company that owns
the minerals in your land owns all the other rights pertaining to it."

By 1950 there were hundreds of "worked-out" ridges along whose
edges ran slender bands of outcrop coal. It was of high quality but
only extended into the hill a hundred feet or so. Tunnel and pillar
mining had long since withdrawn most of the coal, leaving only a
few supporting pillars and barrier walls. In order to remove the
mineral by conventional methods, a thick barrier pillar must be
left intact on the outer fringes of the seam. It comprises the principal
support for the overlying mountain, affording stability and tending
to prevent "squeezes" — those uncontrollable shiftings of the mountain which occur when too much coal is taken out. Then, too, as a
practical matter all the mineral cannot be removed from the inside.
As the miners approach the outside the roof of stone becomes increasingly "rotten" so that on the outer edges it is extremely difficult
to shore up, no matter how thickly timbers and roof-bolts are applied.
Hence the bands of outcrop coal were a loss in so far as the owners
were concerned and were written off as such.

Nor had all the coal in the interior of the mountains been removed.
In the earlier years of the industry some fifty to sixty per cent was
recovered and the rest was required for supports. As techniques and
tools improved the percentage of recovery steadily rose. Finally
in the most thoroughly mechanized mines — those employing roof
bolts, conveyors, shuttle cars and coal moles — recovery soared to
85 or 90 per cent and some operators boasted that they "brought
it clean," removing all except the outcrop. This permitted colossal
"general falls" to bring the roof crashing down behind them as the
machines rapidly chewed their way through the pillars in the pull-
back to the entries. But in all the mines the outcrop remained. In
some places where the Big Bosses had first driven their headings
nearly forty years before the seams had been of extraordinarily high
quality and very thick. For example, Consolidation Coal Company
began its operations in 1912 in seams more than eight feet thick
but by 1948 it had developed especially designed machines to work
in veins only thirty-six inches thick. Engineers were tantalized by
the old workings where thick bands of mineral lay temptingly near

the outside of the mountains. Truck roads could be "dozed" to them at little cost and the rural highway program had already brought roads near countless such hollowed ridges.

But the engineers could devise no means of recovering the coal from the inside. The problem of roof supports was insoluble. Heartened by the powerful new earth-moving machines they resorted to "surface mining." If the coal could not be tunneled out from the interior it could be gouged out from the exterior. Dynamite and bulldozer could remove the "overburden." The coal could be "pop shot" with light charges of explosives, and loaded by giant shovels directly into trucks.

The recovery of coal by the "open-cut" method had previously never been feasible in the mountains, though it had occasionally been practiced in the low hills on the fringes of the plateau. But by 1950, strip mining was not only feasible but was increasingly profitable.

Typically a strip-mine operator needed only a tiny crew of men. He required two bulldozers, one of which could be substantially smaller than the other. He required an air compressor and drill for the boring of holes into the rock overlying the coal. He also required a power shovel for use in loading the coal from the seam into the trucks. These four machines could be operated by as many men. To their wages were added those of a night watchman and two or three laborers, and the crew was complete. With these men and machines the operator first built a road from the nearest highway up the hillside to the coal seam. The bulldozers pursued the seam around the hillside, uprooting the timber and removing all the soil until the coal was reached. Then the dirt was scraped from the sloping mountainside above to expose the crumbling rock. This cut proceeded along the contours of the ridge for half a mile. Then rows of holes were drilled in the rock strata and were tamped with explosives. When the explosives were set off, most of the dirt and rock was blown violently down the mountainside. The remainder lay, soft and crumbly, on top of the coal. The "dozers" then bestrode the shattered "overburden," and with their steel snouts shoved it down the steep slopes. This process left the outer edge of the outcrop exposed. A sheet of coal eight feet thick, fifty feet wide and half a mile long could thus be bared within a few days.

Next, holes were drilled in the glittering black seam of coal. Small charges of dynamite loosened thousands of tons of the mineral, leaving it easily available to the shovel's big dipper. A number of truckers were hired to haul it away, at a cost of perhaps seventy-five cents a ton. It was carried to the nearest ramp or tipple where it was cleaned, sized and loaded into gondolas.

It is instantly apparent that this method of recovery is vastly cheaper than shaft or drift mining. Six or eight men can thus dig more coal from the outcrop than five or six times their number can mine underground. The bulldozers, shovels and drills are expensive, but not more so than their subterranean counterparts. They can produce a ton of coal for little more than half the cost imposed on a competitor in a deep pit. Where the strip mine lies close to the loading ramp so that the haul bill can be minimized the price differential is even more striking.

In the flat country of western Kentucky, where thousands of acres had already been devastated by strip mining, the coal seams lie only thirty to sixty feet beneath the surface. The overburden is scraped off and the coal is scooped out. Inevitably such topsoil as the land affords is buried under towering heaps of subsoil. When the strippers move on, once level meadows and cornfields have been converted to jumbled heaps of hardpan, barren clay from deep in the earth. This hellish landscape is slow to support vegetation and years elapse before the yellow waste turns green again. In the meantime immense quantities of dirt have crept into the sluggish streams, have choked them, and brackish ponds have formed to breed millions of mosquitoes.

The evil effects of open-cut mining are fantastically magnified when practiced in the mountains. Masses of shattered stone, shale, slate and dirt are cast pell-mell down the hillside. The first to go are the thin remaining layer of fertile topsoil and such trees as still find sustenance in it. The uprooted trees are flung down the slopes by the first cut. Then follows the sterile subsoil, shattered stone and slate. As the cut extends deeper into the hillside the process is repeated again and again. Sometimes the "highwall," the perpendicular bank resulting' from the cut, rises ninety feet; but a height of forty to sixty feet is more often found. In a single mile, hundreds of thousands of tons are displaced.

Each mountain is laced with coal seams. Sometimes a single ridge contains three to five veins varying in thickness from two-and-a-half to fourteen feet. Since each seam can be stripped, a sloping surface can be converted to a steplike one.

After the coal has been carried away vast quantities of the shattered mineral are left uncovered. Many seams contain substantial quantities of sulphur, which when wet produces toxic sulphuric acid. This poison bleeds into the creeks, killing minute vegetation and destroying fish, frogs and other stream-dwellers.

Strip mining occurs largely in dry weather. In late spring, in summer, and in early fall the bulldozers and shovels tear tirelessly at the vitals of the mountains while trucks rumble away with their glittering cargoes. Above the operations and their haul roads lie mantles of tawny dust. In the hot sunshine the churned earth turns powder dry and the jumbled spoil-banks lie soft almost to fluffiness.

The seam seldom lies less than a hundred feet above the base of the mountain. Sometimes it is near the top. Again it may lie midway between base and crest. But wherever the seam is situated the spoil bank extends downward like a monstrous apron. Stones as large as army tanks are sent bounding and crashing through trees and undergrowth. Lesser stones find lodgment against trees and other obstacles, and behind them countless tons of soil accumulate.

During the hot season the nearby creek takes on a sallow hue after even the slightest shower. People living along its bank watch apprehensively as the rising highwall deepens the loose earth on the dead and blasted slopes. They remember the horror of other years when flash floods pounded hillsides scratched by hoes and bulltongue plows. They guess what will ensue if a similar downpour falls upon the ravaged slopes which overlook their farms and homes.

Then come the rains of autumn and the freezes and thaws of winter. The descending water flays the loose rubble, carrying thousands of tons of it into the streams and onto the bottoms. The watery scalpel shaves inches from the surface in almost instantaneous sheet erosion. At the same time it carves gullies which deepen until the streams reach the undisturbed soil far beneath. The rain has a kindlier effect, however, and eventually lessens its ravages by compacting the surface. Gradually the beating drops create a hard shell which affords considerable protection to the underlying dirt. Then in late November the saturated spoil-banks freeze. In the icy grip of winter they lie hard as ice and perfectly stable. The freezing water pushes the dirt outward, leaving deep fissures extending far underground. When warmer weather melts the ice the earth crumbles and subsides downhill in tremendous landslides. Snows and rains then saturate the loosened masses again and the process is repeated until the displaced soil reaches the stream beds.

Within a few years after the "strip operator" has slashed his way into the hillside the unresting elements have carried away most of his discarded overburden. The dirt has vanished, leaving immense expanses of sere brown sandstone and slabs of sickening gray slate. A few straggly clusters of broom sage and an occasional spindly sycamore take root and struggle to survive.

Initially the strippers worked only in the outcrop of exhausted mines but as their machines and techniques improved, they pushed into virgin seams. The great cuts appeared on the sides of ridges from which no coal had yet been withdrawn. They scalped away only a thin filament on the outer edges of the hill, leaving the body of the coal bed undisturbed. The coal auger made its appearance as a device for removing that portion of the outcrop which could not be reached by stripping. As a rule of thumb ten feet of overburden can profitably be removed for each foot of coal in the seam. When the highwall rose straight up so far it could not be advantageously increased, much of the outcrop remained. The auger allowed the recovery of a large part of the remaining mineral. It is a gigantic drill which bores straight back into the coal seam, spewing out huge quantities of the mineral with each revolution of the screw. The drills range from seventeen inches to six feet in diameter. When the point has penetrated the entire length of the bit a new section is attached and the drilling continues. Eventually it extends some seventy yards under the hill, piercing the entire barrier pillar.

The bore holes must be somewhat smaller in diameter than the seam is thick, and a few inches are left between the insertions. Consequently, the auger can bring out little more than half the coal. Initially its use was justified on the gound that it prevented the loss of the otherwise unrecoverable barrier pillars, but after the already disemboweled hills were stripped and augered the big bits moved into virgin ridges and began to rend seams which had never felt a pick.

Usually stripping preceded the augers but after a time some auger men dispensed with strip mining altogether. They simply made cuts sufficient to face up the seams, then the monstrous screws were set to work while the lines of trucks labored to carry away their product.

Where augering is done in a previously unmined ridge the crumbly "bloom" and a few yards of weathered roofstone is shoved over the hillside. Then the bore holes follow each other in interminable procession around the meandering ridge. They proceed along the edges of sharp spurs, around the "turn of the point," and back to the main ridge again. When the end of the ridge is passed the cutting and boring continues on its reverse side. Thus the bore holes from one side of the mountain extend toward the ends of those drilled from the other side. Under these circumstances coal production is fantastically cheap. A well-financed operation augering in a four- to six-foot seam can realize a net profit of close to a dollar on the ton even in the depressed coal market prevailing as this is written in 1962. A six-foot auger turning uninterruptedly can load fifteen tons in less than one minute. If the fleet of trucks can keep pace with the bulldozers and augers, the profit can be fabulous, amounting to millions of dollars in a few years. Quite naturally the possibility of such quick and easy enrichment has excited many coal companies and the politicians through whom they dominate the state and county governments.

Strip and auger mining have one very real advantage over conventional methods: they eliminate the need for men to go under the hill. In augering only the revolving steel bits pierce the mountainside, and their human attendants need never follow them. The peril of fire and slate-fall which dogs the underground miners in even the safest pits does not pursue the surface workman. But when this is said, nothing more in defense of the process can be forthcoming.

Augering in virgin ridges is fantastically wasteful. Rarely do the bits extend into the mountain more than a quarter of its width. Hence, even if the boring proceeds from both sides, a solid block is often left in the center of the ridge which contains at least 50 per cent of the seam's original tonnage. When allowance is made for the huge quantities left between the holes and over and under them, another 25 per cent of the seam's content is unretrieved. Competent mining engineers have testified that such an augering project is highly successful if 20 per cent of the total coal is removed. Nor can the remainder be mined at a future time without totally destroying the terrain.

It will at first appear that shafts could be driven into the hill for mining the remaining coal by conventional methods, but unfortunately when the ridge has been augered on both sides this is no longer possible. The bore holes are so close together they leave no pillars of sufficient thickness to support the roof. Within a few years after air is admitted into the seam a chemical reaction causes the remaining coal to crumble. The weight of the overlying rock and soil crushes down through the thin walls remaining between the holes. The coal marooned in the center of the mountain is thus sealed against the outside world. Moreover, tunnel and pillar mining requires ventilation as well as roof supports, and if a reliable air supply is to be maintained at the working faces this exterior wall cannot be reduced under forty feet in thickness without running the risk that the mountain's weight will crack and shatter it, allowing the precious oxygen to leak out. Thus, even if an entry is managed it must operate within the confining limits of a forty-foot barrier pillar following the furthermost penetrations of the auger bits. Generally, when this indispensable safeguard is deducted, too little coal is left to justify the expense of mining it. Thus the auger skims off a thin layer of cream and leaves the balance of a rich and vitally important coal bed in such a state that mining engineers can presently offer no hope for its ultimate recovery. Prudence cannot permit the continued gross wastage of so vital a resource.

Open-cut strip mining does not always follow the meandering borders of the ridge. A different procedure is used when the vein lies near the top of the hill. Then the strippers blast and carve away the stone and soil overlying the coal, shoving it over the brink of the mountain until at last the entire seam lies black and glistening in the sunlight. Such an operation can transform a razorback spur into a flat mesa. Sometimes the hill's altitude is decreased by 20 per cent while its thickness is much increased. When the strippers have departed and the rains and freezes have flayed such a decapitated mountain for a season or two, it takes on an appearance not unlike the desolate, shattered tablelands of Colorado. But these man-made mesas lie in a rainy area and the layers of loose soil cloaking the slopes will not stay *in situ*. Wraithlike the rubble melts away, only to reappear at countless places downstream.

Stripping and augering spread at an accelerating rate through the 1950s. For a long time they were viewed as a tentative and minor industry, one that could deface splotches of land but was unlikely to ever afford serious competition for conventional mines or to constitute a real threat to the region's soil, water and natural beauty. But this casual viewpoint has been dispelled. In 1954 Kentucky's Governor Lawrence Wetherby advocated a mild bill designed to restrain the operators from the worst of their abuses. Immediately the holding companies and the industry reacted as if they had been stung by a huge bee. Lobbyists dragged out all the timeworn arguments again and the lawmakers were solemnly assured that strip and auger mining are good for the region's economy, creating jobs and bringing prosperity to Main Street. A diluted version of an initially weak bill was passed but successive governors have failed to enforce even its mild strictures. For all practical purposes the operators are permitted to conduct their affairs in complete absence of supervision or control. Little effort is made to reclaim or stabilize the land, and indeed, reclamation is rarely possible once the surface has been so violently disturbed.

Under the law strippers are required to replant their wrecked and ravaged acres. The State Department of Conservation recommends short leaf or loblolly pines for the spoil-banks. Conservationists insist that a full year must pass before the young trees are planted. This delay permits the freshly piled soil to settle enough so the trees can take root. The seedlings are approximately five inches long when planted, supposedly at intervals of six feet. Some ten years must elapse before trees growing in such impoverished earth will reach the height of a man's head. In the meantime the rains have clawed the earth about their roots into deep gullies and there is little left for their foliage to protect. Few operators seriously attempt to comply with the reclamation regulations; most are permitted virtually to ignore them.

The effects of strip mining bring an abrupt subsidence of every phase of community life. The community of Upper Beefhide Creek in Letcher County was stripped between 1950 and 1954. Highwalls ten miles long and averaging forty feet in height were created.

Earth and rock were tumbled down the mountainsides and raced through fields of grass and corn and blanketed lawns and vegetable gardens. Stones big as bushels were blasted high into the air like giant mortar shells, to rain down on residences, roads and cornland. One huge rock crashed through the roof of a house, struck a bed dead center and carried the spring and mattress into the earth under the foundation. Another fell on a cemetery, smashing a tombstone and crushing the coffin six feet underground.

Before the avalanches of stone and dirt the population took wings, and seven years after the stripping ceased three quarters of the population had moved away. Before Upper Beefhide Creek was wrecked it comprised a voting precinct and several hundred men, women and children lived reasonably well within its confines. Some were farmers who sold eggs, milk, butter and other produce in nearby towns and camps. Others worked as miners. A few distilled enough moonshine whiskey to win a measure of local renown for their product. Farmers, miners and moonshiners alike forsook the valley leaving it to a corporal's guard of Old Age pensioners and a handful of children and their dispirited parents.

The long-range impact of such wrecking on the economy of an already poor and backward state, is incalculable. While mountain land is now assessed for tax purposes at very low values, strip mining often eliminates it from taxation entirely. Thenceforward the mountaineers who own the surface regard it as worthless for all purposes and decline to pay taxes levied upon it. If the state goes to the expense and effort required to sell the land at a tax sale there are no buyers. Thus the region's schools and other public facilities are deprived of desperately needed revenues, and the taxpayers of more prosperous areas of the state are compelled to produce new funds for support of the "pauper counties" in the plateau. Simultaneously, mud from the spoil-banks congests creeks and rivers and highway culverts and ditchlines. These flood-causing deposits are dredged out by maintenance crews of the Department of Highways, thus draining dollars away from road construction and repair. In effect, the general population is indirectly subsidizing the strippers by paying the bills for much of the damage they inflict.

Practically every ridge, spur and point in the eastern Kentucky coal-

field is a candidate for strip and/or auger mining. Many have already
been "worked," and the remainder are likely to become spoil-banks
within the next few years.

The cumulative effects of the wrecking of a coal-filled mountain
stagger the imagination. Let us suppose the ridge contains three
seams of coal, and that the company first strip-mines the bottommost
seam. A few years later it returns to a higher seam midway up the
mountain and cuts highwalls of fifty or sixty feet in its sides. Then to
crown its enterprise its shovels and bulldozers slice off the top of the
mountain to recover all of the highest seam. Within a dozen years it
has dug millions of tons of coal and made a profit of millions of dollars. But in the process it has totally transformed one of earth's terrain features. A relatively stable mountain, whose soil and water were
to a high degree protected by grass and trees, has been reduced to a
colossal rubble heap.

A few months before this was written I discussed a huge stripping
operation with the engineer who was directing it. He was a veteran
of nearly forty-five years' experience, and he summed up his lifetime
of work in these words: "When I came to this coalfield most of the
hills were covered with fine timber and all were full of topgrade coal.
Since then we have gutted these old mountains and shaved 'em off
clean. Now we are skinning 'em and cutting their heads off!"

Until *circa* 1953 the Tennessee Valley Authority was a benevolent
government agency whose masters gave every evidence of a wise
dedication to public service. Conceived as an immense experiment
in human and resource conservation and rehabilitation, the T.V.A.
accomplished genuine miracles. With its huge dams it disciplined
mighty rivers and savage creeks, and poured out cheap "byproduct"
electricity which brought light and comfort to countless households.
Never before had an agency of government brought so many economic advantages to a large population, while at the same time
widening, rather than limiting, its liberties.

But in 1953 and ensuing years, a subtle change came over the
T.V.A. By degrees it changed direction, converting into a mammoth
corporation which subordinated all other considerations to low costs
and balanced budgets. The Authority had brought into its domain
more refrigerators, electric stoves and factories than it could propel

by hydro-electric power alone. So, quite logically, Congress authorized the T. V. A. to build steam generators to produce electricity at a pace with the mushrooming requirements of the region's factories and mills. It was calculated that the steam generators would burn millions of tons of coal annually and the industry was delighted by the prospect of such a fabulous new customer.

Traditionally, steam generation had required clean fuel and it was assumed that the big pits with their elaborate cleaning plants would receive the lion's share of the orders. But events in the electrical industry were moving rapidly, and thermal engineers had devised new methods of burning coal. It was no longer necessary to feed the fires with fuel that was already free of slate and dirt. In the immense, modern forced-draft furnaces relatively low-grade and dirty coal could be burned efficiently. Fortified by this fact the purchasing agents began buying by thermal units rather than by tons. A given number of thermal units could be extracted more cheaply from low-grade and low-cost coal than from the clean, more expensive product. This dovetailed precisely with the capacities of the strip and auger corporations. They could gouge thousands of carloads from the outcrop and from the poorer seams of mountain ridges, but the augers and shovels scooped up slate and coal together. The voracious furnaces could devour the impure product of auger and bulldozer without a tremor of indigestion. Because of its tremendous fuel requirements, T. V. A. thus became the godparent of the burgeoning industry. The insatiable appetites of the steam-powered generators endlessly multiplied bulldozers, shovels and augers to gnaw at the Appalachians.

On April 12, 1961, the T. V. A. announced that it had accepted bids to supply 16,500,000 tons of Kentucky and Tennessee coal to its plants. One operator contracted to provide coal at only a few cents over $2.00 per ton. On the whole the bids remained under $3.00 a ton. These offers were for coal "free on board" the railroad cars consigned to the T. V. A.'s yards. Even at these fantastically low prices the operators could expect to clear from 75 cents to $1.00 per ton. By comparison it is highly doubtful that the most thoroughly automated and modern underground mining operation in the plateau could produce the fuel at a cost of less then $3.00 per ton, without any profit.

Consequently the T. V. A., the mighty benefactor of the Tennes-see Valley, has become a gigantic co-partner in the destruction of the Cumberland Plateau. Its enormous furnaces have inspired pri-vate power companies to build smaller but similar plants. For example, a thirty-three-million-dollar installation has been built in Lawrence County, Kentucky. It will burn three quarters of a million tons of coal yearly, and in anticipation of its requirements strip-mining companies have leased nearly half the coal in the county. It is almost inevitable that within the next decade or so the county will be chewed to bits to provide fuel for its fires.

Since 1945 many of coal's most important domestic customers have forsaken it. The railroads, formerly prime patrons, have junked their iron horses, replacing them with far more powerful diesel engines. The maritime trade was long ago lost to oil. Millions of coal-burning home furnaces were replaced by oil or gas plants. At a steady pace, the major manufacturing corporations shifted to other fuels. Increased efficiency in foreign pits has curtailed exports of the fuel. So sharp has been the shrinkage of its market that coal is one of the few items in American trade the price of which has remained stable or actually lowered in the last ten years. From the viewpoint of the industry's sales agents there has been only a single bright spot in an otherwise dark sky: the construction of the huge network of coal-consuming electric plants. Detroit, Chicago, New York and many lesser cities have seen such installations arise on their borders, each of their colossal chimneys carrying into the atmosphere smoke from hundreds of tons of coal daily. Without these gigantic new customers the coal industry would have shrunk to a minor one indeed. For a good many years its economists have recognized that strikes or other occurrences which interrupt shipments to the electric utilities could kill King Coal. Hence the sustained efforts of operator and union boss to avoid production stoppages of any kind. Only strip and auger mining can produce fuel cheaply enough to satisfy the T. V. A. and the scores of privately owned power corporations and, at the same time, earn for themselves a reasonable profit. These cir-cumstances are sustaining an industrial tiger which is devouring the Cumberland Plateau and the Southern coalfields in general. T. V. A. has been able to boast of its cheap and stable charge schedule. Other producers of electric power have struggled to remain reasonably close to its price level. Their consumers have been convinced that in cheap electricity they are receiving the best bargain afforded by the American industrial machine. Each week elaborate advertisements proclaim the advantages of electric power and point out the many chores it performs so cheaply and so cleanly for housewife and industrial manager. But the slick advertisements and stable electric bills do not reflect the whole story. The truth is that cheap and abundant electric power is being bought at a titanic hidden and deferred cost, a cost another generation will pay with compound interest.

T. V. A.'s involvement in the electricity industry is gigantic. Its steam plants are located at Colbert and Widow's Creek in northern Alabama; at Shawnee, Kentucky; and at Gallatin, John Sevier, Johnsonville, Kingston and Watts Bar in Tennessee. These plants now burn several hundred thousands of tons of coal weekly. Under construction is the Bull Run plant at Oak Ridge, Tennessee, where four-and-a-fourth railroad gondolas of the fuel will be consumed each hour. When completed the even bigger plant at Paradise, Kentucky will gulp millions of other tons annually. This gargantuan industrial complex recently ordered into effect a rate schedule under which its ordinary homeowner customer will pay only four-and-a-half dollars a month for electricity — one fourth the cost of the same amount of power in New York City. But it is rapidly consuming the coal foundations on which it stands. In its eagerness to raise a hedge around its empire and to make possible still cheaper electricity, the Agency has commenced buying broad tracts of coal. On June 30, 1961, T. V. A.'s General Manager, Louis J. Van Mol, announced the purchase of the coal and mining rights on fifty-nine thousand acres of land in Bell, Harlan, Leslie, Clay and Perry Counties in Kentucky, and the obtaining of an option on fifty-three thousand additional acres in northeastern Tennessee. Since cheap electricity requires cheap coal — and only strip and auger coal appears to be cheap enough for the T. V. A. — this acquisition adds to the plateau's other woes the specter of enormous strip mines owned and operated by the Federal Government.

Inspired by the success of the electric power industry in acquiring cheap coal by the strip and auger processes other large consumers have resorted to the same methods of recovery. A subsidiary of Beth-

322 · THE PURPLE MOUNTAIN MAJESTIES

lehem Steel is augering in Pike and Letcher Counties and United
States Steel is stripping the Big Black Mountain on several levels.
One of its seams is eleven feet thick and occasionally the cut leaves
highwalls ninety feet high.

To sustain the flow of inexpensive electricity the strippers and
augerers are gutting tens of thousands of acres. Buchanan County,
Virginia, has been shredded. A bird's-eye view of it reveals marooned
and isolated farmhouses perched disconsolately on high pillars of
dirt and stone. Towering highwalls make access to them impossible.
Much of the county's total land surface has been stripped of vegetation and reduced to jumbles of stone and gullying spoil-banks.

A similar process has wrecked much of Wise County, Virginia.
It had many of its hills decapitated before January, 1957. In that
month a period of prolonged rain sent cascades of water into streams
from naked hillsides and rubble heaps. The town of Pound, Virginia, which ordinarily sleeps on the banks of a placid little stream,
was overwhelmed by more than twenty feet of water. Pound River,
yellow and monstrously swollen, swept into houses and business
establishments and crested in the second stories of commercial buildings. Similar inundations poured out of Buchanan County into Pikeville, Kentucky, and in a short time that county seat was flooded.
Rescue boats sailed over top of the city's street lights.

But not all the mud and water spewed out by strip mining originated in Virginia. The scarred and ravaged mountains in Letcher,
Harlan, Pike and Perry Counties shed water like so many tin roofs.
Hazard, with a population of seven thousand and the trading center
for several counties, was damaged almost as severely as Pikeville. At
dawn the water was beginning to spill over the river's banks. By noon
it had soared to the ceilings of Main Street retail shops, soaking
merchandise and doing hundreds of thousands of dollars' worth of
damage to real estate. Strangely enough, the whiplash of the flood
caused the prompt rebuilding of these towns on a bigger and better
scale than they had ever known. Four years after the water swept
through them, they appeared more prosperous than before the deluge
arrived. But looks can be deceptive. Each landlord and shopkeeper
who replaced his stock or repaired his building and added a shiny
new front did so with borrowed money, mostly from Federal agencies.
The loans are being reduced, but when outraged nature sends an

even more catastrophic inundation into their establishments it is unlikely they will possess either the resolution or the funds to stage another recovery. And unless men find some way of repealing nature's laws a new calamity cannot be long in coming. The Cumberland Plateau is wet country, receiving an annual precipitation of more than forty-five inches. Even in the dry months of August and September it is seldom that a week passes without rain. This wetness and the law of gravity spell disaster for the plateau and for the towns and cities past which its rivers flow. It is, as Sherlock Holmes might have declared to Dr. Watson, elementary that the normal pattern of rain, snows, freezes and thaws will continue with only slight deviation throughout the present geologic era.

Even if this unremitting abrasion strikes timber and grassy hillsides it will chisel away soil, ultimately reducing mountains to hillocks and then to plains. But when its cutting edge falls on earth from which men have stripped every vestige of vegetative cover the erosive process is incredibly magnified. Once swept into the stream beds the mud cannot be stopped short of the Mississippi Delta. Suspended in water and constantly agitated by rising and falling currents it creeps seaward. Eventually it appears in coal-flecked mud flats which Congressmen vote millions of dollars to have dredged away. But the Southern mountains are numerous and large, and the genius and toil of the Corps of Engineers cannot keep abreast of their off-scourings. Many of the mud flats in the Ohio and Mississippi rivers are monuments to the cheap power which lights the homes along their banks.

Ironically, too, the mountainsides which T. V. A. has done so much to ruin threaten to destroy the magnificent lakes for whose construction the Authority was initially organized. As the yellow pall spreads across the Southern mountains the vile cargo they disgorge creeps into the huge, sparkling lakes on the Tennessee River and its tributary streams. Initially engineers estimated these impoundments would enjoy a life expectancy of centuries, and in some instances, of millennia, but their estimates assumed that the watersheds would be stabilized with timber and cover-crops. As stripping chews up the land from which so much of the Authority's water is derived, it shaves years from the usefulness of the lakes. Someday, even under the best of circumstances, their beds will lie filled with silt and the clear waters will have become sluggish swamps. Then the dams will have to be blasted away so the streams can drain an otherwise pestilential area. But if enough vegetation is removed their life expectancy will be drastically shortened. If the nation's rivers are to be subdued and the string of costly lakes preserved for their recreational and resource value, the mountain slopes must be sheltered with foliage. Cheap power purchased by the ruin of vast land areas and the silting-up of our precious complex of public lakes will prove a costly bargain, indeed. Once the hills are wrecked reclamation can be accomplished only to a limited degree and at fantastic cost. The problems posed by the physical wrecking of the plateau is, in a broader context, a great national one and, so rapidly is it moving toward its climax, that unless a national solution is found for it soon the harm will have been done, perhaps irremediably.

———•———

CHAPTER TWENTY

The Scene Today

THE PRESENT crisis is compounded of many elements, human an⌐ material. They have produced what is probably the most seriously depressed region in the nation — and the adjective applies in much more than an economic sense. They have brought economic depression, to be sure, and it lies like a gray pall over the whole land. But a deeper tragedy lies in the depression of the spirit which has fallen upon so many of the people, making them, for the moment at least, listless, hopeless and without ambition.

The essential element of the plateau's economic malaise lies in the fact that for a hundred and thirty years it has exported its resources, all of which — timber, coal, and even crops — have had to be wrested violently from the earth. The nation has siphoned off hundreds of millions of dollars' worth of its resources while returning little of lasting value. For all practical purposes the plateau has long constituted a colonial appendage of the industrial East and Middle West, rather than an integral part of the nation generally. The decades of exploitation have in large measure drained the region. Its timber wealth is exhausted and if its hillsides ever again produce arrow-straight white oaks, tulip poplars and hemlocks new crops of trees will first have to be planted and allowed to mature. Hundreds of ridges which once bulged with thick seams of high-quality coal have been emptied of all that lay in their vitals and their surfaces have been fragmented for the pitiful remnants in the outcrop. While billions of tons still remain undisturbed they lie in inferior seams and are of poorer quality. The magnificent veins through which

Percheron horses once hauled strings of bank cars have been worked out.

Even more ruinous than the loss of its physical resources is the disappearance of the plateau's best human material. Most of the thousands who left were people who recognized the towering importance of education in the lives of their children, and craved for them better schools than Kentucky afforded. Too many of those who remained behind were without interest in real education as distinguished from its trappings. If their children attended the neighborhood schools the parents had done their duty. Too often they were far less ambitious and such ambition as they possessed was to evaporate in the arms of Welfarism and in the face of repeated failures.

From the beginning, the coal and timber companies insisted on keeping all, or nearly all, the wealth they produced. They were unwilling to plow more than a tiny part of the money they earned back into schools, libraries, health facilities and other institutions essential to a balanced, pleasant, productive and civilized society. The knowledge and guile of their managers enabled them to corrupt and cozen all too many of the region's elected public officials and to thwart the legitimate aspirations of the people. The greed and cunning of the coal magnates left behind an agglomeration of misery for a people who can boast of few of the facilities deemed indispensable to life in more sophisticated areas, and even these few are inadequate and of inferior quality.

Only one facet of the industry ever sought to return to the region any substantial part of the wealth it produced. The United Mine Workers' program of health, welfare and retirement benefits funneled back to the coal counties millions of dollars otherwise destined for the pockets of distant shareholders. To compound the tragedy of the plateau, even this program is today showing unmistakable signs of breakdown and failure. The union and the trustees of its fund were headed for inevitable trouble after the end of the second boom in 1948. Its seeds germinated in the same soil that sprouted the difficulties of the late 1920s: the industry was grossly overexpanded and was prepared to produce twice as much coal as its markets could consume. In 1948 the tremendous new truck-mining industry was overgrown and, hard though they struggled to mechanize their mines with the cast-off relics of their big competitors, the little operators were never really able to compete. A widespread double standard blanketed the coalfields. The big rail mines were sternly forced to comply with the wage and hour contracts negotiated year after year with the United Mine Workers, but John L. Lewis and his associates looked the other way where the truck mines were concerned. Fearing that if these small pits were shut down the resulting labor surplus might break the contracts in the big mines, they tolerated clandestine wage cuts. It became customary for the truck-mine operator to sign the contract and then ignore it. He paid his workmen five or ten dollars per day less than the scale wage and sent only a token contribution to the Health and Welfare Fund. Thus the truck mines existed for a decade, by sufferance of the union.

Then in the spring of 1959 the United Mine Workers undertook to change all this. Wages in many of the truck mines had sunk to ridiculous levels and in others the miners were "gang working" as partners and dividing the meager profits equally. But however they managed and toiled, many were earning no more than eight dollars a day and some as little as four dollars. Despite the pious provisions of the Federal Wage and Hour Law most operators paid as little as the miners could be persuaded to accept. But for a man with a wife and "a gang of young-'uns," with no money, no property and nowhere to go, any income is better than none. Thus when the union suddenly attempted to force the small pits to comply fully and faithfully with the contract their efforts ended in ignominious defeat. The miners in the little "dog-holes" had lost faith in the "organization." It had let them work at ever-lessening wages for ten years, preaching automation and higher pay to men who grew increasingly desperate with each passing year. In their cynical eyes John L. Lewis, once their hero and idol, had become a traitor to their interests.

When the 1959 strike was called, the response was far from uniform. Some of the workmen quit and picketed those who attempted to work. The strike dragged on for months amid recurrences of violence reminiscent of the 1930s. Men were slain, ramps and tipples were blasted and burned, and eventually the state's National Guard was sent into the troubled counties to preserve order. But the strike failed. In the long run practically all the truck miners deserted the union and went back to work. Today they mine many trainloads of coal

daily but pay nothing into the Welfare Fund. Their miners no
longer pay union dues. Their locals have folded up and disappeared. In retaliation against them the U.M.W. Fund trustees
canceled their hospital cards and Welfare benefits and thousands of
truck-mine laborers are now stranded at the mercy of their employers
and the customers who buy their coal. It is a harsh world for everyone, but in all America there is no worker — not even the imported
Mexican "wetback" — who occupies a position more exposed and
helpless than the men who dig coal in these little pits.

The Federal Government makes only a token effort to enforce the
minimum wage requirements of the Fair Labor Standards Act. Almost
always when complaints are called to the attention of the United
States Attorneys they are too busy to deal with them and the miner
in question receives a form letter advising him to bring suit for back-
wages in "a court of competent jurisdiction." But lawsuits cost
money and the miner has none, so the suit is not brought, the
delinquency is not collected and the low wages continue. His union
has ostracized him as a yellow dog and a scab. Some of the magnificent union hospitals stand half-empty while their skilled physicians
resign in disgust because there are so few patients to attend.* The
truck-mine operator is earning little on the coal he sells and competition from the increasing numbers of strip and auger companies
constantly deflates the price of his product. While other Americans
are enjoying prosperity, planning expensive vacations in new automobiles and buying corporate stocks in unprecedented numbers, the
truck miner who is fortunate enough to have a job works for minuscule wages and wonders from payday to payday whether his employer
will be able to pay even the pittances for which he has contracted.

Even worse, the Federal Government treats him as a second-class
citizen when it comes to safety. Of all the things John L. Lewis can
boast of having accomplished for his followers, the Federal Mine
Safety Code is the most important. But Congress gave Lewis only
half a loaf, specifically restricting the act's application to mines
employing fifteen or more men. Small pits were left to the tender
mercies of their bosses and of state inspectors; the carnage continued
in them unabated. Most of the plateau's coal counties now go two

* In October of 1962, the trustees of the Fund announced that four of its
hospitals in the plateau would be permanently closed on June 30, 1963.

or three years at a time without a fatal accident in a railroad mine, but the dreary reports of dead and mangled bodies continue to filter with chilling frequency from the little operations. Truck mines produce approximately 12 per cent of the plateau's coal output and 33⅓ per cent of its killed and injured miners. Strangely enough the state's senior Senator, himself an eastern Kentuckian, is an outspoken defender of this industrial mayhem, and for several years has almost single-handedly staved off Federal safety enforcement in the smaller coal mines.

So the miners, the employed workmen who by hundreds make a skimpy living in the truck mines of the plateau, live on a downward spiral which for several years has appeared to be nearing rock bottom. With low wages, lack of union membership and protection, and in most instances without even Workmen's Compensation coverage, such a miner is fortunate to keep corn bread and beans on the dinner table in the poor shack he so often calls home.

So trifling were his wages that in many instances the "dog-hole miner" could not survive without the free food doled out to him monthly from the great stores of the United States Department of Agriculture. Though his situation was unusually severe, a miner recently remarked to me that for eleven eight-hour shifts of work he collected twenty-nine dollars in wages. It is apparent that he, his wife and three children would starve to death if his labor afforded their only support. It is true that some truck mines are so efficiently organized and have grown so large that they are able to pay decent wages, though few attempt the union scale. The largest ones, however, mine as much as a thousand tons a day and their owners pay twenty dollars for an eight-hour shift. Their miners live reasonably well but it should not be inferred that they set the standards for the industry. In most areas truck mining has degenerated into a ghastly economic mire which holds miner and operator alike enchained. Often the employer is fortunate if he can earn twenty dollars a day for himself, and his employees are lucky if they take home eight or ten dollars. In those pits in which the miners work as partners they are practically unsupervised by safety bosses. Each co-worker thinks of himself as his own boss and of equal voice in the management of the mine and, in consequence, none can enforce safety discipline. Yet they continue to dig coal from the thinning seams, producing it for incredibly low prices and adding to a coal glut which can only depress prices, earnings and wages still further.

Here and there a few rail mines still operate. During the last fifteen years there has been a relentless consolidation as the bigger companies steadily bought up the smaller ones. With roaring machines and shrunken crews, these corporate giants continue to pour coal from the black veins into the clattering tipples. But where nearly eight thousand men once toiled for United States Coal and Coke Company in the Big Black Mountain, fewer than seventeen hundred are now at work. Where five thousand miners once went under the hill for Consolidation Coal Company at Jenkins and McRoberts, nine hundred survivors are still on the payroll. But at neither place has coal production lessened. To the contrary, with advancing mechanization it has steadily swollen.

These fortunate hundreds earn a basic union wage in excess of twenty-four dollars a day and enjoy all the benefits the union contract bestows. They present a sharp contrast to the pauperized doghole miners. The two, and frequently they are blood brothers, are prince and pauper. The workman for Inland Steel, Bethlehem Mines, International Harvester, and United States Steel owns his home in a camp or in one of the rural areas. He has improved the house and installed a furnace and plumbing. His home is neat and well-painted. He drives and owns a late-model automobile and his children attend school regularly. He hopes to send at least some of them to college, perhaps to the University of Kentucky. He has a thousand dollars or so on deposit in a local bank. The magnificent facilities at the Miner's Memorial Hospitals exist primarily for his care. When he or any member of his family is ill or injured, doctors, surgeons and hospitalization cost him nothing. The trustees have lowered the retirement age and when he reaches his sixtieth birthday he can leave the mines and draw from the Fund a monthly retirement check of seventy-five dollars. The mine in which he works is well ventilated and under the orders of Federal Safety Inspectors has been made as safe as human ingenuity can vouchsafe. If, despite the precautions, he is injured, compensation benefits up to a total of $15,300 await him. His union shelters him from coercion by company officials and has long since forced the closing of the scrip office. In most camps the company store is little more than a memory.

But there are portents of trouble for these union miners and their organization. The United Mine Workers has shrunk its membership and raised the living standards of those who remain. In so doing it has kept abreast of progress because progress is bigness, efficiency, technological advancement and organization. At the same time, it has created a favored class, a sort of blue-collar royalty amid a populace of industrial serfs. The combination of giant companies and giant union is driving the truck mines from the scene. Each spring the beginning of the lake trade finds fewer truck mines in operation. Within a few more seasons, the rail-mine operators can confidently expect the last of their small competitors to have been relegated to the scrap heap of history. But they are confronted with competition from other quarters — savage rivalry they cannot dispose of in so cavalier a fashion.

The rising crescendo of strip and auger mining is pouring growing quantities of extremely low-priced coal onto the market. So long as unspoiled ridges invite the bulldozers and big screws, the Big Bosses will face a gruesome dilemma. At great cost to their stockholders they have made ready to market clean and high quality coal. Ironically, this product is now becoming old-fashioned. The trend is toward lower prices and quality, and therefore the huge complex washeries may be little more than outmoded symbols of a departed time. In consequence, the union and its members are losing their economic and political importance. When coal was dug by simple tools and machines the many men who operated them could give fiscal chilblains to industrialists and government officials across the land. The nation was dependent upon coal, and hence on the miner's skills, but this dependence is seeping fast away. In coal production the cornerstone is still the dust-blackened, blue-collar miner, but he is surrendering his primacy to the white-collar expert whose skill and cunning has worked a far-reaching revolution in so short a time. The growing petroleum glut and the network of natural gas pipelines lessen coal's importance with each passing season. Within a few years tireless atomic reactors will provide much of the electric power now made from coal. Though the nation will surely grow steadily, coal is unlikely ever again to be a prime industry. Its path is downward, and the men and communities who are dependent upon it are tied to a descending star. Since coal is, for all practical purposes, the plateau's only industry, the region and its people are tied to an industrial albatross.

In a state where politics is the essence of life, success is measured by the ability to deliver votes. The union once possessed great influence at the polling places, but this too is evaporating. For fifteen years after the union drives were successfully concluded politicians sought the support of union chiefs, and while the rank and file never blindly followed the wishes of their leaders, such endorsements were worth many votes. A great many miners quietly "went along with the organization" and stamped their ballots for candidates who were approved as friends of labor. But such political influence as the shrunken locals still possess is shriveling still further. With the truck miners almost entirely nonunion and thousands of other diggers jobless, the rolls of bona fide, active union members are now relatively small. Too, the once-numerous union pensioners are disappearing fast. The hosts of charter members who retired in the late 1940s have been thinned by death, and most of the survivors are close to eighty years of age. Though they still pay union dues and are grateful to the organization for their monthly checks, they take little interest in the affairs of the locals. They are out of contact with the younger men and are seldom seen at union meetings. They pay little attention to political recommendations, and often fail to vote.

The pendulum has swung so far that union endorsement is now as often a hindrance as a help. The truck miners and their employers are bitterly antagonistic toward the union they once worked so hard to promote. Many miners who scrimped through long strikes in the 1940s to support the great union struggle for shorter hours, higher wages, Federal safety regulations and the Welfare Fund now view the union with aversion. They are more likely to oppose than to support a candidate the U. M. W. of A. has approved.

In fact, the union may be fighting for its very life. In the spring of 1961 a Federal Court in Tennessee awarded damages in the sum of $280,000 to a truck-mine operator who alleged the U. M. W. of A. had conspired with the big operators to force the small pits out of existence. If the judgment is confirmed on appeal, it may well lead to such attrition by lawsuit as to sap ruinously an already seriously weakened organization. So much "nonunion coal" is now on the market that for the last two years the fund has collected much less money than it has disbursed. In the fiscal year ending on June 30, 1961, receipts dropped 10 per cent under those for the preceding year, and disbursements exceeded income by $16,300,000. Already the trustees of the depleted Fund have been compelled to reduce monthly retirement pensions from one hundred to seventy-five dollars and further reductions may soon be necessary. Thus the region's one union —and the only counterpoise to its one industry—is rushing rapidly toward a severe crisis in its affairs. It is by no means inconceivable that within a few more years the U. M. W. of A. will disappear from the plateau, or, at best, be reduced to impotence with small islands of membership in only a few communities.

In community after community one can visit a dozen houses in a row without finding a single man who is employed. Most are retired miners and their wives who live on social security and union pension checks. Hundreds of other houses are occupied by aged widows, some of whom have taken in a grandchild or other youngster for "company" in their old age.

One row of camp houses has twenty-one residences. Seven are occupied by widows, the youngest of whom is fifty-two years of age and four of whom are more than seventy. Five are the homes of aged couples. Four shelter unemployed miners in their early fifties — men "too old to get a job and too young to retire." Three families draw state aid because the men are disabled from mining accidents. Only two houses are supported by men who still have jobs in a nearby mine.

One may walk the streets of camps and wander along winding creek roads for days and rarely find a young man or woman. For years the young and the employable have turned their backs on the plateau. Each spring when warm weather begins to enliven the land the more energetic and ambitious of the young men and women develop a yen for a more hopeful region. One by one they slip away. A year after high-school diplomas are distributed, it is hard to find more than 4 or 5 per cent of the graduates in their home counties.

In the autumn of 1960 one high-school principal assured me that not a single graduate of his school in 1958, 1959 or 1960 was living in the county. A couple of dozen are in military or naval service, but 70 per cent had found jobs (or at least lodgment) in Ohio, Indiana and Michigan. The others were scattered over New York, Illinois and California.

When citizens leave the region at such an early age they rarely return except for short visits. Within a few years they have found spouses, homes and friends elsewhere. Occasionally they come back to attend a funeral or a family reunion, but after a few years such visits generally stop altogether. Poor though its schools are by national norms, the plateau is educating its childrem almost entirely for other and wealthier parts of the nation. The one thing it needs most desperately is an educated and energetic cadre of leaders — imaginative and challenging men and women to grapple with its encrustations of problems and shortcomings. As matters now stand there is little likelihood it can develop such leadership, and its destiny is likely to remain in the hands of the absentee wreckers and their apologists.

The 1960 census discloses some breathtaking facts about the metamorphosis now under way in the character of the Kentuckian and his state. The preceding decade was one of unparalleled dynamism and growth for the nation. While Arkansas, Mississippi and South Dakota lost population, most states, including Kentucky, managed to make at least some population gains. For California, Oregon, Washington, Utah, Arizona, Florida, Ohio, New York and Pennsylvania it was a decade aglow with prosperity. New citizens poured in from other areas. Cities sprang up in waste lands. Some portions of Kentucky — the western and northern areas — shared in the national growth. On the whole, however, the state's census statistics are chilling because of the dreary picture they portray. The total population of Kentucky rose from 2,944,806 in 1950 to 3,038,156 in 1960. The rural population as a whole decreased 9.4 per cent while the urban population rose 24.8 per cent, reflecting the general nationwide movement from the countryside into the incorporated town. A sustained exodus from the state persisted throughout the decade. Most of the emigrés were between twenty-five and twenty-nine years of age. For the state as a whole, that age bracket lost 21.7 per cent, but for the plateau counties the loss ran much higher.

The state as a whole lost 14.6 per cent of its citizens between twenty and twenty-four years of age, but again the loss rate from the Cumberland Plateau was more than twice this figure.

During the same years the number of people eighty-five years of age or older increased in the Cumberlands by 61.8 per cent!

While the energetic, the ambitious and the hopeful were leaving the state, those who remained behind were not idle. The number of children increased by 16.7 per cent. The plateau counties sustained a "fertility ratio" much higher than that of the rest of the state. The poverty-stricken mountain area produced nearly twice as many children per thousand women as did the wealthy and stable Bluegrass. The fertility ratio is determined by the number of children under five years of age per thousand women. In Leslie County this figure was 790. The other plateau counties did not fall much below that level.

Nor should we assume that even the relatively educated highland youth is faring well at the hands of the outside world. Even those with high school diplomas find many doors shut to them. Unfortunately the region's poor schools and the limited cultural facilities have produced whole crops of high school graduates who are poorly pre pared when compared with students who have been educated in good public or private schools elsewhere. Despite twelve years in elementary and high school a majority of the proud young graduates are scarcely literate. They have read little outside their pallid textbooks and have made no real effort in composition. The mathematics classrooms have long been the "sideline" domain of the football and basketball coaches. Physics, chemistry, calculus, algebra and geometry have been so neglected that in some institutions they have practically vanished. Latin and foreign languages, too, disappeared from many curricula during or soon after the Second World War and few students can comprehend a word of any foreign tongue. Infinitely more tragic is their inability to comprehend the best expressions of their own language. Shakespeare and the other poets and playwrights, old and new, are mysterious citadels whose walls few of them have attempted to breach. For years I have talked with high-school students in an effort to discover their knowledge of English and American poetic literature. I can number on the fingers of one hand the few students who have been able to recite from memory even a single stanza from Shakespeare, Shelley, Keats, Browning, Wordsworth, Tennyson, Poe or Whitman. The great novels which spellbound other generations of scholars are regarded as laborious chores to be struggled through out of sheer necessity.

But while genuine learning — where it existed at all — has withered, athletics have found no dearth of official and public support. Rare is the high school whose football coach is not paid far more than its chemistry, mathematics and English teachers. Though decades passed without the building of new classrooms or laboratories the administrators managed to finance gymnasia. In school systems too poor to buy library books, money was always discovered for basketballs and playing floors. In 1947 one school board discussed at length the rising cost of maintaining a chemistry class in each of the county's high schools. Finally, with supreme generosity, the board budgeted fifty dollars for each chemistry teacher to spend on laboratory equipment and supplies. The chemistry teachers were voted annual salaries of $2250. Then, with this vexatious problem disposed of, the board voted to sell bonds in order to spend $257,000 for a gymnasium. The superintendent declared and the board agreed that a strong athletics program would bring the school vigorous support from the community and would keep in the classrooms many students who otherwise might be tempted to go North in quest of jobs.

The region's school system is still hopelessly bogged in politics. Elected school board members hire the superintendents. School board elections occur every two years and invariably the superintendent is one of the most powerful political figures in the county. Almost without supervision by the state he spends hundreds of thousands of dollars annually, all of which can be dispensed to political as well as educational advantage. In 1960 the Legislature enacted a long overdue general 3 per cent sales tax, devoting nearly two thirds of the money to the public schools. This huge and abrupt rise in appropriations has financed substantial salary raises for teachers, and a modest building program.

It has also enabled the school politicians to fortify themselves with massive patronage dispensations. As a rule the school clique is inter-woven with the courthouse political machine which spends county funds and discreetly oversees the local management of the State Aid programs. These powerful allies are thus so well-financed and entrenched that they are extremely difficult to overturn and their foremost objective is political perpetuation. They keep the schools enmeshed in endless political brawls. The tensions generated by the politicians are reflected in cynical teachers who know they are more often hired for their vote-getting power than for their teaching skill. Even more tragically, it is mirrored in dilapidated school buildings, tattered collections of books posing as libraries, comparatively palatial gyms and recurring crops of educationally stunted high school grad-uates.

The Selective Service system deals daily with the products of the weak and politically oriented schools. One county of approximately thirty thousand people (a county in most respects typical) boasts five high schools and is generally rated as having one of the plateau's more effective school systems. In 1960 Selective Service examined one hundred and four young draft registrants from the county. All of them were under twenty-three years of age. Only two failed for physical reasons, but twenty-six failed because they could not pass the mental tests. They were "functional illiterates" who were unable to read or comprehend satisfactorily ordinary printed matter such as newspapers and magazines. Even more shocking, four high-school graduates volunteered and two of them were rejected for the same reason. Selective Service rejections for mental and educational rea-sons are running from 25 per cent in the "better" counties to as much as 50 per cent in the worst.

A fifty-six-year-old jobless miner summed up the hopelessness the shoddy schools sometimes engender. He sat in my law office one rainy Saturday afternoon and described his plight:

I hain't got no education much and jist barely can write my name. After I lost my job in 1950 I went all over the country a-lookin' fer work. I finally found a job in a factory in Ohio a-puttin' televisions inside wooden crates. Well, I worked for three years and managed to make enough money to keep my young-'uns in school. Then they put in a machine that could crate them televisions a whole lot better than us men could and in a lot less time. Hit jist stapled them up in big card-board boxes. I got laid off again and I jist ain't never been able to find nothing else to do.

But I kept my young-'uns in school anyway. I come back home here to the mountains and raised me a big garden ever' year and worked at anything I could find to do. I sold my old car fer seventy-five dollars and I sold all the land my daddy left me and spent the money on my children. They didn't have much to eat or wear, but they at least didn't miss no school. Well, finally last spring my oldest boy finished up high school and got his diploma. I managed to get twenty-five dollars together and give it to him and he went off to git him a job. He had good grades in school and I figured he'd git him a job easy. He went out to California where he's got some kinfolks and went to a factory where they was hirin' men. The sign said all the work hands had to be under thirty-five years of age and be high-school graduates. Well, this company wouldn't recognize his diploma because it was from a Kentucky school. They said a high-school diploma from Kentucky, Arkansas and Mississippi just showed a man had done about the same as ten years in school in any other state. But they agreed to give the boy a test to see how much he knowed and he failed it flatter than a flitter. They turned him down and he got a job workin' in a laundry. He jist barely makes enough money to pay his way but hit's better than settin' around back here.

I reckon they jist ain't no future fer people like us. Me and my wife ain't got nothin' and don't know nothin' hardly. We've spent everything we've got to try to learn our young-'uns something so they would have a better chance in the world, and now they don't know nothin' either!

That his son is not an exceptional example is borne out by the statistics on college freshmen from the plateau. Some, of course, do excellent work in college and have little difficulty in entering the University of Kentucky or colleges outside the state. Most of the hopeful freshmen, however, are shockingly unprepared for college study. The standard College Qualification Test is given annually to seniors in the state's high schools and in those of other states. The test is prepared by the Psychological Corporation, a New York firm, and seeks to measure the high-school graduate's cultural background as well as his scholastic achievement. As its name implies, it is designed to measure the student's preparation for college study. In 1960 students in Virginia and Tennessee averaged above 80 per cent on the test. In areas of Kentucky outside the plateau grades averaged between 55 per cent and 65 per cent out of a possible 100 per cent. If this poor showing is startling what, then, must be one's reaction to the results of the same examination in the counties of the plateau? When the high-school graduates in a broad belt of the coal counties were given the test in 1960, the average grade was only 17.5 per cent.

These undereducated young Americans are the region's fortunate youths, notwithstanding the shortcomings of their schooling. Infinitely worse off are the uncounted children who simply do not go to school. One teacher, for example, began the 1959-1960 school term with fifty-eight enrolled pupils, in four grades. But as the term advanced many difficulties beset her weather-beaten little institution. Some children lived several miles away and had little appetite for the long walk over slippery paths on cold wintry mornings. The drafty building was a breeding ground for cold and influenza viruses and a substantial number were kept away by illness. Most absentees, however, stayed at home simply because their parents could not provide shoes and clothing for them to wear. Consequently, average daily attendance was only thirty-four.

Weak and sporadic elementary-school preparation results in crops of high-school freshmen who are totally unprepared for further studies. Almost one third of the freshmen of 1956 had dropped out of school in 1959.

The incidence of total illiteracy is startlingly high. Every lawyer in the plateau receives clients almost daily who are unable to sign their names to legal documents. On one occasion I went to a coal camp to obtain the signatures of a miner and his wife. Though they were under thirty-six years of age they could not write their names. Under the law their "marks" required attestation by two witnesses. Neither of their nearest neighbors could perform this simple duty and we were compelled to visit the third house before a man and woman were found who could sign as witnesses.

The physical task of providing decent housing for the region's schoolchildren — a prerequisite without which real improvement is unthinkable — is staggering. Though the new retail sales tax is financing the construction of several hundred new classrooms annually, the building rate cannot begin to equal that at which ancient, rickety buildings have to be abandoned. Speaking of the building program in his own county, Pike County Superintendent C. H. Farley told a Congressional committee in March, 1961, that the task of catching-up appeared insuperable without major new sources of revenue. As he termed it, "The hurrieder we go, the behinder we get. Our schools are short on literally everything but children."

The county of approximately thirty thousand people which I have previously mentioned is largely supported by Welfarism of one character or another. As this is written, seven hundred and four Old Age pensioners receive monthly checks from the state capitol. Four hundred and eighty-six families are supported by Aid for Dependent Children checks. Seventy-one blind persons draw checks, and one hundred and twenty-six families are supported because the breadwinner is disabled, has fled or has been imprisoned. Nearly a thousand households receive checks from the United Mine Workers, and more than thirty-five hundred persons draw Social Security checks totalling two million dollars annually. Over a thousand pension and compensation checks reach the county each month from the United States Veterans Administration. At least two hundred families receive compensation checks because the husbands were killed or injured in mining accidents. Two thousand other men are paid unemployment compensation benefits while actively seeking other jobs. On "check days," at the beginning of each month, wastebaskets in county-seat banks are piled high with empty brown envelopes from state and Federal agencies. Sometimes they are inches deep on the floor at the tellers' windows. The millions of dollars thus pumped into the plateau each year keep the people alive and support the merchants and other business establishments. Without such checks a majority of the highlanders would be in abject starvation in a matter of days.

One third of the county's population is on the Commodity Relief rolls. From relatively humble beginnings the commodity distribution program has grown to mammoth proportions. On "giveaway" days queues a hundred yards long form in front of the distribution centers and the huge bags and boxes full of staples are carried to automobiles. Sometimes several people will rent a single car to haul their rations, and its luggage compartment will not hold the entire load.

Other Relief recipients arrive in their own vehicles, ranging from pathetic rattletraps to new Buicks. The late-model cars are the property of miners who were recently idled by layoffs at the rail mines. They worked ten or fifteen years at high wages and still drive cars bought or contracted for in happier times. It is incongruous in the extreme to see a man carry his bag of "giveaway grub" out to a bright red late-model Mercury with synthetic leopardskin seat-covers.

Sixteen hundred of the county's men are still employed in the unionized rail mines (at the height of the Big Boom its rail pits hired ninety-four hundred men), and seven hundred and fifty others work two or three days a week in nonunion truck mines. The county and independent school districts hire nearly five hundred teachers, supervisors, bus drivers, lunchroom cooks, librarians and other personnel for nine months out of each year. Banks, stores, garages, filling stations, machineshops, quarries, sawmills, post offices, restaurants, utilities companies, printers, morticians, railroads and other enterprises provide full or part-time employment to another thirteen hundred men and women. The United Mine Workers' hospital employs a hundred and twenty-five others. Approximately one hundred and fifty persons work for municipalities, the county and the state. Together, the employed support fewer than half the county's population.

An interesting outgrowth of the general aging of the population has been a gradual slipping-away of property from taxation. The old men and women whose children have moved to distant states know their heirs are unlikely to ever return to Kentucky. They know that the houses in which they live are worth only a few hundred dollars. Even a large, renovated camp house with plumbing and central heating will seldom bring more than fifteen hundred dollars.

They "raised" large families and when a twelve- or fifteen-hundred dollar estate is divided among ten or twelve heirs the inheritance is not worth the trouble its settlement will entail. Since the heirs are scattered in several states it is unthinkable that they will hire an attorney to settle an estate which is worth little more than a hundred dollars to each inheritor. Under these circumstances, the aged owners often simply stop paying taxes. They know the sheriffs whose duty it is to collect the levies will not risk the political disfavor enforced collections will bring. If the sheriffs went into the camps and onto the creeks and by attachments and sales compelled people to pay their real-estate taxes they would arouse the animosity of whole communities of voters. Since they have political interests and alliances to protect, they will not hunt trouble. Instead they wait politely in their offices and receive whatever tax payments are brought to them. Hundreds of small parcels of land have now gone for a decade or more without taxes being paid on them.

And when the old couple have died and the house stands empty there is no one to move into it. In lengthening lines deserted houses stretch up the creeks and along camp streets. If a local resident wants to buy such a property the technical difficulties are frequently almost insurmountable. Typically some of the sons and daughters of the last owner have died, leaving children of their own. It is not unusual for a thousand-dollar parcel of real estate to be the property of thirty or forty joint owners, some of whom have not set foot in the county for a decade. Some of them were born in other states and are only five or six years old. The guardians or custodians of such infants cannot convey their land until consent has been obtained from the Circuit Court of the county in which the realty is situated, an expensive, complex and time-consuming process. The state has no effective legislation by which the property can be sold for taxes. Thus as the present owners die off the amount of nontaxpaying property rises, to the increasing detriment of the plateau and of its public institutions.

A trip through the coal counties is a distressing experience. One traverses mile after dreary mile of patched and cratered "highways," their ditches choked with mud and their banks and shoulders thick with weeds. Nearly half the precious bottomland grows nothing more valuable than weeds and broom sage, and some is growing up in thickets. The mountains are strewn with rotted, collapsing coal tipples, chutes and bins and pimpled with ugly slate dumps of every size and shape. The streams have lost their sparkle and are sluggish yellow ropes coiling through the valleys. The hillsides, deserted by hoe and bull-tongue plow, are turning into tangled thickets. In the deep moist coves millions of young poplars have sprung up and constitute one of the region's few potential sources of wealth. But most of the forest land, the points and upper ridges, nourish a disheartening growth of cull gums, beeches, oaks and pines. The generations of wasteful logging and the forest conflagrations that followed in their wake have left little valuable timber. The slashed and burned saplings that survived live on as unhealthy midgets which in the course of decades have grown scarcely at all. In the summertime their green foliage presents the appearance of a vast young forest, but this casual impression is wholly erroneous. One can climb for miles along the coal benches, across the ridges and through the deep coves without encountering a dozen genuinely healthy trees big enough for the sawmill.

Nowhere in the plateau does a single tract of virgin forest remain. All the titanic trees which once towered over its rippling streams have been "worked up" into lumber, mining props or stave bolts. Only a few tiny sawmills persist in a region that once supported scores of mighty band mills. Even a few acres of unspoiled timberland would constitute a priceless heritage for a nation which increasingly idealizes its robust past, but no such acres remain.

Hundreds of worked-out mines have become subterranean lakes. In wet weather water from the overlying mountains seeps into them and in dips or "swags" rises to the crumbling roofs. The unsealed airways and driftmouths disgorge it in foamy torrents, and during the dry summer months the drained hills dry out and turn adobe-hard. They lose their capacity to retain water in normal quantities for the nourishment of the trees struggling on their slopes. Drained of water, the slopes open in deep fissures. These perennial man-made droughts beset the timbered hillsides every summer and choke off growth. In spring the trees have a short burst of vitality but by July they are arrested and stand pale and desiccated, their roots deep in dry hard clay. They are a curious spectacle, little changed year after year, receiving sufficient moisture to preserve life but not enough to nurture vigorous growth.

Along the serpentine roads are the scores and hundreds of abandoned houses. The windows fall out, the chimneys topple, the roofs leak and in the grip of decay they sag ever closer to the earth. Here and there on high, uncertain stilts stands a dilapidated white frame schoolhouse, its playground a grassless, eroded hillside or an undrained mire.

Thousands of highlanders on job-hunting forays into Michigan, Indiana and Northern Ohio bought cheap "junker" cars which they have brought home in the hope of realizing a profit on them. Eventually, these wind up in roadside scrapyards where they are cannibalized for their parts. The mountaineers are inveterate automobile fanciers, but most of them can afford only worn-out, rattling vehicles of ancient vintage. After the last wheezing mile has been wrung from them they come to rest in automobile graveyards. Piece by piece they are stripped for such usable parts as may remain, then eventually they are loaded on trucks and hauled to Ashland, Kentucky, for sale at the great scrapyards of the American Roller Mills Company. The valleys are sprinkled with hideous car dumps where Fords, Chevrolets, Cadillacs and once magnificent limousines lie piled in rusty array. As eyesores they are second only to the ghastly trash dumps.

These latter eyesores abound on roadside and stream-bank. Trash collections outside the towns do not exist and people simply dump refuse wherever impulse directs, usually in the nearest creek or branch. Ancient car bodies, discarded truck beds, rusty bed springs, rotten mattresses, scraps of building materials, tin cans, bottles and paper are heaved onto road shoulders and into rivers and creeks. On a single trip across Knott, Perry, Leslie and Clay counties I counted more than sixty huge trash dumps, each of them plainly visible from the highway. Even when a municipality sponsors a trash-collection system no effort is made toward genuinely sanitary disposal. Instead, the collectors haul it into some ravine not far removed from the main highway. Acres of stinking waste accumulate, sheltering and feeding monstrous rats and buzzing swarms of flies. As the mounds of trash and garbage rise the collectors dump ever closer to the highway. Soon smoke from burning trash ascends from the shoulder of the road.

The city councils and civic organizations appear to be oblivious of the blight cast on their region by private and public dumps. Men who are reputed to be "public-spirited" will cast trunkloads of old newspapers into the river near their homes.

One town labored hard to persuade state officials to establish a state park near its borders. Delegations of city officials, Lions and Rotarians extolled the natural beauty to be seen from a towering mountain crag. Parks commissioners and news reporters were duly escorted to its summit. Through it all, with perfect aplomb, the city trucks carried daily cargoes of litter and waste to a dumping ground below the lookout point. While the community struggled prodigiously to promote "tourism," smoke from its dump sullied one of the region's most picturesque scenic areas.

In the main public standards are symbolized by public buildings.

In the plateau the courthouses and jails are incredibly dilapidated and filthy. They go for years at a time without major repairs or even paint, and today it is scarcely conceivable that such vile and crumbling structures could be found in use in any of the new nations of .Africa — not even in the chaotic Republic of Congo. At most seasons of the year they are festooned with garish signs of all shapes and sizes which proclaim the promises of candidates for innumerable town, county, state and Federal offices.

The strippers are tearing to pieces such natural scenic beauty as the dumps leave undefiled. Many of them work around the clock, their activities illuminated by batteries of powerful lights mounted on tall posts. From the air and from high mountain peaks the strip-lines are mazes of looped and tangled scars. Like great yellow snakes they twist over the tortured hills. Ironically, this destruction by the coal industry is rapidly nullifying the careful efforts of its boosters to develop a new source of income for the plateau.

Slashed and battered though they are, the highlands still afford many areas of breathtakingly rugged natural beauty. The gorge of the Red River is a paradise for lovers of wild flowers, and from crags on top of the Big Black and Pine Mountains one can look down on enchanting hollows. Seen from such eminences the lesser hills and ridges appear as gigantic waves on a primordial ocean. Many people, charmed by such beauty, have sought to establish "tourism" as a secondary "industry" for the region. The state government has created seven state parks at strategic points in the plateau and state officials have exhorted the mountaineers to clean up their roadsides, beautify their towns, build hotels and motor lodges and cater to such travelers as may wander into the area. Thus far the movement has made little headway. Despite the natural beauty to be found in some seasons, tourists will not spend their vacations driving over tortuous roads the sides of which are littered with heaps of junk and trash.

Livestock has almost vanished from the plateau. Between 1950 and 1960 more than half the farms were abandoned. The pastures have been surrendered to broom sage and the cornfields to weeds and brambles. Even the vegetable garden is a disappearing institution. The people have discovered that between giveaway and state aid nobody is going to starve anyway, and it is easier to carry it in than to grow it. In short, the ancient corn and pork subsistence agriculture has been abandoned under pressure from soil erosion, the entice-ment of money wages and a realization that the Welfare state will provide free as much as a man can acquire by backbreaking labor from the soil. Those farmers who learned the new methods of the agricultural agents are also being pushed into surrender. With their reliance upon applications of limestone and fertilizer and better strains of hogs and cattle, they acquired the modern farmer's depend-ence upon cash crops. They had to sell their cattle, hogs, tobacco and other produce for the dollars without which their families could not live. And at sale time their produce is marketed simultaneously with the tremendous avalanche of meat, grain and fiber which annually pours out of the Great Plains. The steep hillsides and nar-row bottoms, no matter how well or intensively used, cannot produce in competition with the big farms in the rich lands of the West and South, and with heartbreaking frequency the mountain farmer is forced to sell at a loss or for a profit that is trifling. The 1960 census revealed the total collapse of the old agriculture with its emphasis on cornfields, plow mules and fattening hogs. In full retreat, too, was the new agriculture. Few farm tractors were discovered anywhere in the plateau and with the coming of the Federal soil bank most farm-ers "banked" their crop land. By this means virtually as much can be realized by a mountain farmer for not working as he can hope to obtain for his family by plowing, planting, harvesting and marketing.

Most saddening of all are the myriads of men, women and chil-dren who sit on the front porches of shacks and houses gazing with listless unconcern at the world. The creeks and yards are littered with tin cans, paper bags and cartons, nearly half of which bear the sten-ciling of the Commodity Credit Corporation. The cloak of idleness, defeat, dejection and surrender has fallen so heavily as to leave them scarcely more than half alive. Their communities are turning into graveyards peopled with the living dead and strewn with the impedi-menta of a civilization which once needed them but does so no longer.

The curse of coal is thus etched indelibly on the land and in the hearts and faces of its inhabitants. Its rapid process of automation and the consolidation of mining operations has stranded as perma-nently jobless most of its laborers. Those who are physically able to work know no skill except mining, and that skill is now hopelessly obsolete. Neither government nor their former employer feels any responsibility to find work — within their capabilities — for their hands. Thus they sit and brood, cynical and bitter but, in most instances, surprisingly well fed. The dole and the wide variety of union and government checks hold at bay the hollow, physical hunger of the early 1930s.

Hellier is a town on Marrowbone Creek in Pike County. It grew up forty years ago as a trading center for the camps that ringed it — Alleghany, Manco, Greenough and Henry Clay. It was a chartered municipality with city hall, police and fire departments and an impressive little high school.

Most of its customers lived in the huge camp called Alleghany. That mining community was built by Hellier Coal and Coke Company fifty years ago. Its rows of two-story frame houses sheltered a multitude of people whose dollars brought prosperity to the stores, poolrooms, garages, barbershops and dives in Hellier.

In the late 1940s the company went through the routine of "freeing" its camp. Then, a few years later, it sold its tipples and coal veins to Blue Diamond Coal Company. With automation the labor force dwindled sharply, but most of the remaining miners lived in the camp. Retired miners and pensioned widows occupied the other houses. The coal reserves were still large and the miners anticipated many years of uninterrupted work.

Then early in 1960 the directors of Blue Diamond negotiated a sale of their mineral rights to a subsidiary of Bethlehem Steel. The steel company desired to withdraw the coal from the opposite side of the hill. It did not want to inherit the commissaries, shops, tipples, coke ovens and portals of Hellier, nor to assume any responsibility for the inhabitants of the town. The results were highly satisfactory for the two corporations, but fell like a sledgehammer on the people of Hellier and Alleghany.

Without previous warning the miners were suddenly informed that the mine was being permanently closed. They received their final wages and "cut-off slips." A few weeks later workmen arrived in the camp and began tearing down the tipple. They were employed by a company dealing in used mining equipment and machinery. They withdrew the machines and tracks from the mine, demolished the shops, coke ovens and commissaries, and hauled away virtually everything the company owned, excepting only the veins of coal. Within a few weeks a bustling community was reduced to a silent, stunned ghost town. The bewildered people required several months to grasp fully the change of circumstances that had so suddenly overtaken them.

Now the stranded town subsists on checks from the U. M. W. of A. and the Welfare state, and such slender earnings as some of the men are able to acquire at truck or auger mines. Those who move away find few buyers for their homes and then only at pitifully low prices. The little city hall stands empty, the government for which it was built having vanished. Auger operations have ripped the hillsides overlooking the town and rains have brought great heaps of mud and rocks down into its creek bed and onto yards, streets and bridges. Stranded Hellier, forlorn and hopeless, symbolizes the coalfield — indifferent and callous economic masters, helpless and despairing people, a narrow twisting valley dependent entirely upon a single industry which has withdrawn its benefits from the families so long dependent upon it.

In the two decades after the building of the railroads the established and relatively conservative Protestant churches took a keen interest in the "unchurched" people of the plateau. They sent ministers and organizers to found churches, "Christian-oriented" schools, and hospitals. They were rewarded with modest success in the county seats, the independent towns and the larger camps. Methodists, Presbyterians and various Baptist groups coalesced and built church houses. The Presbyterians were far more energetic and built a number of small high schools. However, no matter how hard the ministers labored they were rarely able to generate real enthusiasm. They recruited few members in the countryside and lesser camps. The vast majority of the creek and camp dwellers regarded them as "society" or "highbrow" churches and after a few years their membership ceased to grow. For years their pastors have labored with aging congregations to whom few new adherents are ever added. In the meantime the area was not overlooked by the lesser sects. Jehovah's Witnesses, Holiness, Freewill Baptists, Primitive Baptists and Regular Baptists found a larger audience for their less sophisticated creeds.

Their flimsy little frame church houses perched on ungainly foundation props were raised at strategic points in countless communities. Their "hellfire and damnation" doctrines, their promise of eternal life in a heavenly kingdom replete with earthly delights and their reliance on uncomplicated lay preachers appealed powerfully to miner and creek farmer. In a society constantly darkened by the specter of sudden death, and in which worldly security appeared forever unattainable, men and women seized upon religion as a comforting rod. Sometimes their pursuit of salvation led them to incredible lengths. "Holy Rollers" literally "took up serpents" to show the power of their faith — actions which sometimes resulted in death. Some even proclaimed their wholehearted reliance on the Almighty by handling hot coals, a feat which was supposed to show God would protect them from all harm. Their services were filled with quarter-hour long, entreaty-filled prayers, frenzied preaching (sometimes in "unknown tongues") and wild "shoutings" — hysterical experiences in which the "converted" sinners shriek out their "testimony to the power of God." But such sects, too, netted only a tiny part of the total population. Five decades after the first coal drag entered the upper reaches of the plateau no more than 15 per cent of the people claim church affiliation of any kind.

Through a century-and-three-quarters the mountaineers, in the main, have stayed remarkably irreligious. They simply are not joiners, spurning organizations of any kind except the political parties. They have retained a respectful reverence for the Holy Bible and for the Protestant cause but it is a reverence without scholarship, discipline or leadership. When religion comes it is usually with advancing age or as the result of some highly traumatic emotional experience. With the return of health or better times there is a strong likelihood the convert will "backslide." Much, indeed most, religion comes with the shadow of the deathbed. Recently I heard one mountaineer ask another how his sick uncle was faring. The reply was astoundingly candid, "He's a lot better than he was. In fact he's about well enough to backslide!"

There are thousands of mountaineers who go for many years without entering a church of any kind. Such preaching as they hear reaches them from radio evangelists.

The churchless legions present a tremendous challenge to religious orders everywhere in the nation. Materialism has brought them suffering and destitution and they lack spiritual values to support them in their distress. Mingled with this spiritual emptiness and immensely aggravating it is the awareness of futility and ineffectiveness that besets the unskilled in a highly technical and complex world. Out of this background has grown a mass melancholia of ominous and ever-deepening proportions. To escape its grip some commit suicide while others, in numbers we can only guess at, find surcease in the cheap product of tiny household stills. Made from commercial cow or mule feed, this deplorable whiskey is a far cry from the malt-rich corn whiskey of other days; but it enables many jobless miners to stage their "Saturday-night drunks" — sprees which sometimes last through the whole week.

The old fierce pride and sensitive spirit of independence have died from the continuing social trauma of a half-century. In countless instances people who grew up in clean cabins, and whose parents would have starved before they would have asked for charity, now in their old age shamelessly plot to "get by" on public assistance of one kind or another so long as they live. With the demise of their traditional values has come a curious reverse pride, a pride in not having pride. This attitude is extremely difficult to describe but may be illustrated by the fact that one of the finest compliments a mountaineer can bestow upon a stranger is to say that he is "common" or is "not a bit proud."

The Roman Catholic Church has quietly sponsored long-range programs of proselytization in the region and is attempting the incredibly difficult task of recruiting a priesthood from the native stock. The obstacles such an undertaking must overcome are legion, and significant headway may require a century. It can scarcely be doubted, however, that since every society leans heavily upon its spiritual advisers, be they witch doctors, parish priests, or reverend ministers, the mountaineer will approach more closely the norms of American society when he has been brought nearer to the balms religion alone can afford mankind on so many occasions between the cradle and the grave.

The broken and the ill are truly legion. Some suffer from "miner's asthma." They wheeze like dying men, their lungs filled with silica, "rock dust" or fine coal. Some struggle with enlarged and weakened hearts, the results of years of labor in poorly ventilated mines. Others are blind in one or both eyes, display empty sleeves or hobble on artificial legs. Here and there a paralytic sits in a wheel chair on the narrow porch of his little house, a reminder of the sudden slate fall that crushed his spine and made a widow of the fifty-year-old woman who lives around the bend of the creek. These broken men are part of the price America has paid for her industrial pre-eminence, though the Madison Avenue firms never mention them in the expensive advertisements they devise for their coal-consuming clients. Their pain and poverty are a hidden part of the highly touted "American standard of living." Sometimes their suffering is made to outlive their twisted bodies. In a cemetery near the little mining community of Mayking is buried the body of a miner who spent twenty-five years operating a coal-cutting machine. Sandstone dust from the whirring cutter bar gradually congested his lungs and eventually smothered him to death. When he died, a steel cutter bar was set in concrete as his grave marker.

It is scarcely probable, however, that the monstrous industrial exactions have greatly exceeded those of pistol, knife and whiskey. At Pikeville an elderly attorney still maintains an office for the practice of law. In nearly sixty years at the bar he has defended more than a thousand mountaineers charged with "willful murder." A hundred miles away in "bloody Harlan" the Commonwealth Attorney has preserved a record of the murder indictments he has prosecuted. As this is written, his list stands above six hundred. Each of these gentlemen can, almost certainly, claim a record which has never been equaled or surpassed in the world of English jurisprudence. The red violence reflected in their professional careers has also left a sad legacy in crippled men and in widows and orphans.

Only two or three of the plateau's towns have sanitary sewage disposal systems. The others — county seats, coal camps and thousands of individual homes — pour their raw sewage into the stinking streams. Choked with mud and junk, black with coaldust and reeking of filth, the once sparkling creeks and rivers are sluggish open sewers. Swollen with spring rains they sometimes approach the grandeur of the arteries which as late 1910 still admitted steamboats to Pikeville, but the freshets soon subside and in the summer scarcely enough water remains to float a canoe.

CHAPTER TWENTY-ONE

———————◆———————

The Politics of Decay

IN HER CHECKERED history Kentucky has had four written Constitutions. Beginning with the first in 1792 they were extremely democratic documents, vesting in the voters the power to elect almost every man who governs them or has charge of public affairs. The present Constitution, written in 1890, attempted to preserve undiluted the rough frontier equality whose character had been stamped on the state's people a century before. First of all the Constitutional Convention undertook to reserve all real power at the local level. A host of county and city elective officers was established. In a six-year interval the people in a typical plateau county choose the following officials: the state senator, state representative, circuit judge, Circuit Court clerk, Commonwealth attorney, County Court clerk, county judge, county attorney, tax commissioner, sheriff, coroner, eight justices of the peace, eight constables and five members of the Board of Education. In addition the people in each municipality elect a mayor, a police judge, five or six members of the Common Council, and, in some towns, a city attorney and marshal.

At the state level they elect a governor, lieutenant-governor, secretary of state, auditor of public accounts, treasurer, commissioner of agriculture, attorney-general and seven judges of the Court of Appeals. Most ridiculous of all they elect a clerk of the Court of Appeals. This official keeps a record of the proceedings of the state's highest court and has to earn his modest salary by electioneering among three million people in forty thousand square miles of territory.

But the state officials are a façade. The real power of government is at the base. Except for the judicial officers all this great host of local servants are paid by fees. The amount of their compensation is dependent upon their ability to collect charges from the general public. The state officials lack power to remove any of these "fee grabbers" other than the sheriffs, and there is no practical means by which malfeasance at the local level can be punished. To all intents and purposes the governor is little more than a presiding county judge. His ability to lead depends upon his capacity to persuade, because once a governor has fallen into the disfavor of the courthouse cliques his days are numbered. Dealing with a faceless multitude of county-centered and often illiterate voters, the county officials can propagandize endlessly to the detriment of a state administration, assuring its political doom regardless of the worthiness of the governor's aims. The courthouses are one hundred and twenty anchors which perpetually hold developments to the political center of the stream at a virtual standstill. At the bottom of this courthouse conservatism is a relentless determination to prevent any change that might replace fees with salaries or dilute the powers of local offices.

And what is the role of the public servant who holds office in such a setting? What kind of people knock at his door and what standards of public service do they demand of him? By what creed do they expect him to serve the holy principles of Liberty and Justice? In this most democratic of all states, how does Democracy fare?

The office of the county judge is the nerve center of the courthouse. In addition to being a judicial official charged with the trial of misdemeanors and minor civil actions, His Honor is the chief executive officer of the county. He presides over the fiscal court, directs the spending of county funds and is generally the chief "contact man" with Frankfort in political matters pertaining to the county.

His office consists of two dingy rooms. The long unpainted walls are peeling and paint hangs in scales from the ceiling. The rays of the sun struggle with small success to pierce the dirty, rain-streaked windowpanes. In the corner of the outer room a tobacco-stained cardboard box serves as a waste can.

The outer room contains the desk of his secretary and a half-dozen chairs are lined up along the walls. No matter how harassed she may be by the constant procession of callers, his secretary never fails to smile ingratiatingly — because even the smallest frown may offend a voter. From 8:30 in the morning when the office opens until 4:30 when the doors are locked, there is seldom a moment when a group of people are not waiting to "see the judge."

A day spent with the county judge in such an office in a plateau county is a revealing experience. It tells a story of the breakdown of Democracy and of the growing dependence and futility of the population. If Democracy is to eventually prevail over totalitarian ideologies the individual citizen must be able to shoulder a multitude of responsibilities and to discharge them out of a sense of duty. To do this he must possess the ability to meet social and economic problems and the willingness to grasp them. Until a generation ago the mountaineer was accustomed to "turn out" for road workings and other undertakings for community betterment. He was not paid and he did not expect to be. His willingness to work on roads and other essential projects was a holdover from the frontier where no government or government largesse existed. However, as government expanded and its benefits multiplied the old sturdiness began to dissolve. Though many frontier modes and outlooks survive and are sharply impressive, the traumas of fifty years have left a lasting imprint on the character of the mountaineer. His forefathers lived by the frontier maxim "root hog or die." They would be astounded if they could return in the spirit to behold their descendants thronging the office of the county judge to implore his assistance in a multitude of situations which, in an earlier time, would have been met by the citizens without its once occurring to them that help from any quarter was either possible or desirable.

A moment after the judge unlocked the door to his office an elderly woman darted in behind him. The judge greeted her with an affable smile and after a moment of smalltalk about her family and community, he inquired her business. She drew a paper from her purse and displayed it to him. On it was scrawled in longhand: "*We the undersigned persons have contributed to help —— who is sick and has to stay at home.*" Below this caption four or five courthouse officeholders and county-seat merchants had written their names.

Each of them had noted his contribution of $1.00 to the sufferer. The old lady explained that her son had a family and had been sick for a long time. "The doctors," she said, "can't find out what's the matter with him, and, as fer me, I'm almost certain it's cancer. You know, judge, how we've always voted fer you every time you ever run for anything and will again just as shore as you run. If you can help him out now when he's having such bad luck, we shore will appreciate it."

The judge sighed ruefully, because such pleas are routine, but he added his name to the list and handed the woman a dollar bill.

A moment later the secretary arrived and callers began to fill the chairs in the waiting room. Some said they had just dropped by to shake hands with the judge and had no business in particular, but three very determined gentlemen were ushered into his office. Dressed in mud-spattered overalls, they lived on a creek some eleven miles from the county seat. The state had built a rural highway into the community in 1949 and later hard-surfaced it. But long neglect had allowed the road to deteriorate badly. The spokesman for the group, a tall, raw-boned mountaineer, told their story:

"Judge, you know what kind of a shape our road is in and that it's prac'ly impossible to travel it. The ditch lines are all stopped up and there are holes all over it big enough to set a washtub in. One feller broke an axle right in the middle of the road last week. Now you know our precinct has always been one of the best in the county and you never come up there electioneering in your life that you didn't git a big vote, but if you can't do something for us now we'll sure as hell remember it if you ever run for anything else again. We ain't got no governor or he wouldn't let the roads get in the shape they're in now. We've just got to have the ditch lines cleaned out and the holes filled up."

The judge attempted to mollify his angry visitors, for this was not their first visit to his office on the same business. He pointed out very courteously, however, that funds were short and that a new coat of surfacing was out of the question. He promised to send a scraper to clean out the drainage ditches, and pledged an application of gravel for the worst places in the road. He warned them, however: "The roads all over this county are going to pieces, and we simply don't have the money to keep them up. We are doing everything in our power to maintain the roads, but we just don't have the money to do a decent job."

Somewhat mollified, the men departed — but not before dropping another threat of retribution at the polls if some effective relief did not ensue.

As they left, the county attorney rapped on the door and then entered the judge's private office. The Grand Jury had adjourned the day before and, as their predecessors had done for a good many years, the jurors had blasted the county officials for allowing the courthouse and jail to fall into filthy ruin. In a report to the circuit judge they declared that they had inspected the jail and found that structure wholly "unfit for human occupancy." The walls were cracked and broken, the roof leaked and the cells were inadequately heated. The commodes were without seats and the coal-black mattresses were without sheets. The entire facility reeked of excrement, urine and sweat. They recommended that the jail be closed and not reopened until completely renovated. They found the courthouse in almost equally foul condition, and said so in scathing terms.

The judge and the county attorney went over the report together line by line and agreed with the sentiments expressed in it. The county attorney remarked that it was a good report. "They would have been a lot more helpful, though," he said, "if they had told us where to get the money to do something about it." The judge reminded him that in several mountain counties the question of a bond issue for the construction of a new jail and courthouse had been referred to the people and sternly rejected at the polls. The county attorney opined; "If the same issue was placed on the ballot in this county you wouldn't get three votes for it out of that grand jury panel."

While he and the judge talked, proof of the jury's criticism was manifested by a vile stench which crept into the office from the public toilet in the basement of the courthouse.

When the county attorney was gone one of the county's justices of the peace brought his son-in-law to meet the judge. The justice pointed out that the fiscal court would soon have to add another man to the county road crew, and that his son-in-law desperately needed the job. The judge and justice were political allies, and His Honor agreed that the jobless son-in-law was ideally suited for the position. When this happy accord had been reached his secretary informed the judge that a deputy sheriff had arrested a speeder and that the culprit was awaiting trial. Whereupon the judge walked into the unswept little courtroom near his office and sat down behind the judicial desk.

A middle-aged man and his wife were sitting on the front bench in the section of the courtroom reserved for spectators. Nearby sat a man in overalls and an open-collared, blue workshirt. He wore a baseball player's cap and an enormous star-shaped badge was pinned to the bib of his overalls. Strapped to his side was a German Luger pistol, a memento of some distant battlefield. The judge cleared his throat and asked the officer the nature of the charge against the defendant. The deputy stood up and came forward.

"Judge," he said, "this man was driving in a very reckless way. I got behind 'im and follered 'im about four mile, and I seen his car cross the yaller line at least three times. I want a warrant chargin' 'im with reckless driving."

His Honor turned to the offender and asked what he had to say. He was from New Jersey and was on his way to visit his son in Virginia. He and his wife had decided to turn aside and see the Kentucky mountains, about whose beauty they had heard so much. They had driven neither recklessly nor rapidly, and if their automobile had crossed the center line at any time it had been done inadvertently and on a relatively straight stretch of road where no other vehicles were in view.

It was obvious that the judge was impressed by the "violator's" sincerity and that he believed what he had said. He paused for a long moment and reflected upon the situation and, to one versed in mountain politics, his silent cogitations left a plainly discernible track. He weighed the fact that on the one hand he was dealing with a deputy who voted in the county and whose kinsmen and friends were equipped with razor-sharp votes. He knew that if the motorist paid no fine the deputy would be offended. The officer made his living from the fees collected in cases such as this one. If the New Jersey motorist paid a fine he must also pay the costs, six dollars of which would go into the pocket of the deputy. The guardian of the public peace would take unkindly to a dismissal of the case after he had gone to the trouble to capture the man and bring him three

miles to the county seat. Weighed on the other end of the scale was
a stranger who would never be here again and who, even if he paid a
small fine, perhaps unjustly, would not suffer irreparably. These considerations produced the inevitable conclusion. His Honor decreed
the minimum fine allowed under the statute. The total came to eighteen dollars and fifty cents. When justice had thus been meted out
the judge did not return to his office but took advantage of the
opportunity to escape for lunch. When he returned at 1:00 P.M. the
callers had increased in number and their problems had grown even
more vexatious.

A fifty-year-old man, his wife and her father had come to tell the
judge that the Welfare worker had denied his claim for public assistance. He wanted the judge to talk to her and, if necessary, to go to
Frankfort and see if the claim couldn't be straightened out. He said:

"Judge, I just can't work. I can't do nary thing. I'm sick and I've got
a doctor's certificate to prove it. I worked in the mines for twenty-five
years before they shut down but you know I got into bad air and ever
since then when I git hot or a little bit tired I git so nervous I can't
hardly stand it. I don't have a thing in the world to live on and they've
turned down my claim, and I know that if you will get onto the people
at Frankfort you can get it straightened out. There's a sight of people in
this county that ain't as bad off as I am and they didn't have any trouble
gettin' it and I'm sure not a-goin' to give up on it without seeing into it
a little further."

At this juncture the man's father-in-law, a gentleman of approximately seventy-five, chimed in. He had lived with his daughter and
son-in-law for three years and never had known anybody who was a
harder worker. He had seen the man work an hour or two in his
vegetable garden and get so nervous that he would spill his coffee
when he came into the house to rest. He assured the judge that he
would be the first to say so if he thought his son-in-law was "putting
on."

The judge heard this tale of woe with deep respect and assured his
visitors that they had his sympathy and that he would make every
effort to help them. He hedged by pointing out that public assistance is administered by a state agency over which he had no control. The Welfare Department had a lot of stubborn people on its

staff, some of whom, unfortunately, were quite unreasonable. He remembered that the sick man had always been his friend and had stood by him in bygone years. He summed up his gratitude with the assertion, "You've scratched my back in the past and I'll try to scratch yours now. You know, turn about is fair play."

Highly gratified, the nervous man, his wife and his father-in-law left, after again reminding the judge that they sure would appreciate his help.

The next caller had been drawing State Aid but his check had been discontinued because his children had not been attending school regularly. He explained that his young-'uns had been sick. "Not sick enough to have a doctor, but feelin' bad and I just couldn't make 'em go to school a-feelin' bad. As soon as they got to feelin' better they went right back to school, and I don't know what we'll do if we don't git some help fer 'em again."

He promised that if the judge could prevail upon the Welfare worker to restore his check he would make an affidavit to send his children to school on each day when they were well enough to go.

About 3:30 in the afternoon the county truant officer (known officially by the horrendous title of Director of Pupil Personnel) made his appearance. A warrant had been sworn out charging a father with failing to send his children to school and the trial was set for that hour. The defendant was already present in the little courtroom. A few moments later the county attorney appeared to prosecute the case for the state. The truant officer explained that the defendant was the father of six children, all of whom were of elementary school age. They had not been to school in the preceding month despite his pleas that the father keep them in regular attendance. The county attorney asked the Court to impose a fine or jail sentence. The judge asked the defendant why he had not been sending his children to school. The man stalked forward and gazed around him with the uncertainty of a trapped animal. He was dressed in tattered overalls to which many patches had been affixed. He was approximately forty-five years old and it was obvious from his huge hands and stooped shoulders that he had spent many years under the low roof of a coal mine. He pleaded his defense with the eloquence of an able trial lawyer. With powerful conviction he said:

"I agree with everything that's been said. My children have not been going to school and nobody wants them to go any more than I do. I've been out of work now for four years. I've been all over this coalfield and over into Virginia and West Virginia looking for work. I've made trip after trip to Indianny, Ohio and Michigan and I couldn't find a day's work anywhere. I drawed out my unemployment compensation over three years ago and the only income I've had since has been just a day's work now and then doing farm work for somebody. I sold my old car, my shotgun, my radio and even my watch to get money to feed my family. And now I don't have a thing in the world left that anybody would want. I'm dead-broke and about ready to give up. I live over a mile from the schoolhouse and I simply don't have any money to buy my children shoes or clothes to wear. I own a little old four-room shanty of a house and twenty acres of wore-out hillside land. Last spring the coal company that owns the coal augered it and teetotally destroyed the land. I couldn't sell the whole place for five hundred dollars if my life depended on it. Me and my oldest boy have one pair of shoes between us, and that's all. When he wears 'em I don't have any and when I wear 'em he don't have any. If it wasn't for these rations the gover'ment gives us, I guess the whole family would of been starved to death long afore now. If you want to fine me I ain't got a penny to pay it with and I'll have to lay it out in jail. If you think puttin' me in jail will help my young-'uns any, then go ahead and do it and I'll be glad of it. If the county attorney or the truant officer will find me a job where I can work out something for my kids to wear I'll be much abliged to 'em as long as I live."

At the conclusion of this declaration the judge looked uneasily around, eying the county attorney and the truant officer in the hope that some help would come from that quarter. Both gentlemen remained silent. At length the judge plied the defendant with questions. The man had a third-grade education. He had worked in the mines for a total of twenty years and had spent three years as an infantry soldier in the war against Japan. He had been fortunate, however, and had received no wounds. Consequently, he drew no pension or compensation from the Veterans' Administration. The factories to which he had applied for employment had insisted on men with more education than he possessed. They also wanted younger men. Finally the county attorney demanded to know whether he had any skill except mining coal. The answer was an emphatic "No." Then he blurted out:

"Judge, I'm not the only man in this fix on the creek where I live. They's at least a dozen other men who ain't sent their children to school for the same reason mine ain't a-goin'. They can't send 'em cause they can't get hold of any money to send 'em with. Now the county attorney and the truant officer are trying to make an example out of me. They think that if I go to jail for a week or two the rest of 'em will somehow find the money to get their kids into the schoolhouse."

He looked intently at the truant officer and demanded, "Ain't that so?" to which the truant officer hesitantly assented.

The judge mulled the problem over for a moment or two and then "filed away" the warrant. He explained that it was not being dismissed, but was being continued upon the docket indefinitely. "If the case is ever set for trial again I will write you a letter well in advance of the trial date and tell you when to be here," he said. "In the meantime go home and do the best you possibly can to make enough money to educate your children. If they don't go to school they'll never be able to make a living and when they get grown they'll be in just as bad a fix as you are in now."

The defendant thanked the judge, picked up his battered miner's cap and walked to the door. There he paused and looked back at judge, attorney and truant officer for a long moment, as though framing a question. Then he thought better of it and closed the door behind him. His Honor had had enough for one day, and decided to go home. While he was locking the door I glanced at the headlines on the newspaper the morning mail had brought to his desk:

FEDERAL AID TO EDUCATION BILL DIES IN HOUSE COMMITTEE

BILLIONS APPROVED FOR FOREIGN AID

JOBLESS MINER KILLS SELF IN HARLAN

PART VIII

The Future

CHAPTER TWENTY-TWO

The Case for a
Southern Mountain Authority

THE READER who has followed me thus far cannot fail to wonder whether the difficulties which beset the Cumberland Plateau are susceptible of solutions which social and economic planners can devise and which the taxpayers can sustain. So complex and deeply rooted are the region's problems that one may seriously question whether the nation possesses the skill and tenacity to cope with them successfully. Understandable as such a reaction may be it is one of despair ill-suited to a public which has unhesitatingly poured out billions of dollars in an effort to raise living standards, create better social orders and stabilize governments around the globe. If the safety and peace of the American Republic require that we rescue Bolivia, Laos, Tunisia, the Congo and Greece the same considerations must necessitate the succor of these islands of poverty in our own land.

If the Republic is to undertake to rehabilitate the plateau and to give it a productive, full-scale role in the nation's life, its approach must be of a long-range character. Any symptomatic treatment calculated to produce quick and spectacular results would, most probably, be of little lasting benefit and might, indeed, be ultimately harmful. The mountaineer has been surveyed and studied for years. His communities have been invaded by statisticians and sociologists sponsored by state and Federal governments and by private foundations. Reams of reports have been written about him — reports which statistically outline every facet of his life. Nothing more has emerged from the studies, and the highlander is cynical of any proposals to assist him. A short-term and ineffective effort which fails would deepen his already monumental distrust of government and of the industrialists who, in his opinion, dominate its activities. If America is to help him, let its plans be well drawn and let its efforts be serious and sustained.

This is not to say that no short-range efforts should be made. They are essential but they can serve only the tactical purpose of relieving immediate suffering and preventing further deterioration while the strategic plans are being readied.

Nor may we assume that clear-cut and effective answers for the problems of the plateau, and, in larger context, of the Southern mountains, can be devised wholly in advance. A campaign can be planned and initiated, but the reformers must grope toward their goals, changing direction from time to time and seeking new objectives in the light of experience. Solutions can and must be found, but it is scarcely likely that they will be arrived at by rigid adherence to any guidelines which can now be laid down. The same has been true of America's efforts overseas. There our representatives have toiled with varying degrees of success, altering their plans as circumstances required. And on the whole, despite much bungling and waste, their efforts have been fruitful.

A curious facet of America's fabulous foreign aid program since the end of World War II lies in the circumstance that the poor Kentucky mountain counties have been taxed to restore or industrialize foreign countries, few of whose citizens live so poorly as a majority of the inhabitants of the Cumberland Plateau. Coal miners who can scarcely write their names and who struggle to feed large families and to shelter them in crowded shacks have had taxes withheld from their meager wages in order that the people of other lands might have an opportunity to enjoy freedom from want. In so doing the nation's policy was one of enlightened self-interest and cannot be criticized in principle. Common charity and a decent respect for Christian ideals allowed no other choice. Now, however, we must conclude that if charity did not begin at home it should at least end there. In short, we are at last going to have to face squarely the fact that we have at home the same needs and shortcomings we have been struggling so hard to combat abroad, and, call it what we will, a Marshall

Plan for our own chronically and otherwise incurably depressed areas appears to be the only solution. If Communism springs from hunger and hopelessness, we have an abundance of each in the United States, and they are concentrated in strong mixture in the Southern highlands.

Fortunately our nation is not without historic experience as how best to solve the problem of regional decay. The transformation of the Tennessee Valley demonstrates that enlightened government intervention under the auspices of careful planners can accomplish far-reaching economic and social improvements. Thirty years ago the Valley of the Tennessee was as grim and forbidding an expanse of real estate as could be found on this continent. Its yellow hills and disconsolate farmhouses presented the face of poverty reminiscent of the crushed and broken South of 1865. The American Dream had passed the inhabitants by. Frontier precepts and mores, repeated endlessly for generations, had brought them to a cul-de-sac from which nothing in their experience could liberate them. From this dilemma the people and their land were rescued by the Tennessee Valley Authority. This brain child of the great Nebraskan, George W. Norris, achieved genuine miracles in a startlingly short space of time.

Less than three decades after the Tennessee Valley Authority Act was passed by Congress the Valley of the Tennessee is clean and prosperous; its once wasted hills are green. A chain of mighty dams has impounded a spangle of glittering lakes which attract sportsmen and vacationers for a thousand miles. More startling still, the region has given birth to a number of new towns while the old ones scarcely resemble the drab communities which once bore their names. The valley is becoming a new Ruhr and is a showpiece of effective planning and accomplishment of which every American can feel justly proud. The subversion of the T. V. A. in recent years into little more than a gigantic electric power corporation detracts nothing from the illustrious accomplishments of its first two decades.

The problems of the Tennessee Valley in the early 1930s were in many respects vastly different from those of the Cumberland Plateau today. The Tennesseans were afflicted by no industrial overlords who robbed and ravaged the land without check. Its hills were rolling rather than steep, and the Tennessean was less insular in his outlook than his Kentucky kinsman of the 1960s. His physical world was wider, and his sense of isolation and remoteness was less pronounced. Despite these very real contrasts a close similarity between them can be remarked. The Tennessean, too, was a product of the old frontier, and its tenacious influence still persisted to the exhaustion of his lands and of his hopes. Mentally and physically he was closely akin to the mountaineer. His conservative and strongly held opinions presented a formidable barrier to those who sought to help him.

The creation of a Southern Mountain Authority patterned along the lines of its predecessor in the Valley of the Tennessee has been discussed informally for a good many years. Persons and groups familiar with the problems and frustrations of the Southern mountains have realized that only such an authority, with ample funds, long-range planning and competent administration, can bring order out of the chaos created by sustained exploitation, a primitive agricultural system and the tenacious anti-intellectualism bequeathed by the frontier. It is my opinion that if Americans want to rehabilitate this decaying portion of their national fabric the establishment by Congress of a Southern Mountain Authority cannot be much longer delayed.

The experience of the T. V. A. indicates that a Southern Mountain Authority created and financed by Congress for the purpose of bringing the region of the Southern mountains abreast of the nation generally could accomplish the greater part of its mission in two or three decades. I will discuss some of the lines along which it could work for the habilitation of broad areas lying within seven states. For the purposes of this book I have restricted myself to the Kentucky highlands but my proposals apply, with equal force, to similar areas in Virginia, West Virginia, Tennessee, Alabama and, to a lesser extent, Maryland. Since they have never known the oppressive exploitation of the coal barons, the western counties of North Carolina do not present the serious problems imposed by coal mining. However, all the Southern mountains share the difficulties left by generations of primitive agriculture and soil wastage.

It is unquestionably true that the states could achieve many of the objectives I will discuss if their leaders were inclined to do so. Unfortunately nothing in the history of the states betokens that such leadership is likely to materialize. The state capitols lie close to the offices of the rapacious mineral-owning corporations. The coal companies speak with authority in the Chambers of Commerce and exert decisive influences on state officials. The business interests parrot endlessly the nonsense that if the coal market can be expanded the region's ills will evaporate. Governors and legislators exhibit every sign of having fully accepted this premise and such weak leadership as they display rarely rises above discussions of how to "help coal." It cannot be expected that they or their successors will come to grips with the massive problems imposed by blight and stagnation in the highland portions of their states.

For the last decade, the taxpayers in the wealthier sections of Kentucky have been pumping tens of millions of dollars annually into the mountain counties, not for the purpose of curing their ills but merely to sustain their existence. The plateau embraces such a large part of the state and its schools, roads and welfare services impose such a monumental and ever-growing drain upon the state treasury, that they can confidently be expected to bankrupt it within another dozen years. The state is following the fiscal decline charted by Michigan, and for essentially the same reason: the existence within its borders of multitudes of jobless men and the blighted communities in which they live whose support the state must assume over too long a period.

Even if the necessary leadership existed in the state capitols the obstacles to reform are almost insuperable. The courthouses are too powerful and too conservative to permit significant changes. The *status quo* means numerous small counties, each with its swarm of intrenched, fee-paid officials. Public inertia at the local level (an affliction from which Democracy has ever suffered), absence of coordination between such community development programs as are initiated, and lack of regional planning and petty rivalries between counties and communities are potent additional factors which prevent the Cumberlanders from effectively helping themselves.

The American experiment in the Tennessee Valley is not the only example of a planned and designed economy to have been attempted by a democratic national government for the benefit of an agriculturally or industrially depressed and blighted area. In the somber ruin of Wales, the industrial revolution left on the doorstep of the British parliament a disquieting burden strikingly similar to that presented by the Southern coalfield to our own Congress at the present time. So successfully did the Royal Government assail the challenge in the 1920s and 1930s that today Wales is no longer the smoke-stained slum of *How Green Was My Valley*. The Welshman's valleys are green again, and he and his sons and daughters find employment at decent wages in a complex of new factories. More recently Italy has instituted a program to grapple with the centuries-old poverty, ignorance and overcrowding which have made her southern provinces a nightmare land.

Conservative voices will be heard to cry that the Treasury cannot possibly find the billion dollars or so required for a Southern Mountain Project. Some will find such a scheme to subsidize the salvaging of a broad territory and its people fraught with "socialism." Our national stance in foreign and domestic affairs should militate strongly against their fears.

In the first place, most of the country's economic machinery is now subsidized in one form or another by the Federal government: transportation, communications, oil, manufacturing and agriculture benefit from direct or indirect government financial aid. On the other end of the economic ladder are the millions of Public Aid recipients who live on comparatively tiny cash and commodity doles. The subsidized business community can scarcely complain about a program calculated to restore hundreds of thousands of idle or underemployed people to self-supporting productivity and to preserve their land for future usefulness and taxation.

Since 1948 conservatives and liberals in Congress have given unstinted support to "anticommunist" governments around the world. Men whose revolutionary forebears died for the slogan "Death to tyrants!" have voted vast slush funds for Saudi Arabia, an absolute monarchy and one of the few lands where human chattel slavery is still legal. Predictably, much of the money — including some from the ragged pockets of Kentucky coal miners — was lavished on palaces and concubines. Even Marshall Tito, when he became restive under Russian pressure, found fifteen hundred million American dollars flowing into his coffers. The question may then be fairly asked, "If we can afford to subsidize autocratic medieval kings, a communist dictator whose expressed ideology is a detestation of our liberties, and every conceivable shade of political and economic thinking in between, can we fail to spare the funds and efforts required to convert an island of destitution within our own country into a working, self-sustaining partner in the nation's freedom and progress?"

Surely, if justice and logic still have validity, mighty America will answer the query with an affirmative and determined program to do for her own citizens that which she has so generously attempted abroad.

I do not claim to know all, or even most, of the remedies for the ills of the Southern mountains. Indeed, the purpose of this book has been to draw to their problems better heads than my own, in the hope that they will eventually devise the solutions. If my suggestions prove unsound perhaps better ones will be advanced by wiser students. The essential need is that the task be recognized — and attempted.

If the Cumberland Plateau — and the Southern mountains generally — are to be brought abreast of modern America in this century, the nation must first recognize the truth of certain premises about the region:

(1) The savagely individualistic mountaineer of the feud times and of the romantic stories is no more. It has been a long time since the mountaineer was self-supporting. The simple frontier environment which he loved so well has been shattered by the intrusion of exploitive industry and the infinitely more complex social order existing in the surrounding country. The traumas and vicissitudes of more than half a century have left the mountaineer economically dependent upon the nation. When the simple neo-frontier society of which he was a part was undermined he could secure no footing in the varied and highly competitive industrial world. Today he subsists largely on the generosity of the Welfare state.

(2) His history endowed the mountaineer with skills of the simplest and most rudimentary sort, and even these were beneficial only on the neo-frontier. Fifty years of industrial labor taught him nothing more than the coal miner's trade. A modernized coal industry has rendered this new knowledge obsolete and valueless. Conse-

quently he must rely on his labor for a livelihood but is without knowledge that can enable him to go out into the world, find a job and earn a decent living for his family.

(3) The public schools have lagged far behind national norms. For example, in 1960 a study by the University of Kentucky sought to measure the achievement-levels of pupils in Harlan County. It was found that a high-school graduate in that county was three years and five months behind his average counterpart in the nation generally. He had wasted almost one fourth of his time in school. Thus even the fortunate highland youth who has acquired his elementary and high-school diplomas lacks sufficient schooling in mathematics, history, science, literature and the languages to compete successfully in an increasingly college-conscious world.

(4) The rapid automation and consolidation of the coal industry and the decline of coal's importance has *permanently* idled an army of once-valuable coal miners. These men, for the most part between forty-five and sixty years of age, are, in their own expression, "too young to draw Social Security and too old to get a job." They have exhausted their unemployment-compensation benefits and all their savings. Most of them are pauperized. They have tried without success to find jobs in other regions. They are bewildered and embittered by the sudden change of status which sucked away their importance and reduced them to an enforced lifetime of idleness. By a conservative estimate there are, at present, 110,000 such coal miners in the United States and some 60,000 of them are concentrated in eastern Kentucky and in western West Virginia.

(5) The mining communities have based their hopes for future prosperity and usefulness on the possibility of a drastically expanded coal industry. Politicians at state and national levels have fed these hopes with ignorant mouthings to the effect that an upturn in the coal industry will cure the region's ills. Anyone familiar with the basic economic facts in the Cumberland Plateau knows that the manner in which the industry is organized makes such widespread prosperity impossible.

The industry produces three direct categories of income. The first is profits earned from the mining and sale of coal. Approximately 75 per cent of the plateau's output is produced by a relative handful of large corporations. These giants of the industry are, in most instances, "foreign" corporations chartered in other states. Nearly all their stockholders live outside the plateau. This absentee owner-ship of the operating companies promptly drains some three quarters of the production profits out of the area.

The second category of income consists of royalties paid by operat-ing companies to mineral-owning corporations. These holding cor-porations own at least 85 per cent of the region's mineral wealth. They collect from 15 cents to 35 cents for each ton of coal mined from their properties. Their expenditures within the plateau are little more than nominal. At least four fifths of their income is siphoned off to distant shareholders.

The third class of income generated by the coal industry lies in the wages and salaries paid to its employees. These are important, but automation and dwindling markets have reduced the number of essential workmen to a third of those required sixteen years ago. Automation is a continuing process and the payrolls shrink even in years when coal production stands steady or even expands a little. It is extremely unlikely that the market can ever again expand suffi-ciently to permit the re-employment of the thousands of jobless men who now haunt the nation's coalfields.

(6) The coal and logging industries have sown the land with crip-pled men. The ranks of the disabled are swollen by other multitudes who suffer from diseases, and, sometimes, from undernourishment. The physical woes are augmented immeasurably by educational shortcomings. These circumstances have produced an enormous number of persons who cannot be employed in any mass-production industry. They are presently supported by the Welfare state and there is no feasible alternative for them. Charity and justice necessi-tate that we do no less in the future. We must, however, make every effort to avoid the creation of other generations similarly situated.

(7) Living in and among the sick and the disabled are other mul-titudes who are physically and mentally able to work if jobs can be found for their hands and minds. Many of them are drawing checks as disabled persons, but their ailments are largely psychoneurotic. Others are recipients of unemployment-compensation benefits. These doles expire and then from time to time are renewed by legislative and congressional action. Legislators, economists and idle workmen alike pay lip-service to the proposition that developments

in the nation's economy will someday bring them jobs. The truth is, however, that there is no foreseeable prospect of a boom so great that it will put them back to work. Everywhere the blue-collar workman feels his importance declining and offers his skills for sale on an increasingly selective market. In the plateau the able-bodied unemployed workmen are supported by a combination of cash and commodity doles for which they render no service. Thus, being able to work, they do not. They live in idleness on government largesse while around them on every hand lie countless tasks whose doing the national welfare urgently requires. A public policy is scarcely sane when it supports idleness in the midst of a region which desperately needs public improvements. If the taxpayer is going to pay men who are jobless through no fault of their own, every element of common sense requires that he pay them for working rather than for not working. The men would benefit morally, physically and spiritually from constructive employment.

Condescending charity in any form is harmful to the moral fiber of a people. If persisted in long enough, it sees pride and self-respect drain away to be replaced by cynicism, arrogance and wheedling dependence. It undermines good citizenship and contributes toward the thing a democracy can least afford — a class of unproductive and dependent citizens. At the pesent time practically every skilled man in the plateau has regular employment. The few genuinely competent carpenters, masons, mechanics, metal workers and electricians find regular work for their hands. They have jobs at good wages with mining companies and at other essential building and maintenance tasks. While the tiny corps of skilled men are energetically at work, the great army of their unskilled fellows drift about in dejected idleness. Irrefutable logic requires that work be found for their hands and energies also.

(8) The region's women are almost totally unskilled. Aside from a comparatively few female schoolteachers, stenographers, nurses, receptionists and clerks, they find little to occupy their energies outside the home. The limited routines of existence in the quiet mining camps and along the creeks leave them with oceans of idle time upon their hands. While her lot has never been so widely publicized, the frustrations of the highlander's wife are as deserving of attention as are those of her jobless or underemployed husband. If genuine

social and economic advancement are to come to the plateau, wider vistas and more absorbing and profitable horizons must be opened for the thousands of unfortunate women "who help their husbands loaf."

(9) The population of the plateau is too big for its present needs and foreseeable requirements. If the nation enters a new era of surging prosperity — as some government officials have so buoyantly prophesied — there will be areas in which willing hands will be needed. A program to bring useful skills to men who have none could pay enormous and manifold dividends in both material and human terms. A carefully planned and ample program of this nature is essential.

But training in new skills alone is not enough. Such a program must be accompanied by a resettlement campaign. Many of the unemployed are now so totally destitute they could not possibly afford the cost of moving to a job opportunity. As a practicing attorney, I have drafted scores of deeds for miners who were selling their homes for "moving money" — funds with which to finance removal to Ohio, Indiana, Florida or California. Rarely does such a property sell for more than one third of what the seller paid for it. Even such a seller is fortunate, however, because other hundreds of men own no property. Surely if the government can afford to pay an already wealthy farmer the price of a new Cadillac each year to induce him to raise no corn or wheat, it can provide a few hundred dollars to enable a penniless ex-coal miner to transport his family to a useful life in a more fortunate part of the nation.

(10) The means are now at hand for the obliteration of much of the Southern highlands. Technology has brought to the coal barons the means to destroy the region they have hammered at so long and so relentlessly. It is probable that we are in the final decades of King Coal's importance as a fuel, and it may confidently be expected that within another generation the mineral will be far more valuable for its chemical and industrial byproducts than for its heating properties. History will never forgive this generation if it permits the fuel-coal industry in its terminal years to destroy past reclamation a large and potentially important part of the nation's land.

(11) The rain-rich and sunny Southern mountains are the natural habitat of a wide variety of fish, fowl and animals. If permitted to

do so the earth will grow huge crops of superlative and valuable trees. On the other hand, it is not adaptable to conventional farming and cannot support by decent standards a numerous agricultural population.

(12) Last and most important the value to the nation of the Cumberland Plateau and of the entire Southern Appalachians is a very real one. A careful consideration of the nation's present circumstances and potential for growth points up the region's vast importance to millions of future Americans. A gigantic super-metropolis has grown up along the Atlantic seaboard. It stretches from New Hampshire all the way to northern Virginia and embraces some 31,500,000 people. The great and small cities stretch in almost unbroken procession along eight hundred miles of coast. America is in the throes of an immense population upsurge which may, within twenty years, leave more people east of the Mississippi than now inhabit the fifty states. Population experts expect that by the year 2000 the number of Americans will have doubled. When this occurs uncrowded recreational and vacation areas will be priceless. Millions of people will yearn for green and pleasant areas in which to find escape from the anxieties and tensions of competitive and crowded living. Already the super-metropolis has crept to the edge of the Southern mountains, some four hundred miles from the rim of the plateau. The present generation of Americans owes to the next a positive duty to preserve the Southern highlands and to bequeath them in a useful and beneficial condition. With these premises in mind we can proceed to a consideration of how best to perform that duty.

This book has traced the major factors which have operated to impoverish the plateau and its people. It is a biography of a depressed area. I have dwelt purposely on the negative influences because they have given the region its character and have created its difficulties. Nevertheless there have been, in recent years, some important localized efforts at revival. They show what brave men and women can accomplish in the face of adverse circumstances. Unfortunately, the effectiveness of such efforts is limited and they can offer no real hope for the region.

The brightest spot in the plateau is at Hazard in Perry County. Ten years ago it was the dingy capital of a huge coalfield. For forty years its people had been preoccupied with mining almost to the exclusion of all other economic interests. The attention of the community was focused on extraction rather than construction. When the truck-mine boom collapsed, a number of its businessmen and women recognized that continued dependence on a sinking industry was hopeless. They undertook a carefully conceived plan of community improvement. Their scheme was founded on the cardinal fact that the community could never hope to attract other industries until it was made into a far more pleasant place in which to live.

Its civic leaders investigated the Federal programs through which urban renewal and slum-clearance loans and grants could be obtained. With the financial assistance of Federal agencies, a number of off-street parking lots were established and the state was induced to construct a wide, well-designed bypass around the congested Main Street area. These improvements permitted shoppers to find parking space and caused many people who generally "traded" in scattered neighborhood stores to drive to Hazard in quest of lower prices and a wider selection of merchandise.

A number of run-down old buildings were demolished and replaced with new structures. The municipal government sold bonds to finance a sanitary sewage-disposal plant so the filthy North Fork of the Kentucky River which flows through the town could lose a portion of its stench. The voters were persuaded to approve special tax levies for the construction of a new courthouse and jail, and, most striking of all, a handsome new public health center. A public-spirited cinema operator built a beautiful little city park and gave it to the city. Other groups pooled their funds to construct two comfortable motels and launched an advertising campaign to attract people into the county as tourists.

As this is written, Hazard is incomparably the most prosperous town in the plateau, and this notwithstanding the ravages of the savage flood which surged through it in January 1957.

Whitesburg in Letcher County, Paintsville in Johnson County, Hyden in Leslie County, and Cumberland in Harlan County have undergone similar but much less striking transformations. Their civic leaders have toiled unselfishly to build communities acceptable to the industrialists who, it is hoped, will eventually bring them factories of some kind.

Another circumstance which has given the plateau a slight surge of confidence is the increased financing which flowed into the public schools from the state's new general retail sales tax. Beginning in 1960 a fully qualified teacher with a college degree received an immediate salary hike of nine hundred dollars annually and those with inferior qualifications received lesser raises. These pay boosts lifted the morale of teachers and sent hundreds of them crowding into the colleges for summer-school courses. It made better teachers out of men and women who had struggled for years to support their families on as little as two hundred dollars a month. However, we must not accord too much significance to this uplift because even the new salary schedules assure a "degree teacher" with several years of teaching experience only thirty-four hundred dollars a year. The state's revenue structure now embraces practically every category of taxation and no new sources of funds are available. Tennessee, Ohio, Illinois and other states pay much higher salaries and beckon constantly to Kentucky teachers. Unless additional salary increases can be financed in the near future, the flight of schoolteachers will begin anew and the morale of those who remain will plummet again.

Nor do the refurbished county seats betoken improving economic health in the countryside. Once the renovations have been made; when the new sewage system, library, school, health center, courthouse and jail have been built, the prospect for the community remains essentially unchanged. The region upon which it depends for customers continues to decay. The improved community cannot afford really good schools or libraries. It remains bereft of the cultural facilities by which the new industrial managers set much store. It can offer only unskilled workmen to industrialists who demand competence and technical proficiency. In short, isolated, unco-ordinated, community-centered efforts are face-liftings which can alleviate few of the gross problems. To the contrary the bond issues which pay for the overhauls may eventually become detriments as the tax resources relentlessly shrink and the more virile elements of the population continue to ebb away.

The T V. A. demonstrated the means by which many of the world's trouble spots can be rescued. Its example now offers solid assurance that, for low direct cost to the taxpayers, America can successfully attack the ills of the Southern highlands in a campaign that will eventually benefit every one of the fifty states.

The first objective of such a public corporation should be the drafting of an overall plan of development for the region, consonant with its physical resources and population capacities. Such a plan should include a thorough survey and indexing of the region's resources of water and of timber, coal, oil, gas, iron ore, limestone and other minerals, and of land suited to grazing and crop farming. Since, for a good many years at least, a substantial portion of the plateau's wealth will necessarily be derived from the extraction of minerals, it is essential that their mining be continued. However, the Authority should have the power and duty to make certain that their withdrawal is done in accordance with the national welfare. Its minerals should be regarded as an important source of the country's chemical derivatives — products which will be of inestimable value to many generations. The gross wastage of coal through inefficient methods of recovery ought to be terminated. Ordinary self-interest requires the prompt adoption of a sensible national fuels policy, and in the Southern mountains its implementation should be entrusted to the directors of the Southern Mountain Authority. The day of superabundant fuels has already followed the era of superabundant land into history. We can no more afford to waste and ruin huge areas of coal than we can afford to destroy needlessly large segments of our remaining forests. Every American, wherever he resides, has a vital stake in our remaining fossil fuels. We can no longer afford to construe private ownership as including the power wantonly to squander an indispensable resource.

Strip and auger mining on steep mountain slopes is indescribably destructive of coal, soil, water and timber. The long range impact of such operations are incalculable and, if continued, will impose serious direct or indirect burdens on the entire country. Coal so mined is moving in interstate commerce and is subject to the regulatory power of Congress. That power should be speedily invoked to stop this senseless ravaging of an important portion of the nation.

The Authority's plan would be a complex one, dealing in human as well as physical resource engineering. It would seek to preserve the physical utility of the plateau and to raise the mountaineers to full-scale participation in American citizenship. It would undertake to bridge the wide psychological gap separating so many of the mountaineers from their compatriots elsewhere — a gap bequeathed to their ancestors by the frontier and widened by generations of isolation, poor schools and cynical industrial exploitation.

As in the case of the T. V. A. three decades ago, a major role of the S. M. A. would lie in mediation, diplomacy and persuasion. Once the surveys are completed and the plans are drafted the co-operation of county, city and state officials would be required for their effectual implementation. Experience in the Tennessee Valley indicates that generally — though not always — such co-operation would be forthcoming. The prestige of a Federal agency in the offices of local and state officials is great. The problems can be clearly recognized and the man with a plan usually inherits the role of leader — a role easily assumed by a Federal agency but difficult indeed for either of the co-equal states or its governor. Too, the prospect of improvement would inevitably inspire a cadre of leaders in each county seat who would build political fires under balky officials seeking to hinder salvation. On the whole, there is sound reason to believe that state legislatures, governors, local officials and most citizens would rise to the challenge of responsible leadership and give passable support to a comprehensive rescue operation. Some of the needed reforms would come slowly, to be sure, because they would fly in the face of old and time-honored usage. Nevertheless, the Tennesseans yielded to sensible proposals with commendable speed; and basic political reformation might come throughout the Southern mountains, with equal dispatch. If the prime changes in this field could be accomplished in fifteen years there would be no just ground for complaint. Such reforms would have to come about within the framework of our Federal system and without violation of the reserved powers of the states.

Though the crisis everywhere in the Southern Appalachians is acute it is, admittedly, nowhere so desperate as in the Cumberland Plateau region of Kentucky. Nowhere else have the forces of decay and demoralization advanced so far or so rapidly. In no other region would the S. M. A. have to grapple with such heavy burdens of inertia, intrenched local political baronies and complete domination by the coal industry.

To modernize the plateau the Authority would have to tackle the complex task of modernizing the units of government which control its public affairs.

The most difficult and most important objective in this respect would lie in the consolidation of counties. The state is subdivided into one hundred and twenty tiny counties averaging a little more than three hundred square miles in size. In the mountains these units are hopelessly poor and small. Such divisions as Elliott, Morgan, Lee, Estill, Powell, Wolfe, Menifee and Magoffin are little more than expanses of pine and scrub-oak barrens. No justification can be offered for their separate existence. They — and the comparatively wealthy counties as well — ought to be consolidated into much larger entities. By this means the number of officials could be reduced to a third the present number, and the resulting economies would make available to the remaining courthouses funds for essential projects which now receive little or no support.

For seventy years the Kentucky electorate has staunchly resisted Constitutional reform. The process of amending the state charter is long and complex. A proposed amendment must be submitted to the Legislature for consideration by the voters at the general election in an odd-numbered year. It must be approved by a majority of the people voting on the question. No more than two amendments can be submitted for consideration at a single election. The directors of the Southern Mountain Authority would have to attempt the delicate task of persuading the sovereign people to approve needed Constitutional changes, for without them much desperately needed improvement is impossible. It is believed that when such revisions are clearly sanctioned by a Federal agency seeking to elevate the entire region and to help lift an increasingly heavy and unprofitable burden from the shoulders of the taxpayers sufficient support would eventually crystallize throughout the state to assure their adoption.

The consolidation of counties into units of sensible size could be accomplished by act of the Legislature without resort to Constitutional amendment. Vital as this step would be it is only the first

382 · THE FUTURE

one. Kentucky needs desperately to simplify its local governmental apparatus and to unify it into an operable system.

The horde of fee-paid officials spreads demoralization and ineffectiveness everywhere, but its evil effects are immensely emphasized in the mountains. Many of the offices ought to be abolished. The duties of others should be combined and vested in fewer officials.

At present there is no efficient apparatus for the management of county funds. The county judge is nowhere authorized by law to perform many of the functions custom and stark necessity thrust upon him. The authors of the state Constitution designed his office as a judicial one, but the increasing complexity of society slowly transformed it into an administrative one as well. But though the burdens have been deposited on his desk the county judge is without real power to cope with them. At every step he must cajole and wheedle the fiscal court into compliance with his recommendations. For the sake of efficiency and economy that archaic institution should be abolished and its functions turned over to a three-man county commission. If the office of county judge is retained it should constitute a court for probate and other specifically defined judicial affairs. The occupant of that office should be the county's inferior judicial officer with the qualifications of a law judge. The commissioners should be directed to hire a county manager to conduct the fiscal affairs of the county under their guidance.

The office of Commonwealth attorney could advantageously be merged with that of county attorney. This official should be authorized to appoint deputies to assist him when the business of his office justifies their presence on the payroll. The functioning of two elected public attorneys in each county is productive of friction and harmful rivalries.

The posts of constable, jailer and coroner should be abolished. The election of an untrained layman to determine — or guess — the cause of deaths occurring in the county is an exercise in absurdity, and the sheriff ought to be charged with the duty of keeping county prisoners. Surely fewer officers, vested with greater dignity and charged with more clearly defined responsibilities to the electorate, are to be desired over the present fragmentation of power and duties with its attendant buck-passing and dodging of responsibility.

All officers retained by a revised Constitution should be paid reasonable salaries for their services and the unholy fee system should pass into history. It originated in the Middle Ages, in the custom of bribing officials for beneficial favors, and has long overstayed its usefulness.

Court reform is another matter of cardinal importance in the revitalization of the plateau. Now only circuit and appellate judges are required by law to be lawyers. Yet it is elementary that any man or woman who judges questions of law should be schooled in the law. Three to eight justices of the peace function in each county. Most of them never looked into a lawbook prior to their election and quite seldom thereafter. Too often they nurture speed traps and other devices for wringing fines and fees from hapless persons. Their judicial functions should be transferred to the county judge. It is easy to discount these little courts as irritating but not positively harmful, but any erosion of justice is detrimental and should not be condoned.

If a system could be devised whereby judges are appointed for a long term of years without resort to the vagaries and corruptions of the ballot box, much gain would result. For a good many years law enforcement in a number of vital fields has been at a near-standstill. For example, the Legislature has levied certain taxes upon heavy trucks operating on the state's highways. These taxes rise as the weight of the vehicle increases. Almost universally in the plateau the taxes are blithely ignored by truck owners. Overloaded vehicles do great damage to the roads, but judges cannot punish such violations without fear of retribution at the polls. The sheriffs and constables make no arrests for such outrages, and the state police and enforcement officers of the State Department of Motor Transportation make arrests and issue citations to little avail. Time after time they see offenders freed by politically sensitive judges. The same influences work in other vital areas of law enforcement.

Without fair and speedy trials laws lose their vitality and meaning. The Legislature can enact just statutes and bureaucrats can toil for their implementation, but much of their labor will be in vain until the courts are hedged against political reprisals. If the people are to enjoy the benefits a decent respect for law and order brings, reform of their state judiciary is imperative.

Only by Constitutional reform can equitable and sensible property assessment for tax purposes be assured. Until this is accomplished the plateau counties cannot support decent public facilities even if huge amounts of new property were to be enticed into them. They can never benefit from industrial developments until arrangements are made to tax effectively and fairly the property within their confines. At the present time one county taxes its property at 41 per cent of fair market value and another at 17 per cent. Obviously one hundred dollars' worth of property ought to be taxed for as much in one county as in another. The taxpayers and the schoolchildren of the state deserve no less justice than this.

A physical resettlement of much of the plateau's human resources is also essential to the modernization of the region. The mountaineers have spread themselves out over the entire wrinkled landscape. Lonesome houses and shacks have been pushed onto mountain benches and into remote coves. This dispersal of the population was compelled by long dependence on new-ground cornfields. Now the agricultural basis of the social order is shattered. It is impossible for a half million mountainers to live by decent standards on the tiny ribbons of tillable land. The terrain was not designed for the plow and it is time for an enlightened society to devote it to a valuable use in keeping with its capacities.

In the last decade, as we have seen, the general population exodus has been moving the people back down from the lesser tributary streams onto the bigger creeks. During the same years there has been a significant drift from the countryside into the camps, towns and county seats. This movement is a healthy one because economically the continuance of isolated rural living is fantastically wasteful. It lost its justification when the householder ceased to farm.

One of the objectives of the Southern Mountain Authority should be the "metropolization" of the plateau. By the standards of the Federal slum clearance and urban renewal agencies much of the housing in the towns is dilapidated and eligible for replacement. The 1950 census reported that nearly 85 per cent of the region's housing was substandard by national norms and its quality has sunk even lower since that year. If the same housing had existed in any of the nation's major cities the Federal Treasury would have subsidized its replacement years ago. The problems posed by poor housing are no less serious in the mountains than in urban areas, and it is vital to the health, happiness and welfare of the plateau dwellers that they be sheltered in better-planned and more adequately housed communities.

Certain carefully selected county seats should be slated for general reconstruction and expansion through planned housing developments. Areas on their outskirts should be zoned and reserved for orderly future expansion. The rural folk should be encouraged to move into the towns where jobs may be created for them rather than continue their existence on the distant and incredibly rough creeks.

Once a given population is concentrated in a town it can be serviced with schools, libraries, health facilities, and other essential institutions at far less cost than when scattered abroad over a difficult terrain. For example a tremendous portion of each county's school budget is spent to transport children from the isolated creeks and camps to the high schools. In addition the cost of maintaining a passable, all-weather road along each serpentine creek is proving to be beyond the state's financial resources. These burdens are grossly wasteful and, compounding the waste, the widely dispersed abodes contribute nothing to the happiness of the families. Attractive towns with adequate public facilities would be immeasurably more pleasant places in which to live.

There is sound reason to believe that once the Authority commenced a program to improve the towns and to enlarge them the people would begin to abandon their old unprofitable isolation and move into them.

Accompanying the drive to centralize the population should come a second development — one aimed at transforming the dejected face of the land itself. Most of the creeks and hollows still without access roads are worth less *in toto* on the current market than such roads would cost. Only the minerals are of appreciable value. By the construction of strategically situated dams the valleys can be flooded and converted into beautiful lakes. Actually much of the Cumberland Plateau can best serve the nation by being submerged.

Such highland lakes would be valuable for a number of important reasons. They could be utilized to capture and hold portions of the water which so often lashes the region in savage flash floods, saving lower areas the periodic misery of having to clear their cities of flood-borne mountain mud. Reliable and ample water supplies would make it possible for some types of manufacturing industry to operate in the Cumberlands — operations impossible under the prevailing conditions of heavy precipitation and rapid run-off. For example, paper manufacturers have often been enticed by the immense supply of wood available on the hillsides of the plateau but inadequate water sources have baffled them. Most important, however, the lakes would attract fishermen, sportsmen, vacationers, summer residents and, eventually, permanent dwellers in search of comfort and quiet. It is my conviction that the plateau — if its future is not aborted by present rapacity — is destined to become a major recreation area for the nation's teeming millions. As population grows and as wealth and leisure become more commonplace, it is certain that the green hills, the shaded coves and the pleasant climate of the Cumberlands will beckon generations pent up on the fiery concrete and in the fumes-laden atmosphere of urban centers.

A principal feature of the plan of development would be a careful indexing of prospective lake sites throughout the plateau. In many areas the coal has already been removed and the mountains are practically empty of the mineral. In such places the impounding of lakes on the valley floors would not affect the coal industry. Elsewhere the coal remains, and the dams should be so located as to permit access to the seams. Since Europeans have been mining under the sea floor for decades it is unlikely that the creation of relatively small lakes would drastically complicate the problems of coal recovery. The chief problem would be that imposed on transportation, because substantial stretches of railroad would have to be moved to higher ground. Certainly the location and construction of the lakes ought to be consistent in so far as possible with the legitimate rights of the mineral owners, allowing the eventual recovery of as much of the mineral as possible.

Already a number of national forests are scattered over the Southern mountains. Cumberland National Forest is a narrow band of federally owned land stretching across the plateau. It does not lie in the best tree-growing areas and much of it is practically worthless from the forester's viewpoint. Vast new highland areas should be added to the national forest system. The entire length of Pine and Big Black Mountains are admirably suited for forest preserves, and for very little else. They are too rugged and steep for any kind of agricultural use, but their deep coves can produce magnificent stands of trees.

At least 50 per cent of the plateau should be pre-empted by Federal acquisition and set aside as Federal Forests and fresh-water reservoirs. Once the land passes into the hands of the Federal Forest Service, enlightened practices can be adopted to stop the waste of timber and to restore countless acres to the one crop they can successfully produce. As millions upon millions of new Americans crowd into a land which cannot grow to accommodate them by so much as a single inch, the forests can be converted into parks and caused to provide both wood and recreation.

A cry will be raised that the creation of lakes will drown valuable agricultural land. Some rich bottomland will, of course, be destroyed. But if the Tennessee Valley is a sound guide, we may expect that once the lakes are completed and stocked the value of the fish caught from them in a single year will exceed the value of the corn and berries the land could produce in a decade under present methods. The land is geographically suited to become a major playground for nearly a hundred million people by the end of the present century. If that destiny is to be fulfilled the present generation must act with alacrity to set its development under way. Surely recreation and relaxation are commodities of prime importance, and — unless in the meantime a nuclear war sends our people back to the forests as a way of life — under the pressures of the emerging decades they will become absolutely indispensable to continued life.

In short, then, the S. M. A. ought to seek the establishment of a few substantial towns surrounded by a complex of federally owned forests and lakes. In the towns and on the remaining privately owned lands the mountaineers who stay within the region could expect to earn decent livings in industry and by modernized agriculture.

As this is written, only one hundred and twenty-three certified tree farms embracing one hundred thousand acres are in operation in all of Kentucky. By contrast, in Georgia there are more than five million acres in such carefully managed boundaries. These timber-raising plantations are privately owned. The trees are planted as seedlings and are systematically harvested and replanted so as to extract from the soil a never-ending yield. Such orderly forest cropping has gone on in Germany and Scandinavia for more than a century. The nation needs healthy hard and soft woods for an endlessly multiplying variety of purposes. An important goal of the S. M. A. should be to encourage the establishment of privately owned and well-managed tree farms. Unlike the immense tree plantations of Georgia and Alabama such enterprises would not depend almost entirely upon the pine market. The terrain could be utilized in keeping with its varying capacities, simultaneously producing pine, poplar, walnut, hickory, oak and a score of other lumbers. The land is still cheap enough to foster relatively small, family-owned tree farms as well as vast, corporately owned plantations. In sustained-yield tree growing the plateau can find a perennial income without soil exhaustion, scenery defacement or water pollution. It would provide employment for increasingly numerous workmen as wood-using industries are attracted to a large and dependable supply of their chief raw material.

If a portion of the population can be helped to move to job opportunities elsewhere and most of the remaining people can be concentrated in a few relatively large and prosperous towns, the inclination of the mountaineers to retain title to ruinously fragmented small tracts can be dissolved. This will permit businessmen and farmers to acquire large boundaries for tree planting.

Nor would the existence of lakes interfere seriously with timber-cropping on exposed ridges and coves. As the trees on them mature they can be felled and their logs can be floated to collection points for removal to market. Timber growing, coal recovery, light manufacturing and water sports of great value can, with planning, management, restraint and discipline, be conducted side by side without substantial detriment to either.

Forests and lakes would necessarily utilize the greater portion of the land surface. However, in some areas — particularly on the banks of the Kentucky, Cumberland and Big Sandy rivers — important stretches of bottomland would remain available for agricultural use. It is essential that this land be used more wisely than at the present time. It is incongruous in the extreme that in a region whose every inhabitant has strong rural antecedents nearly all the eggs sold in the local stores must be imported from northern Kentucky or elsewhere in the nation. No dairy herds worthy of mention exist within the plateau, though in several areas enough rich bottomland is found to afford ample grazing for hundreds of milk cows. The creation of dairy herds sufficient to meet at least a portion of the region's milk and butter needs should be encouraged by every practicable means.

A substantial part of the river bottoms can be adapted splendidly to the production of berries. With cultivation strawberries, blackberries, raspberries and blueberries can be grown in immense quantities. A glance at the map reveals that Louisville, Cincinnati, Indianapolis, Chicago and a host of other cities to the north and east of the plateau afford a large and convenient market for such succulent delicacies. In any event such farmers as remain within the region will have to turn to novel and drastically more profitable patterns of land use. His traditional modes of agriculture have brought the mountain farmer to despair, futility and bewilderment. His agricultural proclivities must be adjusted to the requirements of the twentieth century. He can no longer farm for the requirements of the frontier.

So tenacious has been the mountaineer's devotion to his primitive agriculture on the one hand and to the mining of coal on the other that a great deal of skepticism may be inevitably expected of him. Too, the enervating influences of Welfarism have eaten deep into his morale and ambition and, in many cases, the highlander who is able to work will resist any effort to get him back to productive labor. This problem will be a thorny one requiring patience, sternness and perseverance. The problem may best be solved by demonstration projects. It will be difficult to convince the mountaineer by lectures or schooling that his living can be earned by unheard-of new methods of agriculture or in some novel minor industry. When their efficacy has been demonstrated by properly conducted and strategically situated pilot projects a more receptive response can be anticipated.

In some parts of the plateau a new climate is crystallizing slowly. Bit by bit a realization is being manifested that the new must be tried because the old has permanently failed. Perhaps this beneficent change will accelerate, clearing the way for a genuine revolution in attitudes. Nevertheless it may be necessary for the Authority to finance the creation of a considerable number of small farms, managed timber tracts, egg production centers and other enterprises adaptable to the region. Once established on a profitable and proven basis they could be sold to individuals or to locally organized corporations. By this means the worth of new methods and ideas can be positively shown and new trends for agricultural and industrial development can be initiated. Once set in motion it can be assumed that the shift from coal and corn to diversification will gather momentum from year to year.

It is certain that the rescue operation should go far beyond the fumbling and red-tape-ridden efforts of the present Area Redevelopment Administration. Launched with the most laudable intentions, this agency — in the Cumberlands at least — has accomplished little beyond a few small loans for minor business enterprises. Most community leaders lost interest in it after attending a few of the interminable planning sessions. Tedious discussions of formulae, objectives and methods discouraged interest and deepened the highlanders' cynicism and disillusionment still further.

Any plan to lift the plateau or to enable the plateau to lift itself must encompass a broad scheme to expand and improve its schools. No longer do its unschooled citizens constitute a drag on Kentucky alone. The family car and the American road transmit the social and economic shortcomings engendered by poor highland schools into every part of the nation. The glitteringly attractive states of California, Hawaii, Arizona, Florida, Massachusetts, Illinois, Ohio, New York, Pennsylvania and Michigan can ill afford the burdens imposed upon them by the influx of uneducated and untrained citizens. It is increasingly apparent that in the future there will be little place anywhere in our country for men or women who have nothing to sell except the services of unskilled minds and hands.

The Authority should encourage the state to modernize its archaic school administrative machinery and to tighten controls over expenditures. In justice the nation cannot be expected to assist the state with funds until reasonable safeguards have been enacted to assure that the new money does not finance fetid local political dynasties or filter into graft-hungry pockets. Research by state agencies has amply demonstrated the nature of the needed reforms. None of them are radical and, indeed, all of them would be deemed conservative in any progressive state. When the safeguards have been provided the Authority should help the counties to finance enough spacious and attractive school buildings to house the region's pupils. As one of the conditions precedent for Federal aid the school boards should be encouraged to locate their schools so as to serve the population centers envisioned by the Authority's master plan. Attractive schools in the major towns and in areas slated for industrial and agricultural development should serve as additional magnets to draw people out of the territories scheduled for conversion into forests and lakes.

The upgrading of schools will constitute one of the most tenacious problems confronted by the Authority. Like the others it cannot be solved quickly or easily. As the region's economic props diversify and as emphasis shifts away from social isolation to something approaching normal community life in urban centers and on productive farms, the popular interest in schools can be expected to grow. It may be anticipated that as the general economic level of the inhabitants rises a deepening awareness of education's importance to present and future will be manifested.

Nor will the improvement of conventional education alone suffice. A system of manual training schools is urgently needed. It can scarcely be disputed that the education of masons, mechanics, carpenters and machinists is of cardinal importance. Such schools would afford many youths who find little of interest in the academic classroom an opportunity to acquire useful and profitable skills. The training of knowledgeable workmen would gradually overcome one of the region's most serious stumbling blocks to industrial diversification. At the same time the advantages of such skills to departing mountaineers can hardly be overstated.

Another major problem to which the Authority would have to address itself lies in the landlocked inaccessibility of the plateau. Modern highways into the area on several fronts are indispensable to its orderly development. Their location should be included in the master plan lest expensive roads and bridges be lost by submergence. Financial assistance for their construction will have to be extended to the state.

The mountaineer has become depressingly defeatist in attitude. Company domination and paternalism and two decades of uninspired Welfarism have induced the belief that control of his destiny is in other hands. To replace this defeatism and dejection with zeal may prove difficult indeed, but upon its accomplishment all other facets of revival will eventually hinge.

The first step in this direction should be to organize projects on which the idle men could work. The Authority should set to work on a wide variety of undertakings. Central junk- and trash-disposal centers should be established and satisfactorily maintained. Roads, schools and dams should engross the labors of others. Practically all the region's timberland would benefit by clearing and replanting operations conducted under the supervision of foresters. The construction of decent public buildings in the planned towns is imperative.

On the whole there is an infinity of desperately needed tasks. To the inevitable cries of "boondoggling" and the more coherent objections to the creation of a new Federal bureaucracy, the answer is compelling: the taxpayers of the nation are already supporting the plateau through a wide range of cash and commodity handouts; the cost is already staggering. The additional expense of maintaining Federal works projects would not be grievous while it would have the advantage of tangible and beneficial results. The present program sustains life but creates nothing. A works program could at least build stepping-stones upward out of the abyss.

Finally I would remind churchmen across the land that the plateau is a great and baffling challenge to them and to their institutions. To thousands of mountaineers the balms of religious associations are virtually unknown. It is among such as these that the Galilean labored so long ago. In their suffering today the highlanders are both a summons and a reproach to the nation's churches.

Indeed, in a broader context, the highlander is a challenge to all Americans everywhere. His sorrowful history has deposited him as a material and spiritual orphan on the nation's doorstep. He will not go away, and, unless he is helped, his situation will not improve. In his mute suffering he appeals to the mind and conscience of his country. He and his tattered land await the genius and glory of America the Beautiful. We will continue to ignore them at peril to ourselves and our posterity.

Postscript

SINCE THE MANUSCRIPT of *Night Comes to the Cumberlands* was completed, more than a year ago, events have moved rapidly in the Cumberland Plateau. The tragedy has deepened, the night has darkened at a pace more rapid than I foresaw when the book was written.

In the autumn of 1962 the United Mine Workers of America abandoned the region. In September the union overlords suddenly began canceling the membership and Welfare cards of miners whose employers were in arrears with payments to the Welfare Fund. Many miners believed the operators for whom they worked were in full compliance with the contract provisions. They were numbed by the letters that told them they had been expelled from the union they had fought and toiled to build. No hearings, no trials were afforded them. By a stroke of a pen they lost the most precious asset left to them.

On October 12 the trustees of the Welfare Fund announced that four of its hospitals — at Whitesburg, McDowell, Hazard and Middlesboro — would be permanently closed as of June 30, 1963, unless some nonprofit organization came forward in the meantime to assume responsibility for their operation. Thus the region was abruptly confronted with the loss of its only top-quality public facility.

In their dismay miners formed groups to "picket" the truck mines in a blind and futile effort to compel adherence to union standards. Somehow, they hoped, the little operators could find the means to pay a decent wage again. But the truck-mine operator could not do the economically impossible. During the century's cruelest winter the plateau counties wallowed in anarchy.

Gun fights and nocturnal explosions rocked the land. More than a million dollars' worth of industrial property was destroyed by explosions which shattered coal tipples, headhouses, substations, railroad bridges, coal augers and bulldozers. No single arrest for these acts was ever effected, though occasionally the home of a miner or operator inside a county seat town was blasted to rubble. New hatreds gripped the hills as the hopeless antagonists grappled over the skinny carcass of what had once been a rich coal industry.

Then, on March 11, 1963, Nature poured out the vials of her wrath on the tortured earth and its despairing inhabitants. Heavy rains beat upon the stripped hillsides for two days. Plunging downward in muddy torrents, the waters swelled the rivers to vast proportions, inundating major sections of Harlan, Pikeville, Hazard and a score of other communities. Soupy with mud, the waters destroyed millions of dollars' worth of real and personal property — much of it collateral for loans owing to the Small Business Administration. Many — the wiser ones — gave up and abandoned hope for the region. Others wearily shoveled out the stinking ooze and undertook to restock their stores, warehouses and homes.

Today the plateau is much worse off than it was a year ago. Hundreds of families have no food — particularly in winter — except the commodity doles. Decay spreads across a land ruined by the abrasion of deluge.

Exhaustion is apparent on every hand — exhaustion of soil, exhaustion of men, exhaustion of hopes. Weariness and lethargy have settled closer everywhere. Nor has a single symptom of improvement manifested itself. The nation — engulfed in its money-making and international politics — has paid no noticeable heed to its darkest area. The plateau, almost unnoticed, continues to lurch toward a day when perhaps 80 per cent of its inhabitants will be Welfare recipients — charges on the national purse.

Where will this course lead us at last? No one here in this deprived corner of the nation's hinterland would be so bold as to hazard an optimistic prophecy in this grim spring of 1963.

HARRY M. CAUDILL

Whitesburg, Kentucky
March 21, 1963